Edward Meyrick Goulburn

Thoughts upon the liturgical Gospels

For the Sundays. Vol. 2

Edward Meyrick Goulburn

Thoughts upon the liturgical Gospels
For the Sundays. Vol. 2

ISBN/EAN: 9783337279875

Printed in Europe, USA, Canada, Australia, Japan

Cover: Foto ©Thomas Meinert / pixelio.de

More available books at **www.hansebooks.com**

THOUGHTS

UPON

The Liturgical Gospels

FOR THE SUNDAYS

ONE FOR EACH DAY IN THE YEAR

With an Introduction on their origin, history, the modifications made
in them by the Reformers and by the Revisers of the Prayer Book,
the honour always paid to them in the Church, and the
proportions in which they are drawn from the
Writings of the Four Evangelists

BY

EDWARD MEYRICK GOULBURN, D.D., D.C.L.

DEAN OF NORWICH

IN TWO VOLS.

VOL. II.

CONTAINING THE GOSPELS FROM
EASTER DAY TO THE TWENTY-FIFTH SUNDAY AFTER TRINITY

RIVINGTONS

WATERLOO PLACE, LONDON

MDCCCLXXXVI

[Second Edition.]

CONTENTS.

BOOK II.

BOOK II.

CHAPTER XXV.

THE GOSPEL FOR EASTER DAY.

St. John xx. 1 *to* 11.

1 The first day of the week cometh Mary Magdalen early, when it
was yet dark, unto the sepulchre, and seeth the stone taken away
2 from the sepulchre. Then she runneth and cometh to Simon Peter,
and to the other disciple whom Jesus loved, and saith unto them,
They have taken away the Lord out of the sepulchre, and we know
3 not where they have laid him. Peter therefore went forth, and that
4 other disciple, and came to the sepulchre. So they ran both to=
gether, and the other disciple did out=run Peter, and came first to
5 the sepulchre; and he stooping down, and looking in, saw the linen
6 clothes lying, yet went he not in. Then cometh Simon Peter
following him, and went into the sepulchre, and seeth the linen
7 clothes lie; and the napkin that was about his head, not lying with
8 the linen clothes, but wrapped together in a place by it self. Then
went in also that other disciple which came first to the sepulchre,
9 and he saw and believed. For as yet they knew not the Scripture,
10 that he must rise again from the dead. Then the disciples went
away again unto their own home.

<table>
<tr><td>[Miss. Sar.</td><td>1549.</td><td>1662 s.b.</td></tr>
<tr><td>In illo tempore, Una sabbati Maria Magdalene venit mane cum adhuc tenebræ essent, ad monumentum. (Vulg. Una autem sabbati, Maria Magdalene, etc.)</td><td>The first day of the sabbaths came Mary Magdalene early (when it was yet dark) unto the sepulchre.</td><td>The first day of the week cometh Mary Magdalen early, when it was yet dark, unto the sepulchre. (Gr. Τῇ δὲ μιᾷ τῶν σαββάτων Μαρία ἡ Μαγδαληνὴ ἔρχεται πρωΐ, etc.)</td></tr>
</table>

The theory of the Easter Gospels in the Missal of Sarum seems to have been that the incidents of the Resurrection given by the different Evangelists should be read through in order, beginning with St. Matthew's account (Chap. xxviii. 1 *to* 8), which was appointed for the Vigil of Easter, and going on to St. Mark's (Chap. xvi. 1 *to* 8), which was appointed for the Festival itself, and so on through the Easter week. The Gospel which in 1549 our Reformers selected for Easter Day was that which they found in the Missal of Sarum as the Gospel for *the Saturday in Easter Week*, to which they added (with their usual propension to pursue a passage of Scripture to its legitimate close), *v.* 10, "Then the disciples went away again unto their own home." As the *Epistle* for Easter Day, they chose the passage, which in the Pre-Reformation Church had served as the Epistle for the Vigil of Easter, Col. iii. 1, 2, 3, 4, adding, however (with admirable judgment), to this doctrinal passage the practical corollary in *vv.* 5, 6, 7, which the Apostle appends to it. And thus in arranging the new Epistle and Gospel for Easter Day, they have adopted the first and last passages of Scripture used by the Pre-Reformation Church, during the Octave which commences with the Vigil of Easter and ends with the Saturday in Easter Week.

The δὲ which appears in the original Greek of St. John xx. 1 is unfortunately ignored in the Authorised Version. The Revised Version, however, represents it by "Now" ;—" Now on the first *day* of the week cometh Mary Magdalene early, while it was yet dark, unto the tomb." The δὲ, both here and in the parallel place of St. Matthew (Chap. xxviii. 1, where again the Authorised Version takes no notice of it, and the Revised Version represents it by "Now"), seems to have its usual adversative force. The last verse of the preceding Chapter has told us of our Lord's burial (in St. Matthew, of the sealing and guarding of His sepulchre) ; "*But*" (think not that He was to sleep for ever in the new sepulchre, within the precinct of the quiet garden ; despite all the precautions used to prevent the removal of the body, it *was* removed), "on the first day of the week cometh Mary Magdalene early," and finds the sepulchre open and empty.

Translation of 1540.—(1) *V.* 1. "The first day of the sabbaths" should be of course, as the Authorised Version renders it, "the first day of the week," the plural σάββατα often denoting a week, the whole period of time embraced by two sabbaths (as, indeed, the singular σάββατον also does, see St. Mark xvi. 9). (2) Throughout *vv.* 1, 2, Cranmer gives us the aorist for the historic present; "Mary Magdalene *came*," "*saw* the stone taken away," "*ran* and *came* to Simon Peter," thus sacrificing the vividness which the present gives to the narrative. The Authorised, first of all the English Versions, exhibits the historic present, which is quite as idiomatic in English as in Greek. (3) The word "grave" is used in *vv.* 1, 2, as a variation on the word "sepulchre" in *vv.* 1, 3, 4, 6, 8. It is noticeable that in the Authorised Version "grave" is not used of our Lord's burying-place (as it is of that of Lazarus), but always either "tomb" (St. Matt. xxvii. 60) or "sepulchre." It is well to discard the word "grave" (from *graben*, to dig) as the translation of μνημεῖον, since it always gives the notion, not of a rock-hewn sepulchre, but of a hole dug in the earth. In our present Gospel, Wycliffe has "grave" throughout as the translation of μνημεῖον; Tyndale, "sepulchre" and "tomb"; Geneva, the same as Tyndale; Rheims, "monument" throughout,—the *monumentum* of the Vulgate. Whatever word be chosen for rendering μνημεῖον, it should doubtless be adhered to throughout. The Revisers of 1881 have chosen "tomb," and use it consistently of Lazarus's burying-place as well as of our Lord's. (4) Following Wycliffe (1380), and Tyndale (1534), Cranmer has in *v.* 9, "that he should rise again *from death.*" For this the Translators of the Authorised Version substituted the more literal concrete expression which they found in the original; "that he must rise again *from the dead,*" ὅτι δεῖ αὐτὸν ἐκ νεκρῶν ἀναστῆναι.]

Sunday. — V. 1. "The first day of the week cometh Mary Magdalene early, when it was yet dark, unto the sepulchre." What a restraint must this holy woman have exercised upon herself during the Sabbath! She was bound to our Lord by special ties of gratitude. Her mind had once been in a state of utter disorder, restlessness, and frenzy; for she had been possessed by seven devils, which had gone out of her at our Lord's bidding.[1] The narrative of our Lord's appearance to her after His resurrection shows that she was of an eager spirit, and ardently devoted to Him. Under these circumstances what a check must the Sabbath have imposed upon her highly-strung sensibilities! She had prepared her spices and ointments[2] on the Friday afternoon, and was longing to pay this last tribute of devotion to One, who had

---

[1] See St. Luke viii. 2 ; St. Mark xvi. 9.
[2] See St. Luke xxiii. 55, 56.

rescued her from the most abject misery a poor soul was ever plunged into. Nevertheless, God's ordinance cannot be dispensed with by her—she must "rest the sabbath day according to the commandment." Let me admire and imitate her self-restraint. We cannot excuse ourselves from our devotions, when the stated hour for them has arrived, without a sensible loss of spiritual strength and peace. Excitement and eagerness about any project, even though it be a project pious and beneficent, must be stilled and soothed, until the prayer has been offered, and the Chapter read and thought over. The hawk will fly all the higher and stronger for having been retained, hooded, upon the falconer's hand a little longer. The mind will address itself to active duties with greater alacrity, with a more elastic spring, after an hour of quiet converse with God. Let me make a study of self-collectedness and self-control under agitating circumstances.

Monday.—V. 2. "She saith unto them, They have taken away the Lord out of the sepulchre, and we know not where they have laid him." The words are those of one dazed and half wild with grief. She had conceived a strong natural affection for her Deliverer; and such an affection often clings to the remains of a departed friend, and makes us think we have not lost him entirely, so long as those remains are with us, or are accessible to us. She clung to a dead Saviour, little dreaming that God had in store for her a living One, and One, of whose present "endless life"[1] and perpetual spiritual Presence with her His death was an essential condition. But the empty sepulchre, which had stupefied her with grief, became the source of her joy, when she ascertained the true cause of its emptiness. God had

<hr>

[1] See Heb. vii. 16.

taken away her Lord, only to replace Him in a better and more enduring form. And so it is with many of the most heart-rending sorrows of God's people; they are seen afterwards to have been, not only preliminaries, but essential conditions, of the joy which has followed them; as it is written, " Ye shall be sorrowful, but your sorrow shall be turned into joy"[1]; " We must through much tribulation enter into the kingdom of God"[2]; " Our light affliction, which is but for a moment, worketh for us a far more exceeding and eternal weight of glory."[3]—O my God, let me take heart, under even the most overwhelming troubles, from the reflexion that "now men see not the bright light which is in the clouds: but the wind passeth, and cleanseth them."[4]

> " Ye fearful saints, fresh courage take ;
> The clouds ye so much dread
> Are big with mercy, and shall break
> In blessings on your head." [5]

Tuesday.—V. 5. " And he stooping down, and looking in, saw the linen clothes lying." The single word translated accurately, but somewhat diffusely, " stooping down and looking in," means to bend the body in order to get a view of something. I note that the same Greek word is employed by St. Peter in describing the interest stirred in the minds of the angels by the preaching of the Gospel,—" which things the angels desire to look into."[6] And this interest taken by the angels in the counsels of God's mercy was signified under the Law by the two golden cherubims, which bent forward over the mercy-

---

[1] St. John xvi. 20. [2] Acts xiv. 22.
[3] 2 Cor. iv. 17. [4] Job xxxvii. 21.
[5] Cowper, in the Hymn, " God moves in a mysterious way," etc.
[6] 1 Pet. i. 12.

seat, or lid of the ark of the covenant, with wings extended over their heads, the extremities of which touched one another.[1] St. John "stooped down" to look into the sepulchre, where that great mystery of our faith, the Resurrection, had been transacted. The cherubims bent over the mercy-seat as if in prayer. Let me learn the true spirit in which mysteries of the faith should be approached. First, we must approach them in deep humility—we must stoop before we look. God has hid these things from the wise and prudent, and has revealed them unto babes; for so it seemed good in His sight.[2] The full flush and pride of intellect disqualifies man for insight into the oracles of God, even as the sun, when it is shining in its full strength, hides from our eyes those diamonds of heaven, the stars.——O Lord, make me as a babe in simplicity and docility, when I read Thy word; for the meek shalt Thou guide in judgment, and the meek shalt Thou teach Thy way.[3]

Wednesday.—Ibid. "stooping down, *and looking in.*" "Which things the angels *desire to look into.*" There must be a holy interest in the counsels of God, and in the mysteries of faith, if there is to be a profitable insight into them. This interest it is which gives a zest to the study of Holy Scripture, and of such books as help to the understanding of the same. "Open thou mine eyes," cries the Psalmist, "that I may behold wondrous things out of thy law."[4] But alas! there are many who are not prepared to see wondrous things in God's law, and therefore never seek such things there. They fancy they know their Bibles by heart, that the Scriptures have nothing new to teach them, and accordingly the reading

---

[1] See 1 Kings vi. 27, 28, and viii. 7 ; Heb. ix. 5.
[2] See St. Matt. xi. 25, 26.   [3] See Ps. xxv. 9.   [4] Ps. cxix. 18.

of the Bible, if practised as a duty, is never engaged in as an interest. Science may interest them, or fiction, or the news of the day—these things they read with avidity, but not God's book. And true it is that the wondrous things in God's book are like a treasure hid in a field; they require digging and delving—patient meditation mixed with prayer—to bring them to light.—O Lord, let me never open Thy book but with the conviction that there is very much to be learned there, which however is not to be learned otherwise than by patient study, under the assurance of reaping a rich reward. Let me seek for wisdom there as silver, and search for her as for hid treasures. So only shall I understand the fear of the Lord, and find the knowledge of God.[1]

Thursday.—V. 5. "He . . . saw the linen clothes lying, yet went he not in." Probably one of the reasons which prevented St. John from entering the sepulchre on the first moment of his arrival there, was a certain awe which inspired him, and which is quite in keeping with his character. He felt he might be in the presence of a great mystery, such as the Resurrection actually was; and he dared not scrutinise. Here, then, is another feature of the spirit in which we should approach the mysteries of God's Word,—not humility only, not interest only, but awe. The cherubims which bent over the ark, as desiring to look into the counsels of God's mercy, veiled their faces with their wings. And let me learn, from the circumstance of St. John's showing this spirit of awe-struck reverence at the Saviour's sepulchre, that reverence consists with, and indeed is but one aspect of, the highest, deepest, truest love. Even with men, the most intimate love never supersedes or excludes, nay always implies and

---

[1] See Prov. ii. 4, 5.

involves, a certain respect.—O my God, when I address myself to the study of Thy word, let me remember that I stand on holy ground, and take off from my feet the shoes of this world's traffic and conversation.[1]

Friday.—V. 8. "Then went in also that other disciple, which came first to the sepulchre, and he saw, and believed,"—believed that our Lord was risen indeed. St. John, with the quick-sightedness of love, was the first to believe in the Lord's resurrection, as St. Mary Magdalene was the first to announce it. St. John's mind was essentially contemplative ; he had been reflecting on what he had heard from Magdalene, on the description given by St. Peter from within the sepulchre of the careful orderly arrangement of the burial linen, (which friendly hands would never have removed at all, and which the hands of foes would never have composed in that decorous manner), and finally on what he had seen with his own eyes, the great stone lifted off the mouth of the sepulchre, and the tenantless cave,—and the result of all these experiences, laid together in his mind, produced conviction,—"he believed." Belief arrived at, or if not arrived at, yet strengthened and fortified by watching the indications of Nature and Providence, the ways of men, the ways of the human heart, and noting the coincidence of these with what we read in the word of God,—how sure and stable is it, as being rooted and grounded in our own mental experience !—Lord, give me that contemplative faith, which may lead me to muse on what I hear, to ponder it in my heart, and inwardly to digest it !

Saturday.—V. 29. "For as yet they knew not the scripture, that he must rise again from the dead." They had been familiar from their childhood upward with the

---

[1] See Exod. iii. 5.

words of Psalm xvi.; "My flesh also shall rest in hope. For thou wilt not leave my soul in hell; neither wilt thou suffer thine Holy One to see corruption. Thou wilt shew me the path of life;"[1] but the words had been dark to them hitherto. Now, what they had heard and seen gave the key to the meaning, at least in the mind of the beloved disciple,—placed a light behind the transparency, and showed what it was intended to represent. The familiar words glowed with a new lustre, when they saw in them a reference to the resurrection of their Master. Scripture prophecy is never fully understood, until the fulfilment clears it up. Thus there were prophecies of a suffering and humiliated, and also of a triumphant and glorified Messiah, which seemed incompatible, and formed an insoluble enigma for the Church under the Law, until "the captain of our salvation" was made "perfect through sufferings,"[2] and having drunk of the brook in the way, afterwards lifted up His head.[3]—O God, Thy providence waits like a handmaid upon Thy word, unfolding it gradually to the apprehensions of Thy people, as the scroll of human history is unfolded. Only let my mind, while fully possessed with the knowledge of Thy word, be quick to note the course of events, and to recognise in them the ordering of Thy hand; and I shall not be without indications that the same hand which indited prophecy is, as time advances, bringing history into agreement with it.

[1] *Vv.* 9, 10, 11.   [2] See Heb. ii. 10.   [3] See Ps. cx. 7.

CHAPTER XXVI

THE GOSPEL FOR THE FIRST SUNDAY AFTER EASTER.

St. John xx. 19 *to* 24
(leaving out " Then," with which *v.* 19 commences).

19   The same day at evening, being the first day of the week, when the doors were shut, where the disciples were assembled for fear of the Jews, came Jesus and stood in the midst, and saith unto them,

20 Peace be unto you. And when he had so said, he shewed unto them his hands and his side. Then were the disciples glad when they saw

21 the Lord. Then said Jesus to them again, Peace be unto you: As

22 my father hath sent me, even so send I you. And when he had said this, he breathed on them and saith unto them, Receive ye the holy

23 Ghost. Whosesoever sins ye remit, they are remitted unto them; and whosesoever sins ye retain, they are retained.

[Miss. Sar.	1549.	1662 s.b.
In illo tempore, Cum esset sero die illo, una sabbatorum, et fores erant clausæ, etc. (*Vulg.* Cum ergo sero esset die illo, una sabbatorum, etc.)	The same day at night, which was the first day of the sabbaths, when the doors were shut, etc.	The same day at evening, being the first day of the week, when the doors were shut, etc. (*Gr.* Οὔσης οὖν ὀψίας τῇ ἡμέρᾳ ἐκείνῃ τῇ μιᾷ τῶν σαββάτων.)

The Gospel of the Sarum Missal for the " Dominica *in Octavis Paschæ* " contained, not only the account of the absolving power conveyed by our Lord to His Apostles on the evening of the day of His resurrection, but also the immediately succeeding narrative of the scepticism and conviction of St. Thomas. Indeed it went beyond this; for it embraced the two final verses of the twentieth Chapter of St. John, which close the original Gospel, the twenty-first Chapter being in the nature of a postscript. The

Reformers in 1549 cancelled the last eight verses of the Chapter, probably because six of them already did duty as the Gospel for St. Thomas's Day. Whether this curtailment was entirely judicious may be doubted. The miracle of feeding the five thousand, in St. John's version of it, appears twice among the Gospels (doubtless from its transcendent importance), and furnishes a precedent for some repetition ; and the narrative of the conviction of St. Thomas has a value and interest altogether independent of the Apostle's personal history, inasmuch as God made the incident conducive to "the more confirmation of the faith" in that cardinal verity, Christ's Resurrection. Thus the narrative is a Gospel appropriate to Eastertide at least as much as to St. Thomas's Day.

The *οὖν*, which connects this Gospel with the story of St. Mary Magdalene's interview with our Lord, is rendered by "Then" in the Authorised Version ("*Then* the same day at evening, being the first day of the week"), by "Therefore" in the Revised Version ("When *therefore* it was evening, on that day, the first *day* of the week"). Unhappily the compilers o.' our Liturgical Gospels have dropped it altogether. Its force is that the interview in the evening of the Resurrection Day with the Ten (and probably others) collectively was the legitimate conclusion of the manifestations, which throughout the day had been granted to, and reported by, individual believers. This is excellently brought out by Professor Westcott *in loc.* "The appearance to Mary Magdalene was (so to speak) necessarily supplemented by an appearance to the Church. The several revelations to individuals (St. Luke xxiv. 31, 34) prepared the way for this manifestation to the body ; and gave occasion for the gathering of the disciples. It could not but be that the tidings, which must have been spread through the company of believers, should cause many to come together, and perhaps to the 'upper room' where the Last Supper was held. Comp. Acts i. 13."

Version of 1540. (1) In the 19th verse, as it appears in Cranmer's Bible ("when the doors were shut (where the disciples were assembled together for fear of the Jews) came Jesus," etc.), the parenthesis confuses the sense. Archbishop Whately used to say he could not bear to hear stupid clergymen reading this verse in such a manner as to convey to the hearer that "the disciples were assembled"—not "the doors shut"—"for fear of the Jews." Cranmer's parenthesis, which groups together the words ("where the disciples were assembled together for fear of the Jews"), as also the punctuation of our own Authorised Version, lends countenance to, if it does not excuse, the error of the "stupid clergymen." The Revised Version of 1881 has corrected the punctuation. (2) In *v.* 21, Cranmer renders καθὼς ἀπέσταλκέ με ὁ πατήρ, "As my Father *sent* me," as if the verb were in the aorist. "The mission of Christ is here regarded" (says Professor Westcott *in loc.*) "not in the point of its historical fulfilment (*sent*), but in the permanence of its effects (*hath sent*)."]

Sunday.—V. 19. "When the doors were shut where the disciples were assembled." There is a wealth of meaning in these words. They remind us of the different promises made by our Lord to private and public prayer. And viewed in connexion with one another, they teach that even public prayer must be in a certain sense private, if it is to be effectual. In prescribing private prayer, our Lord had expressly made mention of closed doors. "Thou, when thou prayest, enter into thy closet, and when thou hast shut thy door, pray to thy Father which is in secret ; and thy Father which seeth in secret shall reward thee openly."[1] It is clear, however, that everybody cannot comply with this precept literally. The very poor have no closet or private chamber, to which they can retire for prayer. The closet, therefore, of which our Lord speaks, must be rather the closet of the heart than of the house. We must retire into our own hearts by collecting the thoughts before we pray, calling them in from the earthly cares and interests amidst which they have been roaming, and fastening them upon God's presence. And we must shut the door, by preventing the intrusion of these worldly cares and interests until the prayer is ended—driving them away to the utmost of our power, as Abram drove away the fowls, which came down upon and would have devoured his sacrifice.[2] And this collection of the thoughts, and guard upon them, is as essential to the reality, and success of public as of private prayer. The doors must be shut, even when the disciples are assembled.

Monday.—*Ibid.* For public prayer we have the distinct

[1] St. Matt. vi. 6.   [2] See Gen. xv. 10, 11.

promise—a promise equally appropriate with the former one to the condition on which it is suspended ; " If two of you shall agree on earth as touching any thing that they shall ask, it shall be done for them of my Father which is in heaven. For where two or three are gathered together in my name, there am I in the midst of them."[1] It would seem that our blessed Lord designed to impress this promise on the minds of His disciples, by visibly fulfilling it to them during the forty days which elapsed between the Resurrection and the Ascension. He would, from time to time, suddenly present Himself in the midst of them during those forty days, to assure them that, even when they did not see Him in their assemblies, He was really there. For, indeed, public worship is an ordinance of great importance, and one upon which it was necessary that Christ should lay especial stress, and put especial honour. It takes up time ; it is attended with more distractions, and more impediments to the concentration of the thoughts, than prayer in the closet. But it is in the nature of a public confession of Christ ; and it is the means of realising upon earth the Communion of Saints ; and, withal, it acts as a check upon that natural selfishness, which is apt to creep into and infect our prayers ; surrounded by others, we are more likely to bear in mind that the Church, though composed of many members, is one body,[2] and that we have common interests, common trials, common needs with others, and must reciprocate prayers and sympathies with them. And, therefore, there was need of a very strong and consolatory promise to enforce the practice of public worship. And yet even with that strong promise, it would seem as if the primitive Christians were sometimes neglectful of the

---

[1] St. Matt. xviii. 19, 20.   [2] See 1 Cor. xii. 12.

duty; for the Apostle thus expostulates with the Hebrews; "Not forsaking the assembling of ourselves together, as the manner of some is; but exhorting one another: and so much the more, as ye see the day approaching."[1]

Tuesday.—V. 19. "Peace be unto you." Our Lord had bequeathed "peace" to His disciples as His parting legacy, when He said to them, "Peace I leave with you, my peace I give unto you."[2] And now, when He returns to them from the grave, as "the first-begotten of the dead,"[3] His greeting is the same as His valediction had been, "Peace be unto you." But for this peace the purchase-money has now been paid in full. He hath "made peace through the blood of his cross,"[4] a fact of which He assures them by pointing them to His hands and His side, through the wounds in which the peace was to flow forth into their hearts and consciences. Their consciences must have needed this peace, as accusing them for having forsaken our Lord, and fled on the moment of His being apprehended.[5] He does not even mention to them, however, this temporary failure in their allegiance to Him. He says, "Peace be unto you,"—a formula of encouragement and comfort, as well as greeting; for we find the steward of Joseph's house using it to calm the agitation of his brethren, "Peace be to you, fear not. . . . I had your money."[6] The word was an assurance to them that their sin in forsaking Him was obliterated by the atoning blood. (Lord, how overflowing is Thy goodness to every returning prodigal, in welcoming him back without a word of remonstrance or rebuke, and fulfilling to him that promise, "All his transgressions that he hath committed, they shall not be mentioned unto him!"[7])

---

[1] Heb. x. 25. [2] St. John xiv. 27. [3] See Rev. i. 5. [4] See Col. i. 20.
[5] See St. Matt. xxvi. 56. [6] Gen. xliii. 23. [7] Ezek. xviii. 22.

It had been a word full of pathos and consolation, when said to them on the eve of His departure. But now with how deep and awful a solemnity is the blessing invested, when it is pronounced by One who, since He last met them, has passed through the experiences of death and resurrection, has been in the lower world, has visited Paradise,[1] has preached to the spirits in prison,[2] and opened their prison-house, and has come forth from the grave triumphant.

Wednesday.—V. 20. "Then were the disciples glad, when they saw the Lord." Thou Thyself, O Lord, hadst just been made glad with the Father's countenance. For, in speaking of Thy resurrection by the Holy Spirit of prophecy, David had said; "Thou wilt not leave my soul in hell, neither wilt thou suffer thine Holy One to see corruption. Thou hast made known to me the ways of life; thou shalt make me full of joy with thy countenance."[3] And now, Thou, in Thy turn, makest Thy disciples glad with the joy of Thy countenance. To catch a glimpse of Thee, O Lord, is the source and secret of all joy to the spirit of man. And the clearer the glimpse, the greater is the joy. We may and do see something of Thee here. Just in proportion as we purify ourselves, even as Thou art pure,[4] is that word of promise fulfilled to us; "Blessed are the pure in heart: for they shall see God."[5] Just in proportion as we are righteous,—righteous by the imputation of Thy merits, and by the impartation of Thy Spirit, —do we " behold thy face in righteousness."[6] But " now we see through a glass, darkly."[7] A time is coming when, if we be faithful, we shall see "face to face,"—yea, shall

---

[1] See St. Luke xxiii. 43.
[2] Acts ii. 27, 28.
[4] See 1 John iii. 3.
[6] See Ps. xvii. 15.
[3] See 1 Pet. iii. 19.
[5] St. Matt. v. 8.
[7] 1 Cor. xiii. 12.

see Thee as Thou art.[1] Then, and not till then, shall Thy perfect image be formed in us, and that word shall receive in us its final fulfilment, "When I awake up after thy likeness, I shall be satisfied with it."[2]

Thursday.—V. 22. "He breathed on them, and saith unto them, Receive ye the Holy Ghost." "The first man Adam," we read, "was made" (by God's breathing into his nostrils the breath of life[3]) "a living soul; the last Adam was made a quickening spirit."[4] Here, first, I find "the second man, the Lord from heaven,"[5] when Himself raised from the dead by the power of the Father, becoming a quickening spirit to His Church; and vindicating to Himself those lofty claims which He had made while on earth; "As the Father hath life in himself; so hath he given to the Son to have life in himself"[6]; "As the Father raiseth up the dead, and quickeneth them; even so the Son quickeneth whom he will."[7]—O Lord, when "good desires are put into" my "heart," let me recognise that it is "by Thy special grace preventing" me,—yea, that these desires are Thy very breath, breathed upon my heart from Thy seat in the heavens, and designed to quicken it into new life, as vernal airs are sent to cherish the earth's vitality, to bring out the bloom of the flower, and the tender green of the leaf. But never let me acquiesce in good desires, O Lord, without good endeavours! Let the holy desires and the good counsels be "brought to good effect" in me "by Thy continual help," — take shape, that is, in "good works,"[8] in a change of life and character.

---

[1] See 1 John iii. 2.   [2] Ps. xvii. 16, P.B.V.   [3] See Gen. ii. 7.
[4] 1 Cor. xv. 45.   [5] See 1 Cor. xv. 47.   [6] St. John v. 26.
[7] St. John v. 21.

[8] See Collect for Easter Day, and Second Collect at Evening Prayer.

Friday.—V. 23. " Whose soever sins ye remit, they are remitted unto them." Christ brings with Him from the cross and grave, from the unseen realm, from the Paradise of God, the forgiveness of sins, to deposit it with His Church for ever, as a treasure of which she is to be the distributor in His name. The great comfort of this fact is the assurance hereby given us that remission of sins is a blessing to be received now, not to be waited for till the great day of final judgment. Christians are to be living in the daily enjoyment of it, sunning themselves daily in the light of God's pardoning love. And it is as a testimony to this present possession of forgiveness by true believers, that in the daily Morning and Evening Prayer of the Church, the keys of the kingdom of heaven are laid out in the sight of the people, after the general confession of sins, the priest standing up, and in virtue of the power and commandment given to him, announcing God's absolution to " all them that truly repent, and unfeignedly believe his holy Gospel." Grant, O Lord, that I, having been once washed in the laver of regeneration in baptism,[1] may wash my feet daily from the dust and defilement, which have accumulated on them in the course of the day's pilgrimage, by a fresh recurrence in repentance and faith to that fountain, which by Thy cross and passion Thou hast " opened for sin and for uncleanness." [2]

Saturday.—*Ibid.* " And whose soever sins ye retain, they are retained." St. Peter in his censure of Ananias and Sapphira, and of Simon Magus ; St. Paul in his rebuke and punishment of Elymas, the sorcerer, in his excommunication of the incestuous Corinthian, and again of Hymenæus and Alexander, exerted this awful power of

---

[1] See St. John xiii. 10.   [2] See Zech. xiii. 1.

retaining sins.[1] It is said in one of these cases, and to
be understood in all of them, that the person exerting
the power was " filled with the Holy Ghost,"[2] while he
exerted it—the retention of sin being thus vitally connected, as our Lord's words connect it, with the reception
of the Spirit. Discernment of spirits was one of the
supernatural gifts of the early Church,[3] and the Apostles
had it in full measure, and were directed by it infallibly
in their sentences of excommunication. The modern
Church is not safeguarded in the same way against error
in her censures; but we may safely make these two
assertions, that the more spiritual any Christian becomes,
the more insight does he acquire into the spiritual
condition of those across whom he is thrown ("He that
is spiritual judgeth all things "[4]); and, secondly, that
there is still a power in the Christian society, wielded
by her ministers as representing her, of retaining as well
as remitting sins, though the exertion of this power is no
longer seconded and facilitated by a miraculous endowment of insight. Whenever an adult is admitted to
Baptism, or re-admitted after grievous sin to the Holy
Communion, a judgment is necessarily passed by the
priest who so admits him upon the genuineness of his
repentance and faith.—Lord, as it has pleased Thee to
endow Thy Church with such awful powers, let me never
be guilty of despising her, or rejecting her authority, even
should these powers fall into the hands of carnal men,
and not always be exercised aright. May I ever remem-

---

[1] See Acts v. 3, 4, 5, 9, 10 ; viii. 20-24 ; xiii. 9, 10, 11 ; 1 Cor. v. 3,
4, 5 ; and 1 Tim. i. 20.

[2] Σαῦλος δὲ (ὁ καὶ Παῦλος) πλησθεὶς Πνεύματος ἁγίου, καὶ ἀτενίσας εἰς
αὐτόν, etc., Acts xiii. 9.

[3] See 1 Cor. xii. 10.   [4] 1 Cor. ii. 15.

ber the solemn words, with which Thou didst second the seventy disciples, in sending them on their mission; "He that heareth you heareth me; and he that despiseth you despiseth me; and he that despiseth me despiseth him that sent me."[1]

[1] St. Luke x. 16.

Chapter XXVII.

THE GOSPEL FOR THE SECOND SUNDAY AFTER EASTER.

St. John x. 11 *to* 17 (but with the words *Jesus said* prefixed).

11 Jesus said I am the good shepherd: the good shepherd giveth
12 his life for the sheep. But he that is an hireling, and not the
shepherd, whose own the sheep are not, seeth the wolf coming, and
leaveth the sheep, and fleeth; and the wolf catcheth them, and
13 scattereth the sheep. The hireling fleeth, because he is an hireling,
14 and careth not for the sheep. I am the good shepherd, and know
15 my sheep, and am known of mine. As the Father knoweth me,
even so know I the Father: and I lay down my life for the sheep.
16 And other sheep I have which are not of this fold; them also I
must bring, and they shall hear my voice; and there shall be one
fold, and one shepherd.

[Miss. Sar.	1549.	1662 s.b.
In illo tempore, Dixit Jesus discipulis suis; Ego sum pastor bonus.	*Christ said*, I am the good shepherd.	*Jesus said* I am the good shepherd.

In the Black-Letter Prayer Book of 1636(39 ?), in which the MS.
alterations were made at the last Revision, the words "Christ said,"
which introduce this selection from St. John's Gospel, are printed, not in
black letter, but in Roman type, probably by way of showing that they
form no part of the sacred text. In 1662 Sancroft (under Cosin's instructions), drew his pen through "Christ," and wrote over it "Jesus."
Rightly : for our Lord in the Gospels is spoken of always by His personal
name, and not by His name of office.—It is interesting to note at what
point of the discourse in St. John x. our Gospel opens. At the beginning
of the Chapter our Lord propounds a threefold allegory of Himself. He is
a door for shepherds, by which they may approach the sheep successfully

(*vv.* 1, 2, 3) ; a door for sheep, by which they have access to God's fold and find pasture (*v.* 9) ; and thirdly, He is Himself the good Shepherd (*vv.* 11, 14). These three thoughts are tangled up one with another in the earlier verses ; but in *v.* 11, and the remainder of our Gospel, the Lord disentangles the last idea from the two previous ones, and exhibits it, in all its fulness and beauty, by itself.—*Translation of* 1540. (1) "*A* good shepherd giveth his life for the sheep" (in *v.* 11) is not wrong, though "*The* good shepherd" expresses the same idea quite idiomatically, as well as literally. When a singular noun is used to express a class, the definite article is prefixed. (See the observations on ὁ σπείρων in St. Luke viii. 5, in the Introduction to the Gospel for Sexagesima Sunday.) (2) In *v.* 16 Cranmer has the old erroneous (and now exploded) translation of καὶ γενήσεται μία ποίμνη, εἷς ποιμήν ; "and there shall be one *fold* and one shepherd," thus confounding ποίμνη (*flock*) with αὐλή (*fold*) of the earlier part of the verse. Cranmer had no excuse, as Tyndale (only five or six years before) had distinguished ποίμνη and αὐλή in his translation ("And other shepe I have, which are not of this *folde.* Them also must I bringe, that they may heare my voyce, and that ther maye be one *flocke* and one shepeherde "). And it is much to be regretted that King James's Translators should have followed suit with Cranmer instead of with Tyndale. "The translation 'fold' for 'flock' (*ovile* for *grex*)," says Professor Westcott (*in loc.*), "has been most disastrous in idea and in influence. The change in the original from 'fold' (αὐλή), to 'flock' (ποίμνη), is most striking, and reveals a new thought as to the future relations of Jew and Gentile. . . . It may be added that the obliteration of this essential distinction between the 'fold' and the 'flock' in many of the later Western versions of this passage indicates, as it appears, a tendency of Roman Christianity, and has served in no small degree to confirm and extend the false claims of the Roman See." The Revised Version of 1881 no doubt gives the true rendering;—"and they shall *become* one *flock*, one shepherd."]

Sunday.—V. 11. "I am the good shepherd : the good shepherd giveth his life for the sheep." I note that this great saying of our Lord's stands midway between certain words of the prophet Isaiah, which it developes more fully, and certain other words of St. Peter, which are the echo of it. Isaiah's words are ; " All we like sheep have gone astray ; we have turned every one to his own way ;

and the Lord hath laid on him the iniquity of us all."[1]
There is no express mention of a shepherd here, but only
of straying sheep, and of the imputation of their iniquity
to one who was wounded for their transgressions. Straying sheep, however, imply a shepherd, whose part it is
to go after and fetch them back. And this implication
is still more clearly brought out in the language of the
119th Psalm (written after the Captivity); "I have gone
astray like a lost sheep; seek thy servant."[2] The person
who seeks a lost sheep, and to whom its piteous bleatings
make an appeal, is its shepherd. Our Lord in the words
before us explicitly calls Himself the Good Shepherd, and
explains that He bare the iniquities of the sheep, when He
laid down His life for them. And in His parable of the
lost sheep, He recognises Himself and His mission as
being the answer to that prayer of the Psalmist; "Seek
thy servant." He is the Shepherd who, having lost one
sheep, leaves the ninety and nine in the wilderness, and
goes after that which is lost until he finds it.[3]—How
welded together is every part of Thy word, O God! It
is one organic living whole, animated by one life, which
indeed is the breath of the Holy Spirit. And what a
growth there is in Holy Scripture, as in the human frame,
so that later passages of it often develope and fill up the
outline of earlier, until at length the truth is displayed in
its full proportions!

Monday.—Ibid. The words of St. Peter, in which he
follows both Isaiah and our Lord, are these: "Who his
own self bare our sins in his own body on the tree, that
we, being dead to sins, should live unto righteousness: by
whose stripes ye were healed. For ye were as sheep
going astray; but are now returned unto the Shepherd

---

[1] Isaiah liii. 6. [2] Ps. cxix. 176. [3] See St. Luke xv. 4.

and Bishop of your souls."[1] The assertion of the Atonement here is more express, and more fully developed, than in the language of either the prophet or our Lord. "Surely he hath borne our griefs . . . he was wounded for our transgressions . . . the LORD hath laid on him the iniquity of us all"[2] . . . "the good shepherd giveth his life for the sheep,"— there is something which goes beyond all this in the words, "himself hath borne our sins in his own body on the tree," if it is only that the Apostle mentions the "body" of Christ as the propitiatory sacrifice ("through the offering of the *body* of Jesus Christ once for all"[3]), and specifies also the tree (or cross) as the place where the sacrifice was made. When Isaiah wrote,—nay, even when our Lord spoke the words of the text,—the crucifixion had not actually taken place, and there could be no explicit mention of the cross, until it had been erected, and the Divine Victim stretched upon it. I am taught here that God's providence waits as a handmaid upon His word, to open it out to the apprehensions of His Church. This is one great principle for our guidance in the study of unfulfilled Prophecy. The Church's fortunes, as they unfold themselves, may be expected to develope more and more of its meaning.

Tuesday.—V. 12. "But he that is an hireling, and not the shepherd, whose own the sheep are not, seeth the wolf coming, and leaveth the sheep, and fleeth." Our Lord, in the course of this wonderful allegory, reckons up three enemies of the sheep, thieves and robbers, hirelings, and wolves. Of the thieves and robbers the Pharisees, and ecclesiastical rulers of the Jews of that day, were specimens. They had just put out of the synagogue a blind man restored to sight, because he had confessed

---

[1] 1 Pet. ii. 24, 25.   [2] Isaiah liii. 4, 5, 6.   [3] Heb. x. 10.

Christ as a prophet sent from God,[1]—that is, they had excluded from the fold of God's ancient Church a sheep which had heard and recognised the voice of the true Shepherd. They were thieves and robbers then, inasmuch as they strove to the utmost to rob the good Shepherd of His due, the allegiance of the people, and to fasten that allegiance on themselves, as sitting in Moses' chair,[2] as "guides of the blind, and lights of them which were in darkness."[3] See the contrast in St. John the Baptist. When he hears that the sheep are trooping away from his baptism to Christ's,[4] he welcomes the tidings, though it imported that his own popularity was on the wane. "He that hath the bride is the bridegroom: but the friend of the bridegroom, which standeth and heareth him, rejoiceth greatly because of the bridegroom's voice: this my joy therefore is fulfilled."[5] Popularity, influence, leadership are naturally dear to us all; and ministers of Christ, especially those who are gifted with influence, must narrowly and anxiously look to it that they do not suffer the minds and hearts of the people to rest upon themselves in any shape, or on the prestige arising either from their gifts or their position—that they do their utmost to centre the gaze of their disciples, as the Baptist did, upon the Lamb of God,[6] and withdraw themselves into the background as much as possible. "We preach not ourselves, but Christ Jesus the Lord."[7] It is a fearful thing to rob the good Shepherd of the allegiance of His sheep.

Wednesday.—V. 13. "The hireling fleeth, because he is an hireling, and careth not for the sheep." A hireling is not a thief, but simply a mercenary, one who will

---

[1] See St. John ix. 17, 33, 34.   [2] See St. Matt. xxiii. 2.
[3] See Rom. ii. 19. [4] See St. John iii. 26. [5] *Ibid. v.* 29.
[6] See St. John i. 29, 36.   [7] 2 Cor. iv. 5.

serve the sheep and tend them, so long as things go smoothly, but serves and tends them for the advantages which accrue to himself from the service, and not from the affection which he bears to them. The test of a hireling is danger; when he " seeth the wolf coming," he " leaveth the sheep, and fleeth." He has none of that real interest in them, which would lead him to stay with his flock at his own risk, and console, and support, and animate them to the best of his ability. He has taken the oversight of God's Church, not " of a ready mind," but " for filthy lucre's sake "[1]; there is not in him the fundamental pastoral grace, a care for souls and a love of them, as being God's choicest handy-work, and the purchase of Christ's blood.—Since Thy flock, O God, has no worse enemies than self-seeking and worldly-minded ministers, let me be diligent in prayer at all times for " those who are called to any office and administration in " [2] Thy Church. " Grant that thy Church, being alway preserved from false Apostles, may be ordered and guided by faithful and true pastors; through Jesus Christ our Lord."[3]

Thursday.—V. 12. " The wolf catcheth them, and scattereth the sheep." As the thief represents " the flesh," —that self-exaltation, self-seeking, self-pleasing, which is the great bane of our corrupt nature; and as the hireling represents " the world,"—secularity of aim and motive in God's ministers; so there can be no doubt that the wolf represents the devil, or chief antagonist of man, elsewhere called " a roaring lion, who walketh about, seeking whom he may devour."[4] And let me observe that he is here represented not only as doing harm to individual sheep, " catching " and biting them, but also as breaking up their

---

[1] See 1 Pet. v. 2 ; and Tit. i. 11. [2] Second Ember Week Prayer.
[3] Collect for St. Matthias's Day. [4] See 1 Pet. v. 8.

organization, and destroying them as a flock,—he "*scattereth the sheep.*"   Christ's design for His church is unity,—
"that they all may be one; as thou, Father, art in me, and I in thee, that they also may be one in us"[1]; or, as we have it in the closing words of this Gospel,—"there shall be one flock" (such is undoubtedly the right translation, not "one fold") "and one shepherd."[2]   The devil, in addition to the mischief which he does to individual souls, strives to break up this unity: heresies, schisms, parties, are of his promoting.—O good Shepherd, true David, who deliverest Thy sheep out of the paw of the lion, and out of the paw of the bear,[3] "keep with thy perpetual mercy thy Church,"[4] as well as each member thereof. "Take away all hatred and prejudice, and whatsoever else may hinder us from godly Union and Concord: that, as there is but one Body, and one Spirit, and one Hope of our Calling, one Lord, one Faith, one Baptism, one God and Father of us all, so we may henceforth be all of one heart, and of one soul, united in one holy bond of Truth and Peace, of Faith and Charity."[5]

Friday.—Vv. 14, 15. "I know my sheep, and am known of mine, even as the Father knoweth me, and I know the Father; and I lay down my life for the sheep." Such is undoubtedly the true rendering of these wonderful words.[6]   I may reach some small part of their profound

---

[1] St. John xvii. 21.   [2] *V.* 16.   [3] See 1 Sam. xvii. 37.
[4] Collect for Fifteenth Sunday after Trinity.
[5] *A Prayer for Unity*, in "the Form of Prayer for the Twentieth Day of June."
[6] The punctuation necessary to give this meaning, and the rendering of κἀγώ as "and I" instead of "even so .. I," are both adopted by the Revisers of 1881. "The affection between the Divine Shepherd and His flock can be compared, for the closeness of its intimacy, with nothing but the affection between the Eternal Father and the Son of His love."—(F. W. Robertson, as referred to in the next note.)

meaning by observing that the words, " I lay down my life for the sheep," are connected by " and " with what goes before. Christ's intimate knowledge of His sheep, and their knowledge of Him (a reciprocal knowledge as intimate—marvellous assertion !—as that which subsists between Him and His Father) is something which leads Him to lay down His life for the sheep, prompts Him to self-sacrifice for them. It must be therefore a knowledge which involves sympathy and love, for nothing short of sympathy and love could have prompted His self-sacrifice. This mutual knowledge, then, is a spiritual instinct which draws both parties together, and is nothing else than " a certain mysterious tact of sympathy "[1] between them. On the one hand, " the Lord knoweth them that are his,"[2] recognises at a glance those who are His in the deepest ground of their heart, however much there may be in them at present which needs correction, and esteems them worthy of the cost which He paid to redeem their souls. And they in their turn know Him intuitively. Not all the authority nor all the threats of the ecclesiastical rulers of his people could persuade the blind man, whose recovery we read of in Chapter ix., that one, who had dealt with Him as Jesus had, was not a prophet sent from God ; a spiritual instinct, from which there was no appeal, taught him that.—Lord, in ascertaining that critical point, whether I am or am not of the number of Thy *true* sheep, bound to Thee by reciprocal ties of sympathy and mutual understanding, let me apply the test of this other word of Thine, " My sheep *hear my voice*, and I know them, and *they follow me.*"[3] That I have

[1] This expression is borrowed from the Rev. F. W. Robertson's Sermon on "the Good Shepherd," Second Series, Sermon xx.

[2] See 2 Tim. ii. 19.   [3] St. John x. 27.

heard Thy voice I know full well; but have I yielded to its attraction? have I listened to it? have I obeyed? have I followed Thee?   Whithersoever Thou callest me by Thy Providence, Thy word, Thy Spirit in my conscience, is it my endeavour to follow Thee, whatever sacrifices may be involved?

Saturday.—V. 16. "And other sheep I have, which are not of this fold" (meaning the Gentiles): "them also I must bring, and they shall hear my voice, and there shall be one flock, and one shepherd."   How profound is the sequence of thought which I trace in the words of Christ! He has been speaking of laying down His life for His sheep. Now Redemption, having been wrought out in human nature, is also *for* human nature.[1]   And so St. John, faithfully echoing his Master's words here recorded by him, tells us of Caiaphas; "He prophesied that Jesus should die for that nation; and not for that nation only, but that also he should gather together in one the children of God that were scattered abroad."[2]   And again; "He is the propitiation for our sins: and not for ours only, but also for the sins of the whole world."[3]   Christ's sympathy travels beyond the Jewish fold, nay, beyond His elect, to all those whose nature He took into union with the Godhead. And hence it is that on Good Friday, the day on which the Shepherd's life was laid down for the sheep, the Church intercedes for "Jews, Turks, Infidels, and Heretics, that God would take from them all ignorance, hardness of heart, and contempt of his Word, and would so fetch them home to his flock, that they may be saved among the remnant of the true Israelites, and be made one fold under

---

[1] "By the anticipation of the Cross (ch. xii. 32) the spiritual horizon is extended."   Professor Westcott in "The Speaker's Commentary."

[2] St. John xi. 51, 52.   [3] 1 John ii. 2.

one shepherd, Jesus Christ our Lord."[1]   How broad are
the sympathies of Thy love, O Lord !   One of the dimen-
sions of Thy love is its *breadth*.   It is broad as the world,
long as eternity, deep as the hell from which it rescues
sinners, high as the heaven to which it proposes to raise
them.[2]   Enlarge my heart, not only to receive and com-
prehend this love, but in my humble measure to exhibit
it to others !

[1] Third Collect for Good Friday.   [2] See Eph. iii. 18, 19.

Chapter XXVIII

THE GOSPEL FOR THE THIRD SUNDAY AFTER EASTER.

St. John xvi. 16 *to* 23
(but with the words *Jesus said to his disciples* prefixed).

16 Jesus said to his disciples, A little while and ye shall not see me; and again, a little while and ye shall see me, because I go to
17 the Father. Then said some of his disciples among themselves, What is this that he saith unto us, A little while and ye shall not see me; and again, a little while and ye shall see me; and Because
18 I go to the Father? They said therefore, What is this that he
19 saith, A little while? we cannot tell what he saith. Now Jesus knew that they were desirous to ask him, and said unto them, Do ye enquire among your selves, of that I said, A little while, and ye shall not see me; and again, a little while and ye shall see me?
20 Verily, verily I say unto you, that ye shall weep and lament, but the world shall rejoyce: and ye shall be sorrowful, but your sorrow
21 shall be turned into joy. A woman when she is in travail, hath sorrow, because her hour is come: but as soon as she is delivered of the child, she remembreth no more the anguish, for joy that a
22 man is born into the world. And ye now therefore have sorrow: but I will see you again, and your heart shall rejoyce, and your joy no man taketh from you.

[Miss. Sar.	1594.	1662 s.b.
In illo tempore, Dixit Jesus discipulis suis; Modicum, et jam non videbitis me, etc.	*Jesus said to his disciples,* After a while ye shall not see mee, etc.	*Jesus said to his disciples,* A little while and ye shall not see me; etc.

Professor Westcott finds in St. John xvi. four sections, connected by an easy and beautiful sequence of thought. 1. *The world and the Paraclete*

(xvi. 1-11); 2. *The Paraclete and the disciples* (xvi. 12-15); 3. *Sorrow turned to joy* (xvi. 16-24); and 4. *After failure, victory* (xvi. 25-33). Our Gospel gives the third of these sections, in which "The prospect of the fulfilment of the work of the Paraclete for the world and for the disciples is followed by a revelation of the condition in which the disciples themselves will be. They are to stand in a new relation to Christ (16-18). A time of bitter sorrow is to be followed by joy (19, 20), by joy springing (so to speak) naturally out of the sorrow (21, 22)." [Commentary on St. John's Gospel, *in loc.*].—*Translation of* 1540. (1) In translating Μικρὸν in *v.* 16 by "After a while," Cranmer followed Tyndale. Wycliffe (in 1380) had been more literal and more vigorous ("A litil and thanne ye schuln not se me, and eftsone a litil and ye schuln se me, for I go to the fadir"). (2) In *v.* 22 Cranmer renders χαρήσεται ὑμῶν ἡ καρδία "Your *hearts* shall rejoyce,"—inaccurately, and forfeiting a fine shade of significance which is given by the singular. They should have but *one* heart in that day, such should be the community and sympathy of feeling existing among them. (Compare Gal. vi. 18 ; Brethren, the grace of our Lord Jesus Christ be with your *spirit,*—μετὰ τοῦ πνεύματος ὑμῶν, ἀδελφοί.) Here again Cranmer followed Tyndale, as against Wycliffe, who gives the singular, ("youre *herte* schal haue ioie ").]

Sunday. —V. 16. "A little while, and ye shall not see me : and again, a little while, and ye shall see me." I will take these words of the Lord Jesus as said by Him to myself. Perhaps, as so said, they mean that, according to the usual count of time, I have but a short time longer to live. I might see it to be so, if I were gifted with insight into the future. The hour of death, brought about perhaps by some quite unforeseen accident, may be imminent, and it may be but a very little while—a week, or a day—and then I shall see my Lord. But possibly I may yet have many years of health and strength before me. Supposing I have as many as twenty or thirty such years, even then it is true that what remains to me of life is but "a little while," little in comparison of what has to be done in it in mortifying sin, gaining a victory over self, and finishing the task allotted to me in the

order of God's Providence.   The Angels at the Ascension
seemed to have thought the long centuries which would
elapse before the Second Advent to be "a little while";
for they will not allow the Apostles to gaze up idly into
heaven for a moment, but tell them that this same Jesus
should come again, as they had seen Him go, as if there
was no time they could afford to waste.[1]   There is then,
I see, a Divine or heavenly count of time, according to
which the longest life is all too short for the perfecting
of the spiritual character.   When time has for us come
to an end, we shall measure it according to this count,
and shall esteem it to have been but "a little while."
But any how, be what remains to me of life long or
short, according to the mere human count of time, what
will the sight of my Lord be to me, when it does come?
See Him I must; for "every eye shall see him."[2]   Am
I so abiding in Him by faith, that, were He to appear
to me to-night, I should "have confidence, and not be
ashamed before him at his coming"?[3]

Monday.—V. 16. " A little while, and ye shall see me,
because I go to the Father."   These words caused perplexity to the disciples; for how could they see their
Master, if He were to go away from them to God? nay,
how could His going away to God be *a reason* for their
seeing Him,—"ye shall see me, *because* I go"?   The
answer is, that the seeing He is speaking of here is not
the mere sight of the eyes, but that of the mind and the
heart; it is that apprehension of Him in His true character,
as the risen and glorified Son of God, to which St. Thomas
gave expression, when, abandoning for ever his unbelief,
and even not availing himself of the evidence of touch
which was offered to him by his Master, he exclaimed,

<hr>

[1] See Acts i. 10, 11.   [2] Rev. i. 7.   [3] See 1 John ii. 28.

"My Lord and my God."[1] For the full recognition of Christ by faith, His death, resurrection, ascension, and the mission of the Comforter, which followed in due course, and which last could not possibly have been without His leaving His disciples ("If I go not away, the Comforter will not come unto you; but if I depart, I will send him unto you "[2])—were absolutely essential. His going away, so far from being a dereliction of His disciples, was really the means of opening their eyes to His true character, and investing them with new faculties and powers; they should see Him more truly than they had ever done before, *because* He had gone away from them. There is some dim shadow of this in our ordinary human experience, according to which we fail to appreciate a friend at his true worth, so long as he is by our side in the battle of life; but no sooner is he disentangled from his earthly surroundings, than the brighter parts of his character begin to stand out in relief to our minds.— Lord, it has not been my lot to see Thee with the eye of flesh, in the days of Thy earthly pilgrimage; and doubtless there were in that fleshly sight drawbacks as well as helps to faith. But it is always open to me to see Thee with the eye of faith, and to see Thee so clearly as to "rejoice" in Thee "with joy unspeakable and full of glory."[3] Make me ambitious of this blessedness.[4]

Tuesday. — Vv. 17, 19. "Then said some of his disciples among themselves, What is this that he saith unto us, A little while, and ye shall not see me: and again, a little while, and ye shall see me: and, Because I go to the Father? . . . Now Jesus knew that they were desirous to ask him, and said unto them, Do ye enquire

---

[1] See St. John xx. 27, 28.   [2] St. John xvi. 7.
[3] See 1 Pet. i. 8.   [4] See St. John xx. 29.

among yourselves of that I said, A little while, and ye shall not see me: and again, a little while, and ye shall see me?" A little glimpse is here given us into the reason why our Lord so often spoke obscurely and enigmatically. It was to elicit and exercise thought on the part of His disciples. No greater boon can be conferred on any one than to lead him to inquire at God's oracles with reverence and humility, seeking light from God, where light is to be had, and, where it is not to be had, acquiescing in mystery.——Lord Jesus, Thou knowest when we are desirous to ask Thee respecting such truths of Thy word as offer difficulties to our understanding. And Thou condescendest now *as graciously* to such desires as Thou didst of old, when Thou wast upon earth ; and *more* effectually, since we have the anointing Spirit sent from Thee, to teach us of all things,[1] and to guide us into all truth.[2]

Wednesday. —— V. 20. "Ye shall be sorrowful, but your sorrow shall be turned into joy." Our Lord uses here the most exact, as well as the most consolatory language. He does not promise that sorrow shall be taken away, and joy placed in its stead, though that would have been true ; and that was in effect what was done. The phrase, "Your sorrow shall be turned into joy," expresses that out of the very materials of the sorrow the joy should be wrought, just as the weak, tasteless water in Cana of Galilee was changed into " wine that maketh glad the heart of man."[3] It was so with the disciples. The pang of being bereaved of their Lord " for a little while " was an essential condition, a necessary preliminary, of the rapture with which they were to look

---

[1] See 1 John ii. 20, 27.   [2] See St. John xvi. 13.
[3] See St. John ii. 9, 10, and Ps. civ. 15.

upon Him again in His glorified form—nay, of all their subsequent much closer spiritual intercourse with Him. He must have died in the flesh, if He was to be given back to them in the Spirit.—O Lord, Thou wouldest have us know that the trials and troubles of Thy sending, are themselves an indispensable instrument of our sanctification. "Our light affliction, which is but for a moment," is not merely unworthy "to be compared with the glory which shall be revealed in us,"[1] but also "worketh for us" (in the hands of Thy grace) "a far more exceeding and eternal weight of glory."[2] Surely then it behoveth us not only to "rejoice in hope of the glory of God, but" to "glory in tribulations also: knowing that tribulation worketh patience; and patience, experience; and experience, hope; and hope maketh not ashamed; because the love of God is shed abroad in our hearts by the Holy Ghost which is given unto us."[3]

Thursday. — V. 21. "A woman when she is in travail hath sorrow, because her hour is come; but as soon as she is delivered of the child, she remembereth no more the anguish, for joy that a man is born into the world." This illustration is not a fanciful one, but deeply seated in the constitution of things, and in the sentence, largely tempered with mercy, which God pronounced upon the original transgressors. The man was doomed to labour[4]; but in useful and productive labour he has, ever since the fall, found his interest and happiness. The woman was to bring forth in sorrow[5]; but mother's pangs were to be the source of mother's joy. Amidst the manifold meanings of this passage (perhaps one of the deepest in the whole Bible) this assuredly is one, that it

[1] See Rom. viii. 18. [2] 2 Cor. iv. 17. [3] Rom. v. 2-6.
[4] See Gen. iii. 17, 18, 19. [5] See Gen. iii. 16.

was through the sufferings of the disciples in the loss of their Lord (sufferings, we may be sure, which led them into themselves and their own hearts with all manner of profitable questionings and ponderings) that the Divine Child was to be born within them, born anew in the apprehensions of their understanding, the convictions of their reason, the affections of their heart. St. Paul employs the same illustration as the Saviour, only adapting it to his own argument, which required that he, not his converts, should be the persons subjected to the preliminary pangs; "My little children, of whom I travail in birth again until Christ be formed in you."[1] —Lord, make me to aspire after the blessedness, and to perceive and thankfully to accept the conditions, of having Christ formed in me. It is only through tribulation and trial, sometimes heart-*rending*, always heart-*searching*, and always (blessed be Thy Name) adapted to our powers of endurance, and light in comparison of "the far more exceeding and eternal weight of glory,"[2] that the Lord Jesus can be engendered in the heart of man. "No throes of anguish, no offspring," is the law of spiritual as of natural birth.

Friday.—V. 22. " Ye now therefore have sorrow." What was the source of their sorrow ? It arose from the absence of their Lord, which was immediately impending. Our Lord had foretold it when He said, " The days will come, when the bridegroom shall be taken away from them, and then shall they fast in those days."[3] Let me seriously ask myself what is the source of my sorrow and my joy, my pleasure and my pain. The great test of character, as distinct from conduct, is, What gives pleasure and pain ? Should I so have loved our Lord, when He

---

[1] Gal. iv. 19.   [2] See 2 Cor. iv. 17.   [3] St. Mark ii. 20.

was upon earth, that I should have joined myself to Him as the disciples did, breaking all worldly and natural ties for His sake, and should have been plunged in the deepest sorrow by His removal? "In his favour is life,"[1] it is said; and again, "Thy loving-kindness is better than life."[2] Do I prize above all things the sense of His favour and gracious presence with me; and when this sense is withdrawn, do I mourn over the withdrawal of it? Is it indeed the thought of being with Him for ever that lends to Paradise and heaven their principal charm in my thought of them? or can I dream of a Paradise and a heaven without a Christ?

Saturday. — V. 22. "But I will see you again, and your heart shall rejoice, and your joy no man taketh from you." Of Christian joy no man can rob us, because its seat is in the heart and character, and because it does not arise from external and adventitious circumstances, which may wholly alter. Christ does not promise happiness, but joy to His followers; for indeed happiness is shown by its very etymology to be something accidental or fortuitous —it lies in a hap, or in something which befalls us from without. But the joy which the spiritual apprehension and sight of Jesus Christ causes in the heart ("I will see you again, and your heart shall rejoice") being internal, and standing in our relationship to Christ by faith, is out of the reach of external accident; it cannot possibly be touched but by some sin, or failure of faith, interrupting and suspending that spiritual relationship. Let me seriously inquire whether I have within me the rudiments of that joy, remembering that faith, if real and vital, cannot fail to produce some measure of it; as it is said, " Whom having not seen, ye love; in whom, though now

---

[1] Ps. xxx. 5.   [2] Ps. lxiii. 3.

ye see him not, yet believing, *ye rejoice with joy unspeakable and full of glory*"[1]; " By whom also we have access by faith into this grace wherein we stand, and *rejoice in hope of the glory of God.*"[2]

[1] 1 Pet. i. 8.   [2] Rom. v. 2.

Chapter XXIX

THE GOSPEL FOR THE FOURTH SUNDAY AFTER EASTER.

St. John xvi. 5 *to* 16 (but substituting the words *Jesus said unto his disciples* for the "But" with which *v.* 5 commences).

5 Jesus said unto his disciples, Now I go my way to him that
6 sent me, and none of you asketh me, Whither goest thou? But because I have said these things unto you sorrow hath filled your
7 heart. Nevertheless, I tell you the truth, it is expedient for you that I go away: for if I go not away, the Comforter will not
8 come unto you; but if I depart, I will send him unto you. And when he is come, he will reprove the world of sin, and of righteous-
9 ness, and of judgement: Of sin; because they believe not on me:
10 Of righteousness; because I go to my Father, and ye see me no
11 more: Of judgement; because the prince of this world is judged.
12 I have yet many things to say unto you, but ye cannot bear them
13 now. Howbeit, when he, the Spirit of truth is come, he will guide you into all truth; for he shall not speak of himself; but whatsoever he shall hear, that shall he speak, and he will shew you
14 things to come. He shall glorifie me: for he shall receive of mine,
15 and shall shew it unto you. All things that the Father hath, are mine: therefore said I, that he shall take of mine, and shall shew it unto you.

[Miss. Sar.	1549.	1662 s.b.
In illo tempore, Dixit Jesus discipulis suis; Vado ad eum, qui me misit, etc. (*Vulg.* Et nunc vado ad eum, qui misit me, etc.)	*Jesus said unto his disciples,* Now go I my way to him that sent me, etc.	*Jesus said unto his disciples,* Now I go my way to him that sent me, etc. (*Gr.* Νῦν δὲ ὑπάγω πρὸς τὸν πέμψαντά με.)

This Gospel is drawn from the first and second sections of St. John xvi., as the preceding one was from the third, and its subject is *The function of the Paraclete to the world and to the disciples.* [*See* Introduction to Gospel for Third Sunday after Easter.] It might have been as well to begin it in the middle of *v.* 4, with the words, "And these things I said not unto you at the beginning, because I was with you," which stand in such close connexion with those which follow, "But now I go my way to him that sent me." This connexion is thus indicated by Professor Westcott (*in loc.*): "Hitherto Christ had Himself borne the storm of hostility, and shielded the disciples : now He was to leave them, and the wrath of His enemies would be diverted upon them, though they would have another Advocate." —*Translation of* 1540. (1) *V.* 6. "Your *hearts* are full of sorrow," instead of, "Sorrow hath filled your *heart*" [*see* the end of preceding Introduction]. (2) "He will *rebuke* the world of sin," instead of, "He will *reprove* the world of sin." Tyndale (1534) had "rebuke." Cranmer followed Tyndale. King James's Translators went back to the "reprove" of Wycliffe (1380). Both "rebuke" and "reproof" yield an idea too exclusively moral,—ignore too much the argumentative process and its result, to which the word ἐλέγχω points. "Convict" (which the Revisers of 1881 have substituted) is for that reason the better word. "The idea of conviction is complex," says Professor Westcott. "It involves the conceptions of authoritative examination, of unquestionable proof, of decisive judgment, of punitive power. Whatever the final issue may be, he who 'convicts' another places the truth of the case in dispute in a clear light before him, so that it must be seen and acknowledged as truth. He who then rejects the conclusion which this exposition involves, rejects it with his eyes open and at his peril. Truth seen as truth carries with it condemnation to all who refuse to welcome it." (3) *V.* 11. "Of judgement, because the prince of this world is judged *already*." And so Wycliffe: "the prince of this world is *now* demed," and Tyndale, "because the chefe ruler of this worlde, is iudged *all ready*." Whence came this "already," as there is no ἤδη in the original? Doubtless from the Vulgate. We are apt to forget how very much the earlier English Translations of the Scriptures were modified by the Vulgate or Latin Translation,—the Version which was in use throughout the whole Western Church. Wycliffe translated *directly* from the Vulgate ; it is exceedingly improbable that he had sufficient knowledge of Greek to enable him to render the New Testament in any other way ; nor, even if he had, would he have been easily able to secure at that early period a manuscript of the Greek Testament from which to translate (it was not till the taking of Constantinople by the Turks in 1453 that Greek manuscripts of the New Testament were carried here and there about Europe by the fugitive Greeks). "Tyndale" indeed "rendered the Greek text directly," but it was "while still he consulted the Vulgate, the Latin translation of Erasmus, and the German of Luther."[1] And, no doubt, "the best learned bishops and others," to whom Cranmer, in arranging for his Bible, sent various portions of "an old English Translation of the New Testament" in so many "paper-books," "to the intent that they should make a perfect correction thereof," had a knowledge of Greek, and revised "the old English Translation" from the original. Still, in every English translation down to the Authorised, the Vulgate was consulted, and allowed a certain amount of influence. And the "already" of Cranmer's Bible in the verse before us is simply the "jam" of the Vulgate ("quia princeps hujus mundi *jam* judicatus est"), which Cranmer's Translators, though it had nothing to represent it in the Greek, did not like to discard. The English exiles at Geneva, whose Translation was published in 1557, and of course also the Rheims Translators of 1582 (who avowedly took the Vulgate as their basis), continued the interpolated word, the first rendering it "already," the second "now." King James's Translators, finding nothing corresponding to it in the Greek, signed its death-warrant. (4) *V.* 12. "But ye cannot bear them *away* now" (ἀλλ' οὐ δύνασθε βαστάζειν ἄρτι). "Bear them *away*" had been Tyndale's Version [1534]. Wycliffe's was simply "bear them." The idea is not that of "carrying off" instruction from a teacher, as people speak of "carrying away something from a sermon"; but simply that of *endurance*,—"Ye cannot at present" (before my Resurrection and the Comforter's Advent) "endure the doctrine of the Cross ; it would be meat too strong and solid for your spiritual digestion."]

Sunday. — Vv. 5, 6. "Now I go my way to him that sent me ; and none of you asketh me, Whither goest thou ? But because I have said these things unto you," (*i.e.*, that the world shall hate and persecute you, put you out of the synagogues, and think the killing you to be an acceptable service done to God[2]), "sorrow hath filled your heart." "Hath *filled* your heart,"—they thought of nothing but that they themselves were to be left behind

---

[1] "Westcott's General View of the History of the English Bible," p. 174. [Macmillan : 1868.]

[2] See Chap. xv. 18, 19, 20 ; xvi. 1, 2, 3.

as butts, at which the shafts of the world's malice, which
had fastened on their Master, so long as He had been
with them, should be aimed.   Had they seriously inquired
whither He was going, and what was the nature and the
object of His departure, they would have found that it
was far better for themselves, as well as for Him, that His
bodily presence should be withdrawn.   Shortly afterwards,
when they saw Him parted from them, and carried up into
heaven, they *did* return to Jerusalem with great joy,[1] both
on His account who was thus glorified, and on their own,
as they felt that they had an Advocate and a Supporter
in the realms above, who would enable them to triumph
over the world's bitterest opposition.   "None of you
asketh me, Whither goest thou ?"   How little curiosity
do men show respecting the things which lie beyond the
grave, the things of eternity !   How little interest do
they take in the counsels of God respecting the salvation
of man and the future of His Church,—things "which
the angels," we are told, "desire to look into."[2]   Every
thing which the senses and ordinary experience of man
cannot reach to—God, Christ, the state after death, the
spiritual world and its agencies,—is vague, unreal, and
shadowy to them ; only this life and its concerns are a
present and pressing reality, absorbing all their care,
interest, and solicitude.—Lord, strengthen in me that
faith, which "is the substance of things hoped for, the
evidence of things not seen,"[3] that I may never be
wholly absorbed in "the things which are seen and are
temporal."[4]

Monday.—V. 7. "Nevertheless I tell you the truth ;
It is expedient for you that I " (*I* emphatic, as distinct

---

[1] See St. Luke xxiv. 51, 52.   [2] See 1 Pet. i. 12.
[3] See Heb. xi. 1.   [4] See 2 Cor. iv. 18.

from "the Comforter,") "go away." Had He not gone away, their sins could not have been atoned for by His death, nor their acquittal declared by His resurrection, nor could they have been visited by the other Comforter, who should abide with them for ever. How little do we know what is really expedient for us! How may the things, which seem to be most adverse, prove to be in the highest degree expedient! When Jacob cries out, "All these things are against me,"[1] he is under the illusion that Joseph has been torn in pieces by wild beasts, altogether ignorant of the fact that he is governor of Egypt, and yearning for his father and his father's home. Similarly the disciples were plunged in sorrow, because it seemed to them that death would swallow up their Master with devouring jaws, and little thought that it was through death that He was to be exalted to God's right hand, there to sympathize with them still, and watch over them with all the tender guardianship of a never-failing Providence. In praying against earthly losses, or for earthly blessings, let me always pray in the consciousness of my ignorance of what is expedient for me. " O God, whose never-failing providence ordereth all things both in heaven and earth ; We humbly beseech thee to put away from us all hurtful " (not all painful) "things, and to give us those things which be " (really and truly, not apparently) "profitable for us."[2] "Fulfil now, O Lord, the desires and petitions of thy servants, *as may be most expedient for them.*"[3]

Tuesday.—V. 7. "For if I go not away, the Comforter will not come unto you." "It was necessary that the order [of things] should be maintained ; that the

---

[1] See Gen. xlii. 36.   [2] Collect for the Eighth Sunday after Trinity.
[3] Prayer of St. Chrysostom.

earth, defiled and profaned by Adam's sin, and by so many crimes and sacrileges, should be purified by the Sacrifice of the Cross, before it could receive the Holy Ghost; that the sin of man should be expiated by the death of the true Victim, before it could be reconciled with God by His Spirit; that his heart should be washed in the Saviour's blood, before it became the temple of the Holy Ghost, and entered into that new covenant with God, whereof Jesus Christ is the Mediator by His blood, and the bond and pledge by His Spirit." (Quesnel.) The above holds good, not only as regards the world, but in the life and experience of the individual soul. Until the sins of each individual soul have been laid upon Christ by faith, and until that soul has thus gained a personal interest in His atoning death, the Comforter cannot come to it; it would be an inversion of the order of God's appointment. Each of us must first know the smiting of the rock, before we can know the gushing forth of the living water.[1]—Lord, make me to look upon Thee, whom I have pierced, and to mourn for Thee in true contrition of heart[2]; and so shall I be made to drink of the spiritual rock.[3] The water that Thou shalt give me shall be in me a well of water springing up into everlasting life.[4]

Wednesday. — V. 7. "If I go not away, the Comforter will not come unto you." These words might often find, in the death of a dear friend or relative, a true and edifying application, albeit a lower one than that which originally belonged to them. Often, if the bereaved person who is left behind could see the truth, he would see that the bodily and temporary separation is necessary

---

[1] See Exod. xvii. 6.
[3] See 1 Cor. x. 4.
[2] See Zech. xii. 10.
[4] See St. John iv. 14.

to ensure the spiritual and eternal re-union. He himself, it may be, has to be awakened from spiritual deadness, and made serious and thoughtful, by the removal of one who seemed all essential to his happiness; or, if he has not been absolutely dead hitherto, he has been loitering and lingering on his spiritual course, and needs quickening, or has been indulging in the idolatry of the domestic affections, and needs to have room made in his heart for the reception of a better Comforter. Let such an one lay to heart this intimation of our Lord that the going away of a true friend may be the indispensable condition of the advent of the Comforter. The heart has only a certain amount of room in it; too often is it like the inn at Bethlehem, in which no harbour for Christ was found; the world, its cares, its intercourse, its vanities, occupy every chamber,—" there is no room for them in the inn."[1] And, even where there is not worldliness of mind, creatures may exclude the Creator. They may be loved more than God,[2] instead of in God, and in subordination to Him. When, under these circumstances, He withdraws them, designing to place Himself in their room, it is not that they may be permanently or in all respects withdrawn, but only that intercourse of a higher kind may be held with them. When we approach the throne of grace even now, we draw near to them spiritually; for, if they have fallen asleep in the faith, they are with Christ in Paradise.[3] And eventually there will be a re-union, which shall know no parting, in the heavenly Zion, as it is said; " He went, and met him in the mount of God, and kissed him."[4] Choose we then which we will have—intercourse with our dear ones according to the flesh, or according to

---

[1] See St. Luke ii. 7.
[2] See St. Matt. x. 37.
[3] See St. Luke xxiii. 43.
[4] Exod. iv. 27.

the Spirit. We cannot have both. Shall the bond, which binds us to them, be earthly and natural, or heavenly and spiritual?

Thursday.—Vv. 8, 9, 10. "And when he is come, he will reprove" (convince) "the world of sin, and of righteousness, and of judgment: of sin, because they believe not on me; of righteousness, because I go to my Father, and ye see me no more; of judgment, because the prince of this world is judged." The Holy Spirit should, it is here predicted, produce a revolution in a man's way of looking at sin, at Christ, and at the false and ungodly system called the world, which is in antagonism to Christ. He should throw a new light upon sin, and exhibit it in much blacker colours, by showing that the root and life of it is unbelief,—an unbelief which finds its climax and culminating point in rejecting God as manifested in Christ. And He should throw a new light upon the system called the world, by showing it to be under the domination of Satan, who, however, is doomed to be cast out and trodden under foot of the world's Redeemer. By way of ascertaining, then, whether the Spirit has done His convincing and converting work upon my heart, I may ask myself what views I entertain of sin and of the world. Am I thinking of sin as nothing more than the breaking of certain rules, which God has laid down for my life and conduct? or do I ever think of it as practical disbelief of His word, which has annexed penalties to the violation of His law? and has it ever struck me that the worst, most hopeless, most irremediable form of sin is the rejection of (or the not closing with) the offers of mercy and love which God makes to me in Christ? And again, do I regard the world as under the power of the devil, animated and inspired by him, and as doomed with him, and now lying under sentence of death ? Ah ! what strangers must they be to the convincing and converting work of the Spirit, who cannot see the operations of evil spirits in the background of the evil which is in and around them ; who question altogether the personal existence of Satan, and resolve all the Scriptural notices of that existence into an allegory ! Surely to keep them in this blindness is one of his own devices.[1]

Friday.—Vv. 12, 13. " I have yet many things to say unto you, but ye cannot bear them now. Howbeit when he, the Spirit of truth, is come, he will guide you into all truth : for he shall not speak of himself; but whatsoever he shall hear, that shall he speak : and he will shew you things to come." It is clearly implied in these words that, when the disciples should be fully placed under the guidance and tuition of the Spirit, they should then be qualified to understand and appreciate those truths which were now beyond them. For which reason I find that St. Paul, writing to the Corinthians, many years after the dispensation of the Spirit had been fully set up, reproves them as carnal, because they could not bear advanced teaching; " I, brethren, could not speak unto you as unto spiritual, but as unto carnal, even as unto babes in Christ. I have fed you with milk, and not with meat : for hitherto ye were not able to bear it, neither yet now are ye able."[2] And the same tone of reproof he adopts with the Hebrews, telling them that respecting the High Priest after the order of Melchisedek " we have many things to say, and hard to be uttered, seeing ye are dull of hearing. For when for the time ye ought to be teachers, ye have need that one teach you again which be the first principles of the oracles of God ; and

---

[1] See 2 Cor. ii. 11.   [2] 1 Cor. iii. 1, 2.

are become such as have need of milk, and not of strong meat."[1]   Nor must it escape me that part of the Spirit's province to the disciples is here expressly stated to be the showing them things to come, as it has pleased Him to do in St. Paul's great oracles respecting the Second Advent,[2] and the man of sin,[3] and in St. John's book of the Revelation, the study of which so many Christians decline, and think it safer to confine themselves to the more elementary truths.——O Lord, since Thou hast placed me under the dispensation of Thy Spirit, let me seek to live fully up to the privileges of my position.   Let me not be a backward scholar in Thy school; but grant that, leaving the principles of the doctrine of Christ, I may go on unto perfection,[4] willing and ready to learn all that the Spirit is ready to teach, and to be guided into whatever truth it may please Him to lead the way.

Saturday.—Vv. 14, 15. "He shall glorify me : for he shall receive of mine, and shall shew it unto you. All things that the Father hath are mine: therefore said I, that he shall take of mine, and shall shew it unto you." Let me meditate on the mutual glorification of the Persons in the Blessed Trinity, of which I have here such a striking instance. Our Blessed Lord in these final discourses leads His disciples to look to the advent and teaching of the Comforter, as something which would do far more than replace His own personal Presence, the precious counsels which He had given, and the lofty example which He had set them. On the other hand, He says that the Spirit, when He came, should glorify not Himself, but Christ,——should take of the things of Christ, and

---

[1] Heb. v. 11, 12.

[2] See 1 Thess. iv. 15 to end.

[3] See 2 Thess. ii, 3, 4.

[4] See Heb. vi. 1.

exhibit to them the treasures of grace and love which were in Him. And yet He shrinks from calling these treasures His own without a reference to the Father's proprietorship in them, in whose love to fallen man the scheme of Redemption originated. While the Father, when He spake directly to man at the Baptism and Transfiguration of the Son, directs us to the Son as His Representative and Exponent; "This is my beloved Son, in whom I am well pleased;" "This is my beloved Son: hear him."[1] What a reproof is there here to the natural vanity of the human heart! In doing any little good, what a tendency do I find in my heart to monopolize the credit, what an eagerness to exhibit self as the doer of it. Lord, cure by Thy grace this radical vice of my heart. Let me seek to hide myself in doing good, as Thou thyself doest; well content, if only I can bless or help others, to bless or help them as from behind a screen.

[1] St. Matt. iii. 17, and St. Mark ix. 7.

Chapter XXX.

THE GOSPEL FOR THE FIFTH SUNDAY AFTER EASTER.

St. John xvi. 23 *to the end*
(leaving out the words, "And in that day ye shall ask me nothing,"
with which *v.* 23 commences).

23 Verily, verily I say unto you, Whatsoever ye shall ask the
24 Father in my Name, he will give it you. Hitherto have ye asked
nothing in my name: Ask, and ye shall receive, that your joy
25 may be full. These things have I spoken unto you in proverbs: the time cometh when I shall no more speak unto you in
26 proverbs, but I shall shew you plainly of the Father. At that
day ye shall ask in my Name: and I say not unto you, that I
27 will pray the Father for you; for the Father himself loveth you,
because ye have loved me, and have believed that I came out
28 from God. I came forth from the Father, and am come into
the world: Again, I leave the world, and go to the Father.
29 His disciples said unto him; Lo, now speakest thou plainly,
30 and speakest no proverb. Now are we sure that thou knowest
all things, and needest not that any man should ask thee: by this
31 we believe that thou camest forth from God. Jesus answered
32 them, Do ye now believe? Behold the hour cometh, yea, is now
come, that ye shall be scattered every man to his own, and shall
leave me alone: and yet I am not alone, because the Father is
33 with me. These things I have spoken unto you, that in me ye
might have peace. In the world ye shall have tribulation; but be
of good cheer, I have overcome the world.

[MISS. SAR.	1549.	1662 S.B.
In illo tempore, Dixit Jesus discipulis suis; Amen, Amen, dico vobis : etc. . . . *down to the end of v.* 30 . . . in hoc credimus quia à Deo existi.	Verily, verily I say unto you . . . *down to the end of the Chapter* (*v.* 33) . . . but be of good cheer, I have overcome the world.	Verily, verily I say unto you . . . *down to,* but be of good cheer, I have overcome the world.

The three verses added on by our Reformers to the old Gospel of the Sarum Missal are a distinct gain. In them our Lord somewhat discounts, as was His wont, the enthusiastic profession of belief just made by His disciples, and shows how little the convictions respecting Him, at which they professed to have arrived, would bear the stress of trial. [See the Thought for *Friday*.] He also sums up the scope of His latest teaching (that delivered to the little circle of the faithful since Judas left the supper-room) in those words, "These things have I spoken unto you, that in me ye might have peace ;" and concludes with the blessed and encouraging assurance of the victory which He had won, and which they in Him should win, over the world ; "In the world ye shall have tribulation : but be of good cheer ; I have overcome the world." "These were," says Professor Westcott, "His last recorded words of teaching before His Passion," and in them "He claims the glory of a Conqueror." Surely it was meet and right that words of such weighty import should find a place in the Liturgical Gospels. — As to the *beginning* of this Gospel, it is well perhaps (at least for those who are acquainted only with the English Translation) that the *earlier* clause of *v.* 23 ("And in that day ye shall *ask* me nothing") is not embraced in it, since the asking of the earlier clause (expressed by the verb ἐρωτάω) is entirely distinct from the asking of the latter expressed by αἰτέω. The former verb denotes the asking for information ; the latter the suing as a suppliant for a gift. Hereupon Archbishop Trench says (*Synonyms of the New Testament*, p. 140); "There is not in this verse a contrast drawn between asking *the Son*, which shall cease, and asking *the Father*, which shall begin : but the first half of the verse closes the declaration of one blessing, namely, that hereafter they shall be so taught by the Spirit as to have nothing further to *inquire ;* the second half of the verse begins the declaration of a new blessing, that whatever they shall *seek* from the Father in the Son's name, He will give it to them." And Professor Westcott, with admirable clearness and terseness ; "*The questioning of ignorance* is to be replaced by *the definite prayer* which claims absolute accomplishment, as being in conformity with the will of God."—*Translation of* 1540. (1) *V.* 25. "These things have I spoken unto you by proverbs. The time will come when, etc." Who foisted in the "but," which appears between "proverbs" and "the time" in all our ordinary modern copies of the Authorised Version ? *It was not in the Authorised Version originally.* It will not be found in the Authorised Version as given in "the Parallel New Testament" [Oxford, University Press : 1882], nor as given in Bagster's "Hexapla" (from an old black-letter copy of 1611). *It never at any time has been in the Prayer-Book* (a discrepancy this between the Prayer-Book and our modern copies of the Bible). It is true that there is a reading of the original Greek, which places an ἀλλ' before ἔρχεται, and that this reading has the sanction of some good manuscripts, and appears in the third edition of Stephanus, published in 1550, which the Translators of 1611 are supposed to have regarded as generally trustworthy ; but it has not approved itself to our Revisers of 1881, and suspicion generally rests upon it. But without entering into the question of the correctness of the reading, how and when did a " But," which King James's Translators did not recognise, find its way into modern copies of a version which professes to be theirs ? (2) *V.* 25. "but I shall shew you plainly *from* my Father." Here we have another instance of the influence of the Vulgate on the early English Translations, even where Greek was known to the Translators. [See the Introduction to the preceding Gospel.] The Vulgate here has, " sed palam de Patre annunciabo vobis," a very correct rendering of the original, ἀλλὰ παρρησίᾳ περὶ τοῦ πατρὸς ἀναγγελῶ ὑμῖν. But the Latin preposition *de*, which here means *concerning, about, on the subject of*, also means *from, down from* (as in the opening of the Litany "Pater *de* cœlis Deus "), and both Tyndale and Cranmer (strangely enough, having the Greek before them) render it thus. Wycliffe, on the other hand, without the Greek to help him, rendered the *de* rightly ; "but opunli *of* my fadir, I schal telle to you." (3) *V.* 26. "I say not unto you, that I will *speak unto my Father for you.*" A free rendering of ὅτι ἐγὼ ἐρωτήσω τὸν πατέρα περὶ ὑμῶν ; but there is something pleasant in this homely phrase, as applied to our Lord's intercession for His people. Cranmer adopted it from Tyndale. One is reminded of, "Wouldest thou be *spoken for* to the king, or to the captain of the host ?" (2 Kings iv. 13). (4) *V.* 30. "And needest not that any man should *ask thee any question.*" A very good way of marking the difference of meaning between ἐρωτάω and αἰτέω. [See the early part of this Introduction.] Cranmer here again adopts Tyndale's Version. In *v.* 23 of this Chapter the Revisers have put *ask me no question* as the representative of ἐρωτάω into their margin. It would perhaps have been well to admit it into the text. (5) *V.* 31. "Jesus answered them, *Now ye do believe.*" The Genevan Translation (1557) was the first

English Version which rendered these words *as a question.* Wycliffe, and Tyndale, and Cranmer, all *exhibit it as an affirmation.* And several eminent modern commentators (among them Dean Alford) maintain that it is so. Thus Stier ("Words of the Lord Jesus" [Edinburgh: MDCCCLVII.], Vol. VI. pp. 415, 416): "Does not the whole of Chap. xvii. most solemnly attribute this" [faith] "to them, and give *testimony* to their believing? And could the same John who wrote Chap. ii. 11 ['His disciples believed on him'], and recorded Chap. vi. 69 ['We believe and are sure that thou art that Christ, etc.'], now be supposed to declare that the Lord at the close of all still doubted the faith of His eleven? . . . Compare, moreover, St. Matt. xvi. 17, 18 ['Blessed art thou, Simon Barjona, etc.']. It had been the aim and object of the whole prophetic ministry of Jesus to make some disciples (not the apostles alone) susceptible for the coming of the Spirit of truth and the benefits of His passion, laying in them the foundation of faith in His own person ;—and was this not attained at the end of all, was it even still a questionable thing? . . . Let all this be well pondered, and the note of interrogation will certainly be renounced as *impossible!* Nor is the most distant irony to be assumed in this earnest and frank indicative; the ἀληθῶς of Chap. xvii. 8 ['they have known *surely* that I came out from thee'] decides against this. . . . The *now* consequently appears to indicate *an end attained* . . . it is 'the great issue of his labours upon them, expressed in one definite word' [Lange]." Powerful as this is, it seems to me to *press too hard upon the language* (on the hypothesis that it is an interrogation). Our Lord did not mean to question the reality of their faith, which is (as Stier justly observes) emphatically asserted to God in the High-Priestly Prayer; but *to themselves He makes the least of it,* predicting how easily shaken it would be with the first stress of trial.—Professor Westcott takes a middle course in his *exegesis:* "The words are half-question, half-exclamation (xx. 29). The power and permanence of their faith are brought into doubt, and not its reality." (6) *V.* 33. "*For* in the world shall ye have tribulation." How the word "for" crept in, it is not easy to say. Cranmer got it from Tyndale; but Tyndale found nothing representing it either in the Greek or in the Vulgate. Probably he inserted it as an *explanatory* particle— "that in me ye might have peace"—"*for,* observe that you will need peace; in the world you shall find nothing but tribulation."]

Sunday.—V. 23. "Verily, verily, I say unto you, whatsoever ye shall ask the Father in my name, he will give it you." These apparently unlimited promises to

prayer are seen, when we examine them closely, to carry
their own limitations with them. A name is expressive
of the character of him who bears it, and to pray in
Christ's name is to pray in acknowledgment of His
revealed character ; it is to pray "*by* Jesus Christ, *with*
Jesus Christ, and *in* Jesus Christ." "*By* Jesus Christ":
it is to come to God through Him, as the revealed door
of access to the Father, through the rent veil—that is to
say, through His flesh, or human nature, which was rent by
death into its two constituent elements of body and soul.
In simpler words, it is to come to God in dependence on
Christ's *sacrifice and righteousness*. "*With* Jesus Christ":
it is to come to God as it were in His company, introduced by Him, presented by Him, taught and having ou1
prayer put in our mouth by Him ; "When ye pray, say,
Our Father"[1]; "My Father, and your Father."[2] In simpler
words, it is to come to God in dependence on Christ's
intercession. "*In* Jesus Christ": the soul of the believer
is in Jesus Christ by faith, much as a living body lives,
and moves, and has its being in the atmosphere, which it
momentarily inhales ; Jesus is its moral atmosphere ; by
communion with Him it lives. To pray in His name is
to pray in the enjoyment of this communion. Laid under
these conditions, a man cannot ask for what would be
spiritually mischievous to him, or not in conformity with
God's will.

Monday.—V. 24. " Hitherto have ye asked nothing in
my name : ask, and ye shall receive, that your joy may be
full." Let us try to realise the great difference, which the
introduction into them of this new element " in my name "
must have made in the prayers of the disciples. Our
Lord had previously taught them to call God their Father

---

[1] St. Luke xi. 2.   [2] St. John xx. 17.

in prayer, and had put words of wondrous significance and comprehensiveness into their mouths, which they could but little understand till the Comforter opened the meaning of them. But, because the veil of Christ's flesh was not yet rent, they could not see the atoning death as giving entrance into the holiest of all; and because the High Priest had not yet entered into the holy place, they could not see Him interceding for them and introducing them there; and because the Spirit had not yet descended upon them, they could not as yet inhale freely and fully the element of communion with their Divine Lord. How must prayer have been a new exercise to them, when these new ideas were thrown into it,—when the true light shone upon it, and lighted it up with this new significance! A peaceful, nay, a pleasant exercise it had always been; but now, the confidence and assurance with which their Saviour's name, the acknowledgment of His character, and of the relations in which He stood to them, enabled them to pray, made their heart brim over with joy in prayer; "ask, and ye shall receive, that your joy may be full,"—literally, " fulfilled," [1]—" filled to the brim."

Tuesday.—V. 25. " These things have I spoken unto you in proverbs,"—or dark enigmatical sayings, such as many of our Lord's were, such as He seems to have made a point of uttering. For example, there is His saying about being born of water and the Spirit, which caused Nicodemus such perplexity[2]; there is the saying about eating His flesh and drinking His blood, which so stumbled some of His disciples that they went back and walked no more with Him[3]; there are His parables, of which He

---

[1] ἵνα ἡ χαρὰ ὑμῶν ᾖ πεπληρωμένη. The Revisers of 1881 have given us " fulfilled " here.

[2] See St. John iii. 5.   [3] See St. John vi. 54, 55, 56, 66.

vouchsafed no explanation to the multitude [1]; nay, there
are certain precepts of Christ, which reason almost forbids
us to suppose He meant us to understand in their literal
sense.[2] Why, so far as we may reverently conjecture His
designs, did He adopt this enigmatical mode of speaking?
Was it to arrest attention, to stir thought, to bring the
mind by force into contact with truth, by presenting that
truth in a form calculated to call it into exercise ?   I find
Almighty God dealing in something of the same way with
the prophets, by causing questions to be put to them on
the subject of the visions exhibited to them; " Son of
man, can these bones live ?" [3]   " What are these which
are arrayed in white robes? and whence came they ?" [4]
Probably part of the design was to prove the spiritual
intelligence, or the faith, or the humility of the hearers—
" this he said *to prove* him." [5]—O my God, let me not be
content with reading Thy Word without any mental
exercise upon it; make me a thoughtful, as well as an
attentive reader; and where the difficulties which it presents are insuperable to my understanding, let them not
stumble my faith, but humble my reason.

Wednesday.—V. 25. " But the time cometh, when I
shall no more speak unto you in proverbs, but I shall
shew you plainly of the Father."   How completely St.
Paul echoes these words of his Divine Master, where
he says; " Now we see through a glass, darkly" (in an
enigma), " but then face to face." [6]   What our Lord calls
a proverb, or dark saying, St. Paul calls an enigma, or
riddle; a dark saying needs an interpretation, a riddle
needs a solution.   Mingled light and darkness is the dis-

---

[1] See St. Matt. xiii. 10-14, 34, 35.

[2] See St. Matt. v. 34, 39, 40; vi. 31, etc.   [3] Ezek. xxxvii. 3.

[4] Rev. vii. 13.   [5] See St. John vi. 6.   [6] 1 Cor. xiii. 12.

pensation under which we now live (" now we know in part"[1];) for nothing else than this would serve the purpose of our probation. There is enough light to enable those to see who desire to see ; enough darkness to confound those who do not desire to see, and to serve them as a pretext for unbelief. But with the ceasing of the state of probation, the dark saying and the enigma will cease also— " I shall shew you plainly of the Father"; "then face to face." [2] I observe, however, that the enlightenment of the disciples was to be, and actually was, gradual,—like the dawn " that shineth more and more unto the perfect day."[3] They were enlightened at and by the Resurrection ; there was a bright diffusion of light at Pentecost; but even then they had many things to learn still, as, for instance, God's purpose of admitting the Gentiles to the fold of the Church, and putting them on the same level of spiritual privilege with the Jews [4]; and since their days we cannot doubt that God's providence in history has thrown much light upon unfulfilled prophecy, and other subjects, so that our present knowledge ought to be much in advance of the knowledge possessed by the Church in her infancy. " The time is coming," says our Lord, "when I shall shew you plainly of the Father"; it is always *coming*; never until probation ceases, and with it dark sayings, will it have fully come.—Lord, while I acquiesce modestly and humbly in the mysteries of Thy Word, make me diligent in availing myself of all those helps for understanding it aright, which either human history or human research may offer.

Thursday.—Vv. 29, 30. " His disciples said unto him, Lo, now speakest thou plainly, and speakest no pro-

---

[1] *Ibid.*   [2] *Ibid.*   [3] See Prov. iv. 18.
[4] See Acts x. 15, 28, 34, 35, 47 ; xi. 17, 18.

verb. Now are we sure that thou knowest all things, and needest not that any man should ask thee: by this we believe that thou camest forth from God." Our Lord, knowing the difficulty to which His words about "a little while" (in v. 16) had given rise in the minds of His disciples, meets it exactly by what He says to them, not so much in the form in which they had stated it, as in that in which they had felt it; for "Christ," as Bacon tells us, "knowing men's thoughts immediately, and not, as we know them, merely through their words, never answered their words but their thoughts."[1] This showed the disciples that He knew the secrets of their hearts, and they burst out at once into an enthusiastic acknowledgment of Him as having come from God, and knowing all things. So Nathanael, convinced that Christ's eye had been upon him in his devotional retirement under the fig-tree, exclaims, "Thou art the Son of God; thou art the King of Israel."[2] So St. Thomas, when convinced that Christ had overheard the presumptuous and irreverent challenge which he had made about the resurrection, is at once subdued to adoration; "My Lord, and my God."[3] There are many analogies between the written and the Personal Word; and one of these is that the Bible, to those who study it devoutly, shows in a thousand passages that it has the clue to the secrets of men's hearts.

> " Eye of God's Word ! where'er we turn
> Ever upon us ! thy keen gaze
> Can all the depths of sin discern,
> Unravel every bosom's maze."[4]

Lord, enable me so to study Thy living oracles, that I

---

[1] "Advancement of Learning." [2] St. John i. 49.
[3] St. John xx. 28. [4] "Christian Year," St. Bartholomew.

may hear Thine own voice in them, dealing with all the subterfuges and evasions of my conscience, and may find Thine eye tracking me home to my business and bosom.

Friday.—Vv. 31, 32. "Jesus answered them, Do ye now believe? Behold the hour cometh, yea, is now come, that ye shall be scattered, every man to his own, and shall leave me alone." It is certainly remarkable—it may be at first sight disappointing—how coldly and discouragingly our Lord replied to warm gushes of enthusiasm in His own favour. There is another instance in Chap. vi. of this Gospel, when to Simon Peter's noble confession, "Lord, to whom shall we go? thou hast the words of eternal life. And we believe and are sure that thou are that Christ, the Son of the living God," He replied, "Have not I chosen you twelve, and one of you is a devil?"[1] And, similarly, to St. Peter professing a readiness to go with Him both into prison and to death, He predicts his shameful denial[2]; and to St. Peter using a sword in His behalf, He issues the injunction to put up the sword.[3]— Lord, what dost Thou design to teach me by this but profound distrust of myself, even when my mind seems to be seized with irresistible convictions of Thy claims, and my heart to swell with gratitude and love in the reception of Thy mercies? If I could sift out this glowing enthusiasm, I should find but a grain or two of gold in it, mixed with a bushel of dust. "Behold, he put no trust in his servants; and his angels he charged with folly: How much less in them that dwell in houses of clay, whose foundation is in the dust?"[4]

Saturday.—V. 33. "These things I have spoken unto you, that in me ye might have peace. In the world ye

---

[1] St. John vi. 68, 70.　　[2] St. Luke xxii. 33, 34.
[3] St. John xviii. 10, 11.　　[4] Job iv. 18, 19.

shall have tribulation : but be of good cheer ; I have overcome the world."   The Lord had been speaking to His disciples a word of censure ; he had predicted their gross infidelity to Himself in His hour of need (" Ye shall be scattered, every man to his own, and shall leave me alone ") ; but He will not part from them thus ; His last sermon to them shall not have so dismal an end ; He will pour into the wounds of their souls, not only the acrid wine of wholesome reproof, but the oil of consolation also. How precious are the last words of a good parent esteemed to be by affectionate and dutiful children !   And these were the last words (or rather the last before His death), which " the everlasting Father "[1] addressed to the little circle of His disciples, whom, in acknowledgment of that endearing relationship, He called " little children."[2]   Let me deeply consider and treasure up in my heart these last words.   He tells them plainly and faithfully what they had to expect from the world (" in the world ye shall have tribulation ") ; but there was a thought in which they might find encouragement, and a sphere in which they might find peace.   The thought was, " I have overcome the world."   But what was that to them ?   If their Lord and they were independent persons, if He stood in no living relation to them, it was nothing to them that *He* had overcome the world.   But if He were the Head of a body, of which they were members, then the same energies which had enabled Him to overcome the world, would give them the victory also ; in other words He would fight *in* them, and *with* them, as He had already fought *for* them, and thus secure their victory. Yes ; He would fight *in* them.   It is not merely an invigorating thought which He offers ; He speaks also of

---

[1] Isaiah ix. 6.   [2] See St. John xiii. 33, and xxi. 5.

the support of an invigorating Presence,—" that *in me* ye might have peace "; not merely, " that *in my words* ye might find encouragement." The good courage was to come, not merely from the assurances of their Master, but from communion with their Master.—Lord, let me but taste peace in communion 'with Thee, from my consciousness of acceptance through Thy blood and Thy righteousness, and that shall minister strength to me against all my spiritual foes, a strength in which I, too, shall overcome the world.

CHAPTER XXXI

THE GOSPEL FOR THE ASCENSION-DAY.

St. Mark xvi. 14 *to the end*
(but substituting the word "Jesus" for "Afterward he" in *v.* 14).

14 Jesus appeared unto the eleven as they sat at meat, and upbraided them with their unbelief and hardness of heart, because they
15 believed not them which had seen him after he was risen. And he said unto them, Go ye into all the world, and preach the gospel to
16 every creature. He that believeth and is baptized, shall be saved;
17 but he that believeth not, shall be damned. And these signs shall follow them that believe: In my Name shall they cast out devils,
18 they shall speak with new tongues, they shall take up serpents, and if they drink any deadly thing, it shall not hurt them; they
19 shall lay hands on the sick, and they shall recover. So then after the Lord had spoken unto them, he was received up into heaven,
20 and sat on the right hand of God. And they went forth and preached every where, the Lord working with them, and confirming the word with signs following.

[Miss. Sar.	1549.	1662 s.b.
In illo tempore, Recumbentibus undecim discipulis apparuit illis *Jesus,* etc. (*Vulg.* Novissime recumbentibus illis undecim apparuit, etc.)	Jesus appeared unto the eleven as they sate at meat, etc.	*Jesus* appeared unto the eleven as they sat at meat, etc. (*A. V.* "Afterward he appeared unto the eleven as they sat at meat, etc." *Gr.* Ὕστερον, ἀνακειμένοις αὐτοῖς τοῖς ἔνδεκα ἐφανερώθη, etc.)

The Ὕστερον ("Afterward"), with which *v.* 14 commences, points back to the two preceding manifestations of the risen Saviour recorded by St. Mark,—that to St. Mary Magdalene (*v.* 9); and that to the two disciples on the road to Emmaus (*v.* 12). I forbear to enter on the controversy respecting the genuineness of the twelve last verses of St. Mark, which is so fully and exhaustively discussed by Bishop Wordsworth in his notes on the Greek Testament, by Canon Cook in the Speaker's Commentary, and above all by Dean Burgon in his valuable treatise, in which he has thoroughly examined every argument brought against this most precious and interesting section of Holy Scripture. The internal evidence (not against its being Scripture, but against its being from the pen of St. Mark) is that "no less than seventeen words and expressions occur in it, which are never elsewhere used by St. Mark" (Dean Alford). This difference in style in the twelve last verses is fully admitted by Bishop Wordsworth, who indeed exhibits the particulars of it; but, after calling his reader's attention to the difference of style between the two Epistles of St. Peter, and between the Gospel and the Revelation of St. John, he observes with singular beauty and force; "So great a change as that wrought by the *Resurrection* of Christ might suggest to St. Mark a change of style; as in music changes are made to mark changes of action and feeling."— *Translation of* 1540. (1) *V.* 14. "he *cast in their teeth* their unbelief," —a strong expression, but not stronger than the original (ὠνείδισε) will warrant. Here again Cranmer follows Tyndale. Wycliffe has the milder word "*reproved.*" The word ὀνειδίζω is also applied to the Saviour's censure of the cities which repented not, although they had seen His mighty works, a censure which begins with "Woe unto thee, Chorazin!" (St. Matt. xi. 21). But such is not the tone in which He objurgates His own people; and we think King James's Translators did well to substitute in our passage the word "upbraid with." (2) *V.* 14. "because they believed not them which had seen *that He was risen again* from the dead,"—a rendering taken from the Vulgate, "quia iis, qui viderant eum resurrexisse, non crediderunt." Wycliffe has the same,—"that hadden *scyn that he was risun* fro deeth." Tyndale,—"had sene him *after his resurreccion.*" (3) *V.* 17. "These *tokens* shall follow them that beleeve." So Wycliffe. (4) *V.* 18. "They shall *drive away* serpents "(ὄφεις ἀροῦσι). Thus Cranmer. Wycliffe,—"*do away*"; Tyndale,—"*kill*"; Geneva,— "*take away*"; Rheims also, "*take away.*" The Vulgate has "serpentes tollent," which of course *may* mean, not only "take up," but "make away with," "destroy" ["*tollet* anum vitiato melle cicuta"—*Hor.*]. Tyndale, in defence of his rendering, might refer to St. Luke xxiii. 18, Αἶρε τοῦτον, and Acts xxii. 22, Αἶρε ἀπὸ τῆς γῆς τὸν τοιοῦτον. But it is better to understand it, as King James's Translators do, of taking up and handling innocuously. (5) *V.* 19. "and *is* on the right hand of God." The Greek is ἐκάθισεν ("sat"). There seems to have been a tendency, in translating this verse, to represent the session of Christ as an event which though it first took place at the Ascension, extends itself throughout all time. Thus the Vulgate has "et *sedet* a dextris Dei"; Wycliffe, "and he *sittith* on the rigthalf of god"; Tyndale, "and *is* set doune," etc.; Geneva, "and *sitteth*," etc.]

Thursday. — V. 14. "Afterward he appeared unto the eleven as they sat at meat, and upbraided them with their unbelief and hardness of heart," etc. It is a strong word, which is here translated "upbraided." In the foregoing Chapter the same Greek word[1] is translated "revile," and is used of the cruel taunts which were hurled at our Lord as He hung upon the cross; "they that were crucified with him *reviled* him."[2] Again, this word is translated "revile" in the Beatitudes of St. Matthew's Gospel, where it is associated with "persecute." "Blessed are ye, when men shall *revile* you, and persecute you."[3] No word that could be called reviling ever fell from the lips of the patient and loving Lord; when He said to the Scribes and Pharisees, "Ye serpents, ye generation of vipers, how can ye escape the damnation of hell?"[4] this was not that language of rancorous, contumelious invective, which hot-tempered persons too often throw out, when they lose their self-control, but a calm, solemn, sorrowful censure, meted out with absolute justice and truth, the awful and yet temperate (more awful, because temperate) expression of

---

[1] ὠνείδισε, from ὀνειδίζω.　　　[2] Ch. xv. 32. ὠνείδιζον.

[3] St. Matt. v. 11, ὅταν ὀνειδίσωσιν ὑμᾶς καὶ διώξωσι. The other renderings of the word in the Authorised Version are : 1. The thieves . . . *cast the same in his teeth* (τὸ αὐτὸ ὠνείδιζον αὐτῷ) St. Matt. xxvii. 44 ; 2. *reproach* (coupled with *separate you from their company*, and *cast out your name as evil*), St. Luke vi. 22 ; see also 1 Pet. iv. 14, "if ye be *reproached*"; and 1 Tim. iv. 10, ὀνειδιζόμεθα, *we suffer reproach*; and Rom. xv. 3, "the reproaches of them that *reproached* thee." The translation is twice *revile* (St. Matt. v. 11 ; St. Mark xv. 32) ; three times *upbraid* (St. Matt. xi. 20 ; St. Mark xvi. 14 ; James i. 5).

[4] St. Matt. xxiii. 33.

" the wrath of the Lamb."[1]   But the fact that this word is sometimes used of sinful reviling, shows that it indicates a stern and sharp rebuke.   The Apostles had deserved such an upbraiding.   Their slowness of heart to believe, not only all that the prophets had spoken,[2] but the re-peated assurances of our Lord that He would rise again the third day, as also the assurances of St. Mary Magdalene and others that they had seen Him after He was risen,[3] deserved doubtless a very heavy word of censure.   But see how His censures are tempered with mercy.   It is " as they sit at meat," and He takes His wonted place among them, that He administers this stern rebuke.   The censure falls not on these elect ones, as it will fall at the last day upon the reprobate, while they are at the bar, and He on the judgment-seat ; but while He is gathered together with them in social and convivial intercourse; " He appeared unto the eleven *as they sat at meat.*"   And, again, He does not leave them with this rebuke ringing in their ears ; He does not part from them with censure, but with blessing, upon His lips.   Immediately before His ascension, He will give them the best proof of His confi-dence by commissioning them as His ambassadors of peace, and assuring them of His presence with them even unto the end of the world,[4] that presence to be attested by the miraculous signs which should follow upon their mission.[5] Nor will I forget in this connexion that other precious passage, in which this same word " upbraid " is said *not* to be characteristic of God's dealings with sinful men ; " Let him ask " wisdom " of God, that giveth to all men liberally and *upbraideth not.*"[6]   Our Lord upbraided His disciples

---

[1] See Rev. vi. 16.   [2] See St. Luke xxiv. 25.
[3] See St. Mark xvi. 11, 13.   [4] See St. Matt. xxviii. 16, 18, 19, 20.
[5] See St. Mark xvi. 17, 18.   [6] James i. 5.

with *want* of faith; but if a man cordially asks God for something of which he feels a need, that asking is an evidence of faith; "for he that cometh to God must believe that he is, and that he is a rewarder of them that diligently seek him"[1]; and accordingly God in such cases never upbraids, however much ground for it there may be in the petitioner's past life and conduct; He never casts his sins in his teeth, nor says, " You refused the other day to listen to the voice of my Spirit in your conscience; and I now refuse to listen to you." " All his transgressions that he hath committed, they shall not be mentioned unto him."[2]

Friday.—V. 15. "And he said unto them, Go ye into all the world, and preach the gospel to every creature." These solemn words were among the last which our Lord spoke upon earth. It was " after he had spoken" these words that " he was received up into heaven," as I see in the 19th verse of this Gospel. Great weight do we attach to a friend's last words,—a weight which is usually (since they are for the most part uttered, when the mind is enfeebled by sickness and pain) very much in excess of their real value. How do dutiful and affectionate children treasure up in their hearts and minds the last wishes of a parent who is being parted from them by death ! How careful are they to carry those wishes into effect in every particular! We have here the last wishes, or rather the last solemn injunction, of Him whose name is called " the everlasting Father,"[3] and who, in recognition of His bearing this relationship to His disciples, called them " little children."[4]—Lord, am I treasuring up in my heart this parting charge of Thine, and acting upon it to the best of my ability ? It is not addressed to the Apostles

---

[1] Heb. xi. 6.

[2] Ezek. xviii. 22

[3] Isaiah ix. 6.

[4] See St. John xiii. 33.

only, though to them it was spoken in the first instance, and their particular destination in life was marked out for them by it. All disciples of Christ are not called to become missionaries or ministers; but all are called to help missions, to show a lively and practical interest in them, and to spread the blessed Gospel by their example and influence. Am I doing this, or at least sincerely endeavouring to do it?

Saturday.—V. 16. "He that believeth and is baptized shall be saved; but he that believeth not" (of those who hear your message, and are privileged to see the miraculous evidences which accompany and attest it) "shall be damned." These last words,—which intimate that the Gospel carries condemnation as well as salvation with it, is the occasion of damnation to some, as well as the cause of salvation to others,—are very awful. I am reminded of what St. Paul says to the Corinthians, where he compares the victorious progress of Christ's apostles through the world, in execution of His commission, to the triumph of an ancient conqueror, in the course of which fragrant incense was offered to the gods as a sacrifice of praise for the victory, and some of the captives, who had been especially reserved for the occasion, were slaughtered as part of the ceremony, while the sky rang again with the acclamations of the people, who owed their deliverance to the hero of the day; "Now thanks be unto God, which always causeth us to triumph in Christ, and maketh manifest the savour of his knowledge by us in every place. For we are unto God a sweet savour of Christ, in them that are saved, and in them that perish: To the one we are the savour of death unto death; and to the other the savour of life unto life."[1] The solemn and awful lesson

[1] 2 Cor. ii. 14, 15, 16.

is, that the hearing of the message of salvation through Christ never can be a thing indifferent. "God's Word," says Bunyan, "has two edges; it can cut back-stroke and fore-stroke. If it do thee no good, it will do thee hurt." "All Christian privileges" (says Bishop Wordsworth on 2 Cor ii. 16), "all the means of grace, Scriptures, Sermons, Sacraments, Sundays . . . and all things that Christ's ministers do and teach in His name, are—according as they are used—either blessings or banes, either physic or poison." Not that there is anything in the Gospel, or the name of Christ, or the means of grace, but what is good, wholesome, remedial, potential for salvation, and only for salvation. But man's freewill too often rejects the remedy which the Gospel proffers; and when it is rejected, the sinner's case becomes hopeless, not because he is a sinner, but because he is a sinner who refuses to be saved. He will not come to Christ, that he might have life.[1] Often have I heard of Christ, and of His gracious invitation to the weary and heavy laden.[2] Have I ever sincerely and with my entire will come to him? If not, the Gospel has been to me "a savour of death unto death."

Sunday.—V. 17. "And these signs shall follow them that believe; In my name shall they cast out devils; they shall speak with new tongues," etc. etc. Our Lord here enumerates some of the miraculous gifts of the Spirit, with which His disciples should be endowed on the day of Pentecost, and which should be to themselves the comfortable, and to the world the convincing, evidence that He was by their side and working with them. Very beautiful were these gifts of the Spirit, and much to be coveted at the period when it pleased God to bestow them; but, beautiful as they were, they were by no means so precious

---

[1] See St. John v. 40.   [2] See St. Matt. xi. 28, 29, 30.

or so earnestly to be sought as the *graces* of the Spirit.
I will think of the miraculous gifts and the ordinary graces
of the Spirit under the image of blossom and fruit.
Beautiful are the apple-blossoms and pear-blossoms in
spring-tide; but they are transitory, and must fall off
before the fruit forms. Even so the gifts of the Spirit, so
far as they were miraculous, disappeared (some sooner,
some later, but all of them) at a very early period of the
Church's history. But "the fruit of the Spirit," which
"is love, joy, peace, long-suffering, gentleness, goodness,
faith, meekness, temperance,"[1] abides and endures still;
and it is by my production or non-production of this
fruit, not by my exhibition of gifts, however brilliant, that
I shall be judged at the last day. He who has planted
me, a worthless fig-tree, in the vineyard of His Church,
comes year after year seeking fruit on this fig-tree.[2] Does
he find it? does He find even promise of it? where in me
are those holy tempers and dispositions, which distinguish
the nominal from the real Christian, and of which our
Lord says, "By their fruits ye shall know them"?[3]

Monday. — V. 17. "They shall speak with new
tongues." The gift of tongues seems to have taken two
different forms. Sometimes (as on the day of Pentecost)
it was a gift of speaking foreign languages, or "*other*
tongues."[4] Sometimes, as seems to have been the case
in the Corinthian Church, it was the gift of elevated
devotional utterances, in which the speaker addressed
himself to God in a *new* language, put into his mouth
by the Spirit for the occasion, and which required an
inspired interpreter to make it intelligible to the congregation. Let me take occasion to reflect that the *grace*

---

[1] See Gal. v. 22, 23.
[3] St. Matt. vii. 20.
[2] See St. Luke xiii. 6, 7.
[4] See Acts ii. 4.

of the Spirit, without any miraculous gift, works a change in the tongue. " Out of the abundance of the heart the mouth speaketh"; . . . " By thy words thou shalt be justified, and by thy words thou shalt be condemned "[1]; " If any man offend not in word, the same is a perfect man, and able also to bridle the whole body."[2]   It is not a little observable that in the Law there is one precept in the first table (the third), and one in the second (the ninth), prescribing the government of the tongue.   Yes; the true disciple, the man who has truly come under the convicting and converting influences of the Spirit, shall "speak with a new tongue."   No corrupt communication shall proceed out of his mouth. " but such as is good for edifying as the need may be, that it may minister grace to the hearers."[3]   God shall open his lips, by touching his heart with gratitude and love, and his mouth shall show forth God's praise.[4]

Tuesday.—V. 18. " They shall take up serpents ; and if they drink any deadly thing, it shall not hurt them "; that is, though they must often come across danger and mischief, as living in a world which is full of both, they shall not take any harm from it.   Christ did not pray for his disciples that they should be taken out of the world, (for how else but by being conversant in it should they win souls for Him ?), but that they should be kept from the evil.[5]   And here He assures them that they shall be secured from physical evil ; poison and poisonous reptiles shall not hurt them.   But here I note, as admonished to do so by another passage of God's Word, that the promise

---

[1] St. Matt. xii. 34, 37.   [2] James iii. 2.

[3] See Eph. iv. 29.   I have adopted the rendering of εἴτις ἀγαθὸς πρὸς οἰκοδομὴν τῆς χρείας, which is given by the Revisers of 1881, and which beyond question is the right one.

[4] See Ps. li. 15.   [5] See St. John xvii. 15.

would afford them no security, if they wantonly ran into danger, courted and trifled with it. It was merely a security against such dangers as crossed their path without any will of their own. When a viper came out of the fire at Melita, and fastened on St. Paul's hand, he would not keep it there in order to prove the truth of the Lord's promise; "he shook off the beast into the fire, and felt no harm."[1] Oh, let me learn that Christ—His promise, providence, and power—will secure me from spiritual mischief, only if I do not trifle with it,—only if I put away sin, as soon as the temptation to it suggests itself. The condition of a motion of lust, or pride, or temper, or covetousness, not harming me is, "that I shake off the beast" by a resolute action of the will into its native element,—"the fire" of hell.—Lord, let me not parley with sin for a single instant. Give me grace to bruise the serpent's head,[2]—to crush sin in that earliest suggestion, which contains in it the germ of the entire act of sin.

Wednesday.— V. 19. "So then after the Lord had spoken unto them, he was received up into heaven, and sat on the right hand of God." How quietly, how modestly, how briefly, do the Evangelists record the Ascension,—not at all as if it were a wonder, but a simple matter of course, the consummation of Christ's career which every one must have anticipated. And this is, indeed, the true view of the case. The wonder lay, O Lord, in Thy descent from heaven, not in Thy return to it, in the amazing condescension and pity which drew Thee down from the Father's bosom, moved Thee to take our creature-nature upon Thee in the Virgin's womb, to make the roughest experience of human life, and the darkest

---

[1] See Acts xxviii. 3, 5.   [2] See Gen. iii. 15, and Rom. xvi. 20.

experience of human death, to visit the realm of the departed, the dreary abode of souls separated from the body, and so to fathom the deepest abyss of man's misery and ruin. That the Sun of righteousness, after sinking into the ocean of death, should once more flush the east with His dawning, and clamber up till He reached the meridian where He was before,—this was only what was to be anticipated from His being the Sun of righteousness,— the source of light and life, aye, and of all activity to the universe. And there Thou sittest, O Lord, at God's right hand,—sittest to *observe* ("The Lord looked down from heaven, and beheld all the children of men: from the habitation of his dwelling he considereth all them that dwell on the earth"[1]); sittest to *judge* ("he hath prepared his throne for judgment. And he shall judge the world in righteousness, he shall minister judgment to the people in uprightness "[2]). May I adore Thee for Thine exaltation; be quickened by Thine observation; prepare myself to appear before Thy judgment-seat!

The Octave.—V. 20. "And they went forth, and preached everywhere, the Lord working with them, and confirming the word with signs following." The close and vital connexion of the Ascension of our Lord with the work of Christian Missions is my thought for to-day. This connexion was figured in the types of the Old Testament. Jonah, emerging from the interior of the fish, and rising out of the depths of the ocean into the life and light of the upper air, goes forthwith to preach to and convert the Ninevites.[3] It was predicted in the Psalms; "Yet have I set my king upon my holy hill of Zion. I will declare the decree: the Lord hath said unto

---

[1] Ps. xxxiii. 13, P.B.V.   [2] Ps. ix. 7, 8.
[3] See Jonah ii. 10, and iii. 4, 5, 10.

me, Thou art my Son; this day have I begotten thee. Ask of me, and I shall give thee the heathen for thine inheritance, and the uttermost parts of the earth for thy possession."[1] The King set upon God's holy hill, the heavenly Zion, desires of God the heathen for His inheritance, and, receiving the grant of this inheritance, proceeds at once to subjugate it by His envoys preaching peace. It is expressly stated by St. Paul; "When he ascended up on high, he led captivity captive, and gave gifts unto men.... And he gave some, apostles; and some, prophets; and some, evangelists; and some, pastors and teachers; for the perfecting of the saints, for the work of the ministry, for the edifying of the body of Christ."[2] I see that the Saviour, though seated and at rest, is still an energizing Saviour; His rest consists with—nay, is the condition—of endless activity; the two things are closely associated, "he sat on the right hand of God," and "the Lord working with them." Whereupon I will take occasion to reflect that peace in the heart and conscience through the blood of the Cross is the secret source of activity in the Christian life; and that to attempt to work up *to* peace of conscience, and not *from* it, is to invert that order of things which God hath appointed.

[1] Ps. ii. 6, 7, 8.   [2] Eph. iv. 8, 11, 12.

CHAPTER XXXII

THE GOSPEL FOR THE SUNDAY AFTER ASCENSION-DAY.

St. John xv. 26 *to* the middle of *v.* 4 in Chapter xvi.
(omitting the "But" with which Chapter xv. *v.* 26 commences).

26   When the Comforter is come, whom I will send unto you from the Father, even the Spirit of truth, which proceedeth from the
27 Father, he shall testifie of me. And ye also shall bear witness,
1 because ye have been with me from the beginning. These things
2 have I spoken unto you, that ye should not be offended. They shall put you out of the synagogues: yea the time cometh, that
3 whosoever killeth you will think that he doth God service. And these things will they do unto you, because they have not known
4 the Father, nor me; but these things have I told you, that when the time shall come, ye may remember that I told you of them.

[Miss. Sar.	1549.	1662 s.b.
In illo tempore, Dixit Jesus discipulis suis; Cum venerit Paraclytus, quem ego mittam vobis a Patre Spiritum veritatis, etc. (*Vulg.* Cum autem venerit Paracletus, quem ego mittam, etc.)	When the Comforter is come, whom I will send unto you from the Father, (even the Spirit of Truth), etc.	When the Comforter is come, whom I will send unto you from the Father, even the Spirit of truth, etc. (*Gr.* Ὅταν δὲ ἔλθῃ ὁ Παράκλητος, etc.)

The force of the "But," with which *v.* 26 of Chap. xv. commences, is obvious to those who look at the context. Our Lord has been speaking of the venomous malignity of the Jews towards Him, a malignity which should after His departure fasten upon His disciples (*v.* 20, "If they have persecuted me, they will also persecute you," etc.), and which was proof even against the convincing evidence of His miracles (*v.* 24, "If I had not done among them the works which none other man did, they had not had sin, etc."). Strange as this malignity was, however, they did but fulfil their own Scriptures in showing it (*v.* 25),—"the word . . . that is written in their law, They hated me without a cause." *But* this malignity was not to prevail. The Christ should have a testimony in His favour, from the Comforter supremely ("he shall testify of me," *v.* 26), and subordinately from the disciples ("and ye also shall bear witness," *v.* 27), which should justify Him triumphantly, all the malice of devils and men notwithstanding. — *Translation of* 1540. (1) xvi. 2. "They shall *excommunicate* you," for which King James's Translators substituted, "They shall put you out of the synagogues." The word *excommunicate* came from Tyndale. Wycliffe, translating from the Vulgate ("Absque synagogis facient vos"), gives the rendering to which the Rhemish Translation [1582] and the Authorised [1611] recurred; "thei schuln make you withouten the synagogis." (2) xvi. 4. "But these things have I told you, that when the time is come, ye may remember *then* that I told you." Thus the text runs in the Black-Letter Prayer Book of 1636 [39 ?], in which the MS. corrections were made at the last Revision. But clearly *then* is a misprint for *them.* Cranmer's translation (as given in Bagster's "Hexapla") is ; "that when the tyme is come, ye maye remember them, that I tolde you." A very accurate rendering of the original (ἵνα ὅταν ἔλθῃ ἡ ὥρα, μνημονεύητε αὐτῶν, ὅτι ἐγὼ εἶπον ὑμῖν), and one to which the Revisers of 1881 have gone back ; "But these things have I spoken unto you, that when their hour is come, ye may remember them, how that I told you." And so Professor Westcott.]

Sunday.—V. 26. " The Comforter." Let me meditate upon this precious title of Comforter, by which our Lord reveals the Holy Spirit to us. The Greek word so translated means also an advocate. And this is the rendering actually adopted by our translators in a passage of St. John's first Epistle ; " If any man sin, we have an *advocate* with the Father, Jesus Christ the righteous."[1] The fact is that there are two Hebrew words of the Old Testament, for which the Greek has only one equivalent, and that one of these signifies a comforter in trouble (as in Job, " miserable comforters are ye all "[2]), while the other means intercessor or advocate. As regards

---

[1] 1 John ii. 1. [2] Job xvi. 2.

God and our relation to Him, the Holy Spirit is our advocate, " helping our infirmities " in prayer, as the Apostle says, and " making intercession for us with groanings which cannot be uttered."[1]   As regards ourselves, and in His relation to us, the Holy Ghost is a " comforter."   And being "the Spirit of truth," He is a *faithful* Comforter, who shows us indeed ourselves, and the truth of our own state as lost and helpless sinners, but who also receives of the things of Christ, of His blood, righteousness, strength, intercession ; and, by showing them also to us,[2] pours into the wounds of our soul and conscience the oil of true consolation.   What a rich mine of comfort and strength there is in the names, under which God is pleased to reveal Himself to us.

Monday.—V. 26. " He shall testify of me."   Christ, in these last discourses with His disciples, testifies everywhere of the Holy Spirit, puts Him in the foreground, tells His followers that it was expedient for them that He Himself should go away, because if He went not away, the Comforter,[3] who should abide with them for ever,—nay, who should be *in* them as well as *with* them, would not come to them.   And when the Comforter came, He testified not of Himself, but of Jesus ; inspired the Apostles to preach Christ crucified,[4] and to know nothing else than Him among their converts ; as the Saviour had said, " He shall glorify me : for he shall receive of mine, and shall shew it unto you."[5] Thus do the Persons of the Blessed Trinity mutually glorify one another ; thus does the Saviour fasten the expectations of the disciples upon the Comforter ; and

[1] See Rom. viii. 26.   [2] See St. John xvi. 14.
[3] See St. John xvi. 7 ; and xiv. 16, 17.
[4] See 1 Cor. i. 23 ; and ii. 2.   [5] St. John xvi. 14.

thus does the Comforter in His turn reveal, not Himself, but the Saviour. May this Divine humility be my model, and one of my criteria in self-examination ! Do I shrink from notice in the little good I try to do, "not letting my left hand know what my right hand doeth ?"[1] Could I bear to found some great enterprise of benevolence, and then, devolving the administration of it upon another, turn the eyes of men to him, and let him have the credit? Or, suppose I were the administrator, could I bear to exhibit the founder only, and be never weary of putting him forward ? Yet this is what Christ did to the Holy Spirit, and what the Holy Spirit does to Christ.[2]

Tuesday.—V. 27. " And ye also shall bear witness, because ye have been with me from the beginning." The Apostles were to witness to the historical facts with which their experience had made them acquainted ; the Holy Ghost in the hearts and consciences of men was to second their testimony. Thus, too, in the present day, the Church bears witness to the genuineness and authenticity of the Holy Scriptures as the written word of God, lodges them in the hands of her children, commends them to their attention, while the Holy Spirit, who alone can do so, applies the word of God to the hearts and consciences of the people. And thus both " the Spirit and the bride say, Come "[3]; the invitation of grace issues from both of them. Let me take occasion to reflect on the way in which the double principle of Divine and human agency runs through the whole scheme of man's salvation. Thou, O God, must act as the master-worker in the matter both of our justification and sanctification, or we sinners are lost for ever.

---

[1] See St. Matt. vi. 3.

[2] See a similar Thought for the Saturday of the week commencing with the Fourth Sunday after Easter. [3] Rev. xxii. 17.

Except Thy Son and Thy Spirit take in hand the work of our salvation for us, there is no hope of its being achieved. But Thou wouldst have us work also, inasmuch as Thou hast endowed us with free wills, and makest the agency of those free wills indispensable to our salvation. Thou biddest us " work out our own salvation with fear and trembling," strong in the assurance that it is Thou " who workest in us both to will and to do of Thy good pleasure."[1]

Wednesday.—Chap. xvi. 1. " These things have I spoken unto you, that ye should not be offended." " Forewarned is forearmed." Our Lord forearms His disciples by assuring them of the internal presence and support of the Comforter. And He forewarns them by telling them plainly of the rancorous hostility, with which their message should be received by the world, so that, when their troubles came upon them, they should be able to say, " This is just what our Master led us to expect, and what we are therefore quite prepared for."—Let me learn a lesson generally of the usefulness of foresight and preparation in the spiritual life. Let me habituate myself to the thought of being (as, in the course of nature, I shall probably be) deprived by God's Providence of several blessings which I now enjoy. How shall I do, when bereaved of this or that dear friend ? It is of no use hiding my eyes from the calamity. Some day we must be parted ; and how then ? could I support the blow, with the internal aid of God the Comforter ?—Nay ; it is a very good and healthful exercise, to look forward in the morning of each day to the temptations we shall probably have to encounter, and the hours when it will behove us to be especially watchful over tongue and temper. How much less often should we

' See Phil. ii. 12, 13.

stumble in our spiritual course, if with some little forecast we prepared ourselves to encounter a stumbling-block!

Thursday.—Chap. xvi. 2. "They shall put you out of the synagogues: yea, the time cometh that whosoever killeth you will think that he doeth God service." The nine days, which elapsed between the Ascension-Day and the Day of Pentecost, were days of expectation. Expectation of our Lord's Second Advent *eventually;* for the angels at the Ascension had held out this hope, and even spoken of the Second Advent as if it were imminent; "This same Jesus, which is taken up from you into heaven, shall so come in like manner as ye have seen him go into heaven."[1] Expectation *in the immediate foreground* of the Advent of the Comforter, whom our Lord had promised to send unto His disciples from the Father. Their Master was to come again and receive them unto Himself[2]; and before and until this took place, they were to receive from the mission of the Comforter all the consolation, and light, and strength, which they could possibly require for the execution of *their* mission. Yet they must not think that it should be all bright. If their future were to be gilded with radiant hope, and if they might expect interior consolation, they were also to look forward to hostility and ill-treatment in their outward circumstances. "In the world," both Jewish and Gentile, " they should have tribulation."[3] They should be excommunicated by the Church in whose bosom they had been bred. Nay, they were to expect, not only spiritual censures, but loss of all things, and of life itself, for Christ's sake. Zealots for the law, or for the idolatrous worship of the heathen, would think it an act of devotion to put them to death.—Let me learn, Lord, that those

[1] Acts i. 11.   [2] See St. John xiv. 3.   [3] See St. John xvi. 33.

who confess Thee bravely before men must not make their account to lead smooth unruffled lives.   If, in days when persecution has ceased, there may not be much trouble without, still the word stands fast that " we must through much tribulation " (through sanctified sorrow, and the stroke of God's hand, if not of man's) " enter into the kingdom of God."[1] None are " counted worthy "[2] of that kingdom save those who are willing to " suffer " for it.

Friday.—Chap. xvi. 3. " And these things will they do unto you, because they have not known the Father, nor me." How loving and lenient is our Lord, in His estimate of men's worst offences ! He knew that the Jews were about to crucify Him.   And here he foretells that after they had crucified the Head, they would show a similar ferocious malignity against the members ; " Whosoever killeth you will think that he doeth God service." And He attributes it to *ignorance* of God, just as at the actual crucifixion He prayed ; " Father, forgive them ; for they know not what they do."[3]   Doubtless they must have recognised both the Father and Him ; for had not the disciples done so ? and had not the other Jews the same opportunities of seeing the Saviour's miracles, and hearing the words of grace which proceeded out of His lips, which the disciples enjoyed ?   But they were blinded by their prejudices in favour of a carnal Messiah, who should set up a temporal kingdom.   Our Lord, however, does not dwell upon their *malice*, awful as it was, but upon their *blindness ;* " they have not known the Father, nor me "; Saul shall have the only excuse made for his persecutions, which his case admits of,—he " did it ignorantly in unbelief."[4]—O Lord, dost Thou not by this Thy lenity read a lesson of charity

---

[1] See Acts xiv. 22.   [2] See 2 Thess. i. 5.
[3] St. Luke xxiii. 34.   [4] See 1 Tim. i. 13.

to Thy disciples ?   If thou canst make excuses for "the blasphemers, the persecutors, the injurious," and allege all the extenuation which their offence admits of, shall not *we* much rather show forbearance to them, who have ourselves so much of perverseness, and so many sins against the light, to be forgiven ?

Saturday.—Chap. xvi. 4. " But these things have I told you, that when the time shall come, ye may remember that I told you of them."   The disciples, finding their experience to correspond exactly with what their Master had predicted, would thence reap two great benefits.   First, a confirmation of their faith in Him,—as He Himself says elsewhere, " Now I tell you before it come, that, when it is come to pass, ye may believe that I am he."[1]   Secondly, a firm persuasion that, as He had foreseen and foretold their troubles, He would assuredly support them when called upon to suffer.   To have foreseen the trouble, what would this be with their loving Lord but to have provided against it,—to have taken steps to enable them to meet it properly?   Though our Lord has never spoken in our hearing, as in that of His Apostles, yet He has given us His written word.   And whenever we find that written word, as happens often to the devout and spiritual mind, to meet our experience,—nay to adjust itself in a wonderful way, not only to our inward needs, but to the very circumstances in which we are placed,—how does this confirm our faith, and tide us with a full wave over our trials and difficulties !   To use the expression of a devout and learned writer; " It seems as if His knowledge, which wrapped us all around, was our very strength against the things He speaks of ; our very tower of refuge, into which

<hr>

[1] St. John xiii. 19.

we may flee as into His Presence.   If we belong to Him, our head is above in heaven, and we, the members of His body, are below: the head is one with the body, careth for it, feels with it by most mysterious, intimate sympathy; guides, protects, and governs it."[1]

[1] The late Rev. Isaac Williams, B.D.   " Devotional Commentary on the Epistles and Gospels;" Vol. I. p. 503 [Rivingtons: 1875].

Chapter XXXIII.

THE GOSPEL FOR WHITSUN-DAY.

St. John xiv. 15 *to the middle of v.* 31
(only prefixing to *v.* 15 the words " Jesus said unto his disciples ").

15 Jesus said unto his disciples, If ye love me keep my command-
16 ments.   And I will pray the Father, and he shall give you another
17 Comforter, that he may abide with you for ever ; even the Spirit
   of truth, whom the world cannot receive, because it seeth him not,
   neither knoweth him ; but ye know him ; for he dwelleth with you,
18 and shall be in you.   I will not leave you comfortless ; I will come
19 to you.   Yet a little while, and the world seeth me no more ; but
20 ye see me : because I live, ye shall live also.   At that day ye shall
21 know, that I am in my Father, and you in me, and I in you.   He
   that hath my commandments, and keepeth them, he it is that loveth
   me ; and he that loveth me shall be loved of my Father, and I will
22 love him, and will manifest my self to him.   Judas saith unto him,
   (not Iscariot) Lord, how is it that thou wilt manifest thy self unto
23 us, and not unto the world ?   Jesus answered, and said unto him,
   If a man love me, he will keep my words : and my Father will love
24 him, and we will come unto him, and make our abode with him.   He
   that loveth me not, keepeth not my sayings : and the word which
25 you hear, is not mine ; but the Fathers which sent me.   These things
26 have I spoken unto you, being yet present with you.   But the
   Comforter, which is the holy Ghost, whom the Father will send in
   my name, he shall teach you all things, and bring all things to your
27 remembrance, whatsoever I have said unto you.   Peace I leave with
   you, my peace I give unto you : not as the world giveth, give I
   unto you.   Let not your heart be troubled, neither let it be afraid.
28 Ye have heard how I said unto you, I go away and come again unto

you. If ye loved me, ye would rejoyce, because I said, I go unto
29 the Father: for my Father is greater than I. And now I have
told you before it come to pass, that when it is come to pass ye
30 might believe. Hereafter I will not talk much with you: for the
31 prince of this world cometh, and hath nothing in me. But that
the world may know that I love the Father; and as the Father
gave me commandment, even so I do.

<table>
<tr><td>[1549.</td><td>1662 s.b.</td></tr>
<tr><td>Jesus said unto his disciples, If ye love me, keep my commandments, and I will pray the Father, etc.</td><td>Jesus said unto his disciples, If ye love me keep my commandments. And I will pray the Father, etc.</td></tr>
</table>

The Sarum Gospel for Whitsun-Day went through two operations at
the hands of the compilers of King Edward's First Book, which ended in
leaving nothing of it remaining. It began in the middle of v. 20 of St.
John xiv. (thus; "*In illo tempore, Dixit Jesus discipulis suis;* Si quis
diligit me, sermonem meum servabit"), and went down (as our present
Gospel does) to the middle of the last verse of the Chapter, "But that the
world may know that I love the Father; and as the Father gave me commandment, even so I do." The Reformers in 1549 seem to have considered
the commencement infelicitous, as indeed it was; for in truth the Gospel
began with the answer to a question from "Judas, not Iscariot," which
question ("Lord, how is it that thou wilt manifest thyself unto us, and
not unto the world?") was not given. That the question should be given,
they may not unreasonably have thought to be essential to the right
understanding of the answer. But the question was linked on closely to
our Lord's promise to manifest Himself to him who had His commandments and kept them; and that again hung on to the preceding verses.
They could not find a sufficient break in the thought till they came to *v.*
15, "If ye love me, keep my commandments"; and there accordingly
they fixed the beginning of the new Gospel. But (probably on the ground
that to have retained the old Gospel with the preceding eight verses prefixed would have made the extract too long) they terminated their new
Gospel with *v.* 21 just before Judas's question,—"I will love him, and will
shew mine own self unto him."—In 1552, however, the compilers of
Edward's Second Book, who were perhaps less scrupulous about lengthy
selections, and possibly also thought that the entire obliteration of the old
Sarum Gospel was to be regretted, carried the Gospel of 1549 down to the
middle of the last verse of the Chapter, thus embracing both the Sarum
Gospel, and the additional verses which in 1549 had been prefixed to it.

And thus it has come about that the Whitsun-Day Gospel is decidedly long,—longer perhaps than any other Sunday Gospel, with the exception of that for the Sunday next before Easter.—The commencement of the Gospel, as it now stands, is excellently chosen (thanks to the Reformers of 1549). At the point where it begins, *there is a real break in the thought.* Our Lord has been speaking of the power of faith ("He that believeth on me, the works that I do shall he do also," *v.* 12), and making large promises to the prayer of faith ("If ye shall ask any thing in my name, I will do it," *v.* 14); and now "Hortatur, statim post fidem, ad amorem" (*Bengel*). "The thought of love follows that of faith. Faith issues 'in works of *power*: love in works of *devotion*'" (*Professor Westcott*).—*Tanslation of* 1540. (1) *V.* 18. "I will not leave you *comfortlesse.*" This word, as the translation of ὀρφανοὺς, was first given by Tyndale, and adopted both by Cranmer and the Genevan Translators. The Rhemish Translators give "orphanes." Perhaps there is no rendering so faithful, and at the same time so significant, as Wycliffe's, "fadirles,"— (bereaved of "the everlasting Father," Isaiah ix. 6). The Revisers of 1881 give us "desolate," with "orphans" in the margin. (2) *V.* 19. "Yet a little while, and the world seeth me no more, but ye see me : for I live, *and ye shall live.*" This rendering of the last clause is that of Wycliffe, Tyndale, Cranmer, the Genevan, and the Rhemish Translators. It was King James's Translators first, who gave the much more pointed and significant rendering, "because I live, ye shall live also." Of the earlier translation Professor Westcott says that, while the original allows of it, "the sense is much feebler ; and the construction is not after St. John's manner. Comp. xiii. 14 ; xiv. 3 ; xv. 20." (3) *V.* 22. "Lord *what is done that* thou wilt shew theyself (*sic*) unto us, and not unto the world ?" And so Wycliffe (after the Vulgate, "Domine, quid *factum est*, quia manifestaturus es nobis teipsum, et non mundo?") "What is done that thou wilt ?" is a more faithful rendering than that of our Authorised Version, "How is it that thou wilt ?", and the Revisers of 1881 have gone back to it ; "Lord, what is come to pass that thou wilt manifest thyself unto us, etc." "The question implies that some change must have come over the plans of the Lord. It is assumed that as Messiah He would naturally have revealed Himself publicly : something then must have happened, so Judas argues, by which the sphere of Christ's manifestation was limited" (*Professor Westcott*). (4) *V.* 27. "Let not your hearts be grieved, neither fear." It is "your heart" in the original (μὴ ταρασσέσθω ὑμῶν ἡ καρδία, μηδὲ δειλιάτω). As believers in Christ, they had *one heart*, and one soul. While Tyndale and the Genevan are equally at fault here, Wycliffe is right ; "be not youre herte afraied, ne drede it"

[*Vulg.* "Non turbetur cor vestrum, neque formidet.") *V.* 28. "If ye loved me, ye would *verily* rejoice." The word "verily" has no representative in the Greek ; yet it is found in Tyndale's and the Genevan and Rhemish Translations as well as Cranmer's. Wycliffe has "*forsothe* ye schulden haue ioie." It is a vestige of the Vulgate, which lingered in the early English Translations ("Si diligeretis me, gauderetis *utique*, quia vado ad Patrem ") till King James's Translators finally extinguished it.]

Sunday.— V. 17. " Ye know him; for he dwelleth with you, and shall be in you." Men knew the Holy Spirit, and were under His influence, before Pentecost. " Holy men of God," under the Old Dispensation, " spake as they were moved by the Holy Ghost."[1] And David cries, " Take not thy holy Spirit from me,"[2] plainly showing that he was in possession of the Spirit. What, then, was the difference between the operations of the Spirit before and after Pentecost? " He dwelleth *with* you " (by your side), " and *shall* be *in* you." And, again, the Spirit under the Old Dispensation is compared to floods poured from without upon a thirsty soil; " I will pour water upon him that is thirsty, and floods upon the dry ground."[3] But under the New it is said ; " The water that I shall give him shall be in him *a well of water* springing up into everlasting life."[4] And again ; " He that believeth on me, as the scripture hath said, out of his belly shall flow rivers of living water."[5] An external shower, refreshing the parched soil, is one thing. A perennial spring, bubbling up from within the earth, is another. True believers under the New Covenant not only have their own thirst slaked, but are made fountains of life and blessing to others.—Am I such a fountain ? Do I even seek to be one ? Is the little patch of human life and society which lies around me, the greener, the fresher, the

[1] 2 Pet. i. 21.   [2] Ps. li. 11.   [3] Isaiah xliv. 3.
[4] St. John iv. 14.   [5] St. John vii. 38.

more spiritually fertile, for my existence ?   By the answer
to this question I shall ascertain whether I have indeed
been made partaker of the great gift of the New Covenant.
When the Comforter first came, He came in the form of
tongues, whereby men were impelled *to speak to others* the
wonderful works of God.[1]

Monday.—V. 18. "I will not leave you comfort-
less."   In the original it is "orphans," or fatherless.   "The
very word," says Canon Westcott beautifully, "which
describes their sorrow, confirms their sonship."   Our
translators would have done well to preserve the exact
idea of the original ; " I will not leave you *fatherless.*"   This
would have connected the Gospel in the minds of readers
with a passage in the sixty-eighth Psalm, one of those
appointed for Whitsun-Day ; " A father of the fatherless
. . . is God in his holy habitation."[2]   Christ had been to
His disciples a Father ; nay, he was their Father in right
of His divine nature.   Among the glorious titles given by
Isaiah to the "child born," and " the son given unto us,"
is that of "the everlasting Father."[3]   And it is immediately
followed by "the Prince of Peace," which title also connects itself with this Gospel in another verse (27), where
our Lord says, " Peace I leave with you, my peace I give
unto you."   And we find that Isaiah, quoted by the
Apostle in the Epistle to the Hebrews, speaks of Christ
and His disciples as " I and the children whom the LORD
hath given me "[4]; to which the Apostle adds, " Forasmuch
then as the children are partakers of flesh and blood, he
also himself likewise took part of the same."[5]   And our
Lord, recognising this relation explicitly in the thirteenth
Chapter of St. John, calls His disciples "little children" ;

---

[1] See Acts ii. 11.   [2] *V.* 5.   [3] See Isaiah ix. 6.
[4] Isaiah viii. 18.   [5] Heb. ii. 14.

"Little children, yet a little while I am with you."[1]
He uses the diminutive to express tenderness and solicitude for them, as who would say; "Ye are not only
children, but young children, needing a parent's care;
children who will perish, if left in orphanhood.   I will
not so leave you."—O Lord, the true consolation of Thy
Spirit is to know by experience Thy fatherly compassion
for us, and the loving-kindness with which, in the exercise
of that compassion, Thou watchest over us from Thy
throne above.

Tuesday.—V. 18. "I will come to you."   In the
original the verb is in the present tense, not the future ;
"I come," or rather, "am coming to you."   I am coming
in my own Person at my resurrection.   I am coming at
Pentecost, in the Person of the Comforter.   I am coming
at the end of the world to "receive you unto myself, that
where I am, there ye may be also."[2]   One name by which
Messiah went among the Jews was "the Coming One,"
—"Art thou he that should come" (ὁ ἐρχόμενος, the
Coming One), "or do we look for another?"[3]   Messiah
was He whose coming had been ever looked for, in
compliance with the original promise respecting the seed
of the woman, who should bruise the serpent's head,[4] and
until whose final coming the serpent's head will not be
effectually bruised.   Observe, also, that His Advent in
the flesh prepared the way for, and opened out into, His
Advent in a spiritual body at His resurrection, and
this again into His Advent by the Comforter, and
this will eventually open out into His final Advent, so
that the word "I am coming" is ever germinant in its
fulfilment.—Lord, may I be living in the spirit of hope,

---

[1] St. John xiii. 33.   [2] St. John xiv. 3.
[3] St. Matt. xi. 3.   [4] Gen. iii. 15.

waiting for Thy Son from heaven,[1] "who shall change our vile body, that it may be fashioned like unto his glorious body, according to the working whereby he is able even to subdue all things unto himself."[2]

Wednesday.—V. 26. "He shall teach you all things, and bring all things to your remembrance, whatsoever I have said unto you." Let me meditate to-day on the action of the Holy Spirit upon the memory. Their Master's words, uttered in their hearing, would have escaped from the Apostles, or would have been inaccurately reported by them, had not their memory been supernaturally quickened to recall His instructions. And when the words were so recalled, the "teaching" of the Holy Ghost, which is also promised in this verse, explained and enforced them, put them in a new light, enabled them to see a beauty and significance in sayings which before were dark.—O Lord, the awful truth is revealed in Thy word,—nay, and in our own experience,—that Satan has a power over the human memory. As the birds carry off the seed, which lies exposed on the surface of the soil, so the devil, Thou assurest us, taketh away the word out of man's heart, lest he should believe and be saved.[3] O Lord, by Thy Holy Spirit counteract his devices. Make my heart soft and receptive, when I read or hear Thy word, that the good seed may sink deep into my soul, and, being cherished there by meditation, may take root and in due time bring forth fruit. And, as thou quickenest memory, so quicken intelligence also, that in the old familiar texts a new significance may continually be discerned by me, and new treasures of edification discovered.

Thursday.—V. 27. "Peace I leave with you" (this

<hr>

[1] 1 Thess. i. 10.   [2] Phil. iii. 21.   [3] See St. Luke viii. 5, 12.

was an ordinary form of farewell, equivalent to our
" good-bye," which Christ here takes up and mints afresh,
and issues it with a higher significance than it had in the
world's mouth) ; " my peace " (literally, " the peace which
is mine ") " I give unto you." How shall we distinguish
between the peace which He leaves, and that which He
gives ? Let us say that the peace which He leaves is the
peace of reconciliation — that reconciliation which was
brought about by His death (" That he might reconcile
both unto God in one body by the cross "[1]; " Therefore
being justified by faith we have peace with God, through
our Lord Jesus Christ "[2]), and that the peace which is
specially His, and which He gives, is the sense of sonship,
of being in Him adopted into God's family—a peace
resulting from the gift of the Spirit of adoption, whereby
we cry, Abba, Father.[3] To be made to feel that Christ is
a propitiation for our sins, this is a source of peace. It
is a further step to be made to feel that God in Him is
not only reconciled, but prepared to deal with us as a
reconciled Father. Then let me repeat Philip's prayer,
only with greater intelligence than he ; " Lord, shew us
the Father, and it sufficeth us."[4] To be shown the Father
will fill up every void in the heart, will give us the peace
which is specially Thine, inasmuch as Thou, who needest
for Thyself no peace of reconciliation, yet livest always in
enjoyment of that unbroken communion with Thy Father,
which is the truest and highest peace.

Friday.—V. 27. " Not as the world giveth, give I
unto you." The better and higher peace, which results
from the sense of sonship, is kept in reserve until we have
first tasted the lower peace, which comes from a sense of

---

[1] Eph. ii. 16.   [2] Rom. v. 1.
[3] Rom. viii. 15.   [4] St. John xiv. 8.

reconciliation. Thus Christ gives His best last. But not so the world. The world gives its best first. Pleasures and excitements and honours, which are very captivating, and have a special charm for us in early life, lose their zest, and begin to pall upon us in our later years. The rule of the world in recompence is, "Every man at the beginning doth set forth good wine; and when men have well drunk, then that which is worse." The rule of Christ is, on the other hand, "But thou hast kept the good wine until now."[1] We need not deny that the world has its pleasures, some of them very fascinating ones; it would have no votaries, if it had nothing to offer in the way of pleasure. But so also has the life of faith and devotion. And the gratifications, which this latter life affords, grow in power and attractiveness as life wears on. More treasures are discerned in the promises of God, as the soul makes fresh experiment of their truth. And the peace, and the good hope through grace, develope themselves more as the goal is more nearly approached.

Saturday.—V. 28. "Ye have heard how I said unto you, I go away, and come again unto you. If ye loved me, ye would rejoice, because I said, I go unto the Father." How selfish are we oftentimes in passionately wishing to detain some dear friend by our side, whose example and influence have been of use to us, and who has bound himself up with our best and holiest associations. It is good for him to be here, we think, looking only to ourselves; why should God remove him? Well, if it *were* clearly good for ourselves to detain him amongst us, is the wish for this detention what true love would dictate, when God is proposing to put him out of harm's way, and to place him in Christ's bosom in Paradise? Surely, if we loved

---

[1] St. John ii. 10.

him, we should rejoice at such a prospect for him. But very possibly God may see that for us also it is good to lose him; that we are leaning more upon him than it is meet to lean upon any creature, and that the bereavement will be the best means of preparing us for future re-union, by leading us to set our affection on things above,[1] and have our treasure in heaven.[2] It was expedient for our Lord to go away, that the Comforter might come; and this, it may be, was only the highest and grandest exemplification of a law which operates also in other bereavements.

[1] See Col. iii. 2. [2] See St. Matt. vi. 19, 20.

Chapter XXXIV

THE GOSPEL FOR TRINITY-SUNDAY.

St. John iii. 1 *to* 16.

1 There was a man of the Pharisees, named Nicodemus, a ruler
2 of the Jews. The same came to Jesus by night, and said unto
him, Rabbi, we know that thou art a teacher come from God: For
no man can do these miracles that thou doest, except God be with
3 him. Jesus answered and said unto him, Verily, verily I say unto
thee, Except a man be born again, he cannot see the kingdom of
4 God. Nicodemus saith unto him, How can a man be born when he
is old? can he enter the second time into his mothers womb, and
5 be born? Jesus answered, Verily, verily I say unto thee, Except
a man be born of water, and of the Spirit, he cannot enter into the
6 kingdom of God. That which is born of the flesh, is flesh; and
7 that which is born of the Spirit, is Spirit. Marvel not that I
8 said unto thee, Ye must be born again. The wind bloweth where
it listeth, and thou hearest the sound thereof; but canst not tell
whence it cometh, and whither it goeth; so is every one that is
9 born of the Spirit. Nicodemus answered and said unto him; How
10 can these things be? Jesus answered and said unto him, Art thou
11 a master of Israel, and knowest not these things? Verily, verily
I say unto thee, We speak that we do know, and testifie that we
12 have seen, and ye receive not our witness. If I have told you
earthly things, and ye believe not; how shall ye believe if I tell
13 you of heavenly things? And no man hath ascended up to heaven,
but he that came down from heaven, even the Son of man, who is
14 in heaven. And as Moses lifted up the serpent in the wilderness:
15 even so must the Son of man be lifted up; that whosoever believeth
in him, should not perish, but have eternal life.

[Miss. Sar.	1549.	1662 a.b.
In illo tempore, Erat homo ex Pharisæis, Nicodemus nomine, etc. (*Vulg.* Erat autem homo ex Pharisæis, Nicodemus nomine, etc.	There was a man of the Pharisees, named Nicodemus, a ruler of the Jews.	There was a man of the Pharisees, named Nicodemus, a ruler of the Jews. (Gr. ἦν δὲ ἄνθρωπος ἐκ τῶν Φαρισαίων, etc.)

Our Authorised Version (following Tyndale, Cranmer, and the Genevan Version) have not represented the δὲ at all. This is a great mistake. The connexion with the preceding Chapter which δὲ marks, is important and interesting. It cannot be better given than in the words of Professor Westcott (*in loc.*). The last verses of Chap. ii. had told us that "Jesus did not commit himself unto them, because he knew all men, and needed not that any should testify of man: for he knew what was in man." Hereupon the Professor remarks, "Nicodemus offered at once an example of the Lord's inward knowledge of men, and an exception to this general rule which He observed in not trusting Himself to them. The word 'man' is repeated to emphasize the connexion with ii. 25." In the Revised Version of 1881, the particle is rendered "Now."—*Translation of 1540*. (1) *V.* 3. "Except a man be born *from above*,"—a rendering which King James's Translators have given us in their margin as an alternative for *again*. Wycliffe has, "born again"; Tyndale, born *anew*. The Translators of 1611 adopted Wycliffe's rendering; the Revisers of 1881 have adopted Tyndale's. The reader is referred to Professor Westcott's learned additional Note (at the end of Chap. III.), in which he sums up the arguments for either rendering thus; "There seems then to be no reason to doubt that the sense given by the Authorised Version is right, though the notion is not that of mere repetition (*again*), but of an analogous process (*anew*)." (2) *V.* 13. "And no man *ascendeth* up to heaven, but he that came down from heaven." The present tense of the verb "ascend" is given in all the four earliest English Versions, Wycliffe's, Tyndale's, Cranmer's, and the Genevan. So manifest an error, when the Greek has the perfect (οὐδεὶς ἀναβέβηκεν εἰς τὸν οὐρανὸν), can only be explained by supposing the Translators to have thought that the accurate rendering of the tense ("No man hath ascended," etc.) would imply that our Lord *had, at the time of speaking, ascended into heaven.* But all that is meant is; "Man, who lives on earth, can only know what is done in heaven, either by ascending to heaven himself, or from the testimony of one who has already been there. Jesus as God had no need to ascend up into heaven in order to learn the things of heaven. By His nature as God He was already in heaven."—Dunwell's "Commentary on St. John's

Gospel," p. 70 [J. T. Hayes, Lyall Place: 1872]. The "but" (εἰ μὴ) excepts our LORD generally from the ignorance of heavenly things attaching to ordinary members of the human race, not from the number of those who had never visited heaven. "How shall ye believe if I tell you of heavenly things?" "*I* am competent to do that, having come down from heaven to earth, and dwelling there even now in virtue of my Divine Nature. But I am the *only* competent Witness on such matters; for no man hath ever ascended up to heaven, and come back to recount his experiences."]

Sunday.—What a beautiful blending of love and truth I observe in our Lord's dealing with Nicodemus! Nicodemus, though under certain convictions, was afraid and ashamed to confess Christ before men, and therefore came to Him under cover of the night. It was an unseasonable hour to come, when doors were shut, and the children of many a householder, like the householder himself, were in bed[1]; but our Lord did not decline to receive and converse with him. It is never out of season to seek Thee, blessed Jesus; and him that cometh to Thee at any hour of day or night, Thou wilt in no wise cast out.[2] Moreover, Thou dost not quench the smoking flax[3]; but from such poor and meagre convictions as Nicodemus had, when he came to Thee, Thou dost seek to lead him on by Thy expostulations to higher and more saving truth. And yet how faithful art Thou in Thy dealings with him! So far from seeming flattered by his visit, as if it were a homage to Thy claims, Thou tellest him plainly of his ignorance of things which most concerned him (ignorance, which in him, as "a master of Israel," was quite inexcusable), and impliest that he must begin his whole spiritual life *de novo*, being born of water and of the Spirit in Baptism, and thus entering into Thy school as a learner,

---

[1] See St. Luke xi. 7.   [2] See St. John vi. 37.
[3] See Isaiah xlii. 3, and St. Matt. xii. 20.

and sitting at Thy feet. Let this prepare me, O Lord, when I too come to Thee for instruction and guidance, to be dealt with faithfully as well as lovingly by One who reads my heart.

Monday.—Some shallow students of Scripture, looking only to our Lord's Sermon on the Mount, and without any sufficient perception of the real drift of that discourse, have said invidiously that doctrine finds no place in our Lord's own teaching, but only in that of His apostles. What do they make of the conversations with Nicodemus, with the Samaritan woman, with the people in the synagogue of Capernaum? Here I find a soul coming to Christ under certain sincere, though inadequate convictions, and with a desire for further instruction. Christ begins with him at once upon doctrines,—preaches to him immediately, as the great truths needful, man's ruin by nature (" Except a man be born again, he cannot see the kingdom of God "); man's redemption by the cross (" even so must the Son of man be lifted up: that whosoever believeth in him should not perish, but have eternal life "); and man's regeneration by the Spirit in the Sacrament of Baptism (" Except a man be born of water and of the Spirit, he cannot enter into the kingdom of God").—Lord, write upon my heart of hearts the conviction of my ruin by nature, my redemption by Thy blood, my regeneration by the first Sacrament of Thy Gospel. For, indeed, these convictions are the beginning of all good in the human soul, and the life of all Christian morality.

Tuesday.—Let me endeavour to see the great appositeness of this Gospel to Trinity-Sunday, the festival for which it is appointed. Nicodemus, as a Jew instructed in the law, knew of God the Father. In the words with which the interview opens, he recognises the First Person of the Blessed Trinity, and owns to the conviction of Christ having been sent by Him; "Rabbi, we know that thou art a teacher come from God: for no man can do these miracles that thou doest, except God be with him." What our Lord declares to him is that, without the agency of the two other Divine Persons, there can be no entrance into God's kingdom for fallen man. The Son of man must be lifted up on the cross as an object of faith, just as the serpent in the wilderness was lifted up for the bitten Israelites to turn their eyes upon.[1] And the Holy Spirit, brooding over the laver of regeneration, as in the first creation He "moved" (or hovered dove-like) "upon the face of the waters," must quicken the soul into spiritual vitality. Thus it needs a function of each Divine Person to save a single soul. There must be, first, the Father's love manifested in the mission (or, rather, in the gift) of the Son ("God so loved the world, that he *gave* his only begotten Son," etc.); this is the *source* of salvation. There must be, secondly, the Son's atoning death; this is the *means* of salvation. And there must be, thirdly, the quickening of the soul by the Holy Spirit; this is the *power which applies salvation to the soul of the individual.* If I desire to see the unity of design and will, which subsists between the sacred Persons of the Trinity, let me observe the glorious harmony in which all concur in the great work of saving a soul from sin and death.

Wednesday.—V. 12. Again I find the appositeness of this Gospel to the Festival of Trinity-Sunday in this verse; "If I have told you earthly things, and ye believe not, how shall ye believe if I tell you of heavenly things?" Regeneration, of which our Lord had been speaking, is an "earthly thing," because, though brought about by Divine

---

[1] See Num. xxi. 8, 9.

agency, it is transacted upon earth, and man has experience of it, and the fruits of it are seen in his life and conversation.   But the Atonement, of which our Lord goes on to speak, is a matter of pure Revelation, altogether outside man's experience, and of which we can know nothing but what God is pleased to tell us.   And much more is this the case with the doctrine of the Holy Trinity, which defines the relations to one another of the three Divine Persons.   This is a purely "heavenly thing," of which our minds can form no conception at all, and for which we are dependent entirely upon the testimony of Him who came down from heaven originally, and who closed His ministry upon earth with the solemn declaration of the Triune Name, and the commission to declare it to all nations, and to bring all to the confession of it; " Go ye and make disciples of all the nations, baptizing them into the name of the Father, and of the Son, and of the Holy Ghost." [1]   Every definition in the Athanasian Creed rests upon Holy Scripture, and may be concluded and proved thereby—that is, it rests upon God's testimony respecting Himself.   Oh that, when we read the Holy Scriptures, we might listen with great intentness to catch the voice of God in them!   Oh that we regarded ourselves, when on our knees with our Bibles, as in the shrine of an oracle, whence issue Divine voices, " for doctrine, for reproof, for correction, for instruction in righteousness "! [2]

Thursday.—V. 4. " How can a man be born when he is old ?" and again (V. 9), " How can these things be ?" " Hows " are a great obstacle in the way of faith.   But if a fact is certain, whether from our experience or from Revelation, it is quite unreasonable that our ignorance of the method in which it is brought about should be an

---

[1] St. Matt. xxviii. 19, R.V.   [2] See 2 Tim. iii. 16.

obstacle to its being believed. This is what our Lord teaches Nicodemus, in what He says about the wind (V. 8); " The wind bloweth where it listeth, and thou hearest the sound thereof, but canst not tell whence it cometh, and whither it goeth." Who doubts the fact of there being a wind, because he cannot understand the laws which regulate the wind, or explain how it is that it should blow at one time or in one place rather than at another ? And similar illustrations may be drawn from every part of Nature ; we know nothing of the " hows " and " whys"; we can never go many steps beyond the facts. We know for certain that the blood circulates, this being a scientific discovery made many years ago, and a discovery which is of the utmost practical service in the art of medicine. But how or why it circulates, what is the principle of that mysterious movement which we call life, who shall say ? The sage here knows no more than the peasant.—O Lord, when I find anything clearly revealed in Thy Holy Word, let me not raise a question how the thing can be ; but making no doubt that it is so, because Thy Word affirms it, let me act upon what is revealed. It is given me as a stimulant, not to speculation, but to practice.

Friday.—V. 12. " If I have told you earthly things, and ye believe not, how shall ye believe, if I tell you of heavenly things ?" Our Lord evidently implies here that certain truths, which rest upon Revelation only, are more difficult to receive than others, which are confirmed by our own reason and experience. I find the same implication in other passages, as, for example, in this ; " Marvel not at this " (*i.e.* at the spiritual resurrection): " for the hour is coming, in the which all that are in the graves shall hear his voice, and shall come forth." [1] Now may we not hence

[1] St. John v. 28.

draw an argument for prompt belief in truths, which make less tax upon our powers of faith than others, which make a much heavier tax, and yet which we receive without question ? Some people unhappily are found in these sceptical days, who profess to receive unhesitatingly the leading doctrines of Christianity, such as the Incarnation and Atonement, but indulge in silly pieces of incredulity about certain Scriptural miracles, say, if you please, Jonah's incarceration in the whale, or the entry of the devils into the swine. Oh, let me beware of these petty incredulities; for they will eat like a canker,[1] until some vital article of faith is touched, and the deposit tampered with. And how essentially foolish and weak such doubts are ! Do I really believe, as the one foundation of all my hopes, that Almighty God " took Man's nature in the womb of the blessed Virgin, of her substance "[2]? If I do not believe this, I am no Christian ; for this is the fundamental doctrine of the Gospel. But if I do, and if the same authority on which I receive this truth, warrants equally the other miracles of the Old and New Testament, what difficulty can these lesser miracles present, which is not infinitely exceeded by the mystery of the holy Incarnation ? To receive the one, and reject the other, is it not to strain out the gnat, while we swallow the camel ?[3]

Saturday.—It is interesting to trace the growth in the religious character of Nicodemus, as this Gospel gives us the means of doing. We find him in the seventh Chapter making a stand against the Sanhedrim, of which he was a member, and demanding that our Lord should at least have a fair opportunity of answering for Himself, (" Doth our law judge any man, before it hear him ?")[4]

---

[1] See 2 Tim. ii. 17.   [2] Second Article of Religion.
[3] See St. Matt. xxiii. 24, R. V. [4] St. John vii. 51.

And the crucifixion of Christ, which had scattered the disciples every man to his own home,[1] seems to have communicated to Nicodemus a certain holy boldness, and to have determined him to confess Christ bravely before men. For we read in Chapter xix. that he " brought a mixture of myrrh and aloes, about an hundred pound weight,"[2] and joined with Joseph of Arimathæa in embalming and paying funeral honours to the body of our Lord. Thus am I taught that grace may be real although feeble, and led to magnify the gentleness and goodness of Him, who, instead of quenching the smoking flax,[3] cherishes it gradually into a flame. And, moreover, the standing forth of several true and brave confessors at the death of Christ, the penitent thief, the centurion in charge, and Nicodemus, is a significant lesson to me that in the Cross alone can I find the strength and courage necessary to carry me successfully through my Christian course, and that it is when fighting under it as my banner that I shall be able to foil my spiritual foes.

[1] See St. John xvi. 32.   [2] *V.* 39.
[3] See St. Matt. xii. 20, and Isaiah xlii. 3.

Chapter XXXV.

THE GOSPEL FOR THE FIRST SUNDAY AFTER TRINITY.

St. Luke xvi. 19 *to the end.*

19 There was a certain rich man, who was clothed in purple, and
20 fine linen, and fared sumptuously every day. And there was a
certain begger named Lazarus, who was laid at his gate full of
21 sores; and desiring to be fed with the crumbs, which fell from the
rich mans table: moreover the dogs came and licked his sores.
22 And it came to pass that the begger died, and was carried by the
angels into Abrahams bosom: the rich man also died and was
23 buried. And in hell he lift up his eies being in torments, and
24 seeth Abraham afar off, and Lazarus in his bosom. And he cried,
and said, Father Abraham, have mercy on me, and send Lazarus
that he may dip the tip of his finger in water, and cool my tongue,
25 for I am tormented in this flame. But Abraham said, Son, remember, that thou in thy life time receivedst thy good things, and likewise Lazarus evil things: but now he is comforted, and thou art
26 tormented. And besides all this, between us and you there is a
great gulf fixed: so that they who would pass from hence to you,
cannot; neither can they pass to us, that would come from thence.
27 Then he said, I pray thee therefore, father, that thou wouldest
28 send him to my fathers house: For I have five brethren; that he
may testifie unto them, lest they also come into this place of
29 torment. Abraham saith unto him, They have Moses and the
30 prophets; let them hear them. And he said, Nay, father Abraham; but if one went unto them from the dead, they will repent.
31 And he said unto him, If they hear not Moses and the prophets,
neither will they be perswaded, though one rose from the dead.

[Miss. Sar.	1549.	1662 s.b.
In illo tempore, Dixit Jesus discipulis suis parabolam hanc ; Homo quidam erat dives, et induebatur purpura et bysso, etc. (*Vulg.* Homo quidam erat dives, qui induebatur purpura et bysso, etc.)	There was a certaine rich man, which was clothed in purple and fine white, etc.	There was a certain rich man, who was clothed in purple, and fine linen, etc. (*Gr.* Ἄνθρωπος δέ τις ἦν πλούσιος, καὶ ἐνεδιδύσκετο πορφύραν καὶ βύσσον, etc.)

No English Translators before the Revisers of 1881 made any attempt to exhibit the δέ, which links this Parable to what went before it in our Lord's discourse. In the Revised Version, however, the attempt is made ; "*Now* there was a certain rich man, and he was clothed in purple and fine linen." The connexion of thought is difficult to seize ; but doubtless it is real. The Pharisees, who were covetous, had derided our Lord's teaching (conveyed in the Parable of the Unjust Steward) on the right use of worldly wealth, and the declaration of the impossibility of serving at the same time God and mammon, with which He had followed up that Parable. "Of the subsequent discourse," says Bengel, "the connexion is this. The justification of oneself before men and [self-righteous] elation of heart nourishes covetousness, and scoffs at heavenly simplicity (*v.* 15); and despises the Gospel " (the calls into God's kingdom, which the Gospel was then making, and successfully with many) "(*v.* 16); and breaks the law " (while making its boast of the law) "(*v.* 17) ; as was shown by an example very necessary to be alleged against the Pharisees" (whose "national judicature, receding from the high standard of God's law, had tolerated the public scandal, which Herod's marriage with his brother's wife had occasioned" [Stier]) "(*v.* 18)." All the above points are embraced in the parable respecting the rich man and Lazarus. As to our Lord's allusion in *v.* 18 to laxity in regard to the marriage law, there seems reason to believe that this was a form of evil prevalent and popular among the Pharisees. Compare the circumstance recorded in connexion with the woman taken in adultery (St. John viii. 7, 9), that "they which heard it " (our Lord's sentence, "He that is without sin among you, let him first cast a stone at her "), "*being convicted by their own conscience,* went out one by one, beginning at the eldest, even unto the last "; and also St. Paul's expostulation with the Jews, who "rested in the law," in Rom. ii. 17, 22 ; "Thou that sayest a man should not commit adultery, *dost thou commit adultery ?*"—*Translation of* 1540. (1) *V.* 19. "which was clothed in purple and *fine white.*" Cranmer stands by himself here. Wycliffe has "whiyt silk"; Tyndale, "fyne bysse "; Geneva (like the

Authorised), "fyne lynnen"; Rheims, merely "silk." (2) *V.* 21, "and no man gave unto him." In interpolating these words, Cranmer followed, not the original, but the Vulgate Translation, which gives *v.* 21 thus; "Cupidus saturari de micis, quæ cadebant de mensa divitis, *et nemo illi dabat:* sed et canes veniebant, et lingebant ulcera ejus." The clause is evidently transferred from the Parable of the Prodigal Son in the adjacent Chapter of the Gospel (xv. 16), where we have another description of the direst physical distress. That Wycliffe, translating from the Vulgate, should have rendered the clause, was of course to be expected. He has, "*and no man yaf to him*, but houndis camen : & likkiden his bilis." But that Cranmer's translator, whoever he was, professing to correct by reference to the Greek that portion of the old English translation, which was allotted to him by the Archbishop, should have represented words which he did not find in the original, especially as Tyndale had not done so before him, is remarkable. Even the original Edition of the Anglo-Rhemish Version, put forth in 1582, ignores the clause, though it seems to have been foisted in (when, and how, I cannot say) to the Douay and Rheims Bible now commonly used by Roman Catholics.[1] It appears in Jerome's Recension of the old Latin Versions of the New Testament, as that Recension is given in the Benedictine Edition of his works; but I do not imagine that there is any authority for it in any existing Greek manuscript. (3) *V.* 25. "remember that thou in thy life time receiuedst *thy pleasure*, and *contrariwise* Lazarus receiued *paine*," (for τὰ ἀγαθά σου . . . . καὶ ὁ Λάζαρος ὁμοίως τὰ κακά) ; and so Tyndale previously, and the Genevan subsequently. King James's Translators put back the literal rendering of ἀγαθά, and the correct rendering of ὁμοίως, which had already appeared in Wycliffe ; "Sone haue mynde, for thou hast resceyued *good thingis* in thi liif : lazarus *also yuel thingis*." The Rhemish Translators had done the same in 1582 ; "thou didst receiue *good things* in thy life time, and Lazarus *likewise euil*." (4) *V.* 26. "*Beyond all this*, between us and you there is a great *space set*." This is adopted from Tyndale. To the Genevan we owe the "Besides all this" and the "great gulf" of our Authorised Version. Wycliffe has, "in alle these thingis : a great *derke place* is stablischid" ("in his omnibus . . . *chaos* magnum firmatum est," *Vulg.*).

---

[1] My edition of this Book is that which has "the approbation of the Right Rev. Dr. Denvir *R.C. Bishop of Down and Connor*," and it is published by Thomas Booker, Manager of the Catholic Company, 53 New Bond Street. Herein *v.* 21 of St. Luke xvi. is thus given ; "Desiring to be filled with the crumbs that fell from the rich man's table, and no none (*sic*) did give him : moreover the dogs came and licked his sores."

Rheims; "is fixed a great chaos." (5) *V.* 28. "Send him to my father's house, *for to warne them.*" And so Tyndale previously, and the Genevan subsequently. Here again Wycliffe's rendering, "that he witnesse to hem," is more literal,—ὅπως διαμαρτύρηται αὐτοῖς ("ut testetur illis," *Vulg.*). (6) *V.* 31. "neither will they *beleeve*, though one rise from death *againe.*" And thus the other four English versions preceding the Authorised. "Will they be persuaded" is more literal, and equally forcible.]

Sunday.—V. 22. "The beggar died, and was carried by the angels into Abraham's bosom." He is exhibited to us as holding after death a restful and blissful communion with Abraham. But Abraham was no beggar. "He was very rich," we read, "in cattle, in silver, and in gold."[1] Thus we learn that it was not the circumstances of the beggar—not his poverty, his rags, his famished state—which brought him to Paradise; nor, on the other hand, the wealth and affluent circumstances of the rich man, which shut him out of Paradise. The rich man lived in and for this world, which was to him the only reality—the world beyond the grave he practically disbelieved in; it exercised no influence upon his character and conduct; he had his "portion in this life."[2] Of wealthy Abraham we read, on the other hand, that "he looked for a city which hath foundations, whose builder and maker is God,"[3] and that not the wealth which he had amassed, but the God whom he worshipped and served, was his treasure. He cared not to share the spoil taken in his successful expedition against the four kings[4]; and, in acknowledgment of his disinterestedness, the Lord said to him, "I am thy shield, and thy exceeding great reward."[5] In a word, Abraham possessed his riches, but the riches of Dives possessed him. Let me learn how Scripture guards everywhere against miscon-

---

[1] Gen. xiii. 2.   [2] See Ps. xvii. 14.   [3] Heb. xi. 10.
[4] See Gen. xiv. 21-24.   [5] Gen. xv. 1.

ceptions of its meaning, and how necessary it is, therefore, to balance its different statements with one another, and not to run away with crude notions fetched from single texts. If the Scripture had only said, " Work out your own salvation," and had not added, " For it is God that worketh in you both to will and to do of his good pleasure,"[1] we should have supposed that salvation was all of human endeavour, and not of grace.

Monday.—V. 23. " And in hell he lift up his eyes, being in torments." Let me reflect upon the remarkable circumstance that it is our Lord and His Apostle St. John who speak so explicitly of the torments of the wicked in a future state of existence. The torments here mentioned are those of their intermediate state (the " hell " being *Hades*, the realm of departed spirits). But in St. Mark ix. our Lord speaks in even more awful terms of the torments of their ultimate state (*Gehenna*), thrice repeating the warning to make any sacrifice rather than be cast " into the fire that never shall be quenched ; where their worm dieth not, and the fire is not quenched."[2] And in the twentieth and twenty-first Chapters of the Revelation St. John exhibits to us " the lake which burneth with fire and brimstone : which is the second death."[3] (I observe, by the way, in connexion with the 15th verse of Rev. xx., " Whosoever was not found written in the book of life was cast into the lake of fire," that Lazarus's name is mentioned in the parable, but *not that of the rich man*). Our Lord, in the Parable before us, spoke from insight into the world beyond the grave ; He told His hearers, in a form adapted to their capacity, exactly what He saw there. And St. John, the Apostle of love, seemed to have shared his Master's insight into

---

[1] See Phil. ii. 12, 13.   [2] *Vv.* 43, 45, 47.   [3] Chap. xxi. 8.

the other world, and to have put on record for our warning what he saw there in an iuspired vision. Both He who is love, and the disciple who lay in His bosom,[1] and who, most remarkably of all the disciples, exemplified the grace of love, seek to work on us by fear, to call into operation in our hearts the dread of God's awful judgments. Let me learn that, since such appeals are made to it in God's Word, fear, though not the highest motive, is yet a motive by which God means us to be influenced; and also that it is a mark of the truest and highest love, not to tamper or trifle with the sins of men, but to tell them plainly and faithfully what is in store for the impenitent and unbelieving.

Tuesday.—V. 23. "And seeth Abraham afar off, and Lazarus in his bosom." From the former part of the verse we learn that in hell there will be positive and acute suffering,—"torments." From this latter clause we gather that, accompanied with this, will be something equally dreadful, the agonizing consciousness of what has been lost. "There shall be weeping and gnashing of teeth, when ye shall see Abraham, and Isaac, and Jacob, and all the prophets, in the kingdom of God, and you yourselves thrust out."[2] The thought of the repose, the blessedness, the glory, the eternal security, which might have been theirs, which was purchased for them as well as for others by the blood and righteousness of Christ, and offered to them as freely as to others, but which they have wilfully bartered away for some sinful indulgence, like Esau selling his birthright for a mess of pottage [3]— with what anguish will this reflexion, brought home to them vividly—perhaps, for aught we know, made palpable

---

[1] See St. John xiii. 23, 25.   [2] St. Luke xiii. 28.
[3] See Gen. xxv. 29-34, and Heb. xii. 16.

to their senses—wring the hearts of the condemned !—O Lord, when I am enticed by any lure of the world, the flesh, or the devil, thus to sell my Baptismal birthright, my sonship and heirship to Thee, dispose and enable me—before I do what my lust, or covetousness, or ambition, solicit me to do—to reckon over in my mind the glory and blessedness, the pure and ravishing delights of communion with Thee and with Thy saints and angels, which I shall thus forfeit.

Wednesday.—V. 25. "But Abraham said, Son, remember that thou in thy lifetime receivedst thy good things." I learn from this that in the disembodied state memory will be on the alert. Perhaps for the very reason that the soul *is* disembodied,—that no activities are now possible to it, because it has laid down the body which is the organ of activity,—it will be all the more impressible by reminiscences of the past; just as, when one lies awake at night, thought is often unusually busy. And what a different appearance will life then present, from what it did while it was passing ! How miserable, how paltry, will the so-called good things of the world,— its pleasures, its indulgences, its honours, for which the sinner bartered away his soul,—appear to be, when they are looked at from the other side of the grave ! And, on the other hand, how will all the trials and sorrows of the true child of God seem to him to be but " light affliction, which is but for a moment "[1]! With what deep gratitude, with what humble adoration of God's Providence, will he review his past, remembering all the way which the Lord his God has led him in the wilderness, to humble him, and to prove him, to know what was in his heart ![2]—O Lord, when I am tempted either to sinful indulgence, or

---

[1] See 2 Cor. iv. 17. [2] See Deut. viii. 2.

to murmuring, give me grace to reflect how this pleasure or this trial will look, when I see it stripped of all its disguises, from the further side of the grave.

Thursday. — V. 29. "Abraham saith unto him, They have Moses and the prophets; let them hear them." Not that they had ever seen Moses and the prophets, or heard them speak. And yet Moses and the prophets in their writings were really and truly expostulating with the brethren of the rich man, and seeking to bring them to repentance. Have I ever fancied that I am at a great disadvantage, because I have never, like the first disciples, seen Christ and His Apostles, and heard the Gospel from those lips which first proclaimed it? Let me reflect that in the precious volume of the New Testament I have Christ and the Apostles. As regards my guidance under the difficulties of life, and my ultimate salvation, it is entirely the same thing as if I were to see and hear them; I have the same advantages as those who did see and hear them; and I am equally responsible. There is no counsel of Christ and His Apostles which it would benefit me to receive, which is not contained somewhere in that holy volume.—Oh then, let me open mine ears to it, while I may, and reflect, when I take it up, that it is indeed the Saviour and His inspired messengers who are addressing me in its pages, and addressing me from glory and from Paradise.

Friday.—(Same verse.) If therefore they had heard Moses and the Prophets—heard them with a " hearing ear and an understanding heart " — they would have received a testimony to a future state of existence, in which the righteous are recompensed and the wicked punished. The books of Moses and the prophets were quite sufficient to give them warning respecting such a state, could have given it to them quite as forcibly, quite as emphatically, quite as unequivocally, as an apparition from the grave could have done. Thus our Lord found the doctrine of the resurrection of the dead in the circumstance that God, speaking to Moses at the bush, calls Himself the God of Abraham, and the God of Isaac, and the God of Jacob, and intimates that the Sadducees did "not know the Scriptures,"[1] because they did not find this meaning in the words. I must strive then, in reading the Holy Scriptures, to discern what lies *beneath* the surface of them as well as what lies *on* the surface, what they imply as well as what they express. And how shall I ever gain this power of discernment, except by the teaching of that Spirit who "searcheth all things, yea, the deep things of God "[2]?

Saturday. — V. 30. "And he said, Nay, father Abraham : but if one went unto them from the dead, they will repent." What contempt this rich man virtually pours upon the Scriptures of the Old Testament ! How little weight and efficacy does he attach to Moses and the Prophets, in comparison with a ghost ! As for the Scriptures, they have palled upon him by repetition ; they are " stale, flat, and unprofitable " ; but a visitant from the dead will not fail to alarm, arrest, arouse to repentance. One of the marks of reprobation visible in this unhappy man is the *slight* account which he makes of God's Word, and the *great* account which he makes of signs and wonders as means of moral suasion. I find in what he says a warning for these times. For in these times, minds that are jaded with this world's vanities, and require some fresh stimulant, instead of

[1] See St. Matt. xxii. 29, 31, 32 ; St. Mark xii. 24, 26, 27 ; St. Luke xx. 37, 38, with Exod. iii. 6.   [2] 1 Cor. ii. 10.

betaking themselves to the Holy Scriptures, which are real communications to us from a higher world, seek a sign from the realm of the grave, and endeavour to hold communication with the spirits of the dead.—May God preserve me from the sin of necromancy, which is an attempt to communicate with the spiritual world by means which He has forbidden, or has never sanctioned; and make me mindful that in the black catalogue of the works of the flesh—that is, the sins to which our corrupt nature is prone—is to be found not only uncleanness and lasciviousness, hatred and wrath, drunkenness and revellings, but also " witchcraft,"[1] and that mixture of human imposture and Satanic delusion, which in these days represents witchcraft, and draws away disciples after it,— as it were spell-bound with their own superstitions.

[1] See GaL v. 20.

CHAPTER XXXVI

THE GOSPEL FOR THE SECOND SUNDAY AFTER TRINITY.

St. Luke xiv. 16 *to* 25 (leaving out the words.
"Then said he unto him," with which *v.* 16 commences).

16, 17   A certain man made a great supper, and bade many; & sent his servant at supper time to say to them that were bidden, Come,
18 for all things are now ready. And they all with one consent began to make excuse : The first said unto him, I have bought a piece of ground, and I must needs go and see it; I pray thee have me
19 excused. And another said, I have bought five yoke of oxen, and I
20 go to prove them; I pray thee have me excused. And another said,
21 I have married a wife, and therefore I cannot come. So that servant came, and shewed his Lord these things. Then the master of the house being angry said to his servant, Go out quickly into the streets and lanes of the city, and bring in hither the poor, and the
22 maimed, and the halt, and the blind. And the servant said, Lord,
23 it is done as thou hast commanded, and yet there is room. And the Lord said unto the servant, Go out into the high=ways, and hedges,
24 and compel them to come in, that my house may be filled. For I say unto you, that none of those men which were bidden, shall taste of my Supper.

[Miss. Sar.	1549.	1662 s.b.
In illo tempore, Dixit *Jesus discipulis suis parabolam hanc;* Homo quidam fecit cœnam magnam, et vocavit multos. (*Vulg.* At ipse dixit ei : Homo quidam fecit cœnam magnam, et vocavit multos.)	A certain man ordained a great supper, and bade many, etc.	A certain man made a great supper, and bade many, etc. (*Gr.* Ὁ δὲ εἶπεν αὐτῷ· Ἄνθρωπός τις ἐποίησε δεῖπνον μέγα, καὶ ἐκάλεσε πολλούς.)

This Parable grew out of a conversation at the table of a Pharisee, where our Lord had taken occasion from the anxiety for precedence, manifested by some of the guests, to speak (under a figure drawn from the social ways of men) of humility towards God (*vv.* 7 *to* 12), and had also exhorted His host to a disinterested hospitality,—the entertainment of the poor and miserable, who could make no requital (*vv.* 12 *to* 15), adding that he should not lose his reward for such generosity ;—"thou shall be recompensed at the resurrection of the just" (*v.* 14). Hereupon one of the guests exclaimed, doubtless in a devout (not a mocking) spirit, "Blessed is he that shall eat bread in the kingdom of God." "The re-surrection of the just," as Archbishop Trench points out in his "Parables," p. 344 [London: 1844], was identified by the Jews with the open setting up of the kingdom of God, and it was "believed that this last would be ushered in by a great and glorious festival, of which all the members of that kingdom should be partakers." Hereupon follows the Parable, addressed primarily to the guest whose remark had elicited it, but through him to all who (as he probably did) flattered themselves on finding in their hearts certain aspirations after a blessedness and glory in the remote future. Our Lord virtually says to such persons ;—"Nay, but the ban-quet of the kingdom is even now thrown open to you ; 'all things are ready,' and the invitations are being issued. Your words imply some anxiety to accept the invitation ; but are you aware how many of you respectable and self-complacent people are even now declining the invita-tion, and causing it to be passed on to guests of the lowest grade, who will thankfully accept such an opportunity ?"—*Translation of* 1540. (1) *V.* 16. "A certain man *ordained* a great supper." And so Tyndale before, and the Genevan after, Cranmer. It would seem as if (looking to the thing figured rather than to the figure) they thought that "made" was too commonplace a word for the occasion,—hardly solemn enough. The Vulgate, however, has "fecit," and Wycliffe, translating from it, gives, "*made* a great soper." (2) *V.* 18. "I have bought *a farm.*" And so Tyndale, Geneva, and Rheims. Wycliffe has "a *toun.*" And, similarly, in St. Luke xv. 15 he represents the same Greek word (ἀγρὸς, a field) by "towne,"—"he sente hym in to his *towne :* to fede swyne." The word "*town*" furnishes an interesting example of a word's coming round in pro-cess of time to mean exactly the opposite of what it originally signified. "In Anglo-Saxon we have the word *tynan*, to hedge. Hence a *tun*, or *ton,* was a place surrounded by a hedge, or rudely fortified by a palisade. Originally it meant only a single croft, homestead, or farm, and the word retained this restricted meaning in the time of Wicliffe." . . . "This usage is retained in Scotland, where a solitary farmstead still goes by the name of the *toun ;* and in Iceland, where the homestead, with its girding wall, is called a *tùn.* In many parts of England the rickyard is called the bar*ton*—that is, the inclosure for the *bear,* or crop which the land bears. There are lone farm-houses in Kent called Shotting*ton,* Wingle*ton,* Goding*ton,* and Apple*ton.* But in most cases the isolated *ton* became the nucleus of a village, and the village grew into a *town,* and, last stage of all, the word TOWN has come to denote, not the one small croft ¡inclosed from the forest by the Saxon settler, but the dwelling-place of a vast population."—[Rev. Isaac Taylor's "Words and Places" (Macmillan : 1865) p. 120]. The "toun," in the celebrated passage of the Prologue to Chaucer's "Canterbury Tales," ("A good man ther was of religioun, That was a poure Persone of a *toun*"), means doubtless a country village with a scattered population—something intermediate between the isolated farm and a country-town with streets. The good parson has far to go in visiting his flock, and takes his staff as for a journey :

> "Wide was his parish, and *houses fer asonder,*
> But he ne left nought for no rain ne thonder,
> In sikeness and in mischief to visite
> The ferrest in his parish, moche and lite,
> Upon his fete, and in his hand a staf."

While there is a certain charm in the plain homeliness of the Authorised Version, "piece of ground," the Revisers of 1881 have probably done well in uniformly rendering ἀγρὸς by "field." (3) *V.* 21. "Then was the *good-man of the house* displeased." This rendering of the Greek word οἰκοδεσπότης King James's Translators have adopted in five places,—St. Matt. xx. 11, xxiv. 43 ; St. Mark xiv. 14 ; St. Luke xii. 39, xxii. 11. The Revisers of 1881 have retained it in two cases (St. Mark xiv. 14, and St. Luke xxii. 11), where it is applied to the man at whose house preparations were made for the Last Supper, but have exchanged it for "householder," or "master of the house," in the other places. Was this because the term "goodman" was applied in Old English *to persons below the rank of gentry,* and they thought perhaps that the man, from whom the Paschal chamber was hired, might fall under that category, but saw no indication of a lower grade in the other instances ? Any how, the οἰκοδεσπότης of the Parable of the Great Supper, if it is only that he is able to give an entertainment on so large a scale, must be supposed to be a person of considerable importance, and above a "goodman." (4) *V.* 21. "Go out quickly into the streets and *quarters*" (εἰς τὰς πλατείας καὶ ῥύμας) "of the citie." Tyndale also has "quarters," the literal translation of *vicos,* which he found in the Vulgate. But both the circumstance of the lowest poor being invited, and the opposition between πλατεῖα and ῥύμη show that "lane" is the true rendering. Wycliffe seized the idea, when he rendered, "Go out swithe in to the greet stretis, and the *smale stretis* of the citie." (5) *V.* 21. "Bring in hither the poor and *feeble*, and the halt, and blinde." "Feeble" is due to the Vulgate, which gives "pauperes, ac *debiles*, et cæcos, et claudos." "Debilis" is properly "de-habilis," a man disabled in some of his limbs or faculties, a crippled or maimed person. But the looser and more general sense of "weak" came to attach to it in the later Latin, and more or less obscured the original force of the word. Tyndale had given "maymed" to represent ἀναπήρους. It is surprising that Cranmer did not follow Tyndale, but went back to Wycliffe's "feble."]

Sunday.—V. 16. "A certain man made a great supper, and bade many." It was at a supper, to which He had been bidden by one of the chief Pharisees (as we see by looking back to the first verse of the Chapter), that our Lord spake this Parable. It was His manner to take occasion for His discourses from the things under His eye. Thus to Nicodemus, who "came to" Him "by night,"[1] He spoke of those who "loved darkness rather than light, because their deeds were evil"[2]; and to the Samaritan woman at the well He discoursed about the "living water"[3]; and, in connexion with the miracle of feeding the five thousand, He preached in the synagogue of Capernaum on "the living bread."[4] It will be a means of sanctifying my senses, if I allow every thing which crosses my path to suggest to me some holy and edifying thought,—if the midnight sky, spangled with a thousand stars, remind me of heaven and its glories, the straying sheep on the downs of the sinner who has gone astray,[5] and must be sought by the Good Shepherd if he is to be brought back again, and the city's turmoil and hubbub of the many hidden saints and servants of God who are

[1] St. John iii. 1, 2.   [2] *V.* 19.
[3] St. John iv. 6, 7, 10, 14.   [4] St. John vi. 11, 26, 32, 51 59.
[5] St. Luke xv. 3-8, and Ps. cxix. 176.

engaged, like St. Matthew, in secular occupations.[1] Thus shall I, with the help of God's grace, be able to copy into my mind a feature of the mind of Christ.

Monday.—The incident, which immediately gave rise to the Parable, was that one of the guests, having heard our Lord speak of " the resurrection of the just,"[2] which the Jews always supposed would be ushered in by a great festival (held to inaugurate the setting up of the kingdom of God), made this pious ejaculation, " Blessed is he that shall eat bread in the kingdom of God."[3] Perhaps he spoke with something of the self-complacency, with which a man occasionally airs a good sentiment. Our Lord answers by the Parable; and the purport of the answer is that, although the heavenly festival was prepared at present, and invitations to it were being issued by Himself, those invitations were not accepted by the persons to whom they were addressed—all of them excused themselves from attending under one plea or another. Our Lord was always somewhat stern and repellent to mere good sentiment, probably by way of proving its genuineness. Thus, when in a gush of pious enthusiasm one said to Him, " Master, I will follow thee whithersoever thou goest,"[4] He as much as answered; " Do you really mean that? Do you know what those warm words are committing you to ?" " The foxes have holes, and the birds of the air have nests; but the Son of man hath not where to lay his head."[5] Mere fine sentiments are often very hollow. Balaam, one of the worst of men in character and conduct, uttered a beautiful sentiment; " Let me die the death of the righteous, and let my last end be like his!"[6]—O Lord, make me

---

[1] St. Matt. ix. 9, 10. [2] St. Luke xiv. 14. [3] *V.* 15.
[4] St. Matt. viii. 19. [5] *V.* 20.   [6] Num. xxiii. 10.

duly mindful that to roll pious sentiments glibly off the
tongue will be no sufficient substitute for having works
of piety and charity upon the hands. "Not every one
that saith unto me, Lord, Lord, shall enter into the kingdom of heaven; but he that doeth the will of my Father
which is in heaven."[1] It is not leaf, nor blossom, but
fruit, which Thou seekest from the fig-trees planted in
Thy vineyard.

Tuesday.—(From Bishop Trower's "Practical Exposi-
tions of the Gospels"). V. 16. "A certain man made a
great supper." "The Gospel blessings are represented
under the image of a feast. . . . The image conveys to
our minds the notion of provision made not only for the
supply of our spiritual necessities, but for the gratification
of every faculty with which our souls are endowed. As
in a feast the entertainer is not satisfied to provide a
sufficiency of the plainest food, but aims at gratifying
every sense, and furnishes the banquet with music and
perfumes, and objects to please the eye, as well as with
sumptuous fare; so in the New Covenant, provision is
made not only for saving us from misery, but for delight-
ing the soul with every exalted pleasure which it is
capable of tasting. . . . The communication of knowledge; the experience of all that Divine tenderness can
do to soothe and gladden us; the active exercise of all
our faculties in the noblest objects, without toil or weari-
ness; all these, and far more than these, are 'ready' at
that table to which God has been inviting sinners by His
ministers from age to age, and to which He now inviteth
them."

Wednesday.—V. 17. "And sent his servant at supper
time to say to them that were bidden, Come; for all

---

[1] St. Matt. vii. 21.

things are now ready." All things had not been ready
hitherto. But when "God sent forth his Son" into the
world, "made of a woman, made under the law,"[1] and
that Son, taking upon Him " the form of a servant,"[2] began
to call men into the kingdom of God, then "the fulness
of the time was come." God had trained men by the
Dispensation of the Law for the appreciation of the blessings of Redemption, and had led them by the Prophets
to look forward in faith and hope to the manifestation of
the Redeemer. And this manifestation was made at a
period of universal peace, and when the whole civilised
world was under one empire, so that the tidings might
spread rapidly. Let me learn that God does nothing,
whether in the history of mankind, or in that of the individual, prematurely. He will not place me on a higher
stage of spiritual life, until I have really mastered the
lower stages of it. All who enter God's school must
begin with the rudiments. There is no royal road to the
higher degrees of illumination and perfection, which are
conferred on patient and laborious students.

Thursday.—Vv. 18, 19, 20. The guests first invited
seem to have been easy and well-to-do persons. They
excuse themselves from attendance,—the first by alleging
the necessity of surveying some newly bought property ;
the second by representing his anxiety as to whether a
purchase of cattle he had made would turn out well; the
third by stating, rather more bluntly, that his having been
recently married made it out of the question for him to
attend. These guests represent those who, from being
absorbed in the cares, or in the riches and pleasures of
this life[3] (according to our Lord's words in explaining the
Parable of the Sower), find no leisure for the concerns of

---

[1] See Gal. iv. 4.   [2] See Phil. ii. 7.   [3] See St. Luke viii. 14.

the soul. Then the invitation, being rejected by these well-to-do folks (who represent the leaders of the Jewish nation), travels on to the poor people in the streets, to the maimed, and the halt, and the blind (who represent the publicans and sinners), and thence is extended beyond the city to the people "in the highways and hedges,"[1] (who represent in the first instance the Gentiles). But there is certainly this secondary application underlying the primary, that when God's offers of grace are rejected by us in prosperity, He makes them to us again more urgently, when we are in trouble; when our circumstances and His discipline have conspired to humble us in our own eyes, and to make us know that we are indeed " wretched, and miserable, and poor, and blind, and naked," then, Lord, and not till then, are we disposed to buy of Thee "gold tried in the fire" (the gold of precious faith), that we may be rich ; "and white raiment" (the raiment of Thy imputed righteousness), "that we may be clothed ;" and to "anoint our eyes with eyesalve" (the eyesalve of spiritual illumination) "that we may see."[2]

Friday.—In the first instance the invitation is a simple bidding by the mouth of a servant; "Say to them, . . . Come" (V. 17). There is more urgency in bidding the people in the streets and lanes; "Go out quickly . . . and bring in hither the poor" (V. 21). There is still more urgency in the conveyance of the invitation to the people in the highways and hedges ; "Go out . . . and *compel them* to come in" (V. 23). In proportion to the lateness of the call is its importunity and urgency, until at length a holy constraint is put upon the invited to fill up the vacant room.—How near am I to my end, O Lord ? "How long have I to live ?"[3] as old Barzillai

---

[1] *Vv.* 21, 23.   [2] See Rev. iii. 17, 18.   [3] See 2 Sam. xix. 34.

asked.   If Thou hast dealt with me in grace for very many years, and hast shown wonderful patience in adjusting Thy discipline to my character, is it not now at length a very urgent matter that I should obey the call to Thy heavenly kingdom with all earnestness and with my whole heart, giving all the little that I have to give—my heart, my affections, my will—for all that Thou, the great and glorious God hast to give, "wisdom, and righteousness, and sanctification, and redemption"[1]?   At all events let me reflect that the later my call is, the more urgent is my obligation to comply with it, the less is the time I have to spare, the fewer my opportunities to come. "Behold, now is the accepted time; behold, now is the day of salvation."[2]

Saturday.—V. 23. "Compel them to come in, that my house may be filled." "Grace, like nature," says Bengel very beautifully, "abhors a *vacuum.*" God will not have any vacant spaces left at His table. There is room for all, if all would come; for He "will have all men to be saved."[3] And let us be sure that whether we accept it or not, His word of invitation shall not, and does not, "return unto Him void."[4] The kingdom of heaven is being silently filled in a manner unknown to us. His grace is compelling men at present to come in, even in the highways and hedges, the nooks and corners of the world.[5] The acceptances of the invitation *which we can see* furnish no test at all of the extent of its acceptance. When Elias complained that he was the only servant of God left, there was a reserve of seven thousand

---

[1] See 1 Cor. i. 30.   [2] 2 Cor. vi. 2.   [3] See 1 Tim. ii. 4.

[4] See Isaiah lv. 11.

[5] This thought is drawn from the late Rev. Isaac Williams' "Sermons on the Epistles and Gospels," though the phraseology has been slightly altered.

men in Israel, who had not bowed the knee to the image of Baal.[1]   And at the end of all things, we are led to believe that there will be an auspicious cast of the net into the waters of the world, which shall fetch in the last great shoal, and a unity which has never been seen before,—the draught and the unity being symbolized by the second miraculous draught of fishes, in which the net was drawn to land "full of great fishes, an hundred and fifty and three : and for all there were so many, yet was not the net broken."[2]   For it is thus that the promise to Thee, O Saviour of men, must be fulfilled; "He shall see of the travail of his soul, and shall be satisfied."[3]

[1] See 1 Kings xix. 18, and Rom. xi. 4.   [2] St. John xxi. 11.
[3] Isaiah liii. 11.

Chapter XXXVII

THE GOSPEL FOR THE THIRD SUNDAY AFTER TRINITY.

St. Luke xv. 1 *to* 11.

1 Then drew near unto him all the publicans and sinners for to
2 hear him. And the Pharisees and Scribes murmured, saying,
3 This man receiveth sinners, and eateth with them. And he spake
4 this parable unto them, saying, What man of you having an hundred sheep, if he lose one of them, doth not leave the ninety and
nine in the wilderness, and go after that which is lost, until he find
5 it? And when he hath found it, he laieth it on his shoulders,
6 rejoycing. And when he cometh home, he calleth together his
friends and neighbours saying unto them, Rejoyce with me, for I
7 have found my sheep which was lost. I say unto you, that likewise joy shall be in heaven over one sinner that repenteth, more than
8 over ninety and nine just persons, which need no repentance. Either
what woman, having ten pieces of silver, if she lose one piece, doth
not light a candle, and sweep the house, and seek diligently till she
9 find it? And when she hath found it, she calleth her friends and
her neighbours together, saying, Rejoyce with me, for I have found
10 the piece which I had lost. Likewise I say unto you, There is joy
in the presence of the angels of God, over one sinner that repenteth.

[Miss Sar.	1549.	1662 s.b.
In illo tempore, Erant appropinquantes *ad Jesum* publicani et peccatores, ut audirent illum. (*Vulg.* Erant autem appropinquantes ei publicani et peccatores, ut audirent illum.)	Then resorted unto him all the publicanes and sinners, for to hear him.	Then drew near unto him all the publicans and sinners for to hear him. (Gr. ἦσαν δὲ ἐγγίζοντες αὐτῷ πάντες οἱ τελῶναι καὶ οἱ ἁμαρτωλοί, ἀκούειν αὐτοῦ.)

Is there any connexion of thought (lurking possibly in the δέ) between this Chapter and the discourse in the preceding ! We find in Chap. xiv. 25 that our Lord's ministry was a popular and attractive one ;—" there went great multitudes with him." Hereupon He took occasion to exhort them to count the cost (*vv.* 28-34). The terms of discipleship were very strict, would often involve a renunciation of natural ties and even of life (*v.* 26), and always a bearing of the cross (*v.* 27). He would have no half-hearted or lukewarm adherents ; there must be in His disciples the spiritual pungency of self-sacrifice and readiness to forsake all for the Master's sake (*vv.* 34, 35); and those, in whom this pungency was not found, He would "spue out of his mouth" (Rev. iii. 16), or, as the image here is, men would cast them out as savourless salt, " neither fit for the land, nor yet for the dunghill."—After reading this, we naturally ask whether the strictness of these terms alienated any of the hearers, made them " go back and walk no more with him" (as St. John vi. 66). Chap. xv. supplies the answer. However Christ might insist upon whole-heartedness in His service, and upon self-sacrifice in His servants, His words rather won than scared. It is as if the sacred writer had said, " Think not such words drove sinners away from Him ; on the contrary they gathered round Him more than ever, —' Now there were drawing near to Him all the publicans and sinners for to hear him.' "—*Translation of* 1540. (1) *V.* 1. " Then *resorted unto him* all the publicanes and sinners." Both Tyndale and the Genevan have *resorted unto him,* missing the force of the tense in ἦσαν ἐγγίζοντες, and the exact meaning of ἐγγίζω. Wycliffe, translating from a Translation, has hit both ; " And pupplicans and synful men *weren nygynge to hym.*" (2) *V.* 6. " He calleth together his *lovers* and neighbours." Cranmer adopted "lovers" from Tyndale. At that period of our language the word "lover" did not denote exclusively (as it now does) one of an opposite sex. Thus we read (1 Kings v. 1) that " Hiram was ever a *lover* of David," and Ps. xxxviii. 11, " My *lovers* and my friends stand aloof from my sore." And so in Shakspere (*Henry VIII.,* Act. IV. Scene i. line 104), " He of Winchester is held no great good *lover* of the archbishop's " ; Brutus to the Romans, " Friends, countrymen, and *lovers !* hear me for my cause" (*Julius Cæsar,* Act III. Scene ii.); and Brutus of Cæsar, " As I slew my best *lover* for the good of Rome, I have the same dagger for myself, when it shall please my country to need my death " (*Ibid.*) (3) *V.* 8. " Either what woman having ten *groats* (if she lose one)." Tyndale and the Rhemish, as well as Cranmer, give us *groats ;* and it is to be regretted that this good old word should nearly have gone out. " Pieces of silver " is the rendering of δραχμὰς in the Genevan, and was adopted by King James's Translators. Wycliffe has *besauntis ;*—" What womman hauynge x *besauntis,* and if sche hath lost oo *besaunte*," etc. The word "*groat*" (if the etymology usually given of it is correct) furnishes one of the many curious instances of a word's coming round to have a meaning the very opposite of that which it had originally. It is said to be fundamentally the same word as "great," and to have been so called because, before Edward III. coined groats (or silver fourpenny bits), the largest silver piece in existence was the *penny*, in comparison of which the groat (being four times as much) was great. What the parable demands as the representative of δραχμή is a piece of money *which to a person in humble life should be something considerable*. "Groat" therefore would answer the purpose very well, so long as any notion of a coin of some value attached to it. But in the days of the Authorised Version (which were also our Shakspere's days), a "groat" had come round to mean a coin of *little* value. Thus Coriolanus says that his mother called the plebeians "things created to buy and sell with *groats*" (*Coriolanus*, Act. III. Scene ii. lines 9, 10) ; and Gloster in 2 *Henry VI.*, Act. III. Scene i., swears,

> "So help me God, as I have watch'd the night,—
> Ay, night by night,—in studying good for England,
> The doit that e'er I wrested from the king,
> Or any *groat* I hoarded to my use,
> Be brought against me at my trial-day !
> No ; many a *pound* of my own proper store,
> Because I would not tax the needy commons,
> Have I disbursed to the garrisons,
> And never ask'd for restitution."

King James's Translators, therefore, did well to discard the "grote" of Tyndale, and substitute "piece of silver."—Wycliffe's "besant" (spelt also *bizant, byzant*) was a gold piece. Johnson (under BIZANTINE) quotes Camden ; "A great piece of gold valued at fifteen pound, which the king offereth upon high festival days ; it is yet called "a bizantine" (Camden lived A.D. 1557-1623), "which anciently was a piece of gold coined by the emperours of Constantinople." If the ordinary bizant was in value at all approaching to the king's presentation-bizant (which query ?) the woman in the parable would (for a humble person) have had a little fortune in her "x. besauntis." What made Wycliffe render the *drachma* of the Vulgate by "besaunte"? Was he acquainted with an hexameter of Joannes de Garlandiâ, which Du Cange cites (*s.v. Byzantius*) ;

> "Dragma Bisantius est, vel Aureus, atque Talentum,"

which asserts definitively that a Bizant, an Aureus, and a Talent, are synonymous with a Drachma ? He *might have been*. John of Garland was an English Grammariau and Poet about the year 1040, who, amongst other grammatical and poetical works, wrote a work on Synonyms (*Opus Synonymorum*) in 707 hexameters, which therefore may be called both a grammatical and poetical work. The above line is from that work. His name and a list of his writings will be found in Fabricius's "Bibliotheca Latina" under *Garlandius.*]

Sunday.—In the sixteenth Chapter of this Gospel, which may be said to form one discourse, interrupted only by the sneers of the Pharisees,[1] with this fifteenth Chapter, our Lord, before whose eyes "hell and destruction"[2] are open, draws aside for a moment the curtain which conceals from us the infernal world, and shows us the rich man "in torments."[3] Here, in the previous Chapter, "He that came down from heaven"[4] draws aside the veil which screens its mysteries, and shows us the heart of the Three Persons of the Blessed Trinity yearning over man in his sinfulness and misery, and the holy angels rejoicing, and striking their golden harps in the praise of redeeming love, as sinners are brought back one by one to God's fold. And in these glimpses of hell and of heaven, we catch sight of one common feature. Both in hell and in heaven interest is felt and expressed for sinners upon earth. The rich man in torments is mindful of his brethren—desirous of their deliverance from the misery in which he finds himself.[5] And in heaven, God, and Christ, and the Holy Ghost, are mindful of sinners, and earnestly desirous of bringing them to glory ; and holy angels manifest a lively interest when they are so brought.—Lord, make me ever to remember that there is an unseen world, in which I am

[1] At Chap. xvi. 14.

[2] See Prov. xv. 11, "Hell and destruction are before the Lord : how much more then the hearts of the children of men !"

[3] St. Luke xvi. 23, 24, 28.   [4] See St. John iii. 13.

[5] St. Luke xvi. 27, 28.

an object of interest——that I am thought of, watched, consulted about, in the council-chambers both of heaven and hell,——that both good angels and bad busy themselves with my eternal destiny.

Monday.——The doctrine of the Holy Trinity is interwoven into many parts of Holy Scripture, where it is not explicitly stated.   The three glorious parables in the fifteenth Chapter of St. Luke, represent to us the sympathy for sinners felt by each of the Sacred Persons——by the Son of God, who came to this world in quest of them; by the Spirit of God, who is ever moving in the Church (or house of God) to recover lost souls; and by the Father lastly, who sees the prodigal son afar off, and runs to meet and greet him.   This Parable of the Lost Sheep represents the work of the Son in seeking and saving the human race. For this purpose He left the ninety and nine sheep——the various orders of angels——in the green pastures of the heavenly fold, and by the Incarnation and Nativity came into this world, and went among the haunts of sinners, and touched their hearts with penitence by His invitations of grace, and, having recovered hundreds of the lost, went back to His home in heaven rejoicing, and announced there the sacrifice which He had made for sinners, and the way which He had opened for every sinner to return to God.   Hence in this first parable, the joy among the angels is spoken of as something future, because the Good Shepherd had not yet returned home, Christ had not yet ascended into heaven, to announce the recovery of fallen man; and so the words are anticipative of what was not at present, but was to be, " I say unto you, that likewise joy *shall be* in heaven over one sinner that repenteth "—— shall be, when I come hither with the sheep upon my shoulder.——O Lord, how wast Thou upheld, in Thy endurance of pain and shame for our sakes, by " the joy that was set before " [1] Thee !

Tuesday.—V. 4. [From the late Rev. Isaac Williams' " Sermons on the Epistles and Gospels," Vol. II. pp. 49, 50]. " *What man of you having an hundred sheep, if he lose one of them, doth not leave the ninety and nine,*" etc.   " As the cry of her own helpless infant is distinguished by a mother amidst a hundred other sounds, as the plaintive call of a lost sheep is heard by the shepherd above the bleatings of the flock, so in the ears of God is the prayer of the distressed penitent. . . . Partaking of this character has, doubtless, often been the prayer of the greatest among saints, the more exalted of God, and enriched by His grace, as they humbled themselves and bewailed their ignorance of Him.   Such was the lament of St. Peter when, as it is said, at the sound of the cock crowing he ever wept[2] ; such that of St. Paul, when he ceased not to bewail himself as one that had been a ' persecutor and injurious '[3] ; such the voice of Mary Magdalene, when earliest and latest she watched at the grave of Him she had lost[4] ; such the feeling of the beloved disciple, when ' he fell at ' his Lord's ' feet as dead.'[5] . . . This penitent cry, of all things upon earth reaches the nearest to God's throne, has the readiest access to the ear of the King of Kings."

Wednesday.— V. 6. " When he cometh home, he calleth together his friends and neighbours, saying unto them, Rejoice with me ; for I have found my sheep which was lost."   Lovely words indeed !   I observe in them, first, that the holy angels, who had been represented just before as ninety-nine sheep left in the wilderness, are here

---

[1] See Heb. xii. 2.   [2] See St. Matt. xxvi. 75.   [3] See 1 Tim. i. 13.
[4] See St. John xx. 11.   [5] See Rev. i. 17.

called Christ's " friends and neighbours," and summoned
in that capacity to rejoice with Him.   They " are called
sheep," says Theophylact, " because every created nature is
as a brute beast, compared with God, but inasmuch as they
are rational, they are akin to God, and therefore are
called also friends and neighbours."[1]   Secondly; What an
exquisite trait is this seeking on the part of the Shepherd
for others to share His joy with.   His joy is so great that
it cannot contain itself, but seeks for utterance and
sympathy.   Thirdly; What a beautiful trait it is, that the
Shepherd does not say, " Rejoice with this sheep; con-
gratulate this poor sinner on his recovery to God's fold,"
but " Rejoice *with me*; for I have found my sheep."   " He
speaks thus," says Gregory the Great, " because our life is
His joy, and, when we are brought home to heaven, we
fill up the festivity of His joy."[2]   And yet, Lord, it
maketh Thee no richer to have the sinner's service and
praise.   Only Thou dost love him so tenderly, that what
is his gain Thou accountest to be Thine.

Thursday.—The Parable of the Lost Coin represents
the action of the Spirit of God in the Church in quest of
lost souls.   The woman, who, having lost one out of ten
coins, lights the candle and sweeps the house, and seeks
diligently till she finds it, is the Church of Christ,
animated, however, and actuated by His Spirit.   It
should be observed that in the East, coins, when strung
together, are employed by women as a head-dress, and it
is doubtless this employment of them, and not their use

---

[1] Theophylact, quoted in the " Catena Aurea " of Aquinas.

[2] " Et notandum, quòd non dicit, Congratulamini inventæ ovi, sed
mihi : quia videlicet ejus gaudium est vita nostra ; et cùm nos ad cœlum
reducimur, solemnitatem lætitiæ ejus implemus." [In Evangelia Homiliæ
Lib. ii. Hom. xxxiv. *Opp.* Ed. Bened. Parisiis, MDCCV. Tom. i. Col.
1602. B.]

as money, which is here adverted to. A coin employed as an ornament, this is the image under which the parable presents the human soul. As a coin bears the image and superscription of the sovereign in whose realm it circulates,[1] so the soul was made originally in the image of God, as it is said, " Let us make man in our image, after our likeness."[2] But the image of God has been well-nigh effaced by the fall, and the superscription, which is "Holiness to the Lord,"[3] has been altogether obliterated. And the coin, until God seeks and finds it, lies in darkness and defilement, the dust of the world having gathered over it and dimmed its brightness. But when reached by the Holy Spirit, and renewed, and purified, the image of God shines out in it again, and it is made meet to be a gem in the diadem of its Redeemer, as it is said, " Thou shalt be a crown of glory in the hand of the Lord, and a royal diadem in the hand of thy God."[4]—O Lord, renew me by Thy grace after the image of Him who created me.[5]

Friday.—Let me observe the fact that the coin was lost *in the house*—within, not outside. The house represents the Church of God, as it is said, " that thou mayest know how thou oughtest to behave thyself in the house of God, which is the church of the living God."[6] Hundreds and thousands of souls in the Church, the great theatre of the ministrations of grace, are lost souls—as completely lost, as thoroughly enveloped in the darkness and defilement of sin, as if they were heathen souls. The enemy has sown tares in God's harvest field,[7] and no watchfulness or precautions can exclude the tares. Ananias and Sapphira, and Simon Magus, crept into the

---

[1] See St. Matt. xxii. 20, 21.　　[2] Gen. i. 26.
[3] See Exod. xxviii. 36 ; xxxix. 30.　[4] Isaiah lxii. 3.　[5] See Col. iii. 10.
　　[6] 1 Tim. iii. 15.　　[7] See St. Matt. xiii. 25, 26, 38, 39.

Church while it was yet under the eye and government of Apostles.[1]   And as soon as the Church had outgrown her childhood, and Infant Baptism had become her rule, of course the number of false professors of Christianity was multiplied, and the house of God became full of lost coins scattered about in the dark corners thereof.—Let me never suppose, O Lord, that because I have been baptized, and admitted outwardly to all the privileges of the Christian Covenant, I need not the converting, renewing, sanctifying influences of Thy grace.   I may be still in the dust of earthliness, in the darkness of spiritual ignorance, in the defilement of sinful habits.   The image of God may yet have to be minted afresh in my heart, and the superscription of " Holiness unto the Lord," to be legibly traced there.   Let me examine into the condition of my soul by the application of this test, " Whose image and superscription hath it ?"[2]

Saturday.—Let me consider to-day the process and the issue of the recovery of the coin. *The process first.* The candle was lighted, the house swept, and diligent search made.   The candle is externally the preached word of God, which is the Holy Spirit's great instrument in seeking and saving souls, and which was emblematized by the seven-branched candlestick in the holy place of the Jewish temple.[3]   " Thy word is a lamp unto my feet, and a light unto my path."[4]   Internally, the light is the conscience, which is called by the wise man the candle of the Lord, and said by him to be used for the purpose of self-examination ; " The spirit of man is the candle of the Lord, searching all the inward parts of the belly."[5]   The

---

[1] See Acts v. 1-12, and viii. 9, 13, 19, 20.
[2] See St. Luke xx. 24.   [3] See Exod. xxv. 31, *et seq.*
[4] Ps. cxix. 105.   [5] Prov. xx. 27.

sweeping and dislodgment of furniture, in order to the search, represents the disturbance which takes place in the conscience, when it is first visited by convictions of sin, and also those Providential disturbances of our lot, by bereavement, poverty, sickness, and so forth, which God finds necessary oftentimes, to prevent our settling down upon the lees of a carnal indifference; " I will search Jerusalem with *candles*, and punish the men that are settled on their lees."[1]—The *issue* of the sinner's recovery is, as in the previous parable, " joy in heaven." But here the joy is spoken of in the present tense, " there *is* joy in the presence of the angels of God," because what is spoken of here is the search which is made for lost souls by the Holy Spirit in the Church, and not the return of Christ to heaven with the souls which He had won upon earth. The angels have always been held to be present in Christian assemblies, on the ground of St. Paul's words as to the reason for the women covering their heads in the congregation ("For this cause ought the woman to have power on her head, *because of the angels* "[2]); and we recognise their presence, and join ourselves to them in accents of praise, when we say, " Therefore with Angels and Archangels, and with all the company of heaven, we laud and magnify thy glorious Name."[3] A holy joy thrills through the hosts of angels, and pervades the whole Church of God, when by the ministry of God's word any fresh soul is reached, and renewed after the image of God, and brought out of darkness and defilement to purity of heart and conscience, and into the light of God's favour.

[1] Zeph. i. 12. [2] 1 Cor. xi. 10.
[3] General Preface in the Communion Service.

Chapter XXXVIII

THE GOSPEL FOR THE FOURTH SUNDAY AFTER TRINITY.

St. Luke vi. 36 *to* 43.

36   Be ye therefore merciful, as your Father also is merciful.
37 Judge not, and ye shall not be judged: condemn not, and ye shall
38 not be condemned: forgive, and ye shall be forgiven: give, and it
   shall be given unto you: good measure, pressed down, and shaken
   together, and running over shall men give into your bosom. For
   with the same measure that ye mete withall, it shall be measured
39 to you again. And he spake a parable unto them, Can the blind
40 lead the blind? shall they not both fall into the ditch? The
   disciple is not above his master; but every one that is perfect shall
41 be as his master. And why beholdest thou the mote that is in thy
   brothers eye, but perceivest not the beam that is in thine own eye?
42 Either how canst thou say to thy brother, Brother, let me pull out
   the mote that is in thine eye, when thou thy self beholdest not the
   beam that is in thine own eye? Thou hypocrite, cast out first the
   beam out of thine own eye, and then shalt thou see clearly to pull
   out the mote that is in thy brothers eye.

[Miss. Sar.	1549.	1662 s.b.
In illo tempore, Dixit Jesus discipulis suis; Estote misericordes, sicut et Pater vester misericors est. (*Vulg.* Estote ergo misericordes, sicut, etc.)	Be ye mercifull, as your Father also is mer-cifull.	Be ye therefore merci-ful, as your Father also is merciful. (*Gr.* Γίνεσθε οὖν οἰκτίρμονες, καθὼς καὶ ὁ πατὴρ ὑμῶν οἰκτίρ-μων ἐστί.)

The Revisers of 1881 have dropped the "therefore," the οὖν not being found in the Sinaitic or Vatican manuscripts, nor in the Codex Bezæ, though it appears in the Alexandrine. I do not know whether for this exploit of criticism they have fallen under the lash so vigorously wielded by a certain Reviewer in "The Quarterly." But at all events,—manuscripts apart,—the discourse seems rather to require the "therefore" as a link of sequence with the foregoing. In *v.* 35 our Lord has been exhorting to a disinterested liberality, which looks for no recompence from man, but the recompence to which shall be sonship to the most High,—the consciousness of a moral resemblance (such as indicates the filial relation) to Him who "is kind unto the unthankful, and to the evil." Is not "therefore" rather desiderated in passing to the injunction, "Be ye merciful, as your Father also is merciful"? All six English Versions, previous to that of 1881, exhibit the "Therefore."—As to the essential difference between the Sermon on the Mount, and the discourse in St. Luke vi. 20 to the end, which has so many similar passages, see Rev. William Pound's "Story of the Gospels," Vol. II. pp. 156, 157 [Rivingtons: 1869]. "The Sermon on the Mount belongs (where it has been placed by the Evangelist) to *the second section of the fourfold system,* the period of miracles, *during which the aspect of the kingdom was blessing only.* The people had not yet held the grace of the kingdom in such contempt or opposition as to cause the recoil of a curse upon their own heads. A cause of curse had not yet arisen ; but the Sermon on the Plain, recorded by St. Luke, and which followed the use of the parables *in the third section,* contains both blessing and curse,"—"Woe unto you " (*vv.* 24, 25, 26), as well as "Blessed are ye."—*Translation of* 1540. (1) *V.* 38. "Good measure, and pressed down . . . shall men give into your *bosoms.*" Again the plural (as so often before), where the original has the singular, the translator probably not seeing how a singular noun could be properly joined with the possessive genitive of a plural pronoun (εἰς τὸν κόλπον ὑμῶν). But in this way is recognised the oneness of believers in Christ, the fact that the Church is "one body " (Eph. iv. 4). Tyndale, Cranmer, and the Genevan have all "bosoms." Not so Wycliffe, —"thei schuln yeve into *youre bosum* a good mesure." And the Rhemish, and afterwards the Authorised, recurred to Wycliffe's singular. (2) *V.* 39. "And he *put forth a similitude* unto them " (Εἶπε δὲ παραβολὴν αὐτοῖς). "Put forth " would be rather παρέθηκεν (as St. Matt. xiii. 24, 31).—Probably it is well to have another word to represent παραβολή, when it is used (as here) loosely for what is not a regular parable, but merely a figurative diction. Wycliffe has, "he seide to hem a *liknes.*" Tyndale, Genevan, and Rhemish, as well as Cranmer, have all *similitude.* King James's Translators were the first to give "parable." (3) *V.* 40. "The disciple is not above his Master. Every man shall be perfect, even as his Master is " (the conjunction *but* left out). This is adopted from Tyndale.

The Authorised Version, when the force of the perfect participle is exhibited, is much better, "Every one, *when he is perfectly instructed*, shall be as his Master" (see the Thought for *Friday*). (4) *V.* 42. "then shalt thou see *perfectly*, to pull out the mote," etc. And so Tyndale and the Genevan. But "clearly" is not only more musical, but a better word than "perfectly," when applied to vision. Thus we have in Milton,— ("Paradise Lost," Book ix. line 705) ;

> "He knows that in the day
> Ye eat thereof, your eyes that seem so *clear*,
> Yet are but dim, shall perfectly be then
> Opened and *clear'd*, and ye shall be as gods,
> Knowing both good and evil, as they know."

The compound verb διαβλέπω (perspicio, *Vulg.*) could not be rendered better than by "see clearly," indicating, as it does, sight passing through something diaphanous, which offers it no obstruction.]

Sunday.—V. 36. "Be ye therefore merciful, as your Father also is merciful." The Gospel of last Sunday exhibited to us our Father's mercifulness,—showed us how the Heavenly Shepherd seeks the lost sheep, and exults over it when He has found and brought it back home, how the Holy Spirit in the Church is ever seeking for lost coins with the light of the Word, and restoring them to God's treasury.[1] The succeeding Gospel opens very appropriately with the lesson that God's mind of compassion towards those who offend is to be our mind also; "Be ye therefore merciful, as your Father also is merciful." If we really believe in God's forgiving and restoring love to ourselves, we cannot but be merciful in our estimate of, and dealing with, others. For by one and the same valve, the heart opens towards God, to receive His mercy for ourselves, and towards our brethren, to distribute mercy to others. And yet so feeble and infirm is the will of man, that the inculcation of motives is not found to be sufficient by itself, without the distinct and independent in-

---

[1] See St. Luke xv. 3-11.

culcation of duties; and therefore we are not only assured of God's mercy to ourselves, but bidden also to extend mercy to others; " Be ye merciful, as your Father also is merciful." And lest we should be discouraged by the arduousness of such a requirement, it may be observed that the word for " be " in the original is a different verb from that for " is," and means rather " Become"; " Become ye what your Father is, merciful." It is a work to be done by degrees, as we grow in grace, and in the knowledge of God and Christ. Young Christians are often harsh, hot, and vehement, like Jonah, when it grieved him that the Ninevites were not destroyed[1]; but as God's work goes on in their hearts, the bloom of the spiritual character, which is love, forms upon them.

Monday.—V. 36. " Be ye merciful, as your Father also is merciful." I will take occasion from these words to reflect on the influence which our conceptions of the character of the God whom we worship must exercise upon our own character. " All people will walk every one in the name of his god," says the prophet Micah, " and we will walk in the name of the LORD our God for ever and ever."[2] The name of God stands in Scripture for the revealed character of God; and the prophet's assertion therefore is that even heathen nations naturally and instinctively mould themselves upon the character, which they attribute to their false gods; and that God's people should mould themselves upon His revealed character. The gods of the heathen were many of them bloody, ferocious, and inexorable, and many of them also licentious and impure. And we find their votaries " walking in their name," striving to propitiate these gods by cruel and lascivious rites, and themselves becoming cruel and

[1] See Jonah iv. 1, 4, 9, 11.　　　　[2] Micah iv. 5.

lascivious in consequence. But let the character of the true God, whose most fundamental attribute is love, and whose "mercy endureth for ever,"[1] be once imbibed by the mind, and mercifulness cannot fail to flow forth into the character of the worshipper, and to tincture all his thoughts, sentiments, and dealings.

Tuesday.—V. 37. "Judge not, and ye shall not be judged: condemn not, and ye shall not be condemned: forgive" (or rather "acquit," "absolve,") "and ye shall be forgiven." Mercy having been prescribed generally in the foregoing words, we have in what follows the attitude of mercy, first towards sin and injury, and next towards want and need. As regards the sin, which everywhere meets our eye, we are not to judge it. Observe that this does not mean that we are to be blind to the faults and failings of those around us. We cannot help seeing or taking notice of such faults, especially when they are prominent, and lie, as many people's faults do, upon the surface. What is forbidden is judgment and condemnation; and these presuppose a controversy, an argument for and against, a trial, a summing up, and ultimately a verdict and a sentence. We have not the materials for such a summing up, for such a verdict and sentence. Very much is hidden from us in the character and conduct of our neighbour, which might make judgment go altogether in his favour, if it were known. Therefore it is an awful presumption to form, even in our minds, a definite judgment of our neighbour's character; it is to thrust ourselves into the place of Him who "shall judge the secrets of men,"[2] and to arrogate His office. And where we can find the slightest extenuating circumstances for a fault or bad action, we are bound to allow full weight to

---

[1] See 1 John iv. 8, 16, and Ps. cxxxvi. passim.   [2] See Rom. ii. 16.

them, and provisionally—pending the great trial of the last day—to hold our brother in our thoughts as acquitted, even where appearances are against him.

Wednesday.—V. 38. Towards want and need, this is to be our rule; "Give, and it shall be given unto you; good measure, pressed down, and shaken together, and running over, shall men " (literally, shall they, meaning the angels, or any one who acts as God's agent in the matter of recompence) "give into your bosom." Where I observe that, although our Saviour forbids us, in our acts of Christian liberality, to look for praise or for more substantial recompence from men,[1] He on the other hand encourages us to look for recompence from God, and to do the act with a view to that recompence. Both the Old Testament and New declare that God returns with large interest what is lent to Him; " He that hath pity upon the poor lendeth unto the Lord: and look, what he layeth out, it shall be paid him again."[2] Simon Peter lent the Lord his boat for the purpose of a pulpit; and his net, by way of repayment, enclosed such a multitude of fishes that it brake.[3] And here we have God repaying those, who give only with their hands, "*into their bosom*,"—giving, that is, lapfuls for handfuls. "There is no such thing as real generosity," says Quesnel, "in any one except God, because He is the only person who does not profit by His own gifts, and because He engages even to pay the debts of His creature with an overflowing interest. Since He promises us such payment, it is the part of piety to hope for it and expect it."

Thursday.—Vv. 39, 40. "And he spake a parable

[1] See St. Matt. vi. 1, 2, and St. Luke xiv. 12, 13, 14.
[2] Prov. xix. 17, as cited in the Offertory Sentences of the Communion Service.   [3] See St. Luke v. 3, 6.

unto them, Can the blind lead the blind? shall they not both fall into the ditch? The disciple is not above his master; but every one that is perfect shall be as his master." In these and the following words our Lord censures the Pharisees and doctors of the law among the Jews, who were confident that they themselves were guides of the blind, lights of them which were in darkness, instructors of the foolish, teachers of babes.[1] He virtually says to these blind guides; "Thou art inexcusable, O man, whosoever thou art that judgest: for wherein thou judgest another, thou condemnest thyself; for thou that judgest doest the same things."[2] And in the words which follow, "How canst thou say to thy brother, Brother, let me pull out the mote that is in thine eye, and thou thyself beholdest not the beam that is in thine own eye?" He strikes the key-note of that passage to the Romans; "Thou therefore which teachest another, teachest thou not thyself? thou that preachest a man should not steal, dost thou steal? . . . thou that makest thy boast of the law, through breaking the law dishonourest thou God? For the name of God is blasphemed among the Gentiles through you, as it is written."[3] Here was the beam in the Pharisees' own eye. The conduct of many of them was so abominably immoral, that it redounded to the discredit among the heathen of the God whom they professed to worship, and the law which they professed to teach. Indeed the whole of the second Chapter of the Epistle to the Romans is but an echo of the words of Christ in this Gospel, and should be read together with them.—O Lord, how do the hidden harmonies of the different parts of Thy word reveal the oneness of the Spirit, by which the holy men of old were

---

[1] See Rom. ii. 19, 20.   [2] Rom. ii. 1.

[3] Rom. ii. 21, 23, 24.

moved to write !¹ Shallow students of Scripture have pretended to discover a difference of tone between St. Paul's Epistles and the Sermon on the Mount. Doubtless the province of the Apostles under the guidance of the Holy Ghost was to speak explicitly truths which, during our Lord's lifetime, had to be touched but briefly and enigmatically, the time not having yet arrived for a full disclosure of them ; but we may safely ask whether Rom. ii. is not a more enlarged paraphrase of part of the Sermon on the Mount.

Friday.—V. 40. "The disciple is not above his master : but every one that is perfectly instructed shall be " (this is the highest point to which he can hope to attain) "as his master." The general maxim in these words is that no pupil can rise in his attainments, whether they be intellectual, or moral and spiritual, above the level of his teacher. The man who is set above me, to raise me up, cannot lift me to a higher platform than he himself stands on. What a great responsibility is laid by this fact upon all who hold the office of teachers of moral and spiritual truth ! The measure of spiritual attainment in their disciples is in their own hand. They determine it, not so much by their lessons as by the way in which they exemplify them. And while thinking of the example set by teachers, I am further reminded of the perfect example of Christ, to which, by the discipline of God's Word and Spirit, every true disciple is making constant approximations. The imitation of Christ, as the one principle of all Christian virtue, was the grand idea of Thomas a Kempis, and how many a saintly life has been framed upon that grand idea ! " Walk *before me,* and be thou perfect,"² said God in the Old Testament. But the New

---

¹ See 2 Pet. i. 21.   ² See Gen. xvii. 1.

Testament has, in exhibiting Christ, revealed even a more golden rule of perfection; " He that *followeth* me shall not walk in darkness, but shall have the light of life"[1]; " Leaving us an *example*, that ye should follow his steps."[2]—Lord, may I daily endeavour myself to follow the blessed steps of thy most holy life![3]

Saturday.—V. 42. " Thou hypocrite, cast out first the beam out of thine own eye, and then shalt thou *see clearly* to pull out the mote that is in thy brother's eye." Spiritual discernment, for the treatment of the spiritual maladies of others, is not otherwise to be gained than by the correction of our own faults of character. That correction will make me not only a good, but a wise and a shrewd man,—spiritually wise and shrewd,—will show me the evasions and subterfuges of the human heart, and give me a knowledge of human character. And next to the knowledge of God, the knowledge of man is the most valuable of all pieces of knowledge. All Solomon's knowledge of natural history was of very little worth,[4] compared with that insight into the human heart, upon which his earliest judgment was founded, and which taught him that a mother's love is the strongest and most unselfish of all instincts.[5]

[1] St. John viii. 12.   [2] 1 Pet. ii. 21.
[3] Collect for Second Sunday after Easter.   [4] See 1 Kings iv. 33.
[5] See 1 Kings iii. 23 *to the end.*

CHAPTER XXXIX

THE GOSPEL FOR THE FIFTH SUNDAY AFTER TRINITY.

St. Luke v. 1 *to* 12
(omitting the " And," with which *v.* 1 commences).

1 It came to pass, that as the people pressed upon him to hear
2 the word of God, he stood by the lake of Genesareth ; and saw two
ships standing by the lake : but the fisher-men were gone out ot
3 them, and were washing their nets. And he entred into one of the
ships, which was Simons, and prayed him that he would thrust out
a little from the land : and he sat down and taught the people out
4 of the ship. Now when he had left speaking, he said unto Simon,
Launch out into the deep, and let down your nets for a draught.
5 And Simon answering, said unto him, Master, we have toiled all
the night, and have taken nothing ; nevertheless at thy word, I
6 will let down the net. And when they had this done, they enclosed
7 a great multitude of fishes, and their net brake. And they beckned
unto their partners which were in the other ship, that they should
come and help them. And they came and filled both their ships,
8 so that they began to sink. When Simon Peter saw it, he fell
down at Jesus knees, saying, Depart from me, for I am a sinful
9 man, O Lord. For he was astonished, and all that were with him
10 at the draught of the fishes which they had taken : and so was also
James, and John, the sons of Zebedee, who were partners with
Simon. And Jesus said unto Simon, Fear not, from henceforth
11 thou shalt catch men. And when they had brought their ships to
land, they forsook all, and followed him.

[Miss. Sar.	1549.	1662 s.b.
In illo tempore, Cum turbæ irruerent *ad Jesum*, ut audirent verbum Dei, et ipse stabat secus stagnum Genesareth. (*Vulg.* Factum est autem, cum turbæ irruerent in eum, ut audirent verbum Dei, et ipse, etc.)	It came to passe, that when the people preassed upon him to hear the word of God, he stood by the lake of Genezareth.	It came to pass, that as the people pressed upon him to hear the word of God, he stood by the lake of Genesareth. (*Gr.* Ἐγένετο δὲ ἐν τῷ τὸν ὄχλον ἐπικεῖσθαι αὐτῷ τοῦ ἀκούειν τὸν λόγον τοῦ Θεοῦ, etc.)

The connecting particle δὲ (rendered "And" in the Authorised Version, "Now" in the Revised Version, but ignored both by Tyndale and Cranmer) indicates that it was in the course of the circuit, which our Lord made in Galilee (which is noticed summarily in the last verse of Chap. iv.), that the incident occurred which forms the subject of this Gospel. In *v.* 43 of Chap. iv. He had told the multitudes who sought to detain Him at Capernaum (where He had now been resident and performing miracles for some time), that He was bound by the terms of His Mission to give to the glad tidings of the kingdom of God a wider circulation. This He did personally, travelling about the district and "preaching in the synagogues of Galilee" (*v.* 44). But his plans had yet to open out still further. His Apostles were to enlarge the sphere of His personal action, and evangelize the world. In the course of this tour it was that He called St. Peter, who was previously a disciple, to be a "fisher of men," and indicated symbolically his extraordinary success, and also the schisms which should attend the multiplication of disciples, by the first miraculous draught of fishes.— *Translation of* 1540. (1) *V.* 4. "*let slip* your nets to make a draught." (Gr. χαλάσατε, *Vulg.* laxate). And so Tyndale. Wycliffe equally well; "*Slack* your nets to take fish." At first one is disposed to regret that the Translators of 1611 did not adopt some word which keeps up the idea of "loosing," "untying," which there is in χαλάω; but they can appeal to other parts of the New Testament, where the word seems to have simply the notion of "lowering." Thus it is used of letting down the paralytic's bed through the roof into the chamber where our Lord was (Mark ii. 4); of letting St. Paul down in a basket from the wall of Damascus (Acts ix. 25; 2 Cor. xi. 33); and of lowering a boat from a ship into the sea (Acts xxvii. 30). In Acts xxvii. 17 also the meaning (which King James's Translators have quite missed) is "lowering"—χαλάσαντες τὸ σκεῦος οὕτως ἐφέροντο. "They lowered the" (heavy) "mainyard, and so were driven." Revised Version, "lowered *the gear.*" (2) *V.* 7. "and filled both the ships, so that they *sunk again.*" This Cranmer adopted from Tyndale.

Wycliffe, translating from the Vulgate, where we have "ita ut *pene* mergerentnr," gives a very vigorous rendering, "so that they were almost drenched." In the expression "they sunk *again*," the *again* expresses not repetition, but mere reaction—action consequent upon,—as when we speak of a shout's making the welkin ring *again*. So Falstaff, in recruiting his soldiers, "'Fore Heaven, a likely fellow!—Come, prick me Bullcalf till he roar *again*" (roar as the effect of being pricked). (2 *Henry IV.*, Act III. Scene ii).]

Sunday.—V. 2. "But the fishermen were gone out of them, and were washing their nets." What a humble, commonplace occupation! And yet it is dignified by a most illustrious manifestation of Divine power, and by a call to the highest of all offices, that of the Apostolate! This was no new thing in the history of the world. God's special calls to high office had often come to men, when engaged in the way of their business or trade. Moses was tending his father-in-law's sheep, when he saw the vision of the burning bush, and heard the voice that issued from it.[1] Similarly with David. "As he was following the ewes great with young ones," God "took him: that he might feed Jacob his people, and Israel his inheritance."[2] Gideon was threshing wheat by the winepress, when the Angel Jehovah saluted him, and inspiring him by his glance as well as by his speech, bade him "save Israel from the hand of the Midianites."[3] Elisha was "ploughing with twelve yoke of oxen before him, and he with the twelfth," when Elijah passed by, and by casting his mantle upon him, designated him as his successor.[4] The wise men were studying the midnight heavens, when the star of Bethlehem, the signal-lamp hung out in the heavens to announce the birth of the

[1] See Exod. iii. 1, 2, 4.　　　[2] Ps. lxxviii. 72, P.B.V.
[3] See Judges vi. 11, 12, 14.　　　[4] See 1 Kings xix. 19, 20.

Redeemer, dawned upon their view.[1] St. Matthew was sitting with his ledger before him at the receipt of custom, when the Lord passed by and called him to be an Apostle.[2] What a consecration has the commonplace work of the secular callings of men received from God! What pains has He taken to show that He approves simple, straightforward, honest-hearted diligence therein! A boy set in the fields to keep off the birds from the corn, and doing his work well and faithfully, is not out of the sphere of Divine manifestations. Miracles have ceased; but nature may make to that poor boy wonderful revelations of God's power, magnificence, and wisdom. When we consider that not a single scribe or teacher of the law—not a single divine of those days—was chosen to be an Apostle, while several fishermen and a tax-gatherer were chosen, how true do we see it to be that

> " We need not bid, for cloister'd cell,
>   Our neighbour and our work farewell,
>   Nor strive to wind ourselves too high
>   For sinful man beneath the sky :
>   The trivial round, the common task,
>   Would furnish all we ought to ask ;
>   Room to deny ourselves ; a road
>   To bring us, daily, nearer God."[3]

Monday. — V. 4. " Now when he had left speaking, he said unto Simon, Launch out into the deep, and let down your nets for a draught." Simon had lent his boat to the Lord, interrupting his work thereby. The work was an anxious, because an uncertain, and occasionally a very disappointing one. All the night, the season most favourable for a large haul of fish, he and his partners

---

[1] See St. Matt. ii. 1, 2.   [2] See St. Matt. ix. 9.
[3] "Christian Year," Morning.

had toiled and had taken nothing.[1]   And probably it was somewhat of a trial to be called off from work under these circumstances.   But Simon had already been made acquainted with our Lord by his brother Andrew, and had received from him a new name,[2] and had doubtless been impressed by His claims and His teaching.   It is to promote the spiritual interests of himself, and those around him, that he is asked to suffer his boat to be converted into a pulpit; and he willingly complies.   And now he is to experience the truth of the proverb of Solomon, that what a man lendeth to the Lord shall be paid him again,[3] and of that saying of the Divine Master's, " Seek ye first the kingdom of God, and his righteousness; and all these things " (what ye shall eat, and what ye shall drink, etc.) " shall be added unto you."[4]   So vast a shoal of fish is to be brought into his net, as might have sufficed for the subsistence of him and his partners for a long time to come.   The narrative is pregnant with instruction both for poor and rich.   If the poor will not excuse themselves from attendance upon God in prayer, public and private, and in the ordinances of His house, food and raiment, more than enough for all their wants, will be secured to them by the word of Him that cannot lie.   And the rich may call to mind that they too, although the Lord Jesus is no longer upon earth, are not deprived of the opportunity of making to Him remunerative loans; for may they not minister to the Head through His members ?[5] and is it not written, " He that hath pity upon the poor lendeth unto the Lord : and look, what he layeth out, it shall be paid him again "?[6]

[1] See *v.* 5.   [2] See St. John i. 40, 41, 42.   [3] See Prov. xix. 17.
[4] St. Matt. vi. 33.   [5] See St. Matt. xxv. 35, 36, 40.
[6] Prov. xix. 17, P.B.V.

Tuesday.—V. 4. "Now when he had left speaking, he said unto Simon, Launch out into the deep, and let down your nets for a draught." What an under-current of the figurative there is running through all the narratives of Holy Scripture! This little boat in which Christ sat so tranquilly, instructing the people with His heavenly doctrine as they stood on the shore, was a figure of the Church, while He was with her in bodily Presence, and His Apostles were sheltered under His wing from the shafts of the world's hostility. It was for them a period of joy; for the Bridegroom was with them[1]; it was for the Church a period of "godly quietness," such as is prayed for in the Collect of the day. But it was to last but a short time. "When" Jesus Himself "had left speaking," being taken up from them into heaven,[2] they were to launch out into the deep sea of the world, and let down their nets for a draught. And the draught should be very plenteous; three thousand souls were entangled in the meshes of the Gospel net by the first Christian sermon.[3] But with this extraordinary success was to come rupture of the net, divisions, heresies, scandals; among believers there were to be found an Ananias and Sapphira,[4] and a Simon Magus.[5] And dreadful storms of persecution were to rock the boat, and threaten to make it founder altogether; and sometimes the Master would seem to be asleep,[6] " His arm shortened, that it could not save; his ear heavy, that it could not hear."[7]—Nay, Lord, this is our want of faith. Thou art always in and with the ship of Thy Church, though for the trial of our faith it is allowed sometimes to be persecuted by the powers

---

[1] See St. Matt. ix. 15.

[2] See Acts i. 11.

[3] See Acts ii. 41.   [4] See Acts v. 1-12.

[5] See Acts viii. 13-25.

[6] See St. Mark iv. 38.

[7] See Isaiah lix. 1.

of the world, sometimes " by schisms rent asunder, by heresies distressed."[1] Thou hast only to say, " Peace, be still,"[2] to " the course of this world," and it shall " be so peaceably ordered by thy governance, that thy Church shall joyfully serve thee in all godly quietness."

Wednesday. — V. 5. " Master, we have toiled all the night, and have taken nothing : nevertheless at thy word I will let down the net." The great interest of the whole narrative turns upon its effect upon the mind of the Apostle Peter, insomuch that it may be properly called (of which more presently) the narrative of his conversion. Every feature of his state of mind therefore is to be carefully noticed. I observe from these words of his that he has already faith in the Saviour, and a faith robust enough to stand a trial. It was putting his faith to the test, when he was required to let down his nets in broad daylight, though in the night-season, which was the opportune time for fishing, nothing had been caught, and he had laboured in vain. This his Master said to prove him, as when to the ten lepers He said, " Go shew your-selves unto the priests,"[3] and to the friends of Lazarus, " Take ye away the stone."[4] And Peter endured the trial. He had already shown, and in a practical form, an interest in divine truth and in things spiritual. Now he shows *faith*—conviction of his Master's power to work wonders,—and in a practical form too; for it is some labour to launch out into the deep, and let down nets for a draught. It is not until the miracle is wrought, that the feature of *repentance* is manifested in him, and he expresses apprehensions of conscience and convictions of

---

[1] " Hymns Ancient and Modern," No. 215, " The Church's one foundation," etc.　　　[2] See St. Mark iv. 39.

[3] See St. Luke xvii. 14.　　　[4] See St. John xi. 39.

sin.   Let us not be too precise and exact in prescribing
the order, in which repentance and faith make their
appearance in the heart.   In the logical order, or order
of thought, repentance comes first; but as a matter of
experience, different characters, when under the guidance
of grace, do not all follow the same method; suffice it
that in the bringing of every soul to God there are these
two essential elements of feeling,—conviction of sin, and
belief in Christ's power and love.   If any man, after a
searching self-examination, has good reason to conclude
that both are present in his heart, happy is he; possessing both, he may appropriate freely all the blessings of
the Gospel, and need not harass himself with the consideration of the order, in which the different phases of
spiritual feeling appeared.

Thursday. — V. 8. " When Simon Peter saw it, he
fell down at Jesus' knees, saying, Depart from me; for I
am a sinful man, O Lord."   It was a rash and indiscreet
prayer, this " Depart from me; for I am sinful "; " as if
the patient should say to the physician, ' Depart from me;
for I am sick.' "[1]   And yet our Lord does not reprove it,
but meets it with a " Fear not," and a promise of a
nobler draught hereafter.   I find that the Gadarenes
preferred a similar request to our Lord, which He met in
a very different way, by simply complying with it.
" Then the whole multitude of the country of the
Gadarenes round about besought him to depart from
them; for they were taken with great fear: and he went
up into the ship, and returned back again."[2]   The two
requests, though expressed in the same words, were as
different as possible in the sentiments from which they

---

[1] Bishop Hall ["Contemplations upon the History of the New Testament," Book II. Cont. iv.]   [2] St. Luke viii. 37.

proceeded. The request of the Gadarenes proceeded from a low panic, mingled with a lower love of gain. Property had been destroyed to a considerable extent, by the perishing of the herd of swine in the waters[1]; they would not have the great Miracle-Worker among them at such a cost as that. And as to the alarm which they manifested, it was simply that of superstition; it did not reach or touch their consciences. And accordingly our Lord withdraws His Presence, where it is declined in this spirit. Strikingly contrasted with this is Simon's request that the Lord would depart from him. He has lost all thought of worldly livelihood, though the means of it were given him in such abundance by the miracle. His alarm and concern are of a purely spiritual character. His whole soul is absorbed in the thought that the holy God is brought very near to him, and he shrinks away from that heart-searching Presence in deep consciousness of his own impurity, like Isaiah crying, " Woe is me ! for I am undone," when he saw this same Lord surrounded by adoring Seraphims in the temple.[2] And so the indiscreetness of the prayer is altogether overlooked; and it is taken as what in truth it was, " the voice of astonishment, not of dislike; the voice of humility, not of discontentment "[3]; it is like the good centurion declining to have Christ under his roof, not because he did not feel the honour and privilege of such a visit, but because he felt unworthy of it.[4] While I hope not to be taken at my word, if I pray indiscreetly, and more especially that God will never give me my desire, while He sends leanness withal into my soul,[5] I see that God is never displeased

---

[1] See St. Matt. viii. 32.   [2] See Isaiah vi. 1-6, with St. John xii. 41.
[3] Bishop Hall, *ibid.*   [4] See St. Matt. viii. 8 ; St. Luke vii. 6, 7.
[5] Ps. cvi. 15, P.B.V

with deep humility, and that just in proportion to my awe of Him, and my sense of my own unworthiness and vileness, will be His readiness to console and exalt me: "Even thereafter as a man feareth, so is thy displeasure."[1] Had St. Peter any remembrance of this critical moment in his life, at which he declined the Saviour's neighbourhood to him, and was met by "Fear not," and the prediction that he should from henceforth catch men,—when in after days he wrote, "Humble yourselves under the mighty hand of God, that he may exalt you in due time"?[2]

Friday. — V. 11. "And when they had brought their ships to land, they forsook all, and followed him." Thus the course, which began with conviction of sin, ends in entire devotion of the whole man to Christ. We may trace here an interesting analogy between the two great Apostles,—the Apostle of the Gentiles, and the Apostle of the Circumcision. We speak familiarly of the conversion of St. Paul; it is an incident which makes a deep impression upon us. Perhaps we do not as often think of the equally interesting conversion of St. Peter, of which we have the account here. The two conversions are strikingly different in their circumstances and their scenes. St. Paul's was much the more sudden and complete change of the two. Up to the moment of his conversion he had been "a blasphemer, and a persecutor"[3]; whereas St. Peter had previously been acquainted with Christ, and had previously recognised Christ's claims, though not in that whole-hearted, self-devoted manner which he afterwards did. And yet notwithstanding all the difference of outward circumstance, we may trace in each character the outlines of the same spiritual process. In each the process begins with fear; each is stricken down in alarm

---

[1] Ps. xc. 11, P.B.V.   [2] 1 Pet. v. 6.   [3] See 1 Tim. i. 13.

when confronted with the Lord. St. Peter cries, "Depart from me," in conscience-stricken awe, and has to be soothed by the word, "Fear not," and exalted by a prediction of his future ministerial success. St. Paul, "trembling and astonished," exclaims, "Lord, what wilt thou have me to do?"[1] and lies at the feet of the Saviour, unable to see for the glory of that light,[2] and forthwith receives a mission for the Gentiles, "to open their eyes, and to turn them from darkness to light."[3] And the process ended in either case with entire devotion of the whole man to the Saviour's service. Peter, having brought his ship to land, "forsook all and followed" Jesus. And St. Paul was able to testify of himself; "What things were gain to me, those I counted loss for Christ. Yea, doubtless, and I count all things but loss for the excellency of the knowledge of Christ Jesus my Lord: for whom I have suffered the loss of all things, and do count them but dung, that I may win Christ."[4]— Alas, how imperfect, and accompanied with how many reserves, is our devotion to our Master! And why but because originally our convictions of sin were so shallow, so inadequate, so little penetrated to the root of our character? The impulse, which was feeble at the outset, cannot be strong in the issue. Lord, touch my heart with contrition and deep self-abasement; else I shall never surrender myself to Thee as I ought.

Saturday.—V. 11. "They forsook all, and followed him." Simon had been previously a believer and disciple, but he did not forsake all and follow Christ, until the sight of this miracle brought him to a complete self-surrender. Though miracles are no longer vouchsafed,

---

[1] See Acts ix. 6.　　　　　[2] See Acts xxii. 11.
[3] See Acts xxvi. 17, 18.　　　[4] Phil. iii. 7, 8.

yet God often nowadays, by some striking dispensation of His Providence occurring in our immediate neighbourhood, brings Himself near to some soul, whom He designs to have for His own. That soul is made to feel that it can no longer keep Him at arm's length, as it had hitherto been doing, by going only ankle-deep into religion; the time is come, as it had now come to Simon, for a deep earnestness, which shall pervade and colour the whole life. It is true of course that the requirement is not nowadays laid upon us actually to forsake, as the Apostles did, our position, our work, our natural ties; but it is equally true that the will is never right, until it sits so loose to these things, that, if the requirement were made, it would be instantly complied with. There is no following Christ without giving all for all, in intention, if not actually, without giving the little we have to give— heart, affections, will—for the much that He has to give,— " wisdom " to enlighten, " righteousness " to justify, "sanctification " to make us " meet for the inheritance of the saints in light,"[1] and consummated " redemption,"[2] to bring us to it. And if we feel that this self-devotion is at present beyond us, the only way to obtain it is to remember that we cannot engender it in our own hearts, and to wait at His footstool for it with the prayer; " Thy people shall be willing,"—willing to be, and to do, and to suffer, whatsoever Thou wouldst have them be, and do, and suffer,—" in the day of thy power."[3]

[1] See Col. i. 12.   [2] See 1 Cor. i. 30.   [3] Ps. cx. 3.

Chapter XL.

THE GOSPEL FOR THE SIXTH SUNDAY AFTER TRINITY.

St. Matt. v. 20 *to* 27
(substituting "Jesus said unto his disciples" for " For I say unto you,
That," at the beginning of *v.* 20).

20 Jesus said unto his disciples, Except your righteousness shall exceed the righteousness of the Scribes and Pharisees, ye shall in
21 no case enter into the kingdom of heaven. Ye have heard, that it was said by them of old time, Thou shalt not kill; and whosoever
22 shall kill, shall be in danger of the judgement. But I say unto you, that whosoever is angry with his brother without a cause shall be in danger of the judgement: and whosoever shall say to his brother, Racha, shall be in danger of the council: but whoso-
23 ever shall say, Thou fool, shall be in danger of hell fire. Therefore if thou bring thy gift to the altar, and there remembrest that thy
24 brother hath ought against thee; leave there thy gift before the altar, and go thy way, first be reconciled to thy brother, and then
25 come and offer thy gift. Agree with thine adversary quickly, whiles thou art in the way with him; lest at any time the adversary deliver thee to the judge, and the judge deliver thee to the officer, and thou
26 be cast into prison. Verily I say unto thee, thou shalt by no means come out thence, till thou hast paid the uttermost farthing.

[Miss. Sar.	1549.	1662 s.b.
In illo tempore, Dixit Jesus discipulis suis; *Amen* dico vobis, quia nisi abundaverit justitia vestra plus quam Scribarum et Pharisæorum,	Jesus said unto his disciples, Except your righteousnesse exceed the righteousnesse of the scribes and Pharisees, etc. . . . *down to* . . .	Jesus said unto his disciples, Except your righteousness shall exceed the righteousness of the Scribes and Pharisees, etc. (*Gr.* Λέγω γὰρ

etc. (*Vulg.* Dico enim vobis, quia nisi abundaverit justitia vestra, etc. The "Amen dico vobis" occurs at *v.* 18, two verses above) . . . *down to* . . . et tunc veniens offeres munus tuum, *v.* 24.	Thou shalt not come out thence, till thou hast payed the utmost farthing. *V.* 26.	ὑμῖν ὅτι ἐὰν μὴ περισσεύσῃ ἡ δικαιοσύνη ὑμῶν πλεῖον τῶν Γραμματέων καὶ Φαρισαίων, etc.), *down to* . . . till thou hast paid the uttermost farthing, *v.* 26.

Our Reformers in 1549 did very well in adding to the old Sarum Gospel *vv.* 25, 26 ("Agree with thine adversary quickly," etc.), which have the closest connexion with the preceding. They illustrate by a figure, drawn from the exaction of an earthly debt, the lesson given in *vv.* 23, 24 of the necessity of reconciliation with a brother whom we have offended. As it is wise speedily to come to terms of friendly understanding with your creditor, before he hands you over to the officials of the law, who will imprison you for your debt, until you have paid every farthing of it, so is it wise to be reconciled to the brother whom we have offended, "to-day while it is to-day," lest we fall into the hands of the Heavenly Judge, when it is too late to seek His favour.—As to the *commencement* of this Gospel, the connexion with the foregoing verses (at which the "For" in *v.* 20 points) is thus explained by the late Dean Mansel ["Speaker's Commentary," *in loc.*] : "This verse is closely joined with the preceding. Christians are not merely bound to acknowledge the obligation of the Law, but to carry it out more fully than its professed expounders and rigid observers, the Scribes and Pharisees, *i.e.* to obey it in the spirit, not merely in the letter, as instanced in the following verses."—*Translation of* 1540. (1) *V.* 21. "Ye have heard that it was said *unto* them of the old time." The five English Versions before the Authorised all have "to" or "unto" instead of "by." *And the Revised Version has gone back to "to."* "The contrast is primarily between the Law as given to the men of old, and as given 'to you'" (Dean Mansel in "the Speaker's Bible"). (2) *V.* 22. "Whosoever is angry with his brother *unadvisedly* shall be in danger of judgement." And thus Tyndale and the Genevan. Jerome repudiates the word translated "without a cause" or "unadvisedly" (εἰκῆ), as not being found in the best Manuscripts. It is not represented in the Vulgate, and accordingly Wycliffe does not represent it,—"each man that is wroth to his brother shall be guilty to doom." And the Revised Version of 1881 excludes it from the text, telling us however in the margin that "many authorities insert *without a cause.*" Bengel (no mean authority) is strongly against the word, says that it is "a gloss which savours of the human understanding," that not even the Pharisees taught that it is lawful to be angry *without a cause*, and that since God bids us love those who are our enemies, He forbids us to hate people (and therefore to be angry with them), *even where there is a cause.* Exceptions to the general rule, he seems to think, (if I rightly understand his very laconic language) are to be sought in other precepts of Holy Scripture, or in the reason of things, just as, when it is said broadly "Thou shalt not kill," this is to be qualified by "he beareth not the sword in vain," which implies that the civil magistrate may take away life, *when there is a cause*, in the interests of society. That there is such a thing as righteous indignation is clear from our Lord's having been angry (St. Mark iii. 5). (3) *V.* 25. "lest . . . the judge deliver thee to the *minister.*" And so Wycliffe, and after him Tyndale. It came from the "judex tradat te *ministro*" of the Vulgate. The Genevan has "sargeant," an admirable translation, according to the original meaning and derivation of the word "sergeant." It is merely the Latin *serviens*, and signifies, according to Johnson, "an officer whose business it is to execute the orders of magistrates." Thus in *Henry VIII.*, (Act I. Sc. i.) Brandon to a Sergeant at Arms ; "Your office, *sergeant ;* execute it,"—who thereupon formally arrests the Duke of Buckingham for high treason. And Hamlet, dying (Act V. Sc. ii.) ; "Had I but time, (as this fell *sergeant*, death, is strict in his arrest) O, I could tell you," etc. In the Authorised Version the word is twice used of the ῥαβδοῦχοι, whom the Philippian magistrates sent to release Paul and Silas (Acts xvi. 35, 38), where the Revised Version judiciously retains the word "serjeants," while exhibiting the more accurate "lictors" in the margin.]

Sunday.—V. 20. "Except your righteousness shall exceed the righteousness of the Scribes and Pharisees, ye shall in no case (*in no wise, R. V.*) enter into the kingdom of heaven." The righteousness of Christ's disciples must exceed that of the Scribes and Pharisees, first, in being *spiritual.* "God is a spirit,"[1] and, because He is so, His law is spiritual,—a law for the heart, conscience, and will, not for the external conduct only. This spirituality of God's law peeps out even in the Decalogue. For though eight of the Commandments are (on the surface) merely restrictions laid upon conduct, and the fifth is

[1] St. John iv. 24.

interpreted by our Lord to prescribe the succouring of parents,[1] which is an external action, the tenth is *purely* spiritual.[2]   No human legislator is able to ascertain whether covetous desires are cherished in the heart; and the presence, therefore, of such a commandment in the code indicates that it comes from a Legislator who searches the heart; and in the Sermon on the Mount, where Christ appears as the Giver of the new Law, the righteousness required by the Sermon is shown at its opening to be spiritual throughout.   For it is upon states of mind, not upon actions, that the beatitudes are pronounced.[3]— Lord, let my heart by Thy grace bring forth to Thee, as a fertile soil, all the fruits of the Spirit,[4] and then my righteousness will be of the true stamp, which Thou wilt recognise at the last day.

Monday.—V. 20. Secondly, our righteousness must exceed the righteousness of the Scribes and Pharisees, in being *moral* as well as ceremonial.   There are those, who insist much upon morality without devotion.   Nothing more is required of us, according to these people, but to be good in all the relations of life, true and just in all our dealings;—this is to ignore the first and great commandment.[5]   Others (and this was the flaw in the Pharisaic righteousness) divorce morality from devotion, and imagine that they can compensate God for careless or even licentious living by punctual observance of His ordinances.   In each of the three first Gospels is our Lord's solemn protest recorded against this dreadful hypocrisy; " Woe unto you, scribes and Pharisees, hypocrites! for ye devour widows' houses, and for a pretence

---

[1] See St. Mark vii. 9-13.   [2] See Rom. vii. 7, and Exod. xx. 17.
[3] See St. Matt. v. 3-12.   [4] See Gal. v. 22, 23.
[5] See St. Matt. xxii. 37, 38.

make long prayer: therefore ye shall receive the greater damnation."[1]   The life of struggle with self, and laborious service of God, is the masculine element in religion; that of devotion and religious contemplation is the feminine; and " neither is the man without the woman, neither the woman without the man, in the Lord."[2]—Lord, let me never put asunder in mine own practice those things which Thou hast made one.[3]

Tuesday.—V. 22. " Whosoever is angry with his brother without a cause[4] shall be in danger of the judgment."   The words " without a cause," even if foisted into the text by a later hand, and therefore not to be received, are certainly to be understood as a qualification. For " the possibility of anger's being sinless is expressly recognised in those words of the Apostle, ' Be ye angry, and sin not '[5] " [Archbishop Trench]; and our Lord Himself is said to have harboured an indignation, which could not be otherwise than righteous (" He looked round about on them with anger, being grieved for the hardness

---

[1] St. Matt. xxiii. 14; and see also St. Mark xii. 38, 40, and St. Luke xx. 46, 47.   [2] 1 Cor. xi. 11.   [3] See St. Matt. xix. 6.

[4] "On the words ' *Whosoever is angry with his brother without a cause,*' Augustine observes, that in the Greek MSS. the last words find no place, and it is simply, and with no exception, ' Whosoever is angry with his brother shall be in danger of the judgment.' This, however, is not the fact with infinitely the largest number of the MSS. which now exist, in which, as in most of the early versions, 'without a cause' is to be found. He must himself naturally have desired it there; for he everywhere recognises the possibility of an holy anger, and ingeniously shows, that even should it be right to omit these words, as probably it is, the prohibition is still not absolute, nor without its qualifications, since it is with thy brother, not with thy brother's sin, that thou art forbidden to be angry." [Archbishop Trench's " Exposition of the Sermon on the Mount, drawn from the writings of St. Augustine," pp. 33, 34.   London : 1844.]   The words *without a cause* are omitted from the text of the Revised Version of 1881, though we are told in the margin that "Many ancient authorities insert " them.   [5] Eph. iv. 26.

of their hearts").[1]   And Bishop Butler has satisfactorily
shown that anger is an original affection of our nature,
which has its functions in the moral system, and which
therefore is not to be suppressed, but only regulated and
controlled.[2]   The danger is that it may be kept in the
heart too long, in which case it will corrupt itself into
feelings of spite, revenge, and hatred, just as the manna,
when kept overnight, bred worms and stank.[3]   The rule
therefore is; "Let not the sun go down upon your
wrath."[4]—Lord, give me grace to observe this rule, by
ever remembering in my evening prayer those who during
the day may have given me offence.

Wednesday.—V. 22. "Whosoever is angry with his
brother without a cause shall be in danger of the judgment: and whosoever shall say to his brother, Raca," [*an
expression of contempt*, Marg. of R.V.], "shall be in danger
of the council: but whosoever shall say, Thou fool," [*a
Hebrew expression of condemnation*, Marg. of R.V.], "shall
be in danger of hell fire."   The general teaching of this
verse is that, as in human law there are degrees of punishment,—some more, some less severe,—so Divine Law
also has its less solemn and severe sentences, each of
them being a damage to the spiritual life, and the loss
of some gem which might have adorned the future crown,
but only the final and most severe being the loss of
the soul itself, its eternal rejection and reprobation.   And
similarly we cannot doubt that there will be various
degrees of blessedness and glory, "an abundant entrance
into the everlasting kingdom" being ministered unto

---

[1] St. Mark iii. 5.

[2] Bishop Butler's "Fifteen Sermons preached at the Rolls Chapel,"
Sermon VIII. "Upon Resentment."

[3] See Exod. xvi. 20.   [4] Eph. iv. 26.

those, who have given all diligence to add to their faith all the graces of the Christian character,[1] while others will be merely saved and no more, saved as firebrands plucked out of the burning.[2] Not that there will be, either among the saved or lost, any felt and conscious deficiency either of happiness or misery. The pursuit of holiness will enlarge a man's capacity for future blessedness; while, on the other hand, every wilful sin will enlarge his capacity of misery. And every vessel will be filled to the extent of its capacity, although the capacities will differ.——O Lord, when I am tempted to indulge my sinful lusts, let it check me to think that this act cannot be indifferent to my hereafter, that, if I am eventually to be saved, it will dash a jewel from my crown; if to be lost, that it will augment my capacity for misery, and so the amount of my future suffering. And in this view of sin's malignity, let me say to each temptation, " Get thee behind me, Satan."[3]

Thursday.——V. 24. " Leave there thy gift before the altar, and go thy way; first be reconciled to thy brother, and then come and offer thy gift." I find that love, whereby we resemble God, is no less essential to the success of our prayers than faith, whereby we throw ourselves in hope and confidence upon His succour. When our Lord showed His disciples the secret by which the word of prayer might become a word of power, He said not only, " What things soever ye desire, when ye pray, believe that ye receive them," but also, " and when ye stand praying, forgive, if ye have ought against any."[4] And in His model-Prayer He teaches us, not only to say " Our Father" in filial confidence; but also to ask, that our

---

[1] See 2 Pet. i. 5-12. [2] See Amos iv. 11, and 1 Cor. iii. 15.
[3] See St. Matt. xvi. 23. [4] See St. Mark xi. 24, 25.

debts may be forgiven us, as we forgive our debtors.[1]
The ground of this is obvious. " God is love"[2]; and
therefore, when out of love, we are in a state of alienation
from Him, and cannot hope that He will respond to us.
But when our hearts are set to the same key as His, He
responds promptly and largely; and this rule holds more
especially in the Holy Communion, which is not only a
feast commemorative of God's love to us, and communi-
cative of Himself in love, but also a feast of brotherly
love with one another; " for we being many are one
bread, and one body: for we are all partakers of that one
bread."[3]—Lord, let me never be guilty of such desecra
tion as to approach Thine altar in a spirit of hostility or
malice to any soul of man.

Friday.—V. 25. " Agree with thine adversary
quickly, whiles thou art in the way with him; lest at
any time the adversary deliver thee to the judge, and the
judge deliver thee to the officer, and thou be cast into
prison." Our adversary is the law of God, with its
claims upon us for perfect love of God, and love of our
neighbour as of ourselves,[4]—which claims we have to
satisfy. The " way " is this life, during which it is open
to us to satisfy the claims of the Law; " behold, now is
the accepted time ; behold, now is the day of salvation."[5]
The "Judge" is "that man, whom" God "hath ordained" to
" judge the world in righteousness" on an "appointed day."[6]
" The officer" is an angel, as it is written; " the angels
shall come forth, and sever the wicked from among the
just."[7] The " prison " is the " furnace of fire," into which

---

[1] See St. Matt. vi. 9, 12.   [2] 1 John iv. 8, 16.
[3] 1 Cor. x. 17.   [4] See St. Mark xii. 29, 30, 31.
[5] 2 Cor. vi. 2.   [6] See Acts xvii. 31.
[7] St. Matt. xiii. 49.

the angels shall cast the wicked.[1]—O Lord, now, while it is the accepted time, let me come to an agreement with Thy law, by throwing myself upon Christ for the expiation of my sins, and for a meritorious righteousness, and by walking, " not after the flesh, but after the Spirit."[2]   Thus shall I be in perfect harmony with Thy law, which shall have nothing to allege against my salvation ; and walking together with it,[3]—by the imputation of Christ's righteousness to me, and by my own spiritual fulfilment of it,— shall finish my course with joy.[4]

Saturday.—V. 48. " Be ye therefore perfect, even as your Father which is in heaven is perfect."   With these words our Blessed Lord summarises the law of *love*, which He lays down in this section of His sermon.   And let me observe that it is the law of *love*, which is thus summarised.   The words before me are, in St. Luke's version of them, rendered thus, " Be ye therefore *merciful*, as your Father also is merciful."[5]   " Above all these things," says the Apostle to the Colossians, having already exhorted them to compassion, humility, and forbearance, " put on love, which is the bond of perfectness,"[6]—the girdle which holds together the whole raiment of the Christian character.   Jonah, though a righteous man, showed that he was not made perfect in love, when he was angry because God did not fulfil His word of threatening against the penitent Ninevites.[7]   And God endeavoured to bring him to His own perfectness of love, by telling him how He yearned over the guilty city, with its six score thousand infants and its much cattle.[8]—Lord, let me love the strictness of Thy law, knowing that it is

---

[1] St. Matt. xiii. 50.   [2] See Rom. viii. 1.   [3] See Amos iii. 3.
[4] See Acts xx. 24.   [5] St. Luke vi. 36.   [6] Col. iii. 12, 13, 14, R.V.
[7] See Jonah iii. 10 ; iv. 1, 2, 3, 4.   [8] *Ibid.* iv. 11.

man's safeguard. If it were relaxed for one, it must be relaxed for another; and the end would be universal licentiousness and disorder,—" all the foundations of the earth out of course."[1] And let me know and feel that this strictness of Thy law is no external Pharisaic punctiliousness as to observances and duties, but simply the love of Thee with all my heart, and mind, and soul, and strength, and the love of my neighbour as of myself, in Thee, and for Thee. Oh, " pour into my heart that most excellent gift of charity, without which whosoever liveth is counted dead before thee."[2]

[1] See Ps. lxxxii. 5.   [2] Collect for Quinquagesima Sunday.

Chapter XLI.

THE GOSPEL FOR THE SEVENTH SUNDAY AFTER TRINITY.

St. Mark viii. 1 *to* 10.

1 In those days the multitude being very great, and having nothing to eat, Jesus called his disciples unto him, and saith unto
2 them, I have compassion on the multitude, because they have now
3 been with me three daies, and have nothing to eat: And if I send them away fasting to their own houses, they will faint by the way;
4 for divers of them came from far. And his disciples answered him, From whence can a man satisfie these men with bread here in the
5 wilderness? And he asked them, How many loaves have ye? And
6 they said, Seven. And he commanded the people to sit down on the ground. And he took the seven loaves, and gave thanks, and brake, and gave to his disciples to set before them, and they did set them
7 before the people. And they had a few small fishes; and he blessed
8 and commanded to set them also before them. So they did eat and were filled: And they took up of the broken meat that was left,
9 seven baskets. And they that had eaten were about four thousand. And he sent them away.

[Miss. Sar.	1549.	1662 a.b.
In illo tempore, Cum turba multa esset *cum Jesu* nec haberent quod manducarent, etc. (*Vulg.* In diebus illis iterum cum turba multa esset, nec haberent quod manducarent, etc.)	In those dayes, when there was a very great company, and had nothing to eat, etc.	In those days the multitude being very great, and having nothing to eat, etc. (Gr. Ἐν ἐκείναις ταῖς ἡμέραις, παμπόλλου ὄχλου ὄντος, καὶ μὴ ἐχόντων τί φάγωσι, etc.)

The narrative is not in the original linked by any connective particle to the preceding Chapter. Mr. Pound thinks that, after the cure of the deaf man who had an impediment in his speech, the last event recorded in Chap. vii., our Lord went along the eastern side of the Sea of Galilee, and ascended the same mountain on which He had previously fed the Five Thousand, and that there the multitudes came to Him, and cast down the lame, blind, dumb, and maimed at His feet, for healing (see St. Matt. xv. 29, 30, 31). The fact that many of these people were Gentiles from Decapolis gives point, he thinks, to the words, "They glorified the God of *Israel*" (St. Matt. xv. 31). The persons previously fed, he says, were "Jews going up to the Passover, and people who had followed from the cities of Galilee." But in the present case, they were "a company of traders and a mixed company of Gentiles and Israelites, who had followed Jesus from the districts of Tyre, Sidon, and Decapolis. If this miracle had a like object with the former Eucharistic miracle, it was probably in some sense a manifestation of the benefits of the Incarnation to the Gentiles" ["Story of the Gospels," Vol. I., p. 257]. See the Thought for *Saturday.— Translation of* 1540. *V.* 4. "*Where* should a man have bread here in the wildernesse, to satisfie these?" It should be "*whence*" (or, as Wycliffe gives it, "where of"="from where"); but Cranmer repeated the "where" from Tyndale, and was in turn copied by the Genevan translator.]

Sunday.—Vv. 2, 3. "I have compassion on the multitude, because they have now been with me three days, and have nothing to eat: and if I send them away fasting to their own houses, they will faint by the way: for divers of them came from far." Love has its fine and delicate features, as well as its more pronounced and obvious characteristics; and one of these is *considerateness.* This feature of love our Blessed Lord exhibited, when after raising Jairus's daughter, He showed Himself mindful of the bodily exhaustion to which the poor girl's illness had reduced her, and " commanded that something should be given her to eat."[1] Again, He showed considerateness, both of the feelings and of the poverty of the married couple at Cana, when, by furnishing a miraculous

[1] See St. Mark v. 43.

supply of wine, He prevented any reflexions from being made on their inhospitality, and also furnished far more wine than could have been necessary for that single occasion.[1] Here He shows Himself considerate of the length of time during which the multitude had been without food, of the distance from which they had come, and which they must again pass over in order to reach their homes.—Lord, make me considerate of the feelings, infirmities, circumstances, and trials of those with whom I have to do, that this feature of the mind of Christ may be reproduced in me.

Monday.—Vv. 2, 3. I observe here, not only our Lord's considerateness, but also that this considerateness extends to bodily needs, such as hunger and fatigue. Who could feel for the wearied and the hungry, so well as He, who sat on Jacob's well in the sultry noontide, " wearied with his journey,"[2] and must have experienced the severest pangs of hunger after his forty days' fast ?[3] The body is an essential part of our nature, not to be annihilated by death, but to be raised up again in incorruption[4]; and on this ground it is, that even the body is to be treated with respect, and its infirmities to be considered. And is not what we have read to be taken as a warning from our Lord Himself, as to the necessity of considering the natural infirmities of those who wait upon Him in His house of prayer, and of not unduly exhausting them by long services and sermons,—the same lesson which is conveyed more explicitly by the narrative of Eutychus ?[5]

Tuesday.—V. 2. " I have compassion on the multitude, because they . . . have nothing to eat." Let me consider the fruit which the words and acts of Christ

---

[1] See St. John ii. 6, 9, 10.   [2] See St. John iv. 6.
[3] See St. Matt. iv. 2.   [4] See 1 Cor. xv. 42.   [5] See Acts xx. 9-13.

have borne in the history of Christendom.   It is difficult
for *us* to imagine a state of civilisation, in which no
provision whatever is made for the poorest classes, when
they are thrown out of work by age or illness.   But, so
far as we know, no such provision was made in the
civilised states of antiquity.   Christ it was who, by His
miracles of healing and feeding the hungry, and by such
words as those now before me, threw into the minds of
men the idea of supplying the wants of the poor and
sick, on a large scale and systematically.—Lord, I desire
to thank Thee for the beneficence of the spirit of Thy
religion, which has remedied so much misery and suffering, about which men were unconcerned and indifferent
before.   There is, alas! far less of Thy spirit than there
ought to be in the hearts and lives of individual Christians.
But we have only to look at Christian philanthropic
institutions to see how much Thou hast done to relieve
the miseries and burdens, under which all of us groan.
These institutions could not have been created except by
a widely diffused spirit of sympathy, and from Thee as
its fountain-head it is that this spirit of sympathy takes
its rise.

Wednesday.—V. 4. "And his disciples answered
him, From whence can a man satisfy these men with
bread here in the wilderness?"   How prone is man to
forget the words and works of God, so that the impression which those words and works have made on him
is obliterated almost as soon as made! Surely this
could not be without some direct action of the evil one
on the heart, such as Christ indicates, when He says,
"then cometh the devil, and taketh away the word out
of their hearts, lest they should believe and be saved?"[1]

---

[1] St. Luke viii. 12.

Could these disciples, without some such action upon their memory, have so soon forgotten the miracle of feeding the five thousand recorded in the sixth Chapter? Surely, had they retained the impression of that miracle, their answer would have been,—not, " From whence can a man satisfy?" but,—" Is anything too hard for Thee, O Lord ?"[1] They speak in the very accents of Moses (who, like them, was, notwithstanding, a true servant of God), when he said; "Shall the flocks and the herds be slain for them, to suffice them? or shall all the fish of the sea be gathered together for them, to suffice them ?"[2] Warned by such examples, let me seek to retain on my mind those words of God, which at any time have sunk into my soul with a peculiar impressiveness, (" Thy word have I hid in mine heart, that I might not sin against thee "[3]), and also any special deliverances and mercies which I may have received at His hand. When the Psalmist's spirit was overwhelmed, and his heart desolate within him, he found comfort and re-assurance of his faith in remembering the days of old, and musing on the work of God's hands.[4]—Lord, let me never be guilty of limiting[5] Thy power, wisdom, and love, in my conceptions of them; but let me expect great things in the future from Thee, who hast done such great things for me in the past.

Thursday.—Vv. 5, 7. "And he asked them, How many loaves have ye ? and they said, Seven. . . . And they had a few small fishes : and he blessed, and commanded to set them also before them." Christ makes the most of existing materials. He did not here create new food, but made the old store, under His miraculous blessing, go as far as was necessary for the occasion. So, in His first

---

[1] See Gen. xviii. 14 ; and Num. xi. 23.　　[2] Num. xi. 22.
[3] Ps. cxix. 11.　　[4] See Ps. cxliii. 4, 5.　　[5] See Ps. lxxviii. 41.

miracle at Cana, He did not create wine, but turned water into wine,[1] using the material which already existed as a basis for the new creation. And this is how God acts in the frame of Nature,—always making the most of existing resources. No particle of matter is annihilated; but when it has fulfilled one function, it takes a new form and fulfils another. Thus the waters of the earth are converted by evaporation into clouds, and the clouds discharge themselves on the earth in the shape of refreshing showers.— Taught by Thy method of proceeding, O Lord, let me make my talents, advantages, opportunities, go as far as ever they will; and in trading with them I shall assuredly find that they will multiply, and meet every emergency which may arise while I pursue my vocation.

Friday.—V. 6. " He took the seven loaves, . . . and *brake.*" V. 20. " When I *brake* the seven loaves among four thousand." Here I find two lessons,—a moral and a spiritual. The moral lesson is, that " in the distribution of our goods we should expect God's blessing, not in their entireness and reservation, ' There is that scattereth and yet increaseth.' " [Bishop Hall.] The spiritual lesson is, that the body of Christ (of the communication of which to His people in the Sacrament of the Eucharist we are here reminded) had need to be broken by His death and passion, before it could become the life-giving, life-maintaining sustenance of the human soul. The living Christ is our *example ;* but it is the bleeding, agonizing, crucified, dying Christ, who is our *life.* " This is my body, which is *broken* for you "[2]; the veil, which is the flesh of Christ,[3] had to be rent asunder[4] by death, into its two constituent elements of body and soul, before men could pass through

---

[1] See St. John ii. 7, 9.   [2] 1 Cor. xi. 24.   [3] See Heb. x. 20.
[4] See St. Matt. xxvii. 51 ; St. Mark xv. 38 ; St. Luke xxiii. 45.

it into the holy of holies, and there hold a life-giving communion with God. And this spiritual sustenance afforded by the broken body of Christ, suffices, and more than suffices, for hundreds of thousands " of all nations, and kindreds, and people, and tongues,"[1] who are all held in communion with God by participation in that broken body. And the outward visible sign of this is, when in the Holy Communion a fragment of the broken loaf passes into, and is assimilated by, the frame of each communicant; " For we being many are one bread, and one body : for we are all partakers of that one bread."[2]

Saturday.—V. 8. " And they took up of the broken meat that was left seven baskets." That this is quite a distinct miracle from the feeding of the *five* thousand is clear from the separate allusion made by our Lord to both of them in verses 19 and 20 of this Chapter.[3] And when we look closely into the language of the original, we find that quite a different word [4] is used for basket in this miracle, from that which is used [5] in recording the feeding of the five thousand. The word here used denotes a large basket, as is seen from its being employed also to denote the basket in which St. Paul was let down by the wall at Damascus (Acts ix. 25).[6] " Hamper " or " Pannier," would perhaps be the more proper rendering of

---

[1] See Rev. vii. 9.   [2] 1 Cor. x. 17.

[3] " When I brake the five loaves among five thousand, how many baskets full of fragments took ye up ? They say unto him, Twelve. And when the seven among four thousand, how many baskets " (panniers ?) " full of fragments took ye up ? And they said Seven."

[4] σπυρίς (See St. Matt. xv. 37 ; xvi. 10 ; St. Mark viii. 8, 20).

[5] κόφινος (See St. Matt. xiv. 20 ; xvi. 9 ; St. Mark vi. 43 ; viii. 19).

[6] λαβόντες δὲ αὐτὸν οἱ μαθηταὶ νυκτός, καθῆκαν διὰ τοῦ τείχους, χαλάσαντες ἐν σπυρίδι.—This basket, however, is called σαργάνη by the Apostle himself in 2 Cor. xi. 33 ; καὶ διὰ θυρίδος ἐν σαργάνῃ ἐχαλάσθην διὰ τοῦ τείχους, καὶ ἐξέφυγον τὰς χεῖρας αὐτοῦ.

the original. The other word denotes a much smaller basket, and one which we find from certain passages in Juvenal,[1] the Jews usually carried about with them in travelling. Perhaps, therefore, it may be the case that by the feeding

[1] Hic, ubi nocturnæ Numa constituebat amicæ,
Nunc sacri fontis nemus et delubra locantur
Judæis, *quorum cophinus fœnumque supellex.*
Sat. iii. 12, 13, 14.

"Here, where [in the olden time] Numa made his assignation by night with [the nymph Egeria] his mistress, now the shrine [of the Camenæ], and the grove [containing] the sacred fountain, are let out to [beggarly] Jews, *whose basket and bundle of hay constitute their whole furniture.*" And again, Sat. vi. 542 ;

Quum dedit ille locum, *cophino fœnoque relictis,*
Arcanam Judæa tremens mendicat in aurem,
Interpres legum Solymarum, et magna sacerdos
Arboris, ac summi fida internuntia cœli ;
Implet et illa manum, sed parcius : ære minuto
Qualiacanque voles Judæi somnia vendunt.

"When [the burly priest] has gone his way, a palsy-stricken old Jewess, *leaving her basket and bundle of hay,* comes begging in a whisper into [my lady's] ear, an interpreter [forsooth] of the laws of Jerusalem, high-priestess of the wood, and a faithful interlocutor with high heaven ; she, too, gets her hand filled, but more sparingly [than the priest had done]: even for a brass farthing your Jew will sell you any sort of dreams you may wish to have."

These passages give us a lively picture of the wretchedness and degradation of the Jews of Rome, at the end of the first and the beginning of the second century of our era. Their being forbidden the city, and obliged to rent Ægeria's grove outside the *Porta Capena* at so much *per* tree ; their abject poverty (nothing in the world but a provision-basket and a few wisps of hay) ; their trading on the superstitions of the heathen, by professing to interpret dreams as Joseph and Daniel had done ; and their using the Revelation made to them, and the practices prescribed by the law, to work upon the religious instinct of the Gentiles, and extort money from them ; all these circumstances, recorded quite incidentally by a pagan satirist, tend to show what a mental and moral blight had fallen upon the people, "who both killed the Lord Jesus, and their own prophets," and on whom in consequence "the wrath of God came to the uttermost." [See 1 Thess. ii. 15, 16.]

of the five thousand is represented the spiritual nourishment of the Jews by the body of Christ, whereas by this miracle may be denoted the administration of the same food to the Gentiles. At all events, the largeness of the basket used on the occasion before us, may furnish a reason why fewer baskets were required than on the previous one, when smaller baskets had been used. But putting all speculations aside, I shall not err in finding, in the distinction between these two miracles, an evidence that God's words, like His works, will bear and repay examination with the microscope. In narratives generally similar we shall yet find instructive differences of detail, just as in nature endless variety of form and function is embraced under the same structural law or general plan.

Chapter XLII

THE GOSPEL FOR THE EIGHTH SUNDAY AFTER TRINITY.

St. Matt. vii. 15 *to* 22.

15 Beware of false prophets, which come to you in sheeps clothing,
16 but inwardly they are ravening wolves. Ye shall know them by their
17 fruits: Do men gather grapes of thorns, or figs of thistles? Even so
   every good tree bringeth forth good fruit; but a corrupt tree bringeth
18 forth evil fruit. A good tree cannot bring forth evil fruit; neither
19 can a corrupt tree bring forth good fruit. Every tree that bringeth
20 not forth good fruit, is hewen down, and cast into the fire. Where-
21 fore by their fruits ye shall know them. Not every one that saith
   unto me, Lord, Lord, shall enter into the kingdom of heaven; but
   he that doth the will of my Father who is in heaven.

[Miss. Sar.	1549.	1662 s.b.
In illo tempore, Dixit Jesus discipulis suis; Attendite a falsis prophetis, etc. (*Vulg.* Attendite a falsis prophetis, etc.), *down to* qui facit voluntatem Patris mei qui in cœlis est, ipse intrabit in regnum cœlorum.	Beware of false prophets, etc.	Beware of false prophets, etc. (Gr. Προσέχετε δὲ ἀπὸ τῶν ψευδοπροφητῶν, etc.)

The particle (δὲ) which connects the first verse of this Gospel with what precedes it in the Sermon on the Mount, has been ousted from the text by the Revisers of 1881, probably on the ground that it is not found in the Vatican Manuscript. None of the English Versions seem to recognise it; but yet surely, if internal considerations are to have any weight in determining the truth of readings, it is quite in place here. In *vv.* 13, 14 our Lord is warning His hearers of the straitness of the gate and narrowness of the way which leadeth unto life ; and then, as Bengel points out, He proceeds to a warning against those who would close the gate upon them. " It is strait enough in its own nature, and by reason of the impediments which you will find in your heart *within.* Take heed that it be not shut up against you by hypocritical scribes and Pharisees (Comp. St. Matt. xxiii. 13), "who will *from without* put an impediment to your entering."—*Translation of* 1540. (*V.* 21.) "but he that doth the will of my Father which is in heaven, *he shall enter into the kingdom of heaven.*" The last clause comes from the Vulgate, not from the original Greek, in which it is not found. It forms part of the Gospel in the Sarum Missal, and appears in Wycliffe's Version and the Rhemish. Why Cranmer inserted it, it is difficult to say. In his Version, as given in Baxter's Hexapla, the clause is in brackets and printed in italics thus,—(*He shall entre in to the kyngdome of heauen*). The Editor tells us (p. 161) that Cranmer's version has been reprinted from a very fine copy of the first edition (1539), in the possession of the Tiustees of the Baptist College at Bristol. In the Black-Letter Prayer Book of 1636 (9 ?) the clause appears in black letter like the rest of the text.]

I. *Sunday.*—Our first thought upon this passage shall be *the reality and urgency of the danger, against which we are here warned ;* " Beware of false prophets." Our Blessed Lord constantly warns His disciples against religious guides whose teaching is unsafe, and will land them, if they follow it, in the quagmire of error. And His three great Apostles catch these accents of His voice, and echo them on. St. Peter; " There were false prophets also among the people, even as there shall be false teachers among you, who privily shall bring in damnable heresies, even denying the Lord that bought them."[1] St. Paul ; " I know this, that after my departing shall grievous wolves enter in among you, not sparing the flock."[2] And again ; " Now the Spirit speaketh expressly, that in the latter times some shall depart from the faith, giving heed to seducing spirits, and doctrines of devils."[3] St. John,

---

[1] 2 Pet. ii. 1.   [2] Acts xx. 29.   [3] 1 Tim. iv. 1.

finally; " Beloved, believe not every spirit, but try the spirits whether they are of God : because many false prophets are gone out into the world." [1]   And he tells us that the appearance of many antichrists is a sign of its being " the last time," [2] which seems to imply that, as the Second Advent draws nearer, swarms of these teachers of error will appear, and succeed in deluding and misleading many, like *ignes fatui* dancing across marshy ground at that critical hour which precedes the dawn, and when the night is blackest.

II. *Monday.*—V. 15. The second thought is, that *no error can gain admission to man's mind, no evil to his will, unless it presents itself under the garb and guise of good.* These false prophets " come to you in sheep's clothing, but inwardly they are ravening wolves."   They could not get a hearing if they came *as* wolves.   It is with every error and sin, as it was with the original error and sin ; " the serpent *beguiled Eve through his subtilty*," [3] " the woman *being deceived* was in the transgression." [4]   " Satan himself is transformed into an angel of light," says St. Paul. " Therefore it is no great thing if his ministers also be transformed as the ministers of righteousness." [5]   " All the ways of a man are clean in his own eyes," [6] says the wise man; that is, however foolish and wicked his conduct may be, he can never bring himself to adopt it without first palming off a deceit upon his own conscience, and investing it with the garb and guise of good, so that to him it appears more or less justifiable.

III. *Tuesday.*—V. 16. The third point is *the test which is to be applied to religious teachers, by way of ascertaining whether they are true or false prophets.*   " Ye shall know

<hr>

[1] 1 John iv. 1.   [2] See 1 John ii. 18.   [3] 2 Cor. xi. 3.
[4] 1 Tim. ii. 14.   [5] 2 Cor. xi. 14, 15.   [6] Prov. xvi. 2.

them by their fruits. Do men gather grapes of thorns, or figs of thistles ? " The fruit of a religious teacher, so far as he is a religious teacher, is the doctrine he brings. When St. John exhorts us not to believe every spirit, but to " try the spirits whether they are of God," the test which he directs us to apply is a doctrinal one ; " Hereby know ye the Spirit of God : every spirit that confesseth that Jesus Christ is come in the flesh, is of God : and every spirit that confesseth not that Jesus Christ is come in the flesh, is not of God : and this is that spirit of antichrist, whereof ye have heard that it should come."[1] And when St. Paul warns us not to " despise " (or disparage) " prophesyings," he immediately adds another warning on the contrary side—not to accept any prophesying, without first applying the touchstone of God's word to it. " Despise not prophesyings. Prove all things ; hold fast that which is " (after such proving is found to be) " good."[2] The test, to which all prophesying is to be submitted, is Holy Scripture, together with that rule of faith which the Church in the Creeds has gathered out of Holy Scripture.

IV. *Wednesday.*—From what has been said it follows, that *we are not to trust implicitly even duly authorised teachers, but to exercise our private judgment on what they teach*, by diligently comparing it with Holy Scripture and the rule of faith. The exercise of private judgment is not so much a privilege as a duty and responsibility, which our Lord and His Apostles have laid upon all Christians. Twice does our Lord warn us to " take heed how " we " hear,"[3] and " take heed what " we " hear."[4] It matters not how fully authorised the prophet may be

---

[1] 1 John iv. 1, 2, 3.   [2] 1 Thess. v. 20, 21.
[3] St. Luke viii. 18.   [4] St. Mark iv. 24.

as to his external credentials. The scribes and Pharisees sat in Moses' seat, and yet they were blind guides.[1] The Bereans are praised as men of "noble" (that is, candid) minds because they did not accept what even an inspired Apostle told them, without bringing it to the criterion of the Old Testament. They "searched the scriptures daily, whether those things were so."[2] Nay, our Lord Himself did not stand exclusively upon His mission and authorisation by the Father; but condescended to appeal to the Old Testament as the criterion of His claims; "Search the scriptures; for in them ye think ye have eternal life: and they are they which testify of me."[3] But how presumptuously have we often heard God's holy Word, and how little have we afterwards tested what we have heard! How often have we trifled and coquetted with error both in books and sermons; going, out of mere curiosity, and to gratify "itching ears,"[4] to hear preachers who maintain some novel and startling doctrine; or glancing over latitudinarian and half-sceptical works, merely to see what the author has to say, entirely forgetful of the "Take heed how," and the "Take heed what ye hear," of which our Master made so great a point!

V. *Thursday.*—V. 16, *et sequent. Let me meditate on that striking and appropriate Scriptural image, according to which men are spoken of as trees, and that which comes from them, in the shape of word or work, as fruit.* In the twenty-first verse, with which the Gospel concludes, our Lord intimates to us that the fruit, which God requires all Christians, and not religious teachers only, to bear, is a cordial doing of God the Father's will; "Not every one

---

[1] See St. Matt. xxiii. 2, 16.   [2] Acts xvii. 11.
[3] St. John v. 39.   [4] See 2 Tim. iv. 3.

that saith unto me, Lord, Lord, shall enter into the kingdom of heaven; but he that doeth the will of my Father which is in heaven." We may profitably complete the image. Fruit-trees bear, not fruit only, but leaf and blossom. What is the leaf which many put forth, who yet have none of the *fruit* of the Spirit to show in their lives? The leaf is the religious profession. Our Lord cursed a barren fig-tree, because, while it made a great show of leaves at a distance, it had no fruit when He came up to examine it.[1] It was a type of the guilty city Jerusalem, where a high profession of religion was found in abundance, but without "judgment, mercy, and faith,"[2] where the religious guides of the people did "all their works for to be seen of men,"[3] and "for a pretence" made "long prayers," while they "devoured widows' houses."[4] Therefore was the city and the temple blighted with God's curse, and the Jewish nation stricken with spiritual barrenness. The reverse of this is described in the first Psalm, where it is said of the man who meditates day and night in the law of the Lord, that "he shall be like a tree planted by the rivers of water, that bringeth forth his fruit in his season; his *leaf* also shall not wither" (his religious profession, instead of shrinking up, and having its hollowness exposed, shall be fresh and fadeless unto the end); "and whatsoever he doeth shall prosper."[5] As for the blossom, which in many fruit-trees is so beautiful, it may represent either those natural amiabilities of character, with which some are endowed, or those supernatural gifts, to which our Lord makes a reference in the twenty-second verse, and which in their miraculous form have not been vouchsafed to the Church

[1] See St. Mark xi. 13, 14.   [2] See St. Matt. xxiii. 23.
[3] See St. Matt. xxiii. 5.   [4] See St. Mark xii. 40.   [5] Ps. i. 2, 3.

since the period of her early childhood. Neither of these furnish any evidence whatever of right principle, or of the heart's being under the influence of divine grace.

VI. *Friday.*—V. 19. *The progressiveness of Revelation* shall be my Friday's thought. Our Lord, we find from this passage, took up His stand on ground previously occupied by St. John the Baptist. He began where His predecessor had left off. The words he uses here, " Every tree that bringeth not forth good fruit is hewn down, and cast into the fire," are taken from one of the Baptist's sermons.[1] The same method is pursued throughout the whole of Revelation. The Law of Moses was a step in advance upon the law of conscience, under which the Patriarchs lived ; the Prophets and Psalms were an advance upon the Law ; the Gospel, as preached by Christ, was a great step in advance upon the Prophets and Psalms, though attested by both ; the Gospel, finally, as explicitly announced by the Apostles under the plenary inspiration of the Holy Ghost, was a yet further developement. There is a gradual unfolding of God's counsel from the first promise in Genesis respecting the Seed of the woman,[2] to the final warning, " Surely I come quickly,"[3] which closes the Book of Revelation.

VII. *Saturday.*—V. 21. The last thought shall be *the great things which are said in Holy Scripture of doing the will of God.* Here our Lord says that he that doeth the will of His Father " shall *enter* into the kingdom of heaven." But from other passages it would appear that such an one shall take high rank there, shall contract thereby affinity with God and Christ, shall be endowed with something of their permanence. " Whosoever shall do the will of my Father which is in heaven, the same

---

[1] See St. Matt. iii. 10. [2] See Gen. iii. 15. [3] See Rev. xxii. 20.

is my brother, and sister, and mother."[1] "The world passeth away, and the lust thereof: but he that doeth the will of God abideth for ever,"[2] says the beloved disciple. The will in any rational and moral being is the deepest thing in him; it is the expression of his character. Therefore, he who identifies himself with the will of God by doing it makes himself one with God,—with Him who is " the same yesterday, and to-day, and for ever."[3] Only we must observe that the "doing" of "the will" here spoken of implies the embracing it with the heart, as well as the mere exhibition of it in the outward conduct. No man does God's will in a way acceptable to God, who does not love it. Balaam, though he observed in the letter the restriction laid upon him by God, yet displeased God, because his heart went not with his action.[4] What need have we to pray, in the language of our Church,—" that we may obtain that which thou dost promise, make us to love that which thou dost command!"[5]

---

[1] St. Matt. xii. 50. [2] 1 John ii. 17. [3] See Heb. xiii. 8.
[4] See Num. xxii. 22. [5] Collect for the Fourteenth Sunday after Trinity.

CHAPTER XLIII

THE GOSPEL FOR THE NINTH SUNDAY AFTER TRINITY.

St. Luke xvi. 1 *to* 10
(except that in *v.* 1 the initial "And" and the word "also" are dropped,
and "Jesus" is substituted for "he.")

1 Jesus said unto his disciples, There was a certain rich man who had a steward, and the same was accused unto him, that he had

2 wasted his goods. And he called him, and said unto him, How is it that I hear this of thee? Give an account of thy stewardship; for

3 thou mayest be no longer steward. Then the steward said within himself, What shall I do? for my Lord taketh away from me the

4 stewardship: I cannot dig, to beg I am ashamed. I am resolved what to do, that when I am put out of the stewardship, they may

5 receive me into their houses. So he called every one of his lords debtors unto him, and said unto the first, How much owest thou unto

6 my lord? And he said, An hundred measures of oyl. And he said unto him, Take thy bill, and sit down quickly, and write fifty.

7 Then said he to another, And how much owest thou? And he said, An hundred measures of wheat. And he said unto him, Take thy

8 bill, and write fourscore. And the lord commended the unjust steward, because he had done wisely: for the children of this world

9 are in their generation wiser than the children of light. And I say unto you, Make to your selves friends of the Mammon of unrighteousness, that when ye fail, they may receive you into everlasting habitations.

[Miss. Sar.	1549.	1662 s.b.
In illo tempore, Dixit Jesus discipulis suis par-	Jesus said unto his disciples, There was a	Iesus said unto his disciples, There was a

abolam hanc: Homo quidam erat dives qui habebat villicum, etc. (*Vulg.* Dicebat autem et ad discipulos suos : Homo quidam erat dives, qui habebat villicum, etc.) | certain rich man which had a steward, etc. | certain rich man who had a steward, etc. (*Gr.* Ἔλεγε δὲ καὶ πρὸς τοὺς μαθητὰς αὑτοῦ· Ἄνθρωπός τις ἦν πλούσιος, ὃς εἶχεν οἰκονόμον, etc.)

There is a beautiful connexion between the three Parables in Chap. xv., and this, with which Chap. xvi. opens. In the Parables of the Lost Sheep, the Lost Coin, and the Lost Son, our Lord had, as it were, pleaded the cause of the publicans and sinners, who thronged to hear Him, and with whom He willingly held intercourse, against the murmurings of the cavilling Pharisees and scribes (see Chap. xv. 1, 2, 3). Here He turns to these publicans and sinners, many of whom doubtless still retained a considerable portion of worldly goods, and addresses to *them* a Parable, the object of which was to instruct them in the right use of wealth. "These disciples," says Bengel on *v.* 1 ("And he said also unto his *disciples*"), "are not those twelve who had forsaken all, and rather were *the friends to be made*, but they who had been publicans. And the Lord now speaks more seriously and sternly *with* disciples who had been publicans, than *for* them to others. The son recovered with joy has not music every day (to celebrate his restoration), but is instructed how to return to his duty."— *Translation of* 1540. (1) *V.* 4. "I *wote* what to do, that when I am put out of the stewardship, they may receive me into their houses." And so Wycliffe, Tyndale, and the Genevan. The Rhemish has, "I *know* what I will do." The translation is not inaccurate, except in so far as "I know," or "I wot," does not sufficiently express the momentariness of the acquisition of the knowledge. The aorist expresses the momentary in past time ; and here the word ἔγνων (as Dean Alford points out) is nearly equivalent to—"It has just struck me what to do." (2) *V.* 6. "And he said, An hundred *tuns* of oil." "Tuns" comes from Tyndale. Wycliffe has, "an hundrid baralis" (barrels) "of oile." The Genevan gives "*mesures* of oyle," which King James's Translators adopted. The Rhemish has "pipes." "Tuns" is a good translation, if the word is taken to imply not any specific measure, but only a large quantity. Looked at in its origin, the word has a vague meaning. It is connected with the Saxon "tynan" (to hedge, enclose), and probably with the Latin *teneo* (to hold), and thus it originally means merely a vessel of a certain capacity, holding or enclosing something. We have the word thus loosely used in Shakspere. Mrs. Ford, of Falstaff (*Merry Wives*, Act II. Sc. i.); "What tempest, I trow,

threw this whale with so many *tuns of oil* in him, ashore at Windsor ?"
And Coriolanus to Aufidius (*Coriolanus*, Act IV. Sc. v) ;

> "Since I have ever followed thee with hate,
> Drawn *tuns* of blood out of thy country's breast,
> And cannot live but to thy shame, unless
> It be to do thee service."

(3) *V. 7.* "And he said, An hundred *quarters* of wheat." And so Tyndale and the Rhemish. The Genevan here again has "mesures," and the Authorised follows the Genevan. Wycliffe Anglicises the Latin word "*coros tritici*," which he found in his Vulgate, and gives "coris of whete." This Latin is the Greek word κόρος Latinised. And the Greek κόρος again is the Hebrew word כֹּר Grecised. "Quarters" is not a happy translation, because the word is never used in a general sense for a large quantity, but always for a specific measure (eight bushels), whereas the "cor," according to the margin of the Authorised, is "about 14 bushels and a pottle." (4) *V. 8.* "For the children of this world are *in their nation* wiser then the children of light." A rendering peculiar to Cranmer. Wycliffe, the Rhemish, and the Authorised have "*generation*"; Tyndale and the Genevan, "in their *kynde.*" The Greek word γενεά has no doubt the meaning of "a race with all its moral and physical peculiarities," "a nation with its characteristics." It would seem to have this meaning in that difficult passage of the Prophecy on the Mount ; "This *generation* shall not pass, till all these things be fulfilled" (St. Matt. xxiv. 34 ; St. Mark xiii. 30), by which we are probably to understand that *the race of the Jews*, characterized, as heretofore, by perversity and unbelief, shall remain on the stage of the world till the time of the end. There "nation" would convey a more accurate idea of the meaning than "generation"; but here the word seems out of place. What is meant,—whether by the "nation," or the "generation," of "the children of this world,"—is people like-minded with themselves.—All the English Versions, down to that of 1881, have missed the force of the preposition εἰς. *Here* it means "in reference to" (as in Acts xxv. 20, ἀπορούμενος εἰς τὴν περὶ τούτου ζήτησιν ; "doubting *in regard to* a question of this sort"; and St. Luke xii. 21, ὁ μὴ εἰς Θεὸν πλουτῶν "he that is not rich *in reference to* God "). The children of this world are, *in regard to* persons like-minded with themselves,—their own kith and kin,—wiser than the children of light. (5) *V. 9.* "that, *when ye shall have need*, they may receive you," etc. Here again "have need" is peculiar to Cranmer. Wycliffe, the Rhemish, and the Authorised all have "fail"; Tyndale and the Genevan, "when ye shall departe." As regards classical usage, the word ἐκλείπω, when intransitive, is applied to an eclipse of the sun, and also to that collapse of the natural powers and

faculties which takes place at death. As regards New Testament usage, the word is used of St. Peter's faith, for which our Lord had prayed that it should not fail (St. Luke xxii. 32), and of the years of the Almighty, "thou art the same, and thy years shall not *fail*" (Heb. i. 12). "Have need" is rather too free a translation. The Revisers of 1881, on the strength of a reading in the Vatican and Alexandrine MSS., have rendered, "that, when *it*" (the mammon of unrighteousness) "shall fail"; and it must be admitted that this harmonizes very well with Chap. xii. 33, where our Lord exhorts His disciples to "provide themselves a treasure in the heavens *that faileth not*" (θησαυρὸν ἀνέκλειπτον ἐν τοῖς οὐρανοῖς). The "mammon of unrighteousness," unlike the treasure in the heavens, sooner or later *does* fail.]

Sunday.—My first consideration shall be the connexion in which this Parable stands, which will be found to throw great light upon the true interpretation of it. It stands midway, then, between two other remarkable Parables,[1]—that of the Prodigal Son, and that of Dives and Lazarus. Our Lord had been cavilled at by the Pharisees for receiving sinners and eating with them[2]; receiving and eating with the many publicans and sinners, who had thronged to hear Him; this was the occasion from which the whole discourse took its rise. He justifies His having done so by representing, in the Parables of the Lost Sheep and Lost Coin,[3] the earnest solicitude with which Almighty God seeks for the lost sinner, and, in that of the Prodigal Son, the warm welcome which every penitent receives to the heart and home of the heavenly Father. The many publicans and sinners who had drawn near to hear Him, and His reception of whom had so scandalized the Pharisees and Scribes, must have taken heart at these gracious words, and doubtless were much touched and softened by them. Their heavenly Father was quite

---

[1] St. Luke xv. 11 *to the end;* St. Luke xvi. 19 *to the end.*
[2] St. Luke xv. 1, 2.   [3] St. Luke xv. 3 *to* 11.

ready to receive them, without so much as a remonstrance
against those dishonest courses in time past, which had
won for them not only the condemnation of their own
conscience, but also a bad name among their countrymen.
But many of these men had enriched themselves with ques-
tionably gotten gains ; and their conscience, quickened by
the Lord's words, tells them that some good use must be
made of the money they had amassed ; and they begin
to crave guidance on this point from their new Master.
The Parable of the Unjust Steward is designed to show
them that they must make as wise and prudent a use, in
reference to their *eternal* interests, of the property which
God still allowed them to retain, as the steward made of
his Master's property in order to secure his *worldly* interests.   They must act on Zacchæus's principle—make
fourfold restitution, where it was possible, of ill-gotten
gains, and give half of their goods to feed the poor.[1]   The
Pharisees, who were covetous, hearing this instruction,
derided our Lord for giving it[2] ; and it was in view of
their covetousness and hardness of heart that He spoke
the parable of Dives and Lazarus, which exhibits in such
awful colours the end of those who, wrapped round in
their own luxuries and comforts, show no sympathy with
the sufferings of God's poor.

Monday.—Out of the above survey of the connexion
in which the Parable stands, arises the thought that
the whole work of grace is not over, when a sinner has
been accepted and forgiven ; that God has a course of
action for him to pursue, after he has found pardon and
peace through the blood of the Cross.   These publicans,
who formerly spent on themselves and their own lusts
all they could wring out of their brethren, were now to

---

[1] See St. Luke xix. 8.   [2] See St. Luke xvi. 14.

make their gains subserve the interests of God's poor, and so their own everlasting salvation. If Christ had given them rest from the burdens of an accusing conscience for simply coming to Him, they, after experiencing that rest, were to take His yoke upon them—the yoke of bearing other's burdens[1]—and to learn of Him.[2] The heavenly Father having welcomed them back home, and bestowed on them the robe of acquittal and the ring of dignity,[3] they were to regard all their earthly substance as *His*, and to act accordingly—they were to give all for all. Christ " died for all, that they which live should not henceforth live unto themselves, but unto him which died for them, and rose again."[4]

Tuesday.—The third reflexion shall be, that God will require from us an account of the manner in which we have discharged the stewardship of our worldly goods, and that, therefore, in self - examination we should be able to give some account to ourselves of the way in which we are administering this stewardship. How can this possibly be, let me ask myself, without systematic beneficence? Have I any clear idea how much I am doing for God's Church and God's poor? how much of my means, whether they be small or great, goes to objects of piety and charity? The majority know no more than this, that they usually give something, when appealed to in behalf of any object which has a reasonable claim upon them. But this kind of haphazard giving,—sometimes from generous or compassionate impulse, sometimes in mere compliance with the importunity of others,—is very unlike the preparation for an audit, and the getting accounts into order to meet a day of reckoning. Yet such

---

[1] Gal. vi. 2.

[2] See St Matt. xi. 28, 29.

[3] See St. Luke xv. 20, 22.

[4] 2 Cor. v. 15.

a day of reckoning we know there will be,—not only for the rich, but for all who have more than they need for the maintenance of themselves and those dependent upon them. How that day can satisfactorily be met, without each man's giving on principle a certain proportion of his means, and looking into his affairs from time to time, to see that he is really and honestly giving that proportion, it is hard to understand.

Wednesday.—Let me observe how other Scriptures, and our Lord's own words, lead us on to a wider application of the word stewardship than it has in the connexion in which it here stands. St. Paul, speaking of himself, Apollos, and Cephas in their ministerial capacity, says; " Let a man so account of us, as of the ministers of Christ, and *stewards* of the mysteries of God. Moreover," he adds, " it is required in stewards, that a man be found *faithful.*" [1] St. Peter adopts the same image, " As every man hath received the gift, even so minister the same one to another, as good *stewards* of the manifold grace of God." [2] Both Apostles borrowed this image from their Master. In the twelfth Chapter of this Gospel, our Lord had spoken of His ministers as stewards over His household; " Who then is that faithful and wise *steward*, whom his lord shall make ruler over his household, to give them their portion of meat in due season ?" [3] And the parable before us, which sets forth only *the wisdom* of a certain steward who acted most *unfaithfully*, is guarded from misapprehension by what follows about the faithfulness, which is the steward's other qualification—" He that is faithful in that which is least is faithful also in much; and he that is unjust in the least is unjust also in much." [4]

---

[1] 1 Cor. iv. 1, 2.　　　　　　[2] 1 Pet. iv. 10.
[3] *V* 42.　　　　　　　　　　[4] St. Luke xvi. 10.

We are taught hereby that those gifts and endowments, which are qualifications for the Christian ministry, are just as entirely gifts of God, and just as independent of man's will, as what we commonly call gifts of fortune, meaning thereby large resources ; and that these higher endowments, like the gifts of fortune, must be laid out in God's service, and made to bear interest for His glory.

Thursday. — My Thursday's thought shall be the mercifulness of God in sending us warnings, and the use which is to be made of them. The steward had not his stewardship taken away at his first interview with his lord. He was allowed a certain period to make up his accounts, and justify his conduct, if it admitted of justification. So God does not usually call us before His judgment seat in an instant of time, but allows us a period to collect ourselves, and consider what account we shall present. By failing health ; or by the removal of some dear friend, who has for many years walked hand in hand, side by side, with us ; or by the growing infirmities of age, making us feel unable " to dig,"—that is, to work any longer with energy in His vineyard ; He says to each of us, " Give an account of thy stewardship ; for thou mayest be no longer steward." How merciful is this arrangement ! In grateful acknowledgment of it, the Psalmist sings, " I will thank the Lord for giving me warning." [1] And in deprecation of any such sudden call to judgment as would preclude the possibility of preparation, the Church prays ; " From murder, and from sudden death, Good Lord, deliver us."

Friday.—V. 2. " Give an account of thy stewardship." I will ask myself whether I hold fairly before the eyes of my mind, and without allowing myself to blink it, the

[1] Ps. xvi. 8, P.B.V.

doctrine of judgment to come according to works. "So then every one of us" (see how individual the scrutiny is to be, so that there will be no hope of passing muster in the crowd) "shall give account of himself to God."[1] "We must all appear" (literally, *be manifested*—all disguises which have here hidden our character, even in some degree from ourselves, will be stripped off) "before the judgment seat of Christ; that every one may receive the things done in the body."[2] It is true, no doubt, that the judgment of the great day is to a certain degree forestalled by the offering of Christ to men's faith, and by their acceptance or non-acceptance of that offer, according to that word to Nicodemus, "He that believeth not is condemned already, because he hath not believed in the name of the only begotten Son of God."[3] But it is quite possible to unite ourselves once to Christ by true faith, and yet not to abide in Him. Whence the force of the exhortation, "Abide in me, and I in you"[4]; "And now, little children, abide in him; that when he shall appear, we may have confidence, and not be ashamed before him at his coming."[5]

Saturday. — V. 8. I will conclude with the great moral of the parable, the superior wisdom of the children of this world in their generation,—that is, in their own earthly sphere,—to that of the children of light in *their* sphere. With what energy, and heart, and singleness of purpose, and self-devotion, will a man toil for earthly honours and distinctions; but how does the energy collapse, when you seek to bring it to bear upon a heavenly crown! How supremely prudent will a man be in making provision long beforehand for the earthly future of himself,

---

[1] Rom. xiv. 12.   [2] 2 Cor. v. 10.   [3] St. John iii. 18.
[4] St. John xv. 4.   [5] 1 John ii. 28.

and those who are to come after him ; while yet he will consent to huddle up all provision for eternity into a week or two preceding death, when the faculties are failing, the mind clouded and rambling, and there are not so much as the dregs of a life to offer to God!   How keenly alive will he be to his own worldly interests, and how culpably negligent or grossly stupid about any thing which menaces his eternal well-being !   Surely in the conduct of worldly men, in their own department of thought and action, we might learn many a holy lesson, which, if we laid it to heart and acted it out in higher concerns, might make us wise unto salvation.

Chapter XLIV

THE GOSPEL FOR THE TENTH SUNDAY AFTER TRINITY.

St. Luke xix. 41, *to the middle of 47.*

41 𝕬𝖓𝖉 𝖜𝖍𝖊𝖓 𝖍𝖊 𝖜𝖆𝖘 𝖈𝖔𝖒𝖊 𝖓𝖊𝖆𝖗, 𝖍𝖊 𝖇𝖊𝖍𝖊𝖑𝖉 𝖙𝖍𝖊 𝖈𝖎𝖙𝖞, 𝖆𝖓𝖉 𝖜𝖊𝖕𝖙 𝖔𝖛𝖊𝖗
42 𝖎𝖙, 𝖘𝖆𝖞𝖎𝖓𝖌, 𝕴𝖋 𝖙𝖍𝖔𝖚 𝖍𝖆𝖉𝖘𝖙 𝖐𝖓𝖔𝖜𝖓, 𝖊𝖛𝖊𝖓 𝖙𝖍𝖔𝖚, 𝖆𝖙 𝖑𝖊𝖆𝖘𝖙 𝖎𝖓 𝖙𝖍𝖎𝖘 𝖙𝖍𝖞 𝖉𝖆𝖞, 𝖙𝖍𝖊 𝖙𝖍𝖎𝖓𝖌𝖘 𝖜𝖍𝖎𝖈𝖍 𝖇𝖊𝖑𝖔𝖓𝖌 𝖚𝖓𝖙𝖔 𝖙𝖍𝖞 𝖕𝖊𝖆𝖈𝖊! 𝖇𝖚𝖙 𝖓𝖔𝖜 𝖙𝖍𝖊𝖞 𝖆𝖗𝖊 𝖍𝖎𝖉
43 𝖋𝖗𝖔𝖒 𝖙𝖍𝖎𝖓𝖊 𝖊𝖞𝖊𝖘. 𝕱𝖔𝖗 𝖙𝖍𝖊 𝖉𝖆𝖞𝖘 𝖘𝖍𝖆𝖑𝖑 𝖈𝖔𝖒𝖊 𝖚𝖕𝖔𝖓 𝖙𝖍𝖊𝖊, 𝖙𝖍𝖆𝖙 𝖙𝖍𝖎𝖓𝖊 𝖊𝖓𝖊𝖒𝖎𝖊𝖘 𝖘𝖍𝖆𝖑𝖑 𝖈𝖆𝖘𝖙 𝖆 𝖙𝖗𝖊𝖓𝖈𝖍 𝖆𝖇𝖔𝖚𝖙 𝖙𝖍𝖊𝖊, 𝖆𝖓𝖉 𝖈𝖔𝖒𝖕𝖆𝖘𝖘 𝖙𝖍𝖊𝖊 𝖗𝖔𝖚𝖓𝖉, 𝖆𝖓𝖉
44 𝖐𝖊𝖊𝖕 𝖙𝖍𝖊𝖊 𝖎𝖓 𝖔𝖓 𝖊𝖛𝖊𝖗𝖞 𝖘𝖎𝖉𝖊, 𝖆𝖓𝖉 𝖘𝖍𝖆𝖑𝖑 𝖑𝖆𝖞 𝖙𝖍𝖊𝖊 𝖊𝖛𝖊𝖓 𝖜𝖎𝖙𝖍 𝖙𝖍𝖊 𝖌𝖗𝖔𝖚𝖓𝖉, 𝖆𝖓𝖉 𝖙𝖍𝖞 𝖈𝖍𝖎𝖑𝖉𝖗𝖊𝖓 𝖜𝖎𝖙𝖍𝖎𝖓 𝖙𝖍𝖊𝖊: 𝖆𝖓𝖉 𝖙𝖍𝖊𝖞 𝖘𝖍𝖆𝖑𝖑 𝖓𝖔𝖙 𝖑𝖊𝖆𝖛𝖊 𝖎𝖓 𝖙𝖍𝖊𝖊 𝖔𝖓𝖊 𝖘𝖙𝖔𝖓𝖊 𝖚𝖕𝖔𝖓 𝖆𝖓𝖔𝖙𝖍𝖊𝖗, 𝖇𝖊𝖈𝖆𝖚𝖘𝖊 𝖙𝖍𝖔𝖚 𝖐𝖓𝖊𝖜𝖊𝖘𝖙 𝖓𝖔𝖙 𝖙𝖍𝖊 𝖙𝖎𝖒𝖊 𝖔𝖋 𝖙𝖍𝖞 𝖛𝖎𝖘𝖎-
45 𝖙𝖆𝖙𝖎𝖔𝖓. 𝕬𝖓𝖉 𝖍𝖊 𝖜𝖊𝖓𝖙 𝖎𝖓𝖙𝖔 𝖙𝖍𝖊 𝖙𝖊𝖒𝖕𝖑𝖊, 𝖆𝖓𝖉 𝖇𝖊𝖌𝖆𝖓 𝖙𝖔 𝖈𝖆𝖘𝖙 𝖔𝖚𝖙 𝖙𝖍𝖊𝖒
46 𝖙𝖍𝖆𝖙 𝖘𝖔𝖑𝖉 𝖙𝖍𝖊𝖗𝖊𝖎𝖓, 𝖆𝖓𝖉 𝖙𝖍𝖊𝖒 𝖙𝖍𝖆𝖙 𝖇𝖔𝖚𝖌𝖍𝖙, 𝖘𝖆𝖞𝖎𝖓𝖌 𝖚𝖓𝖙𝖔 𝖙𝖍𝖊𝖒, 𝕴𝖙 𝖎𝖘 𝖜𝖗𝖎𝖙𝖙𝖊𝖓, 𝕸𝖞 𝖍𝖔𝖚𝖘𝖊 𝖎𝖘 𝖙𝖍𝖊 𝖍𝖔𝖚𝖘𝖊 𝖔𝖋 𝖕𝖗𝖆𝖞𝖊𝖗, 𝖇𝖚𝖙 𝖞𝖊 𝖍𝖆𝖛𝖊 𝖒𝖆𝖉𝖊 𝖎𝖙 𝖆 𝖉𝖊𝖓 𝖔𝖋 𝖙𝖍𝖎𝖊𝖛𝖊𝖘. 𝕬𝖓𝖉 𝖍𝖊 𝖙𝖆𝖚𝖌𝖍𝖙 𝖉𝖆𝖎𝖑𝖞 𝖎𝖓 𝖙𝖍𝖊 𝖙𝖊𝖒𝖕𝖑𝖊.

[Miss. Sar.	1549.	1662. s.n.
In illo tempore, Cum appropinquasset Jesus Hierusalem, videns civitatem flevit super illam, etc. (*Vulg.* Et ut appropinquavit, videns civitatem flevit super illam, etc.)	And when he was come neer *to Jerusalem,* he beheld the citie, and wept on it, etc. (The words "to Jerusalem" are an insertion in the Gospel, as it stands in the Black-Letter Prayer Book of 1636 [39 ?]. They are not found in Cranmer's Bible.)	And when he was come near, he beheld the city, and wept over it, etc. (*Gr.* Καὶ ὡς ἤγγισεν, ἰδὼν τὴν πόλιν, ἔκλαυσεν ἐπ' αὐτῇ, etc.)

The connexion indicated by the "And" between this and the previous verses is obvious. It here indicates mere historical sequence. The disciples who escorted our Lord, and threw their garments under the feet of the colt which carried Him, had recognised Him as "the King that cometh in the name of the Lord," and had praised God with a loud voice for all the demonstrations of beneficent miraculous power which they had witnessed (*vv.* 36, 37, 38). This elicited the remonstrance of the Pharisees, bidding our Lord rebuke His disciples. And this in its turn elicited our Lord's justification of the enthusiastic acclamations of His escort (*vv.* 39, 40). Soon after this, the rocky ledge was reached, from which the city burst into full view, rising out of the deep abyss formed by the gorge of the Kedron and the Valley of Hinnom ; and the spectacle moved our Lord to those tears and utterances which form the main subject of this Gospel. "He wept over the city, not over Himself," says Bengel, and compares His words to the daughters of Jerusalem (xxiii. 28).—*Translation of* 1540. (1) *V.* 41. "He beheld the citie, and wept *on it.*" All the five English Versions which preceded the Authorised have "on" or "upon." This rendering gives to the preposition too exclusively local a meaning ; but at the same time, there is force and significance in the idea that the city, lying below in the ravine, was literally bedewed with the Saviour's tears. (2) *V.* 42. "If thou hadst known those things which belong unto thy peace, even in this thy day, *thou wouldest take heed.*" Wycliffe is the only other English Translator, who gives the clause an apodosis which has no existence in the Greek. *His* apodosis is a very forcible one,—"thou shouldest weep also." But it is a mistake to give an apodosis at all. Bishop Wordsworth (who, however, himself supplies the words, "then how blessed would it be !") calls it "an Aposiopesis full of pathos." *Aposiopesis* (to use Winer's words) ["Idioms of the Language of the New Testament" (Philadelphia : 1840), p. 437, § 66] is "the omission of a clause, in consequence of a peculiar excitement of mind, where the gesticulation of the speaker indicates what is wanting." Such an Aposiopesis is equivalent to "Utinam," "Would God that !" We have another instance in the Septuagint Version of Joshua vii. 7 ; Καὶ εἰ κατεμείναμεν καὶ κατῳκίσθημεν παρὰ τὸν Ἰορδάνην ! rendered by the Vulgate, "Utinam, ut coepimus, mansissemus trans Jordanem !" and by the Translators of 1611, "Would to God we had been content, and dwelt on the other side Jordan !" (3) *V.* 43. "For the dayes shall come unto thee, that thine enemies shall cast a *bank* about thee." The "bank" is from Tyndale. Wycliffe has, "shall environ thee with a *pale.*" The Genevan gives, "cast *rampars* about thee." The Rhemish, followed by the Authorised, a "*trench.*" The Revisers of 1881 have gone back to the *bank* of Tyndale and Cranmer, giving "palisade" as an alternative in their margin. And rightly. Χάραξ (the word here used) originally means a vine-prop or stake ; hence (in fortification) a palisade made with stakes at the top of a mound ; and

hence, the mound so palisaded. The "rampars" of the Genevan Version
is also an excellent translation, but not as vernacular a word as "bank."
The form of the word indicates that the final *t* of the more usual form
(rampart) does not belong to the root ; but came from the tendency of the
tongue to pronounce *d* or *t* after liquids. (Thus the old English "houn"
(a dog) became "houn*d*," and "gown," in the mouth of the vulgar, is apt
to become "gown*d*.") Another antique form of the word "rampart"
was "rampire," which Shakspere has turned into a participle (*Timon of
Athens*, Act V. Scene iv.) ;

> "Set but thy foot
> Against our *rampired* gates, and they shall ope,
> So thou wilt send thy gentle heart before,
> To say thou'lt enter friendly."]

Sunday.—Vv. 41, 45. "And when he was come near,
he beheld the city, and wept over it. . . . He went into
the temple, and began to cast out them that sold therein."
I see that this Gospel consists of two narratives which are
closely connected in thought,—the narrative of our Lord's
weeping over Jerusalem, and that of His cleansing the
temple. He would not indulge His grief over the city,
without doing what admitted of being done to remedy the
evil. The indulgence of pious and pathetic sentiments, unless they find vent for themselves in action, will enervate
and injure the character. When Joshua prostrated himself
before the ark of the Lord, on Israel's sustaining a reverse,
and contented himself with lamenting in prayer what had
occurred, there came to him this stirring reproof; "Get
thee up; wherefore liest thou thus upon thy face ? . . .
thou canst not stand before thine enemies, until ye take
away the accursed thing from among you."[1] Admission
to the Kingdom of Heaven is not given to those who say,
"Lord, Lord," nor even to those who prophesy in Christ's
name, and do many wonderful works by the use of it, but
to those only who do the will of the Heavenly Father[2]

---

[1] Joshua vii. 6-11, 13.   [2] See St. Matt. vii. 21, 22, 23.

True religion is a thing not only of sentiment and aspiration, but of moral endeavour.—Lord, let my religion reach beyond the soul, or emotional part of my nature, to the springs of my character. Let it penetrate to, and lay hold of, my conscience, my spirit, my will.

Monday.—Vv. 41, 42. "And when he was come near, he beheld the city, and wept over it, saying, If thou hadst known, even thou, at least in this thy day, the things which belong unto thy peace!" How opportune was the moment chosen by our Lord, for His tears, and His lugubrious predictions of the city's doom! It was the single moment of triumph which occurred in His whole career, when the multitude, unable any longer to restrain their enthusiasm, burst out into acclamations and Hosannas,[1] recognised Him as the predicted successor to David's throne,[2] and welcomed Him to the sacred metropolis with branches of palm trees borne before Him,[3] or strawed under the feet of the ass's colt.[4] Had He shed tears, and foretold the city's downfall, while the Jews were persecuting Him, or after they had apprehended Him, it might have been thought that He was stirred by anger, and spoke the language of threatening. But as it was, He showed most clearly that He was moved to speak by love and compassion, and by an insight into the future which was perfectly calm, and had in it no element of resentment; for it is when His claims are acknowledged that He weeps, and when the city (as it were) opens its arms to receive Him, that He foretells its doom. There is in His tears and lamentations both the heart of love for the sinner, and the eagle eye which foresees at a glance the sinner's doom.—Lord, let me be

---

[1] See St. Matt. xxi. 9, 15.   [2] See St. Mark xi. 10.
[3] See St. John xii. 12, 13.   [4] See St. Matt. xxi. 8 ; St. Mark xi. 8.

moved by Thy awful warnings (all the more awful, because so calm) to flee from the sins which Thou dost denounce, and allured by Thy compassion for sinners, let me seek that refuge under the shadow of Thy wings, which Thou dost so gladly accord.

Tuesday.—V. 41. " He wept over it." I saw yesterday that these tears proceeded from foresight of the sinful city's doom, and compassion for it. I now find in them another element of feeling, that of patriotism. Patriotism is a particular form of love ; it is a preference for our own race, and for the country of our birth, for its manners, language, institutions. That it is a perfectly lawful affection, and does not necessarily imply any narrowness of sentiment, may be concluded from Christ's having exhibited it in His outburst of tenderness over the holy city ; " O Jerusalem, Jerusalem, thou that killest the prophets, and stonest them which are sent unto thee, how often would I have gathered thy children together, even as a hen gathereth her chickens under her wings, and ye would not!"[1] And St. Paul, reflecting truly the spirit of his Master, speaks the language of the most ardent patriotism in his Epistle to the Romans, when he says ; " I could wish that myself were accursed from Christ for my brethren, my kinsmen according to the flesh : who are Israelites ; to whom pertaineth the adoption, and the glory, and the covenants, and the giving of the law, and the service of God, and the promises ; whose are the fathers, and of whom as concerning the flesh Christ came, who is over all, God blessed for ever."[2] If, then, I would follow the example of Christ and His apostles, I must be alive to patriotic sentiments. Am I thus alive ? And do I show my patriotism, not by vapouring assertions of the supe-

---

[1] St. Matt. xxiii. 37.					[2] Rom. ix. 3, 4, 5.

riority of my own country and its laws and institutions, to those of others, but by a cordial interest in the spiritual welfare of the people, in the prospects and progress of the English Church, and in its continued connexion with the State; and by my earnest prayers for national blessings, the extirpation of national sins, and the increase of national piety, reverence, and faith? " O Lord, save the Queen; Send her help from thy holy place, And evermore mightily defend her."[1] "Be pleased to direct and prosper all the consultations of our Parliament to the advancement of thy glory, the good of thy Church, the safety, honour, and welfare of our Sovereign, and her Dominions; that all things may be so ordered and settled by their endeavours, upon the best and surest foundations, that peace and happiness, truth and justice, religion and piety, may be established among us for all generations."[2]

Wednesday.—V. 42. "If thou hadst known, even thou, at least in this thy day, the things which belong unto thy peace!" Our Lord in these words is probably referring to the meaning of the city's name. Jerusalem signifies, " Ye shall see peace"; and hence the Psalmist exhorts; "Pray for the *peace* of Jerusalem,"[3]—that is, pray that she may realise, and answer to, her name. But Jerusalem did *not* know the things which belonged unto her peace; and therefore she did not see peace.—Let me take occasion hence to reflect on the inconsistency between the profession and practice of men. We all " profess and call ourselves Christians"; but might not our Lord justly take up this lamentation over us, " If ye were indeed followers of Christ, as your name denotes! If ye were indeed disciples of mine, according to my own

---

[1] Versicles and Responds in "the Form of Prayer for the Twentieth of June." [2] Prayer for the High Court of Parliament. [3] Ps. cxxii. 6.

test of discipleship, ' Whosoever doth not bear his cross, and come after me, cannot be my disciple '![1] If ye were indeed, as the name of Christ indicates, anointed in your measure with that Spirit which I possess in its fulness,[2] anointed with the Holy Ghost, and with power[3] to do good works, acceptable to God through me !" O Lord, bring my practice more up to a level with my profession ! "From hypocrisy, good Lord, deliver me."[4] "Grant unto" me and "unto all them that are admitted into the fellowship of Christ's Religion, that we may eschew those things that are contrary to our profession, and follow all such things as are agreeable to the same."[5]

Thursday.—Vv. 43, 44. "For the days shall come upon thee, that thine enemies shall cast a trench about thee, and compass thee round, and keep thee in on every side, and shall lay thee even with the ground, and thy children within thee; and they shall not leave in thee one stone upon another." We read, in the Jewish historian Josephus, not only that these predictions were all fulfilled in the destruction of Jerusalem, but also that they were fulfilled against man's desire and intention. Titus "wished," we are told, "to be spared the labour and delay of making the χάρακες and περικύκλωσις (palisades and line of circumvallation). See *Joseph.* B. J. vi. 7, 13. He wished to spare the City and Temple; and it was with great reluctance that he destroyed the city; and the Temple was burned in contravention of his express command." [Bishop Christopher Wordsworth on Vv. 43, 44.] To this we may add that a destruction so complete as to involve the not leaving one stone upon another was hardly

---

[1] St. Luke xiv. 27.   [2] See Ps. xlv. 7 ; and St. John iii. 34 ; i. 16.
[3] See Acts x. 38.   [4] Second Deprecation in the Litany.
[5] Collect for the Third Sunday after Easter.

likely to occur in the ordinary course of things. But Terentius Rufus, by ordering the ploughshare to be passed over the area of the city, literally fulfilled this prediction also.——How certain is God's Word to come to pass eventually, however much man's perverse will may seem to thwart it, and however much circumstances may seem to stand in the way of its fulfilment. God's Word, as announced in Prophecy, is always surely though secretly working itself out amidst all contradictions and oppositions, and will emerge scathless from the severest trials to which its veracity can be put. " The words of the LORD are pure words ; as silver tried in a furnace of earth, purified seven times."[1]——O Lord, of the many millions of souls who have made experience of the truth of Thy word, both in Paradise,[2] and in the realm of unrighteous departed spirits, not one has ever found it to fail. With how great assurance may I rely upon it, both in its threatenings and in its promises ! With each one of us it will be as it was with our fathers. Thy words and Thy statutes will one day "take hold of" us; and we shall " return and say, Like as the LORD of hosts thought to do unto us, according to our ways, and according to our doings, so hath he dealt with us."[3]

Friday.——V. 44. " Because thou knewest not the time of thy visitation." It is very observable that the miseries and ruin of Jerusalem should be traced up merely to a want of discernment. The Lord says not, " Because thou art so sinful; because thou art so full of hypocrisy, superstition, and profaneness ; because thou hast killed the prophets, and stoned them which are sent unto thee ;" but " Because thou knewest not the time of thy

---

[1] Ps. xii. 6.   [2] See Ps. cxix. 89, P.B.V., with St. Luke xxiii. 43.
[3] See Zech. i. 6.

visitation," thou shalt be utterly destroyed.   The Son of
God had visited them with the offers of mercy and grace;
and they were ruined simply because they did not discern
what God's Providence had brought about, and acknowledge the heavenly Visitant.   This want of discernment,
however, was not a mere intellectual fault; it was rooted
in the will; the evidences of Christ's mission given by His
miracles and teaching were clear and convincing; they
did not discern, because they *would* not, and because they
" loved darkness rather than light."[1]—O Lord, it is not
merely sin, however aggravated, which can destroy any
soul that hears Thy Gospel.   What destroys the soul is
the not embracing the remedy against sin, which the
Gospel proffers, and the not discerning that it must be
embraced at once, and without delay, lest the opportunity
should pass away for ever.   Oh, then, " to-day, while it
is called to-day,"[2] let me not harden my heart!   "The
stork in the heaven knoweth her appointed times; and the
turtle and the crane and the swallow observe the time of
their coming."[3]   Shall man, when wooed to return to
God by the warm breath of His gracious invitation and
promises, be less discerning, less compliant?   "Behold,
now is the accepted time; behold, now is the day of
salvation."[4]

Saturday.—Vv. 45, 46.   "And he went into the
temple, and began to cast out them that sold therein, and
them that bought; saying unto them, It is written, My
house is the house of prayer: but ye have made it a den
of thieves."   This was the second cleansing of the temple.
It took place at the close of our Lord's ministry.   He had
cleansed it previously at the opening of His ministry, as

----

[1] See St. John iii. 19.   [2] See Heb. iii. 7, 8, 13, 15.
[3] Jer. viii. 7.   [4] 2 Cor. vi. 2.

we find from St. John ii. 13-18, and had on that occasion chastised the buyers and sellers with a scourge of small cords made by His own hands.[1]   Then He had called the temple His Father's house[2]; here He calls it a house of prayer.   It was very dear to Him under both titles.   The tabernacle first, and the temple afterwards, were made according to the pattern showed to Moses in the mount[3]; and the priests who officiated there, "served unto the example and shadow of heavenly things."[4]   The temple, therefore, and its worship reminded our Lord of His Father's heavenly house, from which He came to our inhospitable shores, just as the native of a tropical climate, banished to the polar regions, might be reminded of his country by the sight of some beautiful flower, or some bird of gorgeous plumage.   But the temple was dear to our Lord, not only as Son of God, but also as Son of man. As Son of man, and as sinless, He breathed habitually an atmosphere of prayer; the house of prayer, therefore, had a natural congeniality to Him.—O Lord, let the church, which is no less a house of prayer than the temple was, have a congeniality for me also!   Inspire me with some of that hatred of desecration and profaneness, which is a feature of Thine own mind, and let me not fall behind the saints of the old Covenant in love and longing for the places and the exercises of worship!   "How amiable are thy tabernacles, O LORD of hosts !   My soul longeth, yea, even fainteth for the courts of the LORD : my heart and my flesh crieth out for the living God. . . . Blessed are they that dwell in thy house : they will be still praising thee."[5]

---

[1] See St. John ii. 15.   [2] *Ibid.*, *v.* 16.
[3] See Heb. viii. 5.   [4] *Ibid.*   [5] Ps. lxxxiv. 1, 2, 4.

CHAPTER XLV

THE GOSPEL FOR THE ELEVENTH SUNDAY AFTER TRINITY.

St. Luke xviii. 9 *to* 15

(substituting "Jesus" for "And he" in the beginning of *v.* 9).

9 Jesus spake this parable unto certain which trusted in them-
10 selves, that they were righteous, and despised others; Two men
went up into the temple to pray; the one a Pharisee, and the other
11 a Publican. The Pharisee stood and prayed thus with himself,
God, I thank thee, that I am not as other men are, extortioners,
12 unjust, adulterers, or even as this Publican. I fast twice in the
13 week, I give tithes of all that I possess. And the Publican
standing afar off, would not lift up so much as his eyes unto
heaven, but smote upon his breast, saying, God be merciful to me a
14 sinner. I tell you, this man went down to his house justified
rather than the other: for every one that exalteth himself, shall be
abased; and he that humbleth himself, shall be exalted.

[Miss. Sar.	1549.	1662 s.b.
In illo tempore, Dixit *Jesus* ad quosdam qui in se confidebant tanquam justi et aspernabantur ceteros parabolam istam, *dicens,* etc. (*Vulg.* Dixit autem et ad quosdam, qui in se confidebant tamquam justi, et aspernabantur ceteros, parabolam istam : Duo homines, etc.)	Christ told this parable unto certain which trusted in themselves that they were perfect, and despised other. Two men, etc. (*Cranmer.* And he told this parable unto certain which, etc.)	Jesus spake this parable unto certain which trusted in themselves, that they were righteous, and despised others ; Two men, etc. (*Gr.* Εἶπε δὲ καὶ πρός τινας τοὺς πεποιθότας ἐφ' ἑαυτοῖς ὅτι εἰσὶ δίκαιοι, καὶ ἐξουθενοῦντας τοὺς λοιπούς, τὴν παραβολὴν ταύτην, etc.)

We have seen that the 1549 Gospel for the Second Sunday after Easter, began "Christ said"; but there in the Black-Letter Prayer Book of 1636 [39 ?] Sancroft has drawn his pen through the word "Christ," and written "Jesus" over it. Here there is no such erasure.—It is to be regretted that the "And" and "also," which the Received Greek Text exhibits in *v.* 9, are omitted from the Liturgical Gospel. They refer us back to the immediately foregoing Parable of the Unjust Judge, which is introduced by a similar formula, (*v.* 1) Ἔλεγε δὲ καὶ παραβολὴν αὐτοῖς, πρὸς τὸ δεῖν, etc. "And he spake also a parable to them to this end, that men ought always to pray," etc. The sequence of thought between the two Parables is thus given by Archbishop Trench ; "The aim of the last Parable was to teach us the need that prayer should be earnest and persevering, the aim of this is to teach us that it must also be humble ; it furnishes a commentary on the words of St. James : 'God resisteth the proud, but giveth grace unto the humble.'" And thus by Stier (*in loc.*); "Taking the two parables together, we have in conjunction the boldness of faith and the depth of humility which co-exist in all true prayer." See both the boldness of faith and the depth of humility exemplified in the Syrophœnician woman (St. Matt. xv. 22, 25, 27).—*Translation of* 1540. (1) *V.* 9. "Christ *told* this parable unto certain," etc. *Told* is a rendering peculiar to Cranmer. The verb ἔπω is sometimes so translated, though not in similar constructions ; thus, "*Tell* his disciples and Peter that he goeth before you into Galilee" (St. Mark xvi. 7) ; "*Tell* us, when shall these things be ?" (St. Mark xiii. 4) ; "If it were not so, I would have *told* you " (St. John xiv. 2); "*Tell* me where thou hast laid him" (St. John xx. 15). We use the word to "tell" of a story ; and what is the Parable before us but a story ? "If the term Parable were used in its very strictest sense, it would not be here applied ; for there is no comparison here of one set of things with another ; the Pharisee stands for himself, the specimen indeed of a class, and of that class the representative, but not representing any body besides, and in like manner the publican." (Archbishop Trench, "Notes on the Parables.") (2) *V.* 9. "which trusted in themselves that they were *perfect*." Why δίκαιοι should be rendered "perfect" instead of "righteous" (which is its ordinary and every way appropriate meaning) it is hard to say ; but Tyndale rendered it so before Cranmer, and the Genevan followed suit. Old Wycliffe, as so often happens, was much nearer the mark ; "sum men that tristid in hem silf as thei weren *rigtful*" ("quosdam, qui in se confidebant tamquam *justi*," *Vulg.*)]

Sunday.—Vv. 11, 12. What were the defects in the Pharisee's prayer ? Let me try to ascertain them by comparing his language with that of St. Paul, who was a reclaimed and converted Pharisee, and who in his Epistles speaks under the influence of the Holy Spirit.   St. Paul, in the portion of Scripture appointed as the Epistle for this Sunday, says; " I am the least of the apostles, that am not meet to be called an apostle, because I persecuted the church of God. But by the grace of God I am what I am: and his grace which was bestowed upon me was not in vain; but I laboured more abundantly than they all: yet not I, but the grace of God which was with me."[1]   Contrasted as this avowal is with the Pharisee's prayer, there are points of resemblance between them.   As far as his language goes, the Pharisee did not, any more than St. Paul, take to himself the credit of his own righteousness; for he says, " God, I thank thee that I am not as other men are." And, again, St. Paul did not, any more than the Pharisee, conceal what he had done for God, but openly avowed it. " I laboured more abundantly than all the other apostles," says he.   In our approaches to God there is to be no mock modesty, no false humility.   God is " a God of truth,"[2] and with nothing but truth can He be pleased.   As the Pharisee had mortified the flesh by fasting twice in the week, and had given liberally to the support of God's ministers, there was no reason why he should suppress this fact in his prayer, if only he made his religious attainments a subject of thankfulness, as he did ; " God, I thank thee that I am not as other men are."   The perfect truthfulness with which we should approach the God of truth, may well form the subject of my Sunday's meditation.

Monday. — Where, then, was the difference — the enormous, fundamental difference — between the two avowals ?   In this, that in the one there was a poignant

---

[1] 1 Cor. xv. 9, 10.   [2] See Deut. xxxii. 4.

confession of sin and a profound humility, whereas in the other no trace whatever appears of any such sentiment. St. Paul says (and, as he speaks under the inspiration of the Holy Ghost, he speaks truly, and means what he says; his word is a true expression of his thought), " I am the least of the apostles, that am not meet to be called an apostle, because I persecuted the church of God." No doubt St. Peter would have said much the same thing of *himself;* " I am not meet to be called an apostle, because I denied the Master." St. Paul disparages himself in comparison with others, and expressly says that the eminence over others, to which he had eventually attained, was due, not to himself at all, but to God's grace working in him. Peter and John, and the rest, had never persecuted God's church as he had, never imbrued their hands in the blood of martyrs, and though it was true that afterwards he had laboured more abundantly than they all, yet these abundant labours were to be ascribed, not to him, but to the grace of God which was with him. Whereas the Pharisee disparages others in comparison with himself; " God, I thank thee that I am not as other men are, . . . or even as this publican." The profound humility which must characterize acceptable prayer, shall then be my Monday's thought. And, indeed, this is the thread of connexion between this parable and the immediately foregoing one of the Unjust Judge. The lesson taught by that is importunity in prayer. But, however importunate you may be, though you should pray seven times a day, you will never receive anything, unless you pray in a spirit of unfeigned humility, and under a deep sense of need; for, indeed, this sense of need constitutes our receptivity of God's grace; it is the capacity which He has to fill with His blessing.

Tuesday.——Another grand defect in the Pharisee's prayer is the unreasonable and unscriptural doctrine of works of supererogation, which makes its appearance in it. The Jews were only bound by the Law to fast once in the year,——on the day of Atonement.[1]　And it was thought doubtful whether the tithe-law extended beyond the fruit of the field and the produce of cattle.　But this Pharisee ostentatiously alleges that he does more in both these respects than of bounden duty is. required; "I fast twice in the week, I give tithes of all that I possess" (more literally, of everything which I *acquire*, of all my gains in the way of business).[2]　But the first and great commandment of the Law requires that we shall love the Lord our God with all our heart, and with all our soul, and with all our mind, and with all our strength[3]; and it is absurd to suppose that any human obedience, even that which the perfectly sinless Saviour Himself rendered to the Law of God, can go beyond this, can reach a point in advance of this "loving with all the heart, and all the mind, and all the soul, and all the strength."　And with the doctrine of works of supererogation, that of indulgences,——which is the power claimed by the Pope, of making available to the pardon of sins the superfluous merits of the saints,—— falls also to the ground.　Let me, for my Tuesday's thought, read carefully and weigh the Fourteenth Article, "On Works of Supererogation."

Wednesday.——Let me now turn to the publican's prayer.　What were the grounds of its acceptability?　The answer is, that it was the expression of repentance and faith, which are the conditions of our acceptance with

---

[1] See Lev. xxiii. 27, 29, and *cf.* Acts xxvii. 9.

[2] The Revised Version has; "I give tithes of *all that I get.*"

[3] See St. Mark xii. 30.

God. First, of repentance (this shall be my Wednesday's thought). He " stood afar off "—in the background ;—was afraid to draw near ; he " would not lift up so much as his eyes to heaven"; when he came into God's temple, where he had been seldom seen before, the sacredness of the Presence, in which he was standing, made him ashamed of himself and his past life ; he " smote upon his breast," a gesture expressive of self-accusation, as if the person using it would strike his heart, because it had led him astray. And this short, but effective and penetrative, prayer broke from him, " God be merciful to me a sinner " (or, as it is literally, " the sinner"). He is not in a mood for comparisons ; he forgets that other men are sinners too ; only two beings, himself and his God, are present to his mind,—God high and holy and of awful purity,[1] himself all vile and defiled, " the sinful one." Repentance, then, sincere and profound, is one essential element of acceptable prayer. And, in order to learn how we may attain such repentance, we will draw into use another passage, which also makes mention of smiting the breast. " And all the people that came together to that sight " (the crucifixion of Christ), " beholding the things which were done, smote their breasts, and returned."[2] Stand under the cross, gazing up to the figure of thy Lord, and make the reflexion that it was thy sin which drove those cruel nails into the extremities, and drew from the Divine Sufferer the agonizing cry that God had forsaken Him, and then shalt thou, too, with this publican, smite upon thy breast and say, " God be merciful to me a sinner."

Thursday.—There was faith, too, in the publican's prayer,—faith in a Sacrifice which he would fain plead for himself. For I cannot account it an accidental and

---

[1] See Isaiah lvii. 15.   [2] St. Luke xxiii. 48.

insignificant circumstance that the word translated " be
merciful," is a peculiar and rare word,[1] only once again
occurring in the New Testament, where it is translated
" to make reconciliation for," and applied to " the sins of
the people."[2]   One of the cognate substantives is translated " propitiation " in St. John's First Epistle[3]; another
also translated " propitiation " in the Epistle to the
Romans,[4] and "mercy-seat" in the Epistle to the Hebrews.[5]
It was before the mercy-seat that the blood of the sin-
offering was sprinkled, and atonement made; and it is,
therefore, clear that the words of the publican, as we have
them in the original, are designed to express, not a vague
hope in God's mercy, but *a prayer for reconciliation* (an
idea with which every Jew would be familiar), *on the
ground of sacrifice;* " God be propitiated to me the sinful
one."   His prayer is not a half-despairing cry; there is
confidence and hope in it.   And now that the way of
salvation is fully revealed to sinners through the blood
and merits of Jesus, much more does God require confidence and hope as an essential element of every prayer,
which He will condescend to accept and answer.

Friday.—V. 9. My Friday's thought shall turn on
the words " certain which despised others."   Contempt of
others is said by theologians to be the greatest sin which
a man can commit against his neighbour, greater even
than hatred ; because hatred may consist with a lively

---

[1] Ὁ Θεὸς, ἱλάσθητί μοι τῷ ἁμαρτωλῷ. The Revisers of 1881 give us
in their margin the rendering, "Be propitiated."

[2] εἰς τὸ ἱλάσκεσθαι τὰς ἁμαρτίας τοῦ λαοῦ.   Heb. ii. 17.

[3] See 1 John ii. 2, αὐτὸς ἱλασμός ἐστι περὶ τῶν ἁμαρτιῶν ἡμῶν; and iv.
10, ἀπέστειλε τὸν υἱὸν αὐτοῦ ἱλασμὸν περὶ τῶν ἁμαρτιῶν ἡμῶν.

[4] See Rom. iii. 25.   "Whom God hath set forth to be a *propitiation*,"
—ὃν προέθετο ὁ Θεὸς ἱλαστήριον.

[5] See Heb. ix. 5. "cherubims of glory shadowing *the mercy-seat*,"—
Χερουβὶμ δόξης, κατασκιάζοντα τὸ ἱλαστήριον.

appreciation of the power and ability of the person hated ; but contempt is a setting at nought of our neighbour—the making no account of him, morally or intellectually, or both. " Why dost thou set at nought thy brother ?"[1] says St. Paul. This contempt of others is a great snare, which besets all moral and intellectual progress, and against which those who are really making such progress must be carefully on their guard ; for it will spoil all their attainments, just as one dead fly causes the ointment of the apothecary to send forth a stinking savour.[2] What does God tell us of His mind towards those who say, " Stand by thyself, come not near to me ; for I am holier than thou "? He tells us that He hates them ; " These are a smoke in my nose, a fire that burneth all the day."[3] One way of avoiding this sin is seriously to reflect, in the case of every one we feel inclined to despise, that God loved him so dearly as to give His Son for him ; that Christ loved him so dearly as to shed His blood for him ; that the sacrifice of Christ was as really and truly designed for him, as if there had been no other person in the world for whom it was designed but this despised neighbour of ours, whom we forsooth make of no account.

Saturday.—V. 14. The publican " *went down to his house justified,*" having found favour and acceptance with God, and having a sweet sense of that acceptance shed abroad in his heart. My Saturday's exercise shall be one of self-examination as to the frame of mind in which I leave church, and return home. Glad that the service is over, and that the restraint which it laid upon my loquacity, my levity, my high spirits, is at an end ? Or, if not this, yet feeling a sort of satisfaction that I have done a good deed, which will tell in my favour when the account of

---

[1] Rom. xiv. 10.   [2] See Eccles. x. 1.   [3] Isaiah lxv. 5.

my life is summed up before the "great white throne"?[1]
Or have I " gone down to my house " really refreshed and
strengthened, carrying away some new insight into truth,
or, better still, some new impulse in the way of righteousness ?   The publican carried away acceptance from his
prayer in the temple, the Ethiopian eunuch joy from the
administration to him of the Sacrament of Baptism ; " he
went on his way rejoicing."[2]   It ought to be a part of our
devotions, not only to prepare for them reverently beforehand, but also to ascertain what fruit we have reaped
from their performance.

[1] See Rev. xx. 11.   [2] See Acts viii. 39.

Chapter XLVI.

THE GOSPEL FOR THE TWELFTH SUNDAY AFTER TRINITY.

St. Mark vii. 31 *to the end*
(substituting "Jesus" for "And again," with which *v.* 31 commences,
and omitting "he" before "came").

31   Jesus departing from the coasts of Tyre and Sidon, came unto
the sea of Galilee, through the midst of the coasts of Decapolis.
32 And they bring unto him one that was deaf, and had an impediment
in his speech; and they beseech him to put his hand upon him.
33 And he took him aside from the multitude, and put his fingers into
34 his ears, and he spit, and touched his tongue; and looking up to
heaven, he sighed, and said unto him, Ephphatha, that is, Be
35 opened. And straitway his ears were opened, and the string of his
36 tongue was loosed, and he spake plain. And he charged them that
they should tell no man; but the more he charged them, so much
37 the more a great deal they published it, and were beyond measure
astonished, saying, He hath done all things well; he maketh both
the deaf to hear, and the dumb to speak.

[Miss. Sar.	1549.	1662 s.b.
In illo tempore, Exiens *Jesus* de finibus Tyri, venit per Sidonem ad mare Galilææ inter medios fines Decapoleos. (*Vulg.* Et iterum exiens de finibus Tyri, venit per Sidonem, etc.)	Jesus departed from the coasts of Tyre and Sidon, and came unto the sea of Galilee, through the mids of the coasts of the ten cities.	Jesus departing from the coasts of Tyre and Sidon, came unto the sea of Galilee, through the midst of the coasts of Decapolis. (*Gr.* Καὶ πάλιν ἐξελθὼν ἐκ τῶν ὁρίων Τύρου καὶ Σιδῶνος, ἦλθε πρὸς τὴν θάλασσαν τῆς Γαλιλαίας, ἀνὰ μέσον τῶν ὁρίων Δεκαπόλεως.)

The "And again" (dropped in the Liturgical Gospel), with which *v.* 31 commences, refers us back to *v.* 24, "And from thence he arose, and *went into the borders of Tyre and Sidon,* and entered into an house, and would have no man know it : but he could not be hid." Into this house the Syrophœnician woman came to Him, and urged her plea for her possessed daughter with ultimate success. No other incident is recorded during our Lord's residence in this district. Perhaps He did no other great work there, as if to show that He had come into that distant region, bordering on heathendom, in order to give that poor woman her opportunity. His return from the district to the more usual scenes of His ministry is indicated by the "And again" with which *v.* 31 commences. On the authority of the Sinaitic and Vatican MSS. the Revisers of 1881 have adopted the reading ἐκ τῶν ὁρίων Τύρου ἦλθε διὰ Σιδῶνος εἰς τὴν θάλασσαν, etc.,—"he went out from the borders of Tyre, and came *through Sidon* unto the sea of Galilee," etc. Wycliffe, translating from the Vulgate (which has "Exiens de finibus Tyri, venit *per Sidonem* ad Mare Galilææ"), has the same rendering ; "And eftsones ihesus gede out fro the coostis of tire, and cam *thorug sidon* to the see of galile." The Rhemish Version has the same ; "going out of the coastes of Tyre, he came *by Sidon* to the sea of Galilee."—As regards the numerous miracles which our Lord performed on His return, Archbishop Trench says ("Notes on the Miracles" [London : 1856] p. 345) ; "St. Matthew tells us in general terms how when Jesus had returned from those coasts of Tyre and Sidon unto the sea of Galilee, 'great multitudes came unto him, having with them those that were lame, blind, dumb, maimed, and many others, and cast them down at Jesus' feet, and he healed them' (xv. 30) ; but out of this multitude of cures St. Mark selects one to relate more in detail, and this no doubt because it was signalised by some circumstances not usual in other like cases of healing."— This miracle presents a strong contrast to its immediate predecessor,—that wrought upon the Syrophœnician's daughter. Our Lord had to *awaken* in the deaf and dumb man the faith, which was necessary in order to his restoration, which He did (as he could reach his mind in no other way than through the eye and the touch) by putting His finger into his ears and touching his tongue with saliva (see the Thought for *Tuesday*). The Syrophœnician, on the other hand, had her faith fully awake and in exercise, and Christ had nothing to do but to elicit it in all its power, that He might commend and eventually reward it.—*Translation of* 1540. (1) *V.* 31. "Through the mids of the coasts of the ten cities." And so Tyndale. Wycliffe, probably not understanding that "Decapoleos" in his Vulgate ("inter medios fines *Decapoleos*") was a genitive case, gives us, "bitwix the myddil of the coostis of decapoleos." The Genevan, and afterwards the Rhemish, give "Decapolis," which the Authorised follows. Canon Cook in "The Speaker's Commentary" (*in loc.*) says; "Decapolis is not, properly speaking, a district, but a name given generally to the territories of ten great cities, of which lists, differing in some points, are given by Josephus . . .; by Pliny . . .; by Ptolemy . . .; and in the Talmud . . . The principal cities were Damascus, Gadara, Hippo, Pella, and Scythopolis or Bethshean." Dean Mansel in the same Commentary (on St. Matt. iv. 25), says; "The nature of the connexion existing between them" (the ten cities) "is by no means clear. The cities usually named are not geographically contiguous, and it is possible that the union was rather based on community of privileges than on locality." If this be so, perhaps "the Ten Cities" gives a rather more accurate idea of the original than "Decapolis."—(2) *V.* 33. "and *did* spit." And so Tyndale and the Genevan. The Authorised gives "and *he* spit." The verb "to spit" has three forms of the past tense, "he spitted" (*Wycliffe*, "he spettid and touchid his tunge"); "he spat" ("when he had thus spoken, he spat on the ground," St. John ix. 6); and finally "he spit," as here, and in the *Merchant of Venice*, Act I. Scene iii. "Fair sir, you spit on me on Wednesday last," where Knight, in the Library Edition of Shakspere, tells us that "*spet* was the more received orthography in Shakspere's time," and therefore in the time of the Authorised Version, though there the form *spet* is not found.]

Sunday.—V. 32. "They beseech him to put his hand upon him." This was the mode in which our Lord generally wrought miraculous cures; and on that account the people request Him to adopt it in the present case. But it is now His will to proceed in another way, to use significant gestures, to touch only the parts affected (the ears and the tongue), to utter a word of power, "Ephphatha." It shall be my Sunday's meditation, then, that we must not prescribe means to God, when we address Him in prayer; that we should simply represent to Him our felt necessities, leaving Him to supply them how and when He sees best. Very often He will extricate us from our difficulties by means which seem most improbable, in a way which we could not possibly have anticipated. The Virgin's prayer was a good one, when she said to her Divine Son, "They have no wine,"[1] doing no more than calling His attention to the need. She had noted in Him, on previous occasions, indications of Divine wisdom, and of His having a great future in store for Him, which led her to believe that He could help simple folks out of their difficulties. So she throws herself upon Him with the assurance of His ability to counsel or help. But, as she had never yet seen a miracle done by Him, she could not have supposed that He would help in the way He actually did, by turning water into wine. Even when we do not see that God can do anything to help us except by a miracle, let us resort to Him with our trouble, and lay it before Him, whatever it be. The disciples of St. John the Baptist, when their master was beheaded, "took up the body, and buried it, and went and told Jesus."[2] It might seem as if our Lord could do nothing to comfort them, except by raising John the Baptist from the dead. But He saw fit to comfort them in quite another way, by Himself being to them a far better, wiser, more helpful Master than they had lost in John.

Monday.—V. 33. "He took him aside from the multitude." So, in the following Chapter, when about to heal the blind man at Bethsaida, we read that "he took him by the hand, and led him out of the town."[3] A certain amount of seclusion and privacy seems to have been in both cases essential to a cure. Let my Monday's thought, then, be that in the din of this world's business, or when hedged in on all sides by human companionships and secular interests, it is impossible for us to hear the still small voice of God addressing our consciences. In which case, if we are to be recovered from our spiritual deafness,

---

[1] St. John ii. 3.   [2] St. Matt. xiv. 12.   [3] St. Mark viii. 23.

one of two things must be done. Either we, by our own act, must voluntarily "enter into our closet and shut our door"[1]—we must seclude ourselves from the world at stated periods for devotion, and mortify that inordinate clinging to its ties and relationships, as well as its affairs, which obstructs our spiritual sensations,—or, if we have not the moral courage for this, God must, as indeed He often does, take the seclusion into His own hands. He must lay us upon a sick bed, and so place us full in front of eternity; or He must bereave us of those whom we have loved only too fondly, and by this enforced loneliness of spirit throw us back upon communion with Himself, much as He dealt with His ancient Church, when He would unseal her ears to the hearing of His Law, taking her apart into the wilderness of Sinai, and afterwards saying, in reference to that seclusion, "I will allure her, and bring her into the wilderness, and speak comfortably unto her."[2]—Which shall it be in my case? Shall I seclude *myself* from the world and the flesh? or shall God do it for me?

Tuesday.—My Tuesday's thought shall be the indispensability of hope to a spiritual cure. This deaf and dumb man could not be cured, unless, first, the expectation of a cure was awakened in his mind. It was with the view of awakening it that our Lord took him apart from the multitude, and, having thus fixed his attention on what He was about to do, then made expressive signs and gestures, putting His fingers into the ears of the patient, as if to penetrate and thus open them, and touching his tongue with saliva, as if to indicate that it should no longer through excessive dryness cleave to the roof of the mouth. Where the patient was able to hear,

[1] See St. Matt. vi. 6.   [2] Hosea ii. 14.

He quickened by a *word* the expectation of a cure, as to the impotent man at the pool of Bethesda, whose infirmity of nearly forty years' standing, and constant disappointments, had trodden out from his heart all hope of ever getting any better, He said, to rouse him from the indifference of despair, "Wilt thou be made whole?"[1] Just so, in dealing with the begging cripple at the Beautiful gate of the temple, Peter and John, by way of exciting hope in him, fasten their eyes on him, and say, "Look on us."[2] Faith is, as St. Paul has called it, "a looking unto Jesus"[3]; and what does the looking unto Jesus imply, but that we have expectations from Him, that we are confident of His power to grant us spiritual recovery? Let us go to Him in a sanguine spirit, "expecting to receive something of Him,"[4] and saying in our hearts, "Remember the word unto thy servant, upon which thou hast caused me to hope"[5]; and we shall not come away empty.

Wednesday.—V. 34. "Looking up to heaven, he sighed, and saith." So at Lazarus' grave our Lord twice groaned in spirit, groaned in Himself,[6] while there also He lifted up His eyes to heaven, before working the miracle.[7] But, as He was going in one moment to relieve the complaint which was under His eyes, to wipe away the tears of the mourners, why should He sigh and groan? why not rather rejoice and exult? Oh, shallow question ! Christ sighs and groans to show His sympathy with the manifold evils and calamities under which men in general are suffering, as the dismal entail of the fall; and of which He remedied (numerous as His miracles were) only

---

[1] See St. John v. 5, 6.   [2] See Acts iii. 2, 4.
[3] See Heb. xii. 2.   [4] See Acts iii. 5.
[5] Ps. cxix. 49.   [6] See St. John xi. 33, 38.   [7] See *v.* 41.

a very small number. It was by His sympathy with all classes of sufferers that He wound His way into the hearts of those He relieved, and so conferred upon them, together with a temporal cure, a high spiritual blessing. Then let me ask myself, whether, in attempting to imitate Him by doing acts of kindness to others, and helping them under their difficulties, I feel and manifest for them a genuine sympathy. A look of kindness, a word or smile of encouragement, will often make a faster friend than " thousands of gold and silver."

Thursday.—" He saith unto him " (not to his senses, not to his ears, or his tongue, but unto *him*), " Be opened." I will make the reflexion that I live in the midst of a spiritual world, which is all around me, and yet of which my senses give me no notice whatever. Plans and plots are possibly being formed against me in the council-chamber of hell; and some evil spirit undertakes to give them effect. On the other hand, I am given in charge to the good angels, and they busy themselves with ministrations about me, of which I am utterly unconscious. God is watching me, Christ is watching me, " the spirits of just men made perfect "[1] are watching me, to see how I acquit myself in my spiritual race. Conversations are held about me, and deepest interest felt in me, and steps taken both to supplant and succour me, in the great unseen realm. But it *is* unseen. I am as immediately in its neighbourhood as a bird in an egg not yet hatched is in the neighbourhood of all the activities of this busy world. But the din of this world deafens me to the voices of that, and matter and the senses are a block shutting me out from the realm of spirits. Lord, say unto me, " Ephphatha, that is, Be opened."

[1] See Heb. xii. 23.

Open all the avenues of communication between my soul and the unseen world. I am by nature deaf to Thy word, and dumb in Thy praise. Open the ears of my understanding, that I may hear Thy voice addressing me through Thy works and through Thy word. " O Lord, open thou my lips ; and my mouth shall shew forth thy praise." [1]

Friday.—Let me regard this miracle of our Lord as an emblem of the spiritual recovery, which He works for all mankind by means of His Gospel. "Faith cometh," says St. Paul, " by hearing, and hearing by the word of God." [2]   And because faith cometh by hearing, Christ sent forth His Apostles to preach the Gospel to every creature ; and "their sound went into all the earth, and their words unto the ends of the world." [3]   "The ears of the deaf" were "unstopped" [4] to hear those words ; and the effect was that from " the dark places of the earth," which, before they were visited by the Gospel, were " full of the habitations of cruelty," [5] there arose songs of praise, just as the announcement made by the angels on Christ's birthnight woke up from a thousand celestial voices the anthem, "Glory to God in the highest, and on earth peace, good will toward men." [6] The Gentiles, who had an impediment in their speech previously, knowing something of prayer, but of prayer to gods who were the offspring of their own superstition, now " spake plainly" the praises of the Triune God, Father, Son, and Holy Ghost.—Let it be my Friday's reflexion that, before I can speak God's praise aright, I must let His word of grace and reconciliation sink down

---

[1] Versicle and Respond after the first Lord's Prayer in the daily Morning and Evening Office, drawn from Ps. li. 15, P.B.V.

[2] Rom. x. 17.   [3] *Ibid. v.* 18.   [4] See Isaiah xxxv. 5.

[5] See Ps. lxxiv. 20.   [6] St. Luke ii. 13, 14.

into my ears,—must obey that invitation, " Incline your ear, and come unto me : hear, and your soul shall live."[1]

Saturday.—My Saturday's meditation shall be on certain words of the Psalmist, which shall enable me to turn this narrative to greater account. " He that planted the ear, shall he not hear?"[2] and we may add, " He that formed the mouth, shall He not speak?" He that has so often restored these faculties, when they were lost, unstopping the ears of the deaf, and making the tongue of the dumb to sing, must He not Himself be absolute Master of them?—The living God, whom I serve, is a hearing God, and a speaking God; a God who has an ear for the faintest suggestion of evil to the conscience, as well as for the faintest whisper of real prayer; a God of whose voice the whole realm of nature, within and without, is full; One who speaks in His works, who speaks in His word, who speaks in the depth of man's spirit. Oh, may I never turn a deaf ear when He speaks to me, dissuading me from sin, persuading me sweetly and lovingly to holiness !

[1] Isaiah lv. 3.　　　　　[2] Ps. xciv. 9.

CHAPTER XLVII

THE GOSPEL FOR THE THIRTEENTH SUNDAY AFTER TRINITY.

St. Luke x. 23 *to* 38[1]

(leaving out the words, "And he turned him unto his disciples, and said privately," with which *v.* 23 commences).

23, 24   𝔅lessed are the eyes which see the things that ye see. For J tell you, that many prophets and kings have desired to see those things which ye see, and have not seen them; and to hear those

25 things which ye hear, and have not heard them. And behold, a certain lawyer stood up, and tempted him, saying, Master, what

26 shall J do to inherit eternal life? He said unto him, What is

27 written in the law? how readest thou? And he answering said, Thou shalt love the Lord thy God with all thy heart, and with all thy soul, and with all thy strength, and with all thy mind, and thy

28 neighbour as thyself? And he said unto him, Thou hast answered

29 right; this do, and thou shalt live. But he willing to justifie

30 himself, said unto Jesus, And who is my neighbour? And Jesus answering said, A certain man went down from Jerusalem to Jericho, and fell among thieves, which stripped him of his raiment,

31 and wounded him, and departed leaving him half dead. And by chance there came down a certain priest that way, and when he saw

32 him, he passed by on the other side. And likewise a Levite, when he was at the place, came and looked on him, and passed by on the

33 other side. But a certain Samaritan, as he journeyed, came where

---

[1] This is the Gospel for the day in the Sarum Missal; but the modern Roman Use has substituted for it St. Matt. vi. 24-33, which is our Gospel for the Fifteenth Sunday after Trinity. The Parable of the Samaritan is appointed by the Roman Missal as the Gospel for the Eleventh Sunday.

34 he was; and when he saw him, he had compassion on him, and
went to him, and bound up his wounds, pouring in oyl, and wine,
and set him on his own beast, and brought him to an inn, and took

35 care of him. And on the morrow when he departed, he took out
two pence, and gave them to the host, and said unto him, Take
care of him, and whatsoever thou spendest more, when I come

36 again I will repay thee. Which now of these three, thinkest

37 thou, was neighbour unto him that fell among the thieves? And
he said, He that shewed mercy on him. Then said Jesus unto
him, Go and do thou likewise.

[Miss. Sar.	1549.	. 1662 s.b.
In illo tempore, Dixit *Jesus discipulis suis;* Beati oculi qui vident quæ vos videtis. (*Vulg.* Et conversus ad discipulos suos, dixit : Beati oculi, qui vident quæ vos videtis.)	Happy are the eyes which see the things that ye see.	Blessed are the eyes which see the things that ye see. (*Gr.* Καὶ στραφεὶς πρὸς τοὺς μαθητὰς, κατ᾽ ἰδίαν εἶπε· Μακάριοι οἱ ὀφθαλμοὶ οἱ βλέποντες ἃ βλέπετε.)

The connexion of this Gospel with what immediately precedes it must by
no means be put out of sight. Our Lord in the earlier part of the Chapter
had sent forth the seventy disciples with a solemn charge (*vv.* 1-17). The
seventy return from their mission, and express their joy at the success
which had attended their exorcisms of evil spirits in the Saviour's name
(*v.* 17). Hereupon He assures to them that power over the enemy, which
they had felt such pride and pleasure in exercising (*vv.* 18, 19); but
warns them nevertheless rather to rejoice in the security of their personal
relations with God, than in any external triumph (such as entered not
into the province of their inner life) over the powers of evil (*v.* 20).
Then, in full sympathy with their triumph over these powers, He too
rejoices in spirit, and addresses Himself first in accents of thanksgiving to
His Heavenly Father, for having revealed these things to men of low
degree and no account, men who had not the wisdom of this world, nor
the nobility and fame, which it confers upon its great ones (a topic, which
being urged in their hearing, was well suited to prevent their being "exalted by the abundance of the revelations," see and compare 2 Cor. xii.
7, 9, 10) (*v.* 21). And then follows in *v.* 22 a sort of soliloquy, uttered
however aloud, and thus designed to be for the edification of hearers, to
the effect that the disclosures which had been made to them respecting

the Son, and His relations to the Father, were communications not from
flesh and blood, but direct from God Himself. (See and compare St. Matt.
xvi. 17.) And then (still doubtless with the design of making and keeping them duly humble) He speaks to them privately of the high privilege
conferred by this divine illumination, a privilege which prophets, like
Abraham, Isaiah, and Daniel, kings like David and Hezekiah, had yearned
for in vain, and which was awarded therefore, not according to eminence
or merit, but as a matter of. pure grace, to whomsoever God would. He
had spoken in similar words before (St. Matt. xiii. 16) ; but then in reference to the privilege accorded to them of having the mysteries of the
kingdom of heaven opened to them (*Ibid. vv.* 11, 12). Now it is rather
in reference to the supernatural powers with which He had entrusted
them, that He speaks in nearly the same terms.—*Translation of* 1540.
(1) *V.* 23. "*Happy* are the eyes which see the things that ye see." And
so Tyndale before, and the Genevan after, Cranmer. Wycliffe, on the
other hand, gives, "*blessid* ben the iyen." And to "blessed" the Rhemish,
and afterwards the Authorised, returned. "*Blessed*" is no doubt, in this
very solemn asseveration, the better rendering of μακάριος, in which (as
μάκαρ is the word applied in Classical writers to the felicity of the gods,—
μάκαρες θεοί—) there is *usually* a notion of heavenly or spiritual bliss, a
bliss which sometimes (in the very terms of the statement) excludes the
"hap," or bliss of outward circumstance (witness 1 Pet. iii. 14, and iv. 14,
"If ye suffer for righteousness' sake, if ye be reproached for the name of
Christ, happy [μακάριοι] are ye "). But *only* usually. Occasionally the
word seems to be emptied of every higher meaning than "happy," "for-
tunate." Even the Revisers of 1881, though making a point, wherever
they can, of rendering the same Greek by the same English word, have
not ventured to alter "happy" into "blessed" in Acts xxvi. 2 ; "I think
myself *happy*, King Agrippa" (ἥγημαι ἐμαυτὸν μακάριον). They have also
retained "happy" as the representative of μακάριος (and with excellent
judgment) in 1 Cor. vii. 40, "But she is *happier* (μακαριωτέρα) if she so
abide, after my judgment." (2) *V.* 40. "Theeves, which *robbed* him of
his raiment." And so Tyndale and the Genevan. Wycliffe has merely,
"thei *robbeden* hym." "*Robbed* him of his raiment," though a periphras-
tic translation of the single word ἐκδύσαντες, is rather more accurate than
"*stripped* him of his raiment," which is surplusage. To strip a man *is* to
rob him of his raiment (or armour). The Revisers of 1881 have rightly
erased the "of his raiment," and left "stripped him" to stand alone.
(3) *V.* 31. "when he saw him, *he passed by*." Of the five English Versions, which preceded the Authorised, the Genevan alone gives the force
of the first preposition in translating the word ἀντιπαρῆλθεν. The word is

not found anywhere else in the New Testament but in *vv.* 31, 32, of this Chapter; and, the Latin having no single word to exhibit its full force, the Vulgate translation "viso illo *prœterivit*," "cum . . . videret eum, *pertransiit*, is inadequate. 'Αντιπαρέρχομαι expresses not passing by merely, but passing by *on opposite sides* (like armies passing along on opposite banks of a river). The Translators of 1611 rightly followed the Genevan in respecting the ἀντί, and in doing so have not been molested by the Revisers of 1881. (4) *V.* 32. We have nothing to do, except incidentally, with Wycliffe's translation; but I cannot help noticing here his accommodation of the phraseology of the Jewish Church to that of the Christian, in translating the "Levita" of his Vulgate by "deacon,"—"also a *dekene* whanne he was bisidis the place, and saie hym: passid forth." (5) *V.* 34. "and brought him to a *common* inn." And so Tyndale before Cranmer. Wycliffe has "ledde in to an *ostric*," as the representative of the "duxit in *stabulum*," which he found in his Vulgate. The Greek word is πανδοχεῖον; and it is quite possible that, in rendering this "a *commen* ynne," Tyndale wished to give the force of the παν, which is the first element of the word. An inn is a house private to none, *which receives all sorts.*—The *stabulum* (standing-place, stall, stable) of the Vulgate is a little difficult to account for. The word occurs in the Vulgate only three times again, twice of the "sheepfolds" which the Reubenites and Gadites proposed (and which Moses permitted them) to "make for their cattle" on the East of Jordan (Num. xxxii. 16, 24); and once of "the four thousand stalls," which Solomon had for "horses and chariots"(2 Chron. ix. 25). It is clear therefore that in the Latin of the Vulgate it means a *lodging place for cattle.* Probably the translator was guided in the choice of the word "stabulum" by the immediately preceding clause, "and set him on his own *beast.*" The first place to which the Samaritan's mule or ass, with its live burden, would be taken, would be *the stable.* Wycliffe's "ostric" is a stable, not the same word (except fundamentally) as "hostelry." Both are connected no doubt with host, hostel, hostler (*Fr.* hostelier), etc. (6) *V.* 34. "and *made provision* for him" (ἐπεμελήθη αὐτοῦ). And so Tyndale before, and the Genevan after, Cranmer. An inaccurate translation. The *provision* made by the Samaritan for the wounded pilgrim is described in the following verse (35), where he gives direction to the host to tend him at his own cost. By ἐπεμελήθη here is expressed his *personal* tendance of the patient. And so the Rhemish, followed by the Authorised, rightly gives "took care of him." (7) *V.* 35. "Take *cure* of him." And so Tyndale and the Genevan. "Cure" and "care" are fundamentally the same word; but by the time of the Authorised Version *care* had superseded *cure* as a general word for the expression of management and attendance upon, and "cure" had become limited to the responsibilities of the parish-priest (" cure of souls "), and to the effects of the care taken by physician and nurse (" cure of ailments or of patients"). In Shakspere we find the proverb which draws a distinction between the two words ; (*Love's Labour's Lost*, Act V. Scene ii. line 28) ;

> " *Katharine.* You weigh me not ? O, that's you care not for me.
> *Rosaline.* Great reason ; for *Past cure is still past care.*"]

Sunday.—V. 23. " Blessed are the eyes which see the things that ye see : for I tell you, that many prophets and kings have desired to see those things which ye see, and have not seen them ; and to hear those things which ye hear, and have not heard them." These words our Lord said " privately" to his disciples, and there does not seem to be any particular connexion between them and the Parable which follows, and which is addressed to the lawyer. Why are they made to stand at the opening of this Gospel, since they have nothing to do, it would appear, with the main subject of it ? I doubt not there is a meaning, and an edifying one, in this arrangement. The Parable of the Good Samaritan, if it stood by itself, might be,—nay, it has been,—misunderstood. It might be gathered from it that works of love, done in the mere outflowing of natural compassion, might save the soul (a gospel which the natural man would be quite ready to accept) ; and that the spiritual apprehension of Christ by faith was not at all necessary. But these immediately foregoing words teach the blessedness of this apprehension ; for when our Lord says, " Blessed are the eyes which see the things that ye see," He is not to be understood as speaking of the mere bodily or sensuous sight, but of seeing with appreciation and enjoyment of the object seen.[1]—Lord, it is only in the

---

[1] "We must however know this, that *seeing* does not signify the action of the eyes, but the pleasure which the mind receives from benefits conferred. For instance, if any one should say, ' He hath seen good times,' according to the Psalm, *Thou shalt see the good of Jerusalem.* For many Jews had seen

light of Thy love to us that we can do works of love to others. Open our eyes to see that light, and our hearts to feel the glow and warmth of it.

Monday.—V. 25. "Behold, a certain lawyer stood up, and tempted him, saying, Master, what shall I do to inherit eternal life ?" This lawyer showed that he knew perfectly well the terms of inheriting eternal life, which were laid down in the Law; for he quoted those terms quite correctly. And he knew also that one who acted in a neighbourly manner was a neighbour. But, like very many of us, he had never honestly tried to act up to what he knew. This, then, is the first thing which our Lord seeks to lead him to do. As much as if he had said to him; "You have no right to ask Me for new terms of inheriting eternal life, so long as you have old terms which you have never striven to fulfil. Go and do what you know first; and then come to Me for new terms, if you fail."—Lord, when I am prompted to pray for guidance as to what Thou wouldest have me to do, let me make sure in the first place that I am already doing Thy will in other matters, as far as I know it, and also that in this matter I am perfectly prepared to do what is distasteful to myself, should it approve itself to me as Thy will. How often have I asked for guidance hypocritically, when I had no real doubt about the path of duty, but only a great indisposition to walk in it, and a desire that Thou shouldest indicate to me some easier and smoother path ! This is to tempt Thee, Lord, as this lawyer tempted Thee; and for those who

Christ performing divine works—that is to say, with their bodily sight—yet all were not fitted to receive the blessing, for they believed not ; but these saw not His glory with their mental sight." [Theophylact, as quoted in the *Catena Aurea* of St. Thomas Aquinas : "Commentary on the Gospels from the Fathers," Vol. III., Part I., p. 365.]

tempt Thee Thou hast no new revelation of duty, but merely biddest them do what they know already.

Tuesday.—V. 28. "This do, and thou shalt live." But didst Thou, Blessed Lord, by giving this answer, intend to imply that any man ever did, or could, inherit eternal life by keeping the law of love to God and man? Nay; but Thou didst throw this man back upon the Law, in order that "the Law" might be his "schoolmaster to bring" him "unto Christ."[1] He had never tried to keep the Law in all its fulness and strictness; he was under the impression that he had acted fairly up to its requirements, certainly as regarded the love of God, and indeed as regarded the love of his neighbour also, if the word neighbour might be interpreted narrowly, as meaning only a Jew or an orthodox believer. But what indication did the Law give that such a narrow interpretation was the true one? The Law bound him to help his enemy, when his ass was lying under his burden,[2] and if so, surely much more, when his enemy himself was lying on the ground prostrate and wounded. Moreover, a precept of Leviticus enjoined upon the Israelite to "love the stranger, that" dwelt "with" them, "as" himself.[3] Let him say whether he has fulfilled these duties to foes, to foreigners, to heretics; and, when his conscience convicts him of failure, he will be prepared to receive other and more practicable terms of salvation. When I come to the good Physician, in the conceit of my own powers, to earn salvation, He will say to me, "Walk and run in the way of God's commandments," knowing that if I try to walk and run, I shall fail, because I am naturally sick and lame. But if,

---

[1] See Gal. iii. 24.

[2] See Exod. xxiii. 5. "If thou see the ass of him that hateth thee lying under his burden, and *wouldest cease to leave* thy business *for him; thou shalt surely leave* it to join *with him*" (*Marg.*)   [3] See Lev. xix. 34.

under a genuine sense of my infirmity, I come to Him to be made whole, in order that I *may* run and walk, He will then heal me by His blood and His grace.

Wednesday.—V. 28. " This do, and thou shalt live." The love to God and man, which " springs out of a true and lively faith,"[1] is life indeed,—the life of the spirit, life in God's sight. We recognise it as being such, when we pray in our beautiful Collect for Quinquagesima Sunday ; " Send thy Holy Ghost, and pour into our hearts that most excellent gift of charity, . . . without which whosoever liveth is counted dead before thee." " God is love,"[2] and lives the life of love momently ; and therefore he who does not in some measure live this life, though his bodily and mental frame may both be vigorous,—though the roses of health may be on his cheek, and his mind may be exploring new fields of science, and adding to the knowledge and the resources of mankind,—is yet " counted dead before " God. Moreover, works of love are the very soul and animating spirit of love, without which love, when conceived in the heart, very soon evaporates, as two Apostles have been careful to warn us,—St. John ; " My little children, let us not love in word, neither in tongue ; but in deed and in truth. And hereby we know that we are of the truth, and shall assure our hearts before him"[3];—and St. James ; " If a brother or sister be naked, and destitute of daily food, and one of you say unto them, Depart in peace, be ye warmed and filled ; notwithstanding ye give them not those things which are needful to the body ; what doth it profit ?"[4]

Thursday.—V. 29. " And who is my neighbour ?" I observe that our Lord gave no direct answer to this question. He answered the lawyer's thoughts, not his

---

[1] See Art. xii. *Of Good Works.*

[2] 1 John iv. 8, 16.   [3] 1 John iii. 18, 19.   [4] James ii. 15, 16.

words, and in such a manner as to set him right where he was wrong.   The lawyer was thinking; "I hope I can say that I have loved my neighbour as myself; but, until the word neighbour is defined, I hesitate to say I have. I suppose the term does not embrace unbelievers, heretics, Gentile dogs, but only God's own people ?"   This narrow, loveless thought has to be dislodged, and the true notion of a neighbour set up in his mind.   Our Lord virtually says to him; "You know nothing of true love to your neighbour, if you can ask such a question as that."   He tells him a story of a foreigner and heretic, who acted a neighbour's part to a Jew, when two Jews stood aloof, and did nothing for their brother.   And He implies; "If you have the principle of neighbourly love in you, you will do the same as the Samaritan did.   Have you acted as he did, when you have had the opportunity ? or have you acted like the priest and the Levite who hid themselves from their neighbour, would not go into the case, passed by on the other side ?"—O Lord, how must those who confronted Thee with their questionings have been made to feel that Thou knewest the very secrets of their hearts !   Thy written word represents Thee in this; for, when we come up to its light, how does it expose and lay bare for us all the evasions, subterfuges, reasonings of our hearts !   How do we find it to be "quick, and powerful, and sharper than any two-edged sword, piercing even to the dividing asunder of soul and spirit, and of the joints and marrow, and a discerner of the thoughts and intents of the heart "[1] !

[1] Heb. iv. 12.   "Eye of God's word ! where'er we turn,
        Ever upon us ! thy keen gaze
      Can all the depths of sin discern,
        Unravel every bosom's maze."
              ["Christian Year ;" St. Bartholomew.]

Friday.—V. 30. "A certain man . . . fell among thieves." Behind and beyond the primary design of the story of the Samaritan, which was to give instruction to the lawyer in the law of love to our neighbour, the Fathers and all the best Commentators recognise in it a figurative significance, such as makes it a parable, no less than an instructive tale. The traveller who went down from Jerusalem to Jericho represents man, who, having forfeited by the fall the communion with God enjoyed by our first parents in the happy garden, fell under the power of evil spirits, who stripped him of the raiment of original righteousness, and wounded him with severe spiritual wounds,—blindness in his understanding, sensuality in his affections, a wrong bias in his will,—and left him "half dead," that is, with a conscience and moral sense, which might become the nucleus of recovery, a conscience approving what is right, and making him restless in evil courses, but powerless for good without Divine help. In this figurative description of the condition of man after the fall, I will meditate to-day upon this feature—that it was a condition brought about by *external* evil agency,—"he fell among thieves." Here, as elsewhere, the evil which is in man is traced up to the devil and his angels ; man did not go wrong of his own mind ; he was the victim of seduction. Do I give to the doctrine of evil spirits the place in my system of theology which the Scriptures, and the Prayer Book,—nay, and our Lord Himself,—everywhere most unequivocally give to it ? The world, and the flesh,— that is evil self and evil men,—would be comparatively easy foes to deal with, if they were not instigated by, and employed as the instrumentality of, the devil.—Lord, let me not be "ignorant of his devices."[1] Put me on

[1] See 2 Cor. ii. 11.

my guard, both against his subtleties, and his impetuous attacks. "From the crafts and assaults of the devil, good Lord, deliver me."[1]

Saturday.—As the mischief effected an entrance from without, so it is only from without that the remedy can come. The Samaritan represents the Lord Jesus, called a Samaritan by the Jews, ("Say we not well that thou art a Samaritan, and hast a devil?"[2]) who, actuated by that pure compassion which is the loveliest attribute of the Divine nature, came on a journey to the earth to seek and save the lost, and, drawing very nigh to sinners by His Incarnation, went up to them in their haunts, healed the broken in heart, and bound up their wounds,[3] pouring in the wine of His blood and the oil of His grace, and bore the brunt of their sins in His Agony and Bloody Sweat, in His Cross and Passion and precious Death, and provided for them shelter and nourishment in His Church, and has constituted pastors to feed them with His Word and Sacraments, promising to requite the services of those pastors on the re-appearance of Himself the chief Shepherd.[4] But let me remember that, as man's will yielded to Satan, before the ruin of our first parents could be effected, so the will must yield to Christ, if we are to be recovered by Him.[5]   And yet the willingness to be healed by Him is itself from Him.—Lord, "Thy people shall be willing in the day of thy power."[6]

---

[1] See the first Deprecation in the Litany.
[2] St. John viii. 48.   [3] See Ps. cxlvii. 3.   [4] See 1 Pet. v. 2, 3, 4.
[5] See St. John v. 6.   [6] Ps. cx. 3.

Chapter XLVIII.

THE GOSPEL FOR THE FOURTEENTH SUNDAY AFTER TRINITY.

St. Luke xvii. 11 *to* 20
(except that in *v.* 11 "Jesus" is substituted for "he").

11   And it came to pass, as Jesus went to Jerusalem, that he
12 passed through the midst of Samaria, and Galilee. And as he
    entred into a certain billage, there met him ten men that were
13 lepers, who stood afar off. And they lifted up their voices, and
14 said, Jesus master, have mercy on us. And when he saw them, he
    said unto them, Go shew your selves unto the priests. And it came
15 to pass, that as they went, they were cleansed. And one of them,
    when he saw that he was healed, turned back, and with a loud voice
16 glorified God, and fell down on his face at his feet, giving him
17 thanks; and he was a Samaritan. And Jesus answering, said, Were
18 there not ten cleansed? but where are the nine? There are not
19 found that returned to give glory to God, save this stranger. And he
    said unto him, Arise, go thy way, thy faith hath made thee whole.

[Miss. Sar.	1549.	1662 a. b.
In illo tempore, Cum iret *Jesus* in Hierusalem, transibat per mediam Samariam et Galilæam. (*Vulg.* Et factum est, dum iret in Jerusalem, transibat per mediam Samariam, etc.)	And it chanced as Jesus went to Jerusalem, that he passed thorow Samaria, and Galilee.	And it came to pass, as Jesus went to Jerusalem, that he passed through the midst of Samaria, and Galilee. (Gr. Καὶ ἐγένετο ἐν τῷ πορεύεσθαι αὐτὸν εἰς Ἱερουσαλὴμ, καὶ αὐτὸς διήρχετο διὰ μέσου Σαμαρείας καὶ Γαλιλαίας.)

What immediately precedes this incident in St. Luke's Gospel is the
Parable about "Unprofitable Servants" (*vv.* 7 *to* 11). That Parable was

drawn forth from our Lord by the request, on the part of the Apostles, that He would increase their faith (*v.* 5). Our Lord, after magnifying the power of even the smallest measure of genuine faith, seems to intimate by the Parable, that the best way to obtain an increase of it is to wait upon God in the path of our duty, and that, after we have done this, God will give that comfortable and restful increase of faith, which is the recompence of the Christian's service,—a recompence, however, not of debt (for we are at best "unprofitable servants"), but of grace. The miracle wrought upon the lepers illustrates this lesson, inasmuch as they were not healed at once, but bidden to go to the priests, and "as they went, they were cleansed." (See the Thought for *Monday*, and also Chap. xlix.) They acted, in obeying Christ's precept, upon the amount of faith they had ; and every one of them received the blessing for which he sued ; and one of them had his faith so enlarged that it "worked by love," and brought him back to the Saviour's feet in humble acknowledgment of the benefit.—For the commencement of the journey to Jerusalem, in the course of which our Lord performed this miracle, we must go back as far as St. Luke ix. 51, where we read ; "And it came to pass, when the time was come that he should be received up" (in His Ascension, as the crown of His Passion, and the corollary of his Resurrection), "he stedfastly set his face to go to Jerusalem, etc."—*Translation of* 1540. (1) *V.* 11. "And it *chanced* as Jesus went to Jerusalem." And so Tyndale. "It came to pass" is a better rendering of ἐγένετο than "it chanced." But "chanced" is not a bad one. It must not be supposed that there is always in the word "chance" the idea of something causeless, or the cause of which cannot be assigned. It is often equivalent, as here, to "took place," "came to pass." So in Shakspere (2 *Henry IV.*, Act I. Scene i.) ;

> "He that but fears the thing he would not know
> Hath, by instinct, knowledge from others' eyes
> That what he feared is *chanced*."

(2) *V.* 11. "he passed *thorow* Samaria, and Galilee." This again is from Tyndale. Better "through the middle of" (as Wycliffe), or "through the midst of" as the Genevan, Rhemish, and Authorised. The meaning seems to be, not that our Lord walked across the districts of Samaria and Galilee (which would present a difficulty, as Samaria, which is mentioned first, would not be first passed through by a person going to Jerusalem), but that He went along the border-line which separated one of these districts from the other. (3) *V.* 13. "which stood afarre off, and *put foorth* their voyces, and said" (ἦραν φωνήν). And so Tyndale and the Genevan. Much better and more faithful, Wycliffe (representing the *levaverunt*

vocem of the Vulgate) "and *reiseden*" (raised) "hir vois"; and better still the "lifted up" of the Rhemish, Authorised, and Revised. (4) *V.* 15. "One of them, when he saw that he was *cleansed.*" And so all the five English Versions which preceded the Authorised, although the Greek word is not ἐκαθαρίσθη, but ἰάθη. How is this to be accounted for? I suppose by the glamour which the Vulgate (with its "Unus antem ex illis, ut vidit quia *mundatus* est") exerted over the translators. But had Jerome any MS. authority for the word ἐκαθαρίσθη here? (5) *V.* 17. "*Are* there not ten cleansed?" And so Tyndale and the Genevan. The Rhemish, and afterwards the Authorised, give the right tense, "*Were* there not ten cleansed?" Our Lord looks back to the moment of their recovery ;—"Were not all the ten cleansed?" He is not speaking of the present result of the miracle, their state of recovered health, in which case the perfect tense would have been used.]

Sunday.—V. 13. "And they lifted up their voices, and said, Jesus, Master, have mercy on us." It was not an accident which had brought these ten lepers together. Their common misery had for the time sunk even national differences and theological hatreds, and made them conspire to besiege Christ with united prayer for their recovery from a disease, which, in addition to its own loathsomeness, put a ban of excommunication upon them, and excluded them from society. And accordingly, they pray in common, not individually. It is not a separate "Jesus have mercy on *me*," which the Lord hears from each of them, but one loud cry, swollen in volume by every one of them contributing to it; "Jesus, Master, have mercy on *us*." If several men try to draw a heavily laden waggon with a cord or chain, and their force is not applied at the same moment, the waggon remains stationary. But let one of them regulate their movements by giving the time with his voice, so that the force of all is applied simultaneously, and immediately the wheels begin to move. Let me meditate on the prevalence which *united* prayer has with God, not only in virtue of the agreement in certain petitions which characterizes it ("If two of you shall agree on earth as touching any thing that they shall ask, it shall be done for them of my Father which is in heaven"); but still more in virtue of the covenanted presence of our great Interceding Priest in the midst of the petitioners; "For where two or three are gathered together in my name, there am I in the midst of them."[1]　His prayers for His people open heaven to their supplications, and draw down upon them, as they did upon Himself at His baptism, the heavenly Dove of peace and consolation, and whatever else they "faithfully ask according to God's will."[2]

Monday.—V. 14. "And when he saw them, he said unto them, Go shew yourselves unto the priests."　I find that shortly before this miracle, the Apostles had said unto the Lord, "Increase our faith."[3]　And I observe also that the Collect for this Sunday contains a prayer for the increase of faith; "Almighty and everlasting God, give unto us the increase of faith."　I cannot doubt that the way in which our Lord healed these lepers, was designed to give His Apostles a lesson as to the way in which they were to look for an increase of faith.　The lepers were not healed at once, but bidden to go to the priests (an act which implied that they would be healed; for it was the function of the priest to examine a recovered leper, and formally to declare him clean, if he found him so[4]); and " as they went, they were cleansed."[5]　We, too, are to wait upon God in the way of our duty, to act upon that measure of faith which we have, and in doing so we shall receive

---

[1] St. Matt. xviii. 19, 20.

[2] See the Sixth Collect at the end of the Communion Service.

[3] See St. Luke xvii. 5.

[4] See Lev. xiii. 9, 17 ; xiv. 2, 4, 5, 6, etc.　　　[5] *V.* 14.

an increase of faith.[1] How erroneous, then, and how likely to prove fatal, is the notion of those who think that they will wait to enter upon God's service, and upon the fulfilment of their duties to Him and their neighbour, until they experience some great change in themselves which they call conversion. They are waiting for some warm gush of feeling, which assuredly will never come, if sought by listless prayer without effort. Let them act up to what they know of their duty; let them act as the faith, which they profess to covet, would lead them to act; and it shall come to pass that, as they go, they shall be cleansed; as they stretch forth to Christ the withered hand in earnest endeavour, Christ's power shall visit and restore them.[2]

Tuesday.—V. 14. "Go shew yourselves unto the priests." I have already learned a lesson from this Gospel as to the value which God sets upon congregational worship. I will now learn another lesson as to the value which He sets on Ministerial Absolution. The priests could not make the leper clean. Leprosy was the special infliction of God[3]; and it was His special province (for medical skill was avowedly incompetent to reach the disease) to recover the leper, the gift of such healing being occasionally lodged with His inspired messengers, as with Elisha.[4] But, nevertheless, the leper could not, by the

---

[1] May not this be also the underlying meaning of the parable about the "servant ploughing or feeding cattle," with which our Lord makes answer to the request for an increase of faith (*vv.* 7-10)? It is faith which makes duty easy, and seats us (as it were) at a banquet of spiritual good things. We must wait upon our Master in duteous service, before that influx of faith can come, which shall make even the hardest duties appear practicable. We must take and wear Christ's yoke, before we can, and in order that we may, appreciate its easiness. (See St. Matt. xi. 29, 30.) [2] See St. Mark iii. 5.

[3] See 2 Kings v. 7   [4] See 2 Kings v. 10, 14.

law of Moses, be readmitted into society without the
exercise of the priest's office.[1]　It was the priest's part to
examine him thoroughly, and, if he found him cured, to
perform certain symbolical ceremonies, the effect of which
was to pronounce him cured, and to reinstate him in the
communion of the Church.[2]　'It is only the great High
Priest who can, by the application of His blood to the
conscience, and His Spirit to the heart, cleanse the sinner
of the leprosy of guilt; yet God "hath given power and
commandment to his Ministers, to declare and pronounce
to his people, being penitent, the Absolution and Remission
of their sins."　And, this pronouncement being made under
His seal and covenant, Christ will not have it made light
of.　When the conscience is relieved of its burden, He will
still have us seek the absolution of His Church.　And to
faithful souls it cannot fail to be a great consolation to
hear the sentence of God's forgiveness from the mouth of
His authorised ambassador.　The devout Richard Hooker
found it so, when, as he lay on his deathbed, he requested
absolution from Dr. Saravia.[3]

---

[1] See Num. xii. 10, 14, 15.　　　　　　[2] See Lev. xiii. xiv.

[3] "About one day before his death, Dr. Saravia, who knew the very
secrets of his soul, (for they were supposed to be confessors to each other),
came to him, and, after a conference of *the benefit, the necessity, and safety
of the Church's absolution, it was resolved the Doctor should give him both
that and the Sacrament the day following.*　To which end the Doctor
came, and, after a short retirement and privacy, they two returned to
the company ; and then the Doctor gave him and some of those friends
which were with him, the blessed Sacrament of the body and blood of
our Jesus.　Which being performed, the Doctor thought he saw a reverend
gaiety and joy in his face."　And similarly Walton tells us of Sanderson :—
"After his taking his bed, and about a day before his death, *he desired
his Chaplain, Mr. Pullin, to give him absolution : and at his performing
that office, he pulled off his cap, that Mr. Pullin might lay his hand upon
his bare head.*　After this desire of his was satisfied, his body seemed to
be at more ease, and his mind more cheerful ; and he said, *Lord, forsake*

Wednesday.—Vv. 15, 16. "One of them, when he saw that he was healed, turned back, and with a loud voice glorified God, and fell down on his face at his feet, giving him thanks." There is thankfulness here; but there is something beyond and higher than thankfulness—something to which thankfulness leads up. The end of ends which God has in view in Creation and Redemption, in Nature and in Grace, is His own Glory. He may be said to seek glory from His rational creatures. ("There are not *found*," says our Lord—as much as to say, "God seeks, but cannot find"—"that returned to give glory to God, save this stranger.") And we read of this Samaritan glorifying Him with a loud voice when he was healed, just as he had lifted up his voice to cry for healing. The whole of the spiritual life, what is it but a glorifying of God for the cleansing from the leprosy of sin by the blood and grace of Christ, which He bestows on us freely? But then it must be a glorification, not with the mouth only, but with all the faculties of body and soul—such an unfeigned thankfulness of heart "that we may show forth" His "praise not only with our lips, but in our lives, by giving up ourselves to" His "service."[1] In this view of it, thankfulness is the main spring of the regenerate life.

Thursday.—V. 17. "Were there not ten cleansed?" (or rather, "Were not all the ten cleansed?") "but where are the nine?" Let us take occasion to meditate to-day on the fewness of the saved, according to the testimony of our Lord Himself. "Many be called, but few chosen,"[2]— a warning which twice fell from His lips. "Wide is the

---

me not now my strength faileth me; but continue thy mercy, and let my mouth be filled with thy praise." [Walton's Lives of Mr. Richard Hooker and Dr. Robert Sanderson, pp. 189, 363. *Ed.* S.P.C.K., 1847.]

[1] General Thanksgiving.   [2] St. Matt. xx. 16; xxii. 14.

gate, and broad is the way, that leadeth to destruction, and many there be which go in thereat : because strait is the gate, and narrow is the way, which leadeth unto life, and few there be that find it."[1]   Of the hundreds of thousands, who are cleansed from the guilt of original sin in Baptism, and receive the implantation of a new principle of life in that Sacrament, how very small a fraction, when they are come to years of discretion, glorify God in their lives !   And to this effect St. Paul warns his Corinthian converts, when he tells them that though "all" the Israelites " were baptized unto Moses in the cloud and in the sea "; . . . yet " with many of them God was not well pleased "[2]; the fact being, as the history shows us, that only two men out of the whole generation entered on the inheritance of the promised land.[3]——Stir up my will, O Lord, that I may strive to enter in at the strait gate,[4] cutting off the right hand, and plucking out the right eye,[5] rather than retain anything which might risk the loss of my soul.

Friday.——V. 18. " There are not found that returned to give glory to God." The glorifying of God out of gratitude is, as I have already had occasion to observe, the sum and substance of the Christian life.   To-day I will think of ingratitude as the most fundamental sin of man ——the source of all paganism and idolatry.   The Gentiles, says St. Paul, "are without excuse" in their idolatries, " because that, when they knew God " (knew " his eternal power and Godhead " from the evidences given them in the creation of the world), " they glorified him not as God, neither were thankful . . . and changed the glory of the

---

[1] St. Matt. vii. 13, 14.   [2] See 1 Cor. x. 2, 5.
[3] See Num. xiv. 30.   [4] See St. Luke xiii. 24.
[5] See St. Mark ix. 43, 47.

uncorruptible God into an image made like to corruptible man, and to birds, and four-footed beasts, and creeping things."[1]   And he goes on to say that, because man thus degraded God in his conceptions ("changing their glory into the similitude of an ox that eateth grass"[2]), God degraded him by giving him up to uncleanness through the lusts of his own heart—granting to the sensual and animal part a domineering power over the higher faculties.—O God, if ingratitude, and degrading conceptions of Thee, are the point of departure for all evil, how ought I to cherish grateful thoughts, and high lofty conceptions of Thee, as the very spring of all true piety!

Saturday.—V. 19. " Arise, go thy way : thy faith hath made thee whole" (literally, " hath saved thee "). The more literal translation would give the truer notion of our Lord's meaning ; for the nine unthankful lepers were made whole, but only the Samaritan leper was *saved*—only in his case did the healing penetrate from the body to the spirit.   It is faith in Christ which saves us ; but it must be faith working by love.   This it was in his case ; for his healing struck the chord of deep thankfulness in his heart, a thankfulness which constrained him to return, and throw himself at his Deliverer's feet, thanking Jesus, and glorifying God with a loud voice.   As for his comrades (who had seemed equally devout with himself in the time of their adversity), they doubtless believed in the power of Christ to heal them (and were healed in virtue of such faith), but their faith did not go beyond this.   " The devils also believe" in Christ's power ; and, while He was upon earth, they dreaded and deprecated His wrath.[3]   But, in order to be drawn towards Him, we must believe in His

---

[1] Rom. i. 20-24.   [2] See Ps. cvi. 20.
[3] See St. Mark i. 24, and v. 7, with James ii. 19.

love and mercy as well as in His power; in His mercy, I say,—that is, in His love to the evil and ill-deserving. Give me this faith, O Lord, that I may be irresistibly drawn towards Thee, " with cords of a man, with bands of love."[1]

[1] See Hosea xi. 4.

CHAPTER XLIX

ON THE CONNEXION BETWEEN THE COLLECT, EPISTLE, AND GOSPEL FOR THE FOURTEENTH SUNDAY AFTER TRINITY.

THE COLLECT.

Almighty and everlasting God, give unto us the increase of faith, hope, and charity; and that we may obtain that which thou dost promise, make us to love that which thou dost command, through Jesus Christ our Lord.   Amen.

THE EPISTLE.   GAL. v. 16 *to* 25.

I Say then, Walk in the Spirit, and ye shall not fulfil the lust of the flesh.   For the flesh lusteth against the Spirit, and the Spirit against the flesh ; and these are contrary the one to the other ; so that ye cannot do the things that ye would.   But if ye be led by the Spirit, ye are not under the law.   Now the works of the flesh are manifest, which are these, Adultery, fornication, uncleanness, lasciviousness, idolatry, witchcraft, hatred, variance, emulations, wrath, strife, seditions, heresies, envyings, murders, drunkenness, revellings, and such like : of the which I tell you before, as I have also told you in time past, that they who do such things shall not inherit the kingdom of God.   But the fruit of the Spirit is love, joy, peace, long-suffering, gentleness, goodness, faith, meekness, temperance : against such there is no law.   And they that are Christs have crucified the flesh with the affections and lusts.

THE GOSPEL.   ST. LUKE xvii. 11 *to* 20.

And it came to pass, as Jesus went to Jerusalem, that he passed through the midst of Samaria, and Galilee.   And as he entred into a certain village, there met him ten men that were lepers, who stood afar off. And they lifted up their voices, and said, Jesus master, have mercy on us. And when he saw them, he said unto them, Go shew your selves unto the priests. And it came to pass, that as they went, they were cleansed. And one of them, when he saw that he was healed, turned back, and with a loud voice glorified God, and fell down on his face at his feet, giving him thanks; and he was a Samaritan. And Jesus answering, said, Were there not ten cleansed? but where are the nine? There are not found that returned to give glory to God, save this stranger. And he said unto him, Arise, go thy way, thy faith hath made thee whole.

" A THREEFOLD cord is not quickly broken,"[1] says the wise man. When the Collect, Epistle, and Gospel of the day are found to illustrate one another, to give and borrow light reciprocally, as is frequently the case,—always perhaps, more or less, if we would be at the pains to trace the connexion of thought,—great emphasis is given to the instruction which is derived from all three combined.

The Collect is a special prayer for the week, founded on, and rising out of, the consideration of two parts of the New Testament,—one of which contains the writings of an inspired Apostle, and the other the accounts given by the Apostles, or their associates, of the words and deeds of their Master. Thus the Collect may be regarded as the voice of man to God, prompted by some particular communication which God has made to man.

The present Collect is a prayer for the increase of faith, hope, and love. " Almighty and everlasting God, give unto us the increase of faith, hope, and charity." Now if we go back to the earlier part of the Chapter from which the Gospel is taken, we shall find that the Apostles there ask our Lord to " increase their faith,"[2] so as to make

---

[1] Eccles. iv. 12. [2] *V.* 5.

the difficult duty of forgiveness of injuries light and easy
to them. In answer to this petition, He tells them that
a little faith will go a long way,—the tiniest grain of it
would enable them to overcome the most stupendous
difficulties,—to uproot trees from the earth, and plant
them in the sea.[1] And then follows the Parable about
the servant who, when he comes in from his drudgery in
the field, has still to wait upon his master at table, before
he is allowed to take his own meal. As if our Lord
had said; " It is true that faith will tide you easily
over all spiritual difficulties ; if it were strong, no duty,
however arduous, would present any difficulty to you ;
but you must not snatch at this high estate of spiritual
feeling, as if God would make it over to you simply
for the asking ; you must wait upon Him patiently for
it, not only in prayer, but in the way of His service,
in the way of His commandments ; and then you shall
be refreshed by a large influx of faith in His own good
time, at the end of your service, but not before it is
rendered,—' afterward thou shalt eat and drink.' However," He adds, " you are not to think much of your
service, as though it established a claim of merit upon
God—you owe it from first to last to Him ; you have
but done that which was your duty to do." And then
follows the incident of the Cleansing of the Ten Lepers,
which forms the Gospel, in which our Lord seems to have
been minded to impress upon His disciples by His method
of acting, what He had just taught them in words. He
did not heal the lepers at once ; but bade them take a
journey of some length, to show themselves to the priests.
This implied that He would heal them in His own good
time (for of what use would it have been to show them-

[1] *V.* 6.

selves to the priests, unless they were first healed ?), but that, for the present, they were to wait upon Him in the way of His commandment,—simply to do His bidding. They entered upon their journey accordingly; and " it came to pass that, as they went, they were cleansed." Now turn to the Collect, and observe how the prayer for an increase of faith, hope, and charity, in the earlier part of it is qualified and conditioned by the latter clause,—" and that we may obtain that which thou dost promise, make us to love that which thou dost command." Faith and hope look forward eagerly to God's promises, —enable us in some measure to realise them, before their fulfilment ; but it is important to remind ourselves that our recompence is not to come till our service is over, and that this will only cease with our lives. The faithful service of God in this life, as last week's Collect reminded us, is essential to our finally attaining His heavenly promises ; or, as *this* Collect puts it, there is no obtaining that which God promises without loving, and doing out of love, that which He commands. I clearly see, when I look closely into it, this subtle thread of connexion, which links together the prayer of the Collect with the incident recorded in the Gospel.

And now let me turn to the Epistle. " Give unto us the increase of charity (or love)," says the Collect. " The fruit of the Spirit," says St. Paul in the Epistle, " is love," love first and foremost, but not love alone,—several other dispositions also associated with, and flowing out of, love —" joy, peace, long-suffering, gentleness, goodness, faith, meekness, temperance." It will be observed that in this catalogue faith does not stand first. The faith of which mention is here made, is not the faith of which an increase is asked in the Collect, and which stands at the very foundation of the Christian life, but loving trustfulness towards God and man, a characteristic and exhibition of love, as we have it in the celebrated panegyric of love in 1 Cor. xiii.[1]; "Charity believeth all things," *i.e.* is full of loving trust both to God and man. Why, then, does not the Apostle mention in this catalogue of fruits of the Spirit the fundamental faith in Christ, out of which all graces spring? We must put ourselves in his point of view, to seize his meaning. And his point of view is very much the same as his Master's in the fifteenth Chapter of St. John's Gospel. By faith, co-operating internally with the Sacrament of Baptism externally, we are grafted into the true Vine, and become branches in Him. But, if we are to have any profit of this engrafting, we must be fruit-bearing branches; "for every branch" in Christ "that beareth not fruit" the heavenly Husbandman "taketh away: and every branch that beareth fruit, he purgeth it, that it may bring forth more fruit"[2]; and again; "He that abideth in me, and I in him, the same bringeth forth much fruit: for without me ye can do nothing."[3] Now the fruit is love, and all the gracious dispositions associated with love, as it is said, "faith which worketh by love."[4] The Apostle is addressing those who by faith and Baptism have been grafted into Christ. And therefore he needs not to press upon them the fundamental faith; for that they had; he directs their minds to the fruit which they must bear, in order to give evidence of their faith; "The fruit of the Spirit is love." Observe, too, how the Epistle illustrates the word "increase" in the Collect. The Collect prays for an increase of love. The Epistle speaks of love as a fruit. And fruit is something which grows; which becomes riper, and ruddier, and more abundant as

---

[1] *V.* 7.   [2] *V.* 2.   [3] *V.* 5.   [4] Gal. v. 6.

the year goes on; fruit is the great instance of increase which Nature exhibits,—an increase, not by addition from without, but by the unfolding from within of the life of the tree. Now the precious addition which the Epistle makes to the ideas of the Collect is just this, that the increase, for which the Collect petitions, can only be by the Spirit,—by His outpouring in larger measure upon our hearts. The increase is " the *fruit* of the Spirit." If you cause the sap to rally more strongly in the roots of a tree, you will have more fruit; if you cause the Holy Spirit to operate more powerfully in the heart of the Christian, you will have a larger increase of faith, hope, and love.— Observe also that the story of the lepers gives us an instance of a faith accompanied by love, and a faith not so accompanied. The nine unthankful lepers had faith in Christ's power to heal their bodies, and were healed accordingly; but only the Samaritan had the faith, which brought him in grateful love to the feet of His Redeemer; and we are to understand, therefore, that only his faith was of any special avail to him, contributed aught to the saving of his soul.

Finally, does not the Collect suggest a searching question, which we shall do well, before we offer it, to put to our consciences,—namely, whether we have the rudiments of faith, hope, and love in our hearts; whether we really possess them in a measure? For to ask for their increase, unless we are conscious of possessing them already to some extent, is surely to use an " idle word " before God; for how can that be increased which does not exist? " Be not rash with thy mouth, and let not thy heart be hasty to utter any thing before God."[1] " Every idle word that men shall speak, they shall give account thereof in the day of judgment."[2]

[1] Eccles. v. 2.   [2] See St. Matt. xii. 36.

CHAPTER L.

THE GOSPEL FOR THE FIFTEENTH SUNDAY AFTER TRINITY.

St. Matt. vi. 24 *to the end.*

24 No man can serve two masters: for either he will hate the one, and love the other; or else he will hold to the one, and despise the
25 other. Ye cannot serve God and Mammon. Therefore I say unto you, Take no thought for your life, what ye shall eat, or what ye shall drink; nor yet for your body, what ye shall put on: Is
26 not the life more than meat, and the body than raiment? Behold the fowls of the air; for they sow not, neither do they reap, nor gather into barns; yet your heavenly Father feedeth them: Are ye
27 not much better than they? Which of you by taking thought can
28 add one cubit unto his stature? And why take ye thought for raiment? Consider the lilies of the field how they grow: they toil
29 not, neither do they spin: And yet I say unto you, that even Solomon in all his glory was not arayed like one of these.
30 Wherefore if God so clothe the grass of the field, which to day is, and to morrow is cast into the oven; shall he not much more
31 clothe you, O ye of little faith? Therefore take no thought, saying, What shall we eat? or what shall we drink? or where-
32 withall shall we be clothed? (for after all these things do the Gentiles seek) for your heavenly Father knoweth that ye have need
33 of all these things. But seek ye first the kingdom of God, and his
34 righteousness, and all these things shall be added unto you. Take therefore no thought for the morrow; for the morrow shall take thought for the things of it self: sufficient unto the day is the evil thereof.

[MISS. SAR.	1549.	1662 S.B.
In illo tempore, Dixit Jesus discipulis suis; Nemo potest duobus dominis servire . . . . *down to the end of v.* 33, et hæc omnia adjicientur vobis. (*Vulg.* Nemo potest duobus dominis servire, etc.)	No man can serve two masters : . . . *down to the end of the Chapter,* (*thus embracing v.* 34) Sufficient unto the day is the travell thereof.	No man can serve two masters : . . . *down to the end of the Chapter,* (*thus embracing v.* 34) sufficient unto the day is the evil thereof.

The Reformers in 1549 did well in completing the old Sarum Gospel by adding to it the 34th verse, which summarises, and puts the crown upon, the whole section about anxiety. How the Gospel can ever have stopped short of this verse it is difficult to understand. Three is a mystical and perfect number in Holy Scripture ; and by embracing *v.* 34, we get a solemn threefold prohibition of anxiety by our Blessed Lord, Μὴ μεριμνᾶτε, *v.* 25 ; Μὴ οὖν μεριμνήσητε, *v.* 31 ; Μὴ οὖν μεριμνήσητε, *v.* 34. (See the Thought for *Sunday.*) The difference of the tense may be explained, but cannot be expressed in English. In *v.* 25 (where the prohibition is in the present tense) anxiety *as a general mental condition* is forbidden. In *vv.* 31, 34 it is the outbreak of anxiety at some point of time, and in definite form, which is forbidden, as, for example, when we say, "What are we to eat, drink, etc.?" (see *v.* 31).—The connexion of this Gospel with what immediately precedes is easy and obvious. Our Lord has been speaking of almsgiving, and exhorting to lay up treasure in heaven, not on earth (*vv.* 19, 20, 21). Alms must be given with a single eye (or intention), not in order to secure the praise of man (*vv.* 22, 23, and compare *v.* 1 *to* 5). "Now therefore follows the assurance of the folly of attempting the double service, an attempt which might flow out of the double eye" (Archbishop Trench's "Exposition from St. Augustine of the Sermon on the Mount" [Parker, 1844] p. 119, on *v.* 24).—*Translation of* 1540. (1) *V.* 24. "or else *lean to* the one, and despise the other." (Gr. ἢ ἑνὸς ἀνθέξεται). And so Tyndale and the Genevan. Wycliffe and the Rhemish, following the Vulgate ("aut unum *sustinebit,*") have "sustain." "Hold to" came in with the Authorised, and is probably the best rendering. The same Greek word is used of "*holding fast* the faithful word" (Tit. i. 9), and of "*supporting* the weak" (1 Thess. v. 14).—Milder words are required in this than in the first clause,—"either he will hate the one, and love the other,"—which is intended (according to Augustine) to be the case of the godly man, who abhors Satan, and loves God. The succeeding clause,—"or else he will hold to the one, and despise the other "—is the case of the *ungodly*, who sides with Satan, and practically despises God, by indulging his lusts in spite of the Divine threatenings. This "subtle remark" on "the nice selection of words here" "clears the passage even from the appearance of a repetition." (See Archbishop Trench, as above, p. 119.) There is, however, another way of "clearing the passage from the appearance of repetition," by supposing that the first clause represents the case of *strong characters* ("good haters and good lovers," as Dr. Johnson phrased it), the second of *weaker and more languid ones.*—Any how, in reading the passage aloud, the " or else " should be made much of, in order to call the hearer's attention to the fact that two different cases are contemplated in the two clauses. (2) *V.* 25. "*Be not carefull* for your life" (μὴ μεριμνᾶτε); *v.* 31, "Therefore *take no thought*, saying" (μὴ οὖν μεριμνήσητε); *v.* 34, "*Care not then* for the morrow" (μὴ οὖν μεριμνήσητε). Thus in three different ways (within a very few verses of one another) does Cranmer render the very same Greek verb. And so Tyndale and the Genevan. Of the three different renderings, "Be not careful" is clearly the best, and had this been adopted instead of "Take no thought" by King James's Translators in all three places, the Revisers of 1881 (who give us, "Be not anxious," which to modern English ears conveys the meaning even more accurately than "Be not careful") would probably have made no alteration. I cannot help noticing Wycliffe's rendering of the "Ne soliciti sitis," "nolite ergo soliciti esse," which he found in his Vulgate; "that ye ben not *bisie* to youre liif"; "therfor nyle ye be *bisie* seiynge"; "nyle ye be *bisie* in to the morewe," as showing the meaning which the word *busy* had in his day (a meaning which probably might be illustrated from the writings of Chaucer). The word occurs only once in the Authorised Version, in 1 Kings xx. 40; "As thy servant was *busy* here and there, he was gone" (*Vulg.* "Dum autem *turbatus huc illucque me verterem,* subito non comparuit"; *Sept.* Καὶ ἐγενήθη, περιεβλέψατο ὁ δοῦλός σου ὧδε καὶ ὧδε, καὶ οὗτος οὐκ ἦν); which passage gives exactly the notion of *distraction amid different objects and pursuits*, which is the fundamental notion of μέριμνα, anxiety. (See Archbishop Trench's note in the little volume above quoted, p. 120.) (3) *V.* 25. "Is not the life more worth then meat ! and the body more of value than raiment?" And so Tyndale and the Genevan. Our Authorised Version is more literal; and, as the meaning does not want expanding, and cannot be mistaken, ours is preferable. "Will He who gave the life and the body as the greater gift, keep back the food and clothing which those gifts need 1" (Stier *in loc.*) It is a line of argument very parallel with that in Rom. viii. 32; "He that spared not his own Son, but delivered him up for us all, how shall he not with him also freely give us

all things !"   (4) *V.* 26. "neither do they reap, nor *carry* into the barns."
And so Tyndale and the Genevan.   Not nearly as faithful a rendering of
συνάγουσιν as our own "gather," inasmuch as it takes no notice of the
συν.   How Tyndale came to alter the (perfectly correct) "nether gaderen
in to bernes" of Wycliffe is not clear.   Perhaps the word "carrying" was
so familiarly applied to harvest operations in England that he thought it
would come home more to simple folks.   (5) *V.* 26. "*and* your heavenly
Father feedeth them" (*Gr.* καί).   Every English Translation before the
Authorised rendered καί "and."   The Authorised first substituted "yet."
The Revisers of 1881 have replaced "and."   Have they done rightly ?
Winer (Grammar of the Idioms of the Greek Testament [Philadelphia:
1840] Part III., § 57, p. 343) tells us what justifies them.   He says that
"the *accent* or *tone* in the old languages rendered many things clear,
which we (having the reader in view while writing) express by the structure
of the sentence.   We too enunciate the sentence ; *I have saved thee from
death*, and *thou hast betrayed me*, differently from this : *I come to thee*, and
bring my friend with me."   In such cases Winer says that "the *translator*
who would not injure the complexion of the language *must retain the
particle he finds in the original*, whilst the *interpreter* should exchange it
for a special conjunction."   In several places, where "*yet*" seems to be
implied by καί, even King James's Translators have allowed "*and*" to
stand.   Thus St. John iii. 32 ; "What he hath seen and heard, that he
testifieth ; AND no man receiveth his testimony"; and St. Matt. x. 29,
"Are not two sparrows sold for a farthing ? AND one of them shall not
fall on the ground without your Father."   (6) *V.* 27. "Which of you by
taking carefull thought, can adde," etc.   And so the Genevan.   A fourth
variation of the way of rendering the verb μεριμνάω [see (2) above].   (7)
V. 29. "Even Solomon *in all his royalty* was not clothed like one of
these."   And so Tyndale and the Genevan.   The Rhemish returned to
"glory," which Wycliffe had already given.   (8) *V.* 30. "Which *though
it stand to day*, is to morrow cast into the *furnace*."   "Though it stand
to day" is very vigorous, but not literal enough.   "Furnace" is from
Tyndale.   The Genevan went back to "oven," the right translation of
κλίβανος, which Wycliffe had already given.   Κάμινος is a *furnace*,—used
for smelting metals, not for baking bread.   (8) "all these things shall be
ministred unto you" (προστεθήσεται ὑμῖν).   So Tyndale and the Genevan.
Wycliffe rendering his Vulgate (as was his wont) *very literally*, gives,
"shall be *cast to you*" ("hæc omnia *adjicientur* vobis").   Rheims has,
"shall be given you besides."   Ours is as literal as possible ; and yet there
cannot be any mistake as to the meaning.   (9) *V.* 34. "for *tomorrow day
shall care for itself*."   The Genevan and the Rhemish have "*the morrow*

day." The word "morrow" is said to be only the Saxon *morgen* = morning. Johnson says (ART. Morrow); "The original meaning of *morrow* seems to have been *morning*, which being often referred to on the preceding day, was understood in time to signify the whole day next following." He also says; "*To morrow* is sometimes, I think improperly, used as a noun." *To-morrow* and *to-day* are doubtless properly adverbs; and when "*to-morrow* is used as a noun," the full construction is "the to-morrow day" (or, if the assigned derivation be correct, "the day which begins in the morning"). From this full expression Cranmer has dropped the definite article, and the Rhemish the "to." Similarly in Greek αὔριον and σήμερον are properly adverbs (= to-morrow, to-day), and we have the full expression ἡ ἐς αὔριον ἡμέρα (the to-morrow day) in Sophocles Œd. Col. 565, 566, where Theseus says,

$$\text{ἐπεὶ}$$
$$\text{ἔξοιδ' ἀνὴρ ὤν, χὤτι τῆς ἐς αὔριον}$$
$$\text{οὐδὲν πλέον μοι σοῦ μέτεστιν ἡμέρας.}$$

(Since I know myself to be a man, and that I have no larger share in *the to-morrow day* than thyself.)]

Sunday.—V. 25. "Therefore I say unto you, Take no thought for your life, what ye shall eat, or what ye shall drink." Our Lord in this Gospel forbids all anxious thought about the supply of our bodily wants,—all such thought as shall distract the mind[1] from the service of God as the "one thing needful."[2] He forbids it, I observe, with special emphasis, repeating the words, "Take no thought" three times over, here in V. 25, and again in Vv. 31 and 34. And I observe further that He prefaces the words here with that solemn formula, with which He was

[1] Μὴ μεριμνᾶτε, μὴ μεριμνήσητε. It is much to be observed that the words μεριμνάω, μέριμνα, indicate by their etymology division or distraction. This throws great light upon the connexion between *v.* 24, "No man can serve *two* masters," etc., and *v.* 25, "Therefore I say unto you, Take no thought for" [Be not distracted about] "your life," etc. You can only serve one master at a time. Do not attempt, therefore, to divide your service. Do not allow worldly cares to distract you from the earnest, single-minded quest of God's kingdom and His righteousness.

[2] See St. Luke x. 42.

wont to usher in the weighty sentences of His new Law;
"I say unto you."   Who is this "I," who forbids, with
such emphasis, anxious thought about food, and drink, and
raiment?   Is it One who, from never having known want
Himself, cannot sympathize with the poor?   Nay; though,
as God, "he was rich" in the possession of all things,
"yet for" our "sakes he became poor, that" we "through
his poverty might be rich"[1]; He condescended to live upon
the alms of His creatures,[2] and often "had not where to
lay His head"[3];—so keen was His experience of the
want of necessary things.   And again, is He One, who is
unable to supply those needs, which He will not have to
engross us?   Nay, Lord, Thou art Thyself the "bread of
life"[4]; Thou biddest him who thirsts to come unto Thee
and drink[5]; Thou counsellest those, who have nothing
better to show than the "filthy rags"[6] of their own
righteousness, to buy of Thee white raiment, that they
may be clothed[7] indeed.   And if Thou art able to feed
and clothe the soul, shall we not believe that Thou art
much rather able to supply the body's necessities, as Thou
Thyself in this Gospel dost reason; "Is not the life more
than meat?"   He, therefore, who gives the life, is it not
easy for Him to give the meat which merely sustains it?

Monday.—V. 26. "Behold the fowls of the air: for
they sow not, neither do they reap, nor gather into barns:
yet your heavenly Father feedeth them."   Our Lord's lesson
is against anxious care, which distracts the mind from
God's service, not against prudent foresight and thrift.   If
the birds are proposed to us as a model of freedom from
care, we must remember that by the same Divine Wisdom,

---

[1] See 2 Cor. viii. 9.   [2] See St. Luke viii. 3.
[3] See St. Matt. viii. 20; St. Luke ix. 58.   [4] St. John vi. 35.
[5] See St. John vii. 37.   [6] See Isaiah lxiv. 6.   [7] See Rev. iii. 18.

speaking to us in the Book of Proverbs, the ants are proposed to us as a model of provident industry. " Go to the ant, thou sluggard; consider her ways, and be wise: which having no guide, overseer, or ruler, provideth her meat in the summer, and gathereth her food in the harvest."[1] And our Lord Himself, who exerted His miraculous power on more than one occasion to multiply food, would not have the food so multiplied, wasted, or thrown away; He showed a care that it should be thriftily dealt with; " Gather up the fragments that remain, that nothing be lost."[2] And His Apostles, who everywhere echo His precepts, warn us " that if any would not work, neither should he eat."[3] It is not therefore thrift, or industry, or even the foresight of, and provision against, wants which will arise in the future (for is not this foresight and provision the very basis of all civilisation, which Christ cannot be held to condemn?), but simply distraction of mind from the great all-absorbing aim of God's service, which is here condemned.

Tuesday.—V. 26. " Are ye not much better than they?" (the fowls). As He says in another place, " Ye are of more value than many sparrows."[4] The very capacity of understanding and being moved by an argument such as this, that He who makes provision for the birds, and controls the destiny of each one of them, will much more make all necessary provision for far nobler creatures, proves of itself the superiority of man to the fowls of the air. It is only reason which can be lifted up to apprehend, and take courage from, the superintending Providence of God. Let me observe how our Lord preaches and maintains, as necessary to the moral eleva-

---

[1] Prov. vi. 6, 7, 8.

[2] St. John vi. 12.

[3] 2 Thess. iii. 10.

[4] St. Matt. x. 31.

tion of man, the dignity of human nature. Man's capabilities are vast indeed, if it were only that he has the power of knowing and loving God. Man was made in God's image originally; and it was this fact which made the Incarnation,—that is, the union of the divine with the human nature in the Person of the Son,—practicable. How humbling is the thought that we have degraded by sin a nature of such great capabilities, to a level lower than that of the beasts which perish! For how often has man thrown his powers of imagination and invention into his vices! Animals, in pursuit of their prey, often inflict suffering or fear on other animals. But what animal ever employed its intelligence, as men have often done, to invent instruments of torture, and methods of prolonging life amidst exquisite sufferings? The ingenuity of reason has been called in, to give a higher zest to cruelty.

Wednesday.—Vv. 28, 29. " Consider the lilies of the field, how they grow; they toil not, neither do they spin: And yet I say unto you, That even Solomon in all his glory was not arrayed like one of these." We have here our Lord's expressed admiration of one of God's works of nature,—the flowers. Is not admiration of God's works of nature one of the traits demanded in the character of the Perfect Man? I call to mind that, when our Lord's attention was called to a work of art, and His admiration solicited for it; " Master, see what manner of stones and what buildings are here!", He had no word of commendation, but only of threatened judgment; " Seest thou these great buildings? there shall not be left one stone upon another, that shall not be thrown down."[1] I call to mind also the depreciation of a work

---

[1] St. Mark xiii. 1, 2.

of art in comparison of a work of nature in St. Mark's description of the Transfiguration; "His raiment became shining, exceeding white as snow; so as no fuller on earth can white them."[1] And in our Lord's choice of the flowers for special commendation I find one of the many traits of "the meekness and gentleness of Christ."[2] When God in the Old Testament would convict His servant Job of impotence and nothingness, He calls His attention to the works of *power* manifest in nature, both animate and inanimate, to the sea,[3] the stars,[4] the clouds,[5] the lightnings,[6] to the unicorn,[7] the ostrich,[8] the war horse,[9] the eagle,[10] the behemoth,[11] the leviathan.[12] But God, in the New Testament, seeking to win by sweet persuasiveness, rather than to overwhelm with fear, takes a tuft of the wild lilies, which grew on the Galilæan hills, and, holding them up before the eyes of His hearers, asks whether they can suppose that He, who clothes the perishable grass of the field in such lovely hues, will be unmindful that the curiously constructed bodies of His own children need covering to protect them.

Thursday.—V. 30. "Wherefore, if God *so* clothe the grass of the field." The main lesson of these words, and indeed of the whole passage of which they form a part, is one of trust in God's Providence. But there is a subordinate lesson, lying under the surface, against vanity and display in costume. God clothes the grass of the field *from within.* Those beautiful hues of the flower cannot be detached from the body which they adorn; they are not a raiment put on from without, but a natural

---

[1] St. Mark ix. 3. [2] 2 Cor. x. 1. [3] Job xxxviii. 8, 9, etc.
[4] *Vv.* 31, 32, etc. [5] *V.* 34. [6] *V.* 35. [7] Job xxxix. 10, 11, etc.
[8] *V.* 13. [9] *V.* 19, etc. [10] *V.* 27, etc. [11] Job xl. 15, etc.
[12] Job xli. 1, etc.

grace unfolded out of the flower's life. I am irresistibly reminded of St. Peter's warning against want of simplicity in apparel; " Whose adorning let it not be that outward adorning of plaiting the hair, and of wearing of gold, or of putting on of apparel; but let it be the hidden man of the heart, in that which is not corruptible, even the ornament of a meek and quiet spirit, which is in the sight of God of great price."[1] The "meek and quiet spirit," though (like the life of the flower) an inward endowment, will show itself outwardly by calmness, gentleness, modesty, retirement into the background; just as the flower's life shows itself outwardly in the delicately-painted blossom.—O God, what a mine of thought underlies Thy holy Word in every part, so that not only its superficial meanings are edifying, but those meanings also which it requires meditation to bring to light !

Friday.—V. 32. " For your heavenly Father knoweth that ye have need of all these things." " Heavenly,"—here is God's omnipotence; unlike human parents, who are always disposed to help, but often have not the power, He, being a heavenly Parent, " is able to do exceeding abundantly above all that we ask or think."[2] " Father," —here, in the centre between the other two great attributes, is the love of God, the source and spring of all His blessings, whether in nature, providence, or grace,—a love which blends the tenderness of a mother's affection with the far-seeing providence of a father's; for is it not said, " Can a woman forget her sucking child, that she should not have compassion on the son of her womb? yea, they may forget, yet will I not forget thee."[3] And then " knoweth";—here is God's omniscience; He " knoweth what things ye have need of, before ye ask

---

[1] 1 Pet. iii. 3, 4. [2] Eph. iii. 20. [3] Isaiah xlix. 15.

him."[1]   We pray, not to inform Him of our needs, but as a discipline of our own characters, and because He loves to hear from His children an acknowledgment of their dependence on Him.   What support, comfort, help, may we not expect from His fatherly love, seconded as it is by His omnipotence and omniscience !

Saturday.—V. 34. " Take therefore no thought for the morrow : for the morrow shall take thought for the things of itself.   Sufficient unto the day is the evil thereof."   Care, as distinct from sorrow, involves in its very nature a reference to the future, an apprehension of troubles or loss expected to accrue to-morrow.   This apprehension our Lord here cuts off, teaching us to live, not indeed *for* the present, but *in* the present, and not to let our thoughts busy themselves about a morrow which may never come, and which will provide for itself, if it does come.   What an emphasis is lent to these counsels of our Lord by the Old Testament precept about the manna, " Let no man leave of it till the morning."[2]   When the people violated this precept, and kept it over night, " it bred worms, and stank."[3]   The attempt to lay up the manna in store for the morrow was in vain, and defeated itself.—Teach me, O Lord, while I live for an eternal future, to live *in the present*, not in the past by sentimental regrets, still less in the future, by dismal and depressing apprehensions.

[1] See St. Matt. vi. 8.   [2] Exod. xvi. 19.   [3] *V.* 20.

CHAPTER LI.

THE GOSPEL FOR THE SIXTEENTH SUNDAY AFTER TRINITY.

St. Luke vii. 11 *to* 18
(except that in *v.* 11 "Jesus" is substituted for "he").

11 And it came to pass the day after, that Jesus went into a city
called Naim,* and many of his disciples went with him, and much

12 people.   Now when he came nigh to the gate of the city, behold,
there was a dead man carried out, the only son of his mother, and

13 she was a widow; and much people of the city was with her.   And
when the Lord saw her, he had compassion on her, and said unto

14 her, Weep not.   And he came and touched the biere, (and they that
bare him stood still) and he said, Young man, I say unto thee, Arise.

15 And he that was dead, sat up, and began to speak: and he delivered

16 him to his mother.   And there came a fear on all, and they glorified
God, saying, that a great Prophet is risen up among us, and that

17 God hath visited his people.   And this rumour of him went forth
throughout all Judea, and throughout all the region round about.

<table>
<tr><td>[Miss. Sar.</td><td>1549.</td><td>1662 s.b.</td></tr>
<tr><td>In illo tempore, Ibat Jesus in civitatem quæ vocatur Naim, et ibant cum eo discipuli ejus, etc. . . . down to the end of v. 16, "quia Deus visitavit plebem suam." (Vulg. Et factum est, deinceps ibat in civitatem, quæ vocatur Naim; et ibant cum eo discipuli ejus, etc. etc.)</td><td>And it fortuned, that Jesus went into a citie called Naim, and many of his disciples went with him, etc. . . . down to the end of v. 17, thorowout all the regions which lie round about.</td><td>And it came to pass the day after, that Jesus went into a city called Naim, and many of his disciples went with him, etc. . . . down to the end of v. 17, throughout all the region round about. (Gr. Καὶ ἐγένετο ἐν τῇ ἑξῆς, ἐπορεύετο εἰς πόλιν καλουμένην Ναΐν· καὶ συνεπορεύοντο αὐτῷ οἱ μαθηταὶ αὐτοῦ ἱκανοί, etc. etc.)</td></tr>
</table>

---

* In Mr. Stephens' Edition of the Sealed Book for the Chancery, the last letter of
the word "Naim" is printed blue.

Our Reformers in 1549 did well in adding the seventeenth verse to the old Sarum Gospel. It enhances our idea of the miracle, and of the impression which it made, to be told how far the fame of it spread. Nain was in Galilee, two miles from Capernaum (according to Jerome); but the fame of the miracle "as being a greater marvel of power than any which Jesus had previously exhibited," (the resuscitation of Jairus's daughter, which preceded it in point of time, took place much sooner after life was extinct, for the corpse was still in the death-chamber), circulated widely and rapidly, so that "His name was spread abroad, not only in the immediate neighbourhood of the town in which the miracle was wrought, but throughout Judæa also" ("Speaker's Commentary," *in loc.*); and the rumour even penetrated the walls of the castle of Machærus, and reached John in his prison-cell (see *v.* 18). The addition of this verse moreover emphasizes a distinguishing feature of the miracle,—*its designed publicity.* The raising of Jairus's daughter had been transacted with the utmost privacy (St. Mark v. 37, 40); and a strict command had been issued "that no man should know it" (St. Mark v. 43; St. Luke viii. 56), although even in this case "the fame hereof went abroad into all that land" (St. Matt. ix. 26). Here, on the other hand, the miracle is wrought under the eyes of a multitude (see the Thought for *Sunday*); and to have forbidden the publication of it would have been entirely out of keeping with the circumstances. The fame of the lifegiving Saviour, who was thus made (even before His own Resurrection) "a quickening spirit," flew around, as on the wings of the wind.

> Like circles widening round
>   Upon a clear blue river,
> Orb after orb, the wondrous sound
>   Is echoed on for ever. [1]

> Waft, waft, ye winds, His story,
>   And you, ye waters, roll,
> Till like a sea of glory,
>   It spreads from pole to pole. [2]

—This Gospel carries with it in its first verse a note of time, referring to what precedes it in St. Luke's narrative. King James's Translators, adopting the reading τῇ ἑξῆς, indicate the resuscitation of the Widow's Son as having taken place "the day after" the healing of the centurion's servant. But the reading of the Alexandrian and Vatican Manuscripts (τῷ ἑξῆς) which indicates a connexion of time by no means so strict, has

---

[1] "The Christian Year." (Christmas Day.)
[2] Bishop Heber in the Hymn "From Greenland's icy mountains."

been accepted by Bengel and Lachmann, and is apparently that which Jerome adopted ; for the rendering of the Vulgate is *deinceps*. The Revisers of 1881 also prefer this reading, and render, "It came to pass *soon afterwards*, that he went to a city," etc. We can discern more than one contrast between the miracle wrought on the centurion's servant and that wrought on the widow of Nain's Son, which may serve as mental couplings between the one and the other. The first was an exertion of miraculous power by an act of our Lord's will in a place which He never visited, and where the case of the sufferer only came before Him by the representations and intercessions of friends. In the second, the case of bereavement and consequent sorrow, which was relieved, was thrown directly across His path. Again ; in the one case, the tie which bound together the person on whom the miracle was wrought, and the person interested in him, was the social bond of master and servant. In the other the tie was that of nature,—the relationship of parent and child. And again ; in the first miracle no outward sign of any kind was employed (the extraordinary faith of the centurion needing none) ; in the second Christ "touched the bier," thereby arresting the attention, and probably awakening the expectations, of the mourners.—*Translation of* 1540. (1) *V.* 11. "And it *fortuned*, that Jesus went into a citie." And so Tyndale before, and the Genevan after, Cranmer. Wycliffe has, "it was don"; the Rhemish first rendered "it came to passe." As early probably as Cranmer's time the idea of chance was beginning to fade from the verb "to fortune," as it has faded from the synonymous "to happen." Probably in the mind of a translator of that day "it fortuned" was equivalent merely to "it occurred," "it happened." We have the verb once in Shakspere. Soon after his time probably it died out. See *Two Gentlemen of Verona*, Act V. Scene iv. (*last line but four*) ;

> "Please you, I'll tell you as we pass along,
> That you will wonder *what hath fortunèd*."

(2) *V.* 14. "And he came *nigh* and touched *the coffin*." The Revisers of 1881 have restored the "nigh," as contributing to make the rendering of προσελθὼν slightly more accurate. "Came nigh" had been already given by Wycliffe and the Rhemish as well as by Cranmer. But Tyndale dropped the "*nigh*," and in doing so was followed by the Genevan and Authorised.—King James's Translators took their word "bier" from Wycliffe ("touched the bere"). Tyndale, Cranmer, the Genevan, and the Rhemish, all have "coffin." Though the word "coffin" in the time of the Authorised Version, did not always mean a closed coffin, (as is clear from the well-known passage, "My heart is *in the coffin* there with Cæsar,"

compared with "Look! in this place ran Cassius' dagger through : See what a rent the envious Casca made," etc. [*Julius Cæsar*, Act III. Scene ii.]) yet now we always mean by coffin a chest shut and nailed down, before it is laid in the earth, and which, as it appears at a funeral, allows no view of the person of the deceased. "Bier" therefore is the better word. —(3) *V.* 17. "And this rumour of him went forth thorowout all *Jury*." Tyndale, the Genevan, and the Rhemish, all have "Jewrie." King James's Translators went back to Wycliffe's "alle *iudee*." We may still hope to retain the word "Jewry" in the Prayer Book Version of Ps. lxxvi. (*v.* 1). "In Jewry is God known : His Name is great in Israel." The Revisers of 1881 have struck it out from St. Luke xxiii. 5 and St. John vii. 1, in both which places of the Authorised Version it still lingers ; and it is probable that the Old Testament Revision Company may extinguish it in Dan. v. 13 ; but even so an instance of the word will still remain in the Book of Common Prayer. It must be admitted that, as meaning merely a district (whether city or country), in which Jews dwell, it is hardly as accurate a rendering as "Judea." Yet in the time of the Authorised Version it seems to have been often used as exactly equivalent to Judæa. Thus we find "Herod the king of Judea" four times called "Herod of Jewry" by Shakspere ; and the "wives of Jewry" who "with their howls confused" did "break the clouds At Herod's bloody-hunting slaughter-men" (*Henry V.*, Act III. Scene iii.) are evidently the mothers of "the children that were in Bethlehem, and in all the coasts thereof" (*i.e.* in Judea). [See St. Matt. ii. 16.] In *Antony and Cleopatra*, however, (Act IV. Scene vi.), "Jewry" is used more loosely for Palestine ; "Alexas did revolt ; and went to Jewry On affairs of Antony."]

Sunday.—V. 11. "Many of his disciples went with him, and much people." The publicity with which this miracle of raising the dead was wrought, contrasts strikingly with the privacy, which our Lord insisted upon in the case of Jairus's daughter. In that case, He closed the door upon " the minstrels and the people making a noise,"[1] and suffered only the three chosen Apostles, and the father and mother of the maiden, to witness the miracle.[2] Here the miracle is wrought " in the chief place of concourse,

---

[1] See St. Matt. ix. 23, 24, 25.
[2] See St. Mark v. 37, 40 ; St. Luke viii. 51.

in the openings of the gates," [1] and in the confluence of two crowds—a crowd of people who followed our Lord, and another crowd who, in token of respect for the dead and sympathy with the bereaved mother, attended the funeral.[2]　I observe an exquisite appropriateness in each miracle to the circumstances under which it was wrought. There is a solemn stillness in the death-chamber, which it jars upon us to disturb.　Even sobbing, and wailing, and loud ebullitions of grief, are felt to be somewhat out of place ; we say " Hush !" we hurry away those who cannot command their feelings.　But a funeral is in its very nature a public occasion ; the period of domestic seclusion is ended ; the corpse is carried openly to the grave ; and whether by the Service, or by words spoken to them, we seek to carry home a lesson to the hearts of those who witness what is done.　The sermon which our Lord preached at this funeral, and which impressed all the bystanders with awe and convictions,[3] was a sermon on His sympathy with man's sorrows, and His power to save from death.　The larger the number present, the more there were to be edified by the sermon.—Lord, in every-thing that Thou doest there is a delicate suitability to the occasion, which escapes those who do not look below the surface.　And the same I observe in everything that Thou sayest.　" The Lord God hath given " thee " the tongue of the learned, that " thou shouldest " *know how to speak a word in season* to him that is weary."[4]　I must bear this in mind as a warning against separating Scriptures too much from their context, and not looking at them in the connexion in which they occur.

Monday.—V. 12.　" She was a widow : and much

---

[1] See Prov. i. 21.　　　　　[2] *Vv.* 11, 12.
[3] See *v.* 16.　　　　　[4] See Isaiah l. 4.

people of the city was with her." This large attendance at the funeral of her son indicates that the widow was a person of consideration in the city,—rich, perhaps, and noble. Another widow, who came across our Lord's path at a later period, was in abject poverty. "Two mites, which make a farthing," were "all that she had, even all her living."[1] For that widow the Saviour had *a word of commendation,*—the Divine tribute to her self-sacrificing munificence; "Verily I say unto you, That this poor widow hath cast more in, than all they which have cast into the treasury."[2] For this, whose heart was wrung with sorrow, He has *a word of consolation,* "Weep not," and, since all God's words take effect, and none of them is spoken into the air, an *act of consolation* also; "He delivered" the living son "to his mother." Here is another instance of the suitability of Christ's words and acts to their occasion. And hence also arises the consideration that riches, rank, influence, though to many they prove such deadly snares, that our Lord says "it is easier for a camel to go through the eye of a needle, than for a rich man to enter into the kingdom of God,"[3] yet may be possessed in such a manner as by no means to shut out their possessors from Divine compassion and Divine consolation. Wherever there is the open avenue of faith, whether in rich or poor, these pass into the soul.

Tuesday.—V. 13. "When the Lord saw her, he had compassion on her." Our Lord usually wrought His miracles in answer to an application for relief from the patient or his friends, in order, doubtless, forcibly to impress upon men the lesson, "Ask, and it shall be given you; seek, and ye shall find."[4] It was not so here, nor in the

---

[1] See St. Mark xii. 42, 44. [2] *Ibid. v.* 43.
[3] St. Mark x. 25. [4] St. Matt. vii. 7 ; St. Luke xi. 9.

case of the woman bowed together by a spirit of infirmity in the thirteenth chapter of this Gospel, whom He summoned to Him without any application on her part.[1]   " While we have to do with the Father of mercies," says Bishop Hall, " our afflictions are the most powerful suitors.   No prayers can move Him so much as His own commiseration."   The cry of need and distress is itself a prayer, which reaches and moves the heart of the Father of mercies, even when it comes from irrational creatures; and accordingly we read of the young ravens crying unto God, and God giving them food.[2]   How much more is the cry of need and distress a prayer, when it comes from a rational creature with an immortal spirit; " Are ye not much better than they ?"[3]   And so it is written; " Lord, thou hast heard the *desire* of the humble "[4]; and again, " It shall come to pass, that before they call, I will answer."[5] —I will take comfort, then, if in any sudden great emergency or trouble I do not feel able to throw my prayers into form, am all abroad, dazed, and stunned, do not know what to pray for.   The mere exposure of the heart to God with all its grief, needs, achings, longings, this is accounted prayer by my heavenly Father; it is " the desire of the humble," and He will hear it.   So rare were Christ's miraculous resuscitations of the dead (probably the raising of Jairus's daughter was the only one which had yet occurred) that perhaps the widow would not have ventured to ask this.   As there is an importunity in prayer, which God loves, when the thing asked for is clearly according to His will, so there is a modesty and reticence in prayer, which particularly wins Him, when

---

[1] See St. Luke xiii. 11, 12, 13.
[2] See Job xxxviii. 41 ; Ps. cxlvii. 9 ; St. Luke xii. 24.
[3] St. Matt. vi. 26.   [4] Ps. x. 17.   [5] Isaiah lxv. 24.

we merely expose our needs to Him, to deal with us as He pleases, feeling that "we know not what we should pray for as we ought."[1]

Wednesday.—V. 13. "When the Lord saw her, he had compassion on her, and said unto her, Weep not." What a store of thought there is in these two short words! What an essential feature the miracle would lose, if they had not been said! First; we should have lost the expression of the tenderness of Christ for human sorrow, which, combined as it is with the exercise of His power reaching even into the domains of the dead, is so peculiarly consolatory. A tenderly sympathizing omnipotence is the character of Him "with whom we have to do."[2] Then again, secondly, we should have lost the precious practical lesson of giving relief sympathetically, and with an expression of sympathy. Even where we can do little or nothing to alleviate the distress of a sufferer, such an expression, if genuine (and mourners have a wonderful instinct for detecting its genuineness), finds its way to a sufferer's heart with a soothing and healing power. And then, again, there is in these words the recognition of a law, which pervades all the miraculous relief given by God to man —that man must more or less anticipate and expect it, before it can be bestowed. Without hope, without faith, in blank despair, he is not susceptible of relief. Hence, before the relief is administered, something is said or done to put the mind on the alert, to quicken expectation; " Wilt thou be made whole?"[3] " Peter, fastening his eyes upon him with John, said, Look on us "[4]; and here, the word of consolation spoken by the Wonder-worker, and the touching of the bier.—Ah, Lord, how profound and how

1 See Rom. viii. 26.   2 See Heb. iv. 13.
3 See St. John v. 6.   4 Acts iii. 4.

manifold are the meanings of Thy slightest word! As we may apply the microscope to Thy humblest works of nature, and discover ever new wonders, so is Thy briefest utterance also inexhaustible in its significance.

Thursday.—V. 14. " And he came and touched the bier " (or open coffin). The following thought is from Quesnel; " Christ touches the living coffin of a dead soul, when He smites its body with some sore sickness, or its senses with certain objects, or its ears with certain words, which conduce by means of grace to its conversion." There is here a wide field for meditation on the access which God gains to the inward (the spirit of man being imprisoned in a body of flesh and blood) through the outward. The works of nature preach to the eye (" the heavens declare the glory of God; and the firmament sheweth his handy-work "[1]); the word of God to the ear (" so then faith cometh by hearing, and hearing by the word of God"[2]). And how often have bodily pain and sickness been made instrumental in solemnising, softening, subduing the soul!

Friday.—V. 15. " And he that was dead sat up, and began to speak." In other miracles of resuscitation, other symptoms of the receiving of life are specified: sneezing and opening the eyes in the case of the Shunammite's child,[3] walking in the case of Jairus's daughter,[4] coming forth from the sepulchre in the case of Lazarus,[5] opening the eyes in the case of Dorcas[6]; here, and only here, we have mention of *speaking*, an act not purely physical, but denoting an exercise of the mind. I will take occasion to reflect that the first act of the soul, which is raised by the grace of Christ from the death of sin to the life of

---

[1] Ps. xix. 1.   [2] Rom. x. 17.   [3] See 2 Kings iv. 35.
[4] See St. Mark v. 42.   [5] See St. John xi. 44.   [6] See Acts ix. 40.

righteousness, is to confess its sins to God,—the first symptom this of restored vitality. "While I held my tongue : my bones consumed away through my daily complaining."[1] . . . "I said, I will confess my sins unto the Lord : and so thou forgavest the wickedness of my sin."[2] On reaching his home, and being welcomed, the first thing which the prodigal does is to say, "Father, I have sinned against heaven, and in thy sight,"[3]—the evidence this that the son who was dead is alive again.[4]

Saturday.—V. 15. "And he delivered him to his mother." It is very observable that in the case of the widow of Zarephath's son, of the Shunammite's son, of Jairus's daughter, and here also, there was a restoration of a child to parents,[5] who were mourning its loss. "Women," says the Apostle to the Hebrews, looking back at the Old Testament resuscitations wrought by Elijah and Elisha, "received their dead raised to life again."[6] If we can augur anything from these miraculous resuscitations, as to the proceedings of the general resurrection, must we not suppose, that one of those proceedings will be the restoration to their friends of those who have fallen asleep in Jesus, — a restoration which shall wipe away the mourner's tears ? It is not only a deeply-seated instinct of our nature, but also several incidental notices of Scripture, which hold out this blessed hope of mutual recognition, and re-union in a land beyond the grave ; "them which sleep in Jesus shall God bring with him."[7] In that day the long separated brothers shall meet again, and greet one another; as it is written, "he went, and met him in the mount of God, and kissed him."[8]

1 Ps. xxxii. 3, P.B.V.   2 Ps. xxxii. 6, P.B.V.
3 St. Luke xv. 21.   4 See *Vv.* 24, 32.
5 See 1 Kings xvii. 23 ; 2 Kings iv. 36 ; St. Luke viii. 51, 56.
6 Heb. xi. 35.   7 1 Thess. iv. 14.   8 Exod. iv. 27.

CHAPTER LII

THE GOSPEL FOR THE SEVENTEENTH SUNDAY AFTER TRINITY.

St. Luke xiv. 1 *to* 12
(leaving out "And," and substituting "Jesus" for "he" in *v.* 1).

1 It came to pass, as Jesus went into the house of one of the
chief Pharisees to eat bread on the sabbath-day, that they watched
2 him. And behold, there was a certain man before him who had
3 the dropsie. And Jesus answering, spake unto the lawyers and
4 Pharisees, saying, Is it lawful to heal on the sabbath-day? And
they held their peace. And he took him, and healed him, and let
5 him go; and answered them, saying, Which of you shall have an
ass, or an ox fallen into a pit, and will not straight-way pull him
6 out on the sabbath-day? And they could not answer him again
7 to these things. And he put forth a parable to those who were
bidden, when he marked how they chose out the chief rooms, saying
8 unto them, When thou art bidden of any man to a wedding, sit not
down in the highest room, lest a more honourable man than thou
9 be bidden of him: And he that bade thee and him, come and say to
thee, Give this man place; and thou begin with shame to take the
10 lowest room. But when thou art bidden, go and sit down in the
lowest room, that when he that bade thee, cometh, he may say unto
thee, Friend, go up higher: then shalt thou have worship in the
11 presence of them that sit at meat with thee. For whosoever
exalteth himself, shall be abased; and he that humbleth himself,
shall be exalted.

[Miss. Sar.	1549.	1662 s.b.
In illo tempore, Cum *introisset* Jesus in do-	It chanced that Jesus went into the house of	It came to pass, as Jesus went into the

mum cujusdam principis Pharisæorum sabbato manducare panem, etc. (*Vulg.* Et factum est cum intraret Jesus in domum cujusdam principis Pharisæorum sabbato manducare panem, etc.)

one of the chief Pharisees, to eat bread on the sabbath day, etc.

house of one of the chief Pharisees to eat bread on the sabbath day, etc. (*Gr.* Καὶ ἐγένετο ἐν τῷ ἐλθεῖν αὐτὸν εἰς οἶκόν τινος τῶν ἀρχόντων τῶν Φαρισαίων σαββάτῳ φαγεῖν ἄρτον, etc.)

It is to be regretted that the "And," with which Chap. xiv. opens, should have been dropped in the Liturgical Gospel. It connects the invitation given to our Lord by "one of the chief Pharisees" with a plot of theirs to get rid of Him which had failed, and the failure of which had doubtless irritated them ; and thus shows (what indeed is not obscurely intimated in the words "they watched him," *v.* 1) the hypocrisy which underlay this show of courtesy and friendliness. (See the Thought for *Sunday.*) In Chap. xiii. 31, we read, "The same day there came certain of the Pharisees, saying unto him, Get thee out, and depart hence : for Herod will kill thee." Herod, already troubled with alarms of conscience occasioned by his murder of the Baptist (St. Matt. xiv. 2 ; St. Mark vi. 16), a crime which he was averse to commit (St. Matt. xiv. 5 ; St. Mark vi. 20), and to which he had been driven only by a regard to his rash oath and his character as a prince who kept his word (St. Matt. xiv. 9), was not likely seriously to intend to kill our Lord. But he would gladly have got rid of Him out of his dominions, and with that view intrigued with the Pharisees to frighten Him away from the tetrarchy. (Similarly Amaziah the priest of Beth-el had sought to banish the prophet Amos from Beth-el, and to induce him to flee into the land of Judah and prophesy there,—see Amos vii. 12, 13.) Our Lord instantaneously saw through the intrigue, and sent a message to Herod, the wily "fox," who had set it on foot, the scope of which was that "the times and seasons" were in higher hands than those of men (see Acts i. 7), that when the time came for laying down His life, He would lay it down, but that, so long as any thing remained for Him to do, and while yet it was day, He must work the works of Him that sent Him (see St. John ix. 4). To this He adds, by way of reply to the hypocritical counsellors who had feigned a concern for His safety, that His life must needs be secure so long as He was not yet in Jerusalem, which had ever been the slaughter-house of God's true prophets ("it cannot be that a prophet perish out of Jerusalem," *v.* 33). Then follows the pathetic lament over Jerusalem, with the prediction of the utter desolation of the temple ("*your* house,"—no longer God's, *v.* 35),—words which would intensify the bitterness already

existing towards Him in the mind of the Pharisees.   The result was that
they immediately plotted against Him in another form, issuing a friendly
invitation, with the purpose of lying in wait for Him "to catch something
out of his mouth, that they might accuse him" (see St. Luke xi. 54),—
thus entitling themselves to the appellation of "this fox," which our
Lord had given to Herod, and which Bishop Christopher Wordsworth
thinks to have been intended for them as much as for the tetrarch.—
Translation of 1540.   (1) *V.* 1. "It *chanced* that Jesus."   Cranmer here
follows Tyndale.   Wycliffe has "it was don"; and the Genevan was the
first to render, "it came to passe."   The same remark might be made of
the "it chanced" as of "it fortuned" in the Introduction to the preceding Gospel,—that the idea of fortuitousness had more or less worn away
out of it in Cranmer's time, and that the word was beginning to be simply
equivalent to "it occurred."   Thus Shakspere uses it more than half a
century later :

> "Now in London place him
> .   .   .   .   and omit
> All the occurrences, whatever chanced,
> Till Harry's back-return again to France."
>   (HENRY V., *Chorus at the beginning of Act V.*)

(2) *V.* 1. "It chanced that Jesus went into the house . . . *and* they
watched him."   This simple mode of rendering ἐν τῷ ἐλθεῖν αὐτὸν εἰς
οἶκον . . . καὶ αὐτοὶ ἦσαν παρατηρούμενοι αὐτὸν is borrowed from Tyndale.
Wycliffe had rendered the ἐν τῷ ἐλθεῖν, etc., rightly, "*whanne he* hadde
entrid in to the hous," but he retains the "*and*" ("and thei aspieden
hym"), making the English unidiomatic.   The Rhemish, too, while giving
"when" in the former clause, inserts the "and," probably because the
Vulgate does so, "Et factum est *cum intraret Jesus* in domum, etc. . . .
et ipsi observabant eum."   The Genevan was the first English version
which dropped it, and the Authorised followed suit.   It should be dropped
in an idiomatic translation.   The redundant "and" is to be explained as
arising from a mixture of two constructions, the one that given by
Cranmer, "He went into the house, AND they watched him," the other,
"When He went into the house, they watched Him."   [See Winer's
Grammar of New Testament Greek, edited by Rev. W. F. Moulton, D.D.
Edinburgh : 1877.   Sec. LIII. 3 (f), and Sec. LXV. 3.]   (3) *V.* 7. "He put
forth also a *similitude* to the *ghests*."   And similarly Tyndale and the
Genevan.   "Parable" is here obviously better than "similitude," as
being often used in a laxer sense.   The parable here is simply a moral
instruction (like one of the Proverbs of Solomon), with a deeper spiritual
significance lying under the surface.   "Claim only a low place, and your

fellow-men will put you in a higher." The underlying significance is that humility of heart *in dealing with God* will be followed by exaltation. As society deals with those who *profess* humility, so will God deal with those who *have* it. This is the only "similitude." (See the Thought for *Friday.*) (4) *V.* 7. "when he marked how *they preassed to be in the* highest roums." And so Tyndale and the Genevan. Wycliffe, truer to the original, rendered, "hou thei *chesen* the first sittynge placis." The "*chose out*" of the Authorised is truer still (ἐξελέγοντο). (5) *V.* 10. "Friend, *sit* up higher." It is difficult to account for this rendering of προσανάβηθι by all the English Versions previous to the Authorised, with the exception of Wycliffe, who has, "frend come higer." The "Amice, *ascende* superius" (= mount higher) of the Vulgate gives us no clue to the solution.]

Sunday.—V. 1. "And it came to pass, as he went into the house of one of the chief Pharisees to eat bread on the sabbath-day, that they watched him." Our Lord had been invited by this Pharisee, as by Simon in the seventh Chapter.[1] And He knew that under the courtesy there was latent a hostile intention; His enemies were seeking to use His words and actions as a handle against Him; for we are told that "they watched him." Yet He did not decline the invitation, nor allow "the eyes of suspicion and hatred which rested upon Him to dry up the ever fresh fountain of His love" (Rev. Isaac Williams). We do not read that He ever declined any invitation which was addressed to Him.—Lord, Thou art ever more willing to be our guest than we are to bid Thee. Thou proposest Thyself to us (oh, wonderful act of grace and condescension!) as to Zacchæus of old; "To day I must abide at thy house."[2] Thou standest at the door of our hearts, and by Thy voice in the conscience, by Thy preached word, by providences, by chastisements, by mercies, Thou knockest for admittance. We have Thine own word to assure us of Thy longing to enter; "If any

---

[1] See Chap. vii. 36, 40. [2] St. Luke xix. 5.

man hear my voice, and open the door, I will come in to him, and will sup with him, and he with me."[1]　It was in pledge of this willingness to enter into every heart which opens itself to Thee, that, when even malignant Pharisees bade Thee to their houses, Thou didst forthwith cross the threshold.

Monday.—V. 2. " And, behold, there was a certain man before him which had the dropsy." This poor man did not solicit a cure. Probably he dared not do so on the sabbath, and when on the premises of a Pharisee. But he hoped that, if he placed himself in our Lord's way, he might attract His notice, as so many other suffering patients had done, and in this hope he entered before our Lord into the court, round which the house was built, and there awaited Him as He passed on towards the dining-room. And he gained his object. " One in distress or infirmity was to Christ what the sight of a great man may be to us, something that immediately attracted his attention " (Isaac Williams). "It suffices oftentimes," says Quesnel, "that our misery should be exposed to the eyes of the Divine mercy. That mercy is apt to prevent us, and, without waiting to be solicited, is disposed to do us good." Sometimes our minds are in such a tangled state, that we cannot pray in words, however much we desire it. But we can at all events place ourselves by an act of self-recollection in Christ's Presence, and, as it were, court His eye. He is prompt to note such an act, and if we persevere in it patiently, simply turning our eyes towards His power and mercy without any definite petition, He will interpret for us our wishes, and give the relief we need.—And, as another application of the same idea, is it not one of the advantages, which men reap from con-

---

[1] Rev. iii. 20.

scientiously attending Public Worship, that they thereby throw themselves as it were across Christ's pathway, and may thus come in for a share of the blessings which He does not fail to distribute " where two or three are gathered together in " His " name "[1]?

Tuesday.—V. 4. " And he took him, and healed him." " He took him,"—that is, took hold of him, took him by the hand, or laid His hands upon him. We must not overlook the significance of this "taking." Our Lord sometimes did miracles by a simple act of volition, as when at a distance he healed the son of the nobleman of Capernaum,[2] the servant of the centurion of Capernaum,[3] and the daughter of the Syro-Phœnician woman.[4] In such cures His Divine nature displayed itself; for God's will takes immediate effect, without words or visible signs, in the remotest parts of His universe. But in the greater number of His cures, our Lord used His hands in some form or other, thus bringing the patient into contact with His own person. Hereby He indicated two things. First; that not merely as God, but as man also, He had the power of healing; for whenever the will of man acts upon matter, and modifies or counteracts the forces of nature, it is upon the condition that he uses his body; without that instrumentality he can produce no impression. Secondly; that His human nature—of which His body was the external part and the symbol—is the great instrument of healing, the means which He uses for our recovery. It is through the suffering and glorified humanity of Christ that mercy and salvation pass to sinners; there is no other avenue through which they can pass. And hence it is

[1] See St. Matt. xviii. 20.
[2] See St. John iv. 46, 47, 50, 53.   [3] See St. Luke vii. 1, 2, 3, 10.
[4] See St. Mark vii. 26, 29, 30.

said ; "Except ye eat the flesh of the Son of man, and drink his blood, ye have no life in you."[1]

Wednesday.—V. 5. " And answered them, saying." So above (V. 3), " And Jesus *answering* spake unto the lawyers and Pharisees."   But the lawyers and Pharisees are not said to have put any question, or made any observation.   No; but they were watching Him, to see how He would act in the matter of the dropsical man. And He, reading their thoughts, made an answer which was exactly to the point, the gist of which was that if it was right to rescue on the Sabbath an animal in distress —a work involving some labour, the bringing of ropes to the place, the adjusting them, the effort of pulling—much more must it be justifiable to relieve one of God's rational creatures, endowed with a rational soul, especially when this latter was done (as God does all things) with the utmost ease, promptitude, and freedom.[2]   Our Lord, in dealing with us, reads our thoughts.   " Unto Him all hearts be open, and every act of the will speaketh "[3] (such is the literal translation of the words, with which the first Collect in the Communion Service commences).   And His " answers " are to be found in various parts of Holy Scripture, many passages of which come home to the devout and thoughtful student with such peculiar appositeness to his circumstances, that they seem to have been written in contemplation of his case.   And, indeed, in the design of the Holy Spirit,—who foresaw and foreknew all things, when causing those words to be written, —it was so.

[1] St. John vi. 53.   [2] See *v.* 5.

[3] " Deus, cui omne cor patet, et *omnis voluntas loquitur,* et quem nullum latet secretum, etc. etc."   Original of the Collect for Purity at the opening of the Communion Service as it stands in the Sarum Missal.

Thursday.—V. 7. " And he put forth a parable to those which were bidden, when he marked how they chose out the chief rooms." Are the miracle and parable of which this Gospel consists, strung together by any thread of thought, or is their juxtaposition merely fortuitous ? Clearly there is a deep connexion. The dropsical man had attracted our Lord's attention, and had been healed by Him. And now He marks among the guests a worse than bodily dropsy, the morbid tumour and inflation of pride, which He addresses Himself to heal by His heavenly doctrine. But the connexion is, I believe, even deeper than this. The Pharisees had shown a miserable want of love, by grudging this poor patient his cure on the sabbath. They had not that compassion for his distress, which they would have shown for the distress of an ox and ass being their own property. Now want of love springs from pride. Pride is the great solvent of human society, which breaks it up and disintegrates it. All dissensions have their root in pride. And therefore the reproof of want of love is most appropriately followed by a reproof of pride. I see that, as it is with the Lord's Prayer, so it is (more or less) with the whole Scripture ; there is as much of significance and instruction in the connexion of the parts, and in the way in which one part opens out from another, as in the parts themselves.

Friday.—V. 7. " And he put forth a *parable* to those which were bidden, when he marked how they chose out the chief rooms ; saying unto them." Our right understanding of what follows depends upon our observing that the saying is called, and therefore is to be considered as, a *parable*—a parable drawn, as several of our Lord's are, from the ways and habits of men. It is not necessarily implied in such a parable that these ways of men are justifiable, or what they ought to be ; suffice it if we can draw from the parable a wholesome lesson as to what God's ways may be expected to be. In the Parable of the Unjust Judge, the human judge's want of sympathy and piety is by no means commended to us for imitation ; but the lesson is, if a hard and bad man can be won by importunity, how much more shall He be so won, who is "always more ready to hear than we to pray"[1]? Here the parable is a maxim of worldly wisdom, drawn substantially from the Book of Proverbs, which abounds with such maxims ; " Put not forth thyself in the presence of the king, and stand not in the place of great men : for better it is that it be said unto thee, Come up hither ; than that thou shouldest be put lower in the presence of the prince whom thine eyes have seen."[2] Our Lord does not mean, neither does the Holy Spirit who spake by Solomon mean, that the worldly policy of putting one's self in a lower place, with the view of being asked to take a higher, is a form of humility which ought to be imitated, (for indeed it is no humility at all, but only pride aping humility) ; but merely that, as it is the fashion of human society to place the unpretentious man lowest, and to give pretentiousness a rebuff ; so God in His eternal kingdom will assuredly exalt to the highest places those who are really lowly in their own eyes, and abase those who have a high conceit of their own goodness and strength. Thus, incidentally, our Lord teaches us how to understand Solomon's Proverbs, and how to turn every one of them,— even where the maxim seems thoroughly worldly on the surface, and has a worldly ring about it,—into a spiritual lesson. " Withdraw thy foot from thy neighbour's house ;

---

[1] Collect for Twelfth Sunday after Trinity, and see St. Luke xviii. 1-9.
[2] Prov. xxv. 6, 7.

lest he be weary of thee, and so hate thee."[1] It is not prudent, that is, in paying a visit, to outstay your welcome. But this is not all we are meant to find in the proverb. It, too, is a parable. There is one who never wearies of us, however often we seek His Presence,—nay, who delights to have us with Him, and never finds our visits unseasonable. Barzillai thought he might be "a burden unto my lord the king," if he went and lived at David's court.[2] In the court of the King of heaven we can never be burdensome.

Saturday.—V. 11. " Whosoever exalteth himself shall be abased ; and he that humbleth himself shall be exalted ;"—a maxim which, on account of its transcendent importance, our Lord often repeated.[3] Here is a thought from Isaac Williams ; " Many are the forms of humility, or the ways in which it shows itself, which our Lord sets forth in different parables ; on this occasion it is taking the lowest place at a feast; at another, it is one who in prayer stands afar off, not daring to lift up his eyes to Heaven ; in another, it is one who comes with the words, ' Father, I am not worthy to be called thy son, make me as one of thy hired servants' ; in another parable, it is one who loved much because he felt he had been forgiven much ; in another, it is one who, even at the last Day, says with surprise, ' Lord, when saw we thee an hungered, and ministered unto thee ?' as if quite unconscious of any good in himself that should claim so great a reward. Many also are the examples which set forth the same in different aspects, but this one expression embraces all.— There seems some great mystery on this subject of humi-

---

[1] Prov. xxv. 17. [2] See 2 Sam. xix. 32, 33, 35.

[3] See Chap. xviii. 14 (where the saying occurs at the end of the Parable of the Pharisee and Publican) and St. Matt. xxiii. 12.

lity, as connected with our justification, with the atonement of Christ and our faith. Perhaps the less we say to explain it, the less likely shall we be to fall into error; for it is one on which the most wise have fallen, but the meek will be guided aright in the way of peace."[1]

The pride whereby Lucifer fell, and the profound humiliation whereby the Son of God wrought out human redemption, connect themselves with the profoundness and mysteriousness of this Divine aphorism. On the one hand, "How art thou fallen from heaven, O Lucifer, son of the morning![2] . . . For thou hast said in thine heart, I will ascend into heaven, I will exalt my throne above the stars of God . . . I will be like the most High." On the other, "Who made himself of no reputation, and took upon him the form of a servant, and was made in the likeness of men : and being found in fashion as a man, he humbled himself, and became obedient unto death, even the death of the cross. Wherefore God also hath highly exalted him."[3]

[1] "Sermons on the Epistles and Gospels, by the Rev. Isaac Williams, B.D." Vol. II., p. 216. (Rivingtons, 1875.)

[2] Isaiah xiv. 12 13, 14.   [3] Phil. ii. 7, 8, 9.

CHAPTER LIII.

THE GOSPEL FOR THE EIGHTEENTH SUNDAY AFTER TRINITY.

St. Matt. xxii. 34 *to the end*
(omitting "But," and substituting "Jesus" for "he" in *v.* 34).

34   When the Pharisees had heard that Jesus had put the Sadduces
35 to silence, they were gathered together. Then one of them, who was
36 a lawyer, asked him a question, tempting him, and saying, Master,
37 which is the great commandment in the law? Jesus said unto him,
   Thou shalt love the Lord thy God with all thy heart, and with all
38 thy soul, and with all thy mind. This is the first and great com-
39 mandment. And the second is like unto it, Thou shalt love thy
40 neighbour as thy self. On these two commandments hang all the
41 law and the prophets. While the Pharisees were gathered together,
42 Jesus asked them, saying, What think ye of Christ? whose son is
43 he? They say unto him, The son of David. He saith unto them,
44 How then doth David in Spirit call him Lord, saying, The Lord
   said unto my Lord, Sit thou on my right hand, till I make thine
45 enemies thy footstool? If David then call him Lord, how is he
46 his Son? And no man was able to answer him a word, neither
   durst any man (from that day forth) ask him any moe questions.

[Miss. Sar.	1559.	1662 s.b.
In illo tempore, Accesserunt ad Jesum Pharisæi ; et interrogavit eum unus ex eis legis doctor, etc. (*Vulg.* Pharisæi autem audientes quòd silentium imposuisset Sadducæis, convenerunt in unum : Et interrogavit eum unus ex eis, etc.)	When the Pharisees had heard that Jesus had put the Sadduces to silence, they came together, etc.	When the Pharisees had heard that Jesus had put the Sadduces to silence, they were gathered together. (*Gr.* Οἱ δὲ Φαρισαῖοι, ἀκούσαντες ὅτι ἐφίμωσε τοὺς Σαδδουκαίους, συνήχθησαν ἐπὶ τὸ αὐτό.)

The loss of the "But," with which *v.* 34 commences, is not much felt, because *v.* 34 itself contains an explicit reference to the discomfiture of the Sadducees which had just preceded.   Our Gospel contains the last of a series of questions put to our Lord, the three first of which were hostile in intent.   The first (Chap. xxi. 23) was from the ecclesiastical heads of the people, "the chief priests and the elders," as to the authority under which He was acting in cleansing the temple, etc.—The second was from a mixed deputation of Pharisees and Herodians (Chap. xxii. 15, 16), as to the lawfulness of giving tribute to Cæsar,—an acknowledgment of the Roman supremacy, which the first repudiated on the theocratic ground, and the second on the secular ground of still maintaining such vestiges of a national polity and independence, as the rule of the Herodian princes seemed to offer.   The third was from the rationalistic party of the day, the Sadducees (Chap. xxii. 23), as to the domestic relations in the future state of parties who had been more than once married.   In answering this question our Lord's profound argument from the Book of Exodus in proof of the Resurrection made its mark on the mind of at least one of the hearers.   One of the scribes, who had heard them reasoning together, "perceived that He had answered them well" (see St. Mark xii. 28). That scribe,—the "lawyer" of St. Matt. xxii. 35—impressed by what he had heard, and dropping all hostile intent, proceeded to put to Him a question which had perplexed rival theological schools, with a sincere intent of eliciting the true solution.   "Here, as in St. Luke x. 25, the expression *tempting* does not necessarily imply an evil intention.   It simply means 'trying Him'—endeavouring to test His wisdom as a teacher."   ("Speaker's Commentary," *in loc.*; and see the Thought for *Sunday*).—*Translation of* 1540.   (1) *V.* 35.   "And one of them which was *a doctor of the law.*"   And so Tyndale and the Rhemish.   Wycliffe has, "a *teacher* of the lawe;" the Genevan, "an *exponder* of the lawe." The Revisers of 1881 have retained the "lawyer" of the Authorised Version, probably because thus a distinction is drawn between νομικὸς (the word used here) and νομοδιδάσκαλος, a word found only once in the Gospels (St. Luke v. 17) but occurring again Acts v. 34 (of Gamaliel) and 1 Tim. i. 7 ("desiring to be *teachers of the law*").   (2) *V.* 36.   "Which is the *greatest* commandment in the law?" and again *v.* 38, "This is the first and *greatest* commandment."   So stand the words in the Photo-zincographed facsimile of the Black-Letter Prayer Book of 1636 [39 ?], in which were entered the corrections of 1662.   But in Cranmer's Bible we have the positive in both cases,—"greate."   The copy I consult is that in Bagster's Hexapla, which (we are told on p. 161) was "reprinted from a very fine copy of the first edition, 1539."   And the edition of 1541 has "great" also.—I note therefore this discrepancy between Cranmer's Version of the New Testament as it was first published, and as portions of it were transferred to the Book of Common Prayer in 1549, ten years afterwards.—(3) *V.* 43. "How then doth David *in spirit* call him Lord?" And so all the English versions including the Authorised. It was reserved for the Revisers of 1881 to insert the definite article, "How then doth David *in the Spirit?*" etc. Eph. ii. 22; vi. 18, and Col. i. 8, furnish other instances in which *after a preposition* the word Πνεῦμα, though denoting the Holy Spirit, loses the definite article. (See Winer's Grammar of New Testament Greek, Ed. Moulton. Part III. Sec. xix. p. 151.)]

Sunday.—Vv. 35, 36. "Then one of them, which was a lawyer, asked him a question, tempting him, and saying, Master which is the great commandment in the law?" That this question was not put captiously, or with the intention of "entangling our Lord in His talk" (like those in an earlier part of the Chapter[1]), is clear from the fuller account of the incident given us by St. Mark, who tells us that this lawyer was struck with the wisdom of the answer which had been given to the Sadducees,[2] and afterwards with the wisdom of that which was given to himself,[3] and that our Lord told him that he was not far from the kingdom of God.[4] Just as the queen of Sheba came to Solomon's court "to prove him with hard questions,"[5] desirous of making experiment for herself of his extraordinary wisdom, the report of which had reached her in her own land[6]; so this lawyer, having had one specimen of Christ's wisdom, desired to make a further exploration in that mine. I must beware, in my study of God's word, of raising questions of mere curiosity; and far be it from me at all times to raise captious and sceptical questions, seeking as it were "to entangle" Holy Scripture

---

[1] See *vv.* 15, 17, 23-29.

[2] See St. Mark xii. 28.

[3] See St. Mark xii. 32, 33.

[4] *V.* 34.

[5] See 1 Kings x. 1.

[6] See *vv.* 6, 7.

"in its talk"; but if in some passages I have had glimpses opened to me of a rich vein of spiritual wisdom lying under the surface, I shall do well to search more deeply for edification in a mine which has already yielded it. Let my simple desire in searching Holy Scripture be to make experience of a truth and a wisdom, of the existence of which I am well persuaded, and have had an inkling,— to be able to say, "Like as we have heard, so have we seen,"[1] "It was a true report that I heard of . . . thy wisdom,"[2]—and I shall assuredly find on further exploration that "the half was not told me,"[3] that in God's written, as in His Personal Word, "are hid all the treasures of wisdom and knowledge."[4]

Monday.—V. 37. "Jesus said unto him, Thou shalt love the Lord thy God." It has been well said; "Love is the most personal of all affections. One may fear an event, one may hope for an event, one may rejoice in an event; but one can love only a person."[5] Thus the fact that we are bidden, as the most fundamental of all duties, to love God,—this of itself shows the personality of God, just as the precept not to grieve the Holy Spirit[6] proves the personality of the Comforter; for how can we grieve an influence or an emanation? If the Holy Spirit is capable of being grieved, He must be a Divine Person. Those who deny the Personality of God, conceiving of Him as the aggregate of all natural powers or forces, or as a certain tendency in human affairs which makes for righteousness, not only degrade Him below the level of His rational creatures, but rob Him of the highest tribute which those

---

[1] See Ps. xlviii. 7, P.B.V.
[2] See 1 Kings x. 6 ; and see also St. John iv. 42.
[3] See 1 Kings x. 7.   [4] Col. ii. 3.
[5] Dr. David Brown's "Commentary on the Gospels."
[6] See Eph. iv. 30.

creatures can make to Him,—love and trust. To know that in the long run virtue will meet with its reward, and vice with its penalty,—because the system of human affairs naturally works itself out in these results,—is but a feeble moral restraint on those who are bent on doing evil. But to be assured that a Personal All-Seeing Judge "shall bring every work into judgment, with every secret thing, whether it be good, or whether it be evil,"[1] is a formidable sanction of morality, and much less easily evaded.—O my God, quicken my sense of Thy personality; for such a sense lies at the very root of the spiritual life !

Tuesday.—V. 37. "Thou shalt love the Lord thy God with all thy heart, and with all thy soul, and with all thy mind." By the "heart" I understand the moral powers,—the conscience, and the will. Am I loving God with these ? Conscience is as the eye of the soul, which receives the light of heaven. Am I admitting that light freely, or partially excluding it, on account of some un-worthy bias or prepossession of the will ? And again, have I in my will no reserves with God ? Am I heartily willing to surrender everything on which He lays His ban, to adopt into my practice everything which He bids me do ? The "soul" is the seat of feeling and emotion. Is there fervour and enthusiasm in my service of God ? or, while my religion is an outward restraint on me, does it lack warmth and glow,—that warmth which can only be given by a grateful sense of the love which has been shown to me ? By the "mind" is meant the intelligence, —the reflective and reasoning powers. God has made us reasonable creatures, and will therefore not have from us a blind devotion, but a reasonable service. Do I yield to Him the love of the reason, submitting my reason to the

---

[1] Eccles. xii. 14.

dictates of His word, and acquiescing in mysteries as the necessary condition of a Divine Revelation; but still seeking light, where it may be had, and striving to grow in knowledge as well as in grace? Will, emotion, intelligence, are a trinity of faculties in man, and the Holy Trinity must be adored and loved with one and all of them.

Wednesday.—V. 39. "And the second is like unto it, Thou shalt love thy neighbour as thyself." Love to God involves and contains in itself the love of our neighbour, just as sunlight contains in itself moonlight. Moonlight is sunlight, only coming to us not direct from the sun, but reflected by the moon. And so the love of our neighbour, if true, is the love of God's image and handiwork in our neighbour; and accordingly it is said, "Every one that loveth him that begat loveth him also that is begotten of him. By this we know that we love the children of God, when we love God."[1] Nevertheless our Saviour, the Personal Word of God, and the written Word of God everywhere, seem to consider that the love of our neighbour, however much involved in the love of God, requires a distinct and separate statement,—it would not do to leave so weighty a matter to inference. Our Lord is only asked which is the greatest commandment in the law. He indicates which it is; but goes on at once, and in the same breath, to add, "And the second is like unto it, Thou shalt love thy neighbour as thyself."—What knowledge of human nature, and of the tendency of the heart to evade what is difficult to flesh and blood, is shown in God's Word! We are justified by faith, and living faith involves works, just as a living fruit-tree will certainly bring forth fruit in its

---

[1] 1 John v. 1, 2.

season. But there are many human theologians, who, if they mention good works at all, mention them only in a parenthesis, or as a corollary, and huddle them away out of sight as soon as possible. Not so the Bible. Our Lord, St. Paul, St. James, all press good works, moral, social, political, with emphasis and in detail. Though virtually wrapped up in faith, they require distinct and independent pressing.

Thursday.—V. 39. " As thyself." It is observable that the love of self, which rests upon the same ground with the love of our neighbour, (for it is God's image in ourselves, no less than in our neighbour, which we are to love) *is* prescribed by inference only, and not directly; for the reason no doubt that it is sufficiently secured by the constitution of our nature; for where is the man that does not seek good to himself, and is not alive to his own interests? It is, however, prescribed inferentially; for if we are to love our neighbour as ourselves, that implies that we are to love ourselves as our neighbour. Again, self-love is constantly appealed to in Scripture, whenever punishment is threatened against wrong-doing, and "the hope which is laid up for you in heaven"[1] is proposed as the recompence of virtue and constancy, which appeal would not be made, if self-love were not designed to actuate us. And when the Apostle says that grace teaches us to "live soberly, righteously, and godly, in this present world,"[2] it is plain that the first word expresses our duty to self, the second that to our neighbour, the third that to God. Rational self-love,—the self-love which seeks supremely heavenly blessedness, and shuns supremely God's wrath and everlasting damnation,—is by no means more prevalent among men, as Bishop Butler intimates, than it

---

[1] See Col. i. 5. [2] See Tit. ii. 11, 12.

ought to be.[1] When people, making an intellectual confusion between selfishness and self-love, strive and strain to get rid of self altogether (as one of their phrases is), a thing which the constitution of their nature prevents their doing, their piety degenerates into a morbid pietism.—O Lord, among the manifold perversions of religion which now everywhere abound, keep me sound in faith and practice !

Friday.—Vv. 41, 42. "While the Pharisees were gathered together, Jesus asked them, saying, What think ye of Christ? whose son is he?" I recognise a deep connexion between this question as proposed by Christ, and the answer which He had just given on the subject of "the great commandment." The lawyer, as we are informed by St. Mark, manifested a cordial approval of our Lord's doctrine that the love of God and our neighbour was "more than all whole burnt-offerings and sacrifices," and was told by our Lord that he was "not far from the kingdom of God."[2] "Not far," because he fully appreciated the nature and extent of God's requirements, and doubtless was earnestly praying and honestly striving to come up to them. But why was he not in the kingdom of God? What he wanted, in order

---

[1] "Self-love in its due degree is as just and morally good, as any affection whatever. . . . Neither does there appear any reason to wish self-love were weaker in the generality of the world than it is. . . . Upon the whole, if the generality of mankind were to cultivate within themselves the principle of self-love ; if they were to accustom themselves often to set down and consider, what was the greatest happiness they were capable of attaining for themselves in this life, and if self-love were so strong and prevalent, as that they would uniformly pursue this their supposed chief temporal good, without being diverted from it by any particular passion ; it would manifestly prevent numberless follies and vices." —Preface to Bishop Butler's Sermons. Pp. xxv., xxvi. [Oxford : University Press, MDCCCL.]   [2] See St. Mark xii. 32, 33, 34.

to be within it, was an acknowledgment of the Divine-Human Saviour,—and a looking for salvation to the power and sympathy given Him by His composite nature. The lawyer (and the better class of Jews generally, whom he represented) were " going about to establish their own righteousness "; and they were therefore to be taught that " Christ is the end of the law for righteousness to every one that believeth," and that salvation was to be had only by confessing Him with the mouth, and believing in Him in the heart.[1]—O my Lord, grave upon my heart this last lesson of Thy public ministry to the Jews, that no mere moral striving can bring me to God, without looking to Thee, who in Thine own Person hast fulfilled the law.

Saturday.—Vv. 43, 44, 45. " He saith unto them, How then doth David in spirit call him Lord, saying, The LORD said unto my Lord, Sit thou on my right hand, till I make thine enemies thy footstool. If David then call him Lord, how is he his son ?" Let me not think that the calling Jesus Lord (as David did by anticipation) is an easy thing,—the mere verbal recitation of a formulary. David himself only did it " in spirit,"[2] that is, in the Holy Spirit, when breathing the atmosphere of inspiration. That Jesus is the Christ, the Son of the living God, was revealed to St. Peter, not by flesh and blood, but by Christ's Father in heaven.[3] And St. Paul expressly lays down, as a principle for ascertaining the genuineness of an operation of the Spirit, " No man can say that Jesus is the Lord, but by the Holy Ghost."[4] Have I been brought to a deep internal conviction of this great truth by an

---

[1] See Rom. x. 3, 4, 9, 10.

[2] The rendering of the Revised Version of 1881 is ; " How then doth David *in the Spirit* call him Lord !"

[3] See St. Matt. xvi. 16, 17.   [4] Cor. xii. 8.

operation upon my heart and conscience ?   Should I believe it and confess it, even if all the society around me disclaimed all participation in the conviction, and made my avowal of it a reason for ridiculing and persecuting me ?   And am I confessing Jesus as my Lord, by actively obeying His every precept, by submitting with cheerful and thankful heart to His every dispensation ?   To confess *with the mouth only* that " Jesus is the Lord," is nothing.   To make the avowal *with the mind* is not enough ; mental conviction may be produced by evidence ; and evidence may be set before us by our follow-men. The moral powers, the conscience, heart, and will, must be the seat of the avowal.   How much have these moral powers had to do with my profession of Christianity ?

Chapter LIV.

THE GOSPEL FOR THE NINETEENTH SUNDAY AFTER TRINITY.

St. Matt. ix. 1 *to* 9
(substituting the name "Jesus" for "And he" in *v.* 1).

1 Jesus entred into a ship, and passed over, and came into his own
2 city. And behold, they brought to him a man·sick of the palsie,
lying on a bed. And Jesus seeing their faith, said unto the sick of
3 the palsie, Son, be of good cheer, thy sins be forgiven thee. And
behold, certain of the Scribes said within themselves, This man
4 blasphemeth. And Jesus knowing their thoughts, said, Wherefore
5 think ye evil in your hearts? For whether is easier to say, Thy
6 sins be forgiven thee? or to say, Arise, and walk? But that ye
may know that the Son of man hath power on earth to forgive sins,
(then saith he to the sick of the palsie) Arise, take up thy bed, and
7 go *into thine house. And he arose, and departed to his house.
8 But when the multitude saw it, they marvelled, and glorified God,
who had given such power unto men.

Miss. Sar	1549.	1662 s.b.
In illo tempore, Ascendens *Jesus* in naviculam transfretavit, et venit in civitatem suam, etc. (*Vulg.* Et Ascendens in naviculam, transfretavit, et venit in civitatem suam, etc.)	Jesus entred into a ship, and passed over, and came into his own city, etc.	Jesus entred into a ship, and passed over, and came into his own city, etc. (*Gr.* Καὶ ἐμβὰς εἰς τὸ πλοῖον, διεπέρασε, καὶ ἦλθεν εἰς τὴν ἰδίαν πόλιν.)

The connexion of *v.* 1 with the preceding Chapter, indicated by "And" (which has unfortunately been dropped in the Liturgical Gospel) is so close that Dean Mansel ("Speaker's Commentary," *in loc.*) thinks that this verse "should be placed at the end of the preceding Chapter, as

---

* In Mr. Stephens' Edition of the Sealed Book for the Chancery the first letter of the word "into" (in "into thine house") is printed blue.

being properly connected with the previous narrative." It was at the unanimous request of the Gergesenes, who had been panic-stricken by the casting out of the devils into the swine, and who also doubtless were under apprehensions of a further loss of property, should this Wonder-worker continue in their district, that our Lord re-embarked (see Chap. viii 18), and crossed again to the Western side of the lake ;—"And, behold, the whole city came out to meet Jesus : and when they saw him, they besought him that he would depart out of their coasts." Chap. viii. *last verse. The Lord took them at their word,* and removed from them the Divine Presence, of which in a low panic, and a still lower clinging to their earthly possessions, they had shown themselves so unworthy. " He obtrudes not His blessings on the unwilling," says Bengel. Nevertheless, as this incomparable Commentator does not omit to notice, the Lord in judgment remembered mercy, and made provision for the evangelization of the Gergesenes by sending back to his home one of the restored demoniacs, and bidding him "show how great things God had done unto him." And the man published his recovery by the mercy of the Saviour "throughout the whole city" (see St. Luke viii. 38, 39). Another very beautiful remark of Bengel's upon the first verse of this Gospel is that our Lord's habit of not staying very long in any one place tended to kindle in people's hearts a more ardent desire of His Presence.—The text of Stephens' 3d Edition (of 1550), which is "presumed to have been accepted by the Translators of 1611" (see Archdeacon Palmer's "Greek Testament with the Revisers' Readings"), exhibits the definite article before the word "ship,"— "And he entered into *the* ship,"—*the* ship being that which Christ had virtually ordered, when giving "commandment to depart unto the other side" (Chap. viii. 18) and in which He had crossed the lake (Chap. viii. 23), and had been beset by the tempest (Chap. viii. 24),—"the walking school," as Bengel so beautifully terms it, "in which the disciples were much more solidly instructed, than if they had lived under the roof of a college without any anxiety and temptation." [See our Thoughts on the Gospel for the *Fourth Sunday after the Epiphany.*]—*Translation of* 1540. (1) *V.* 2. "And when Jesus *saw the faith of them.*" And so Wycliffe and Tyndale. A little more emphasis than in the Authorised Version is thus given to the fact that it was the faith of the sufferer's *friends, not of himself,* that our Lord took note of. The Genevan first gave "seeing *their* faith." [See the Thought for *Monday.*] (2) *V.* 4. "And when Jesus *saw* their thoughts." The five English versions before the Authorised give "had seen" or "saw," showing that their translators adopted the reading ἰδών. This too is the reading adopted in the Vulgate, which has, "Et cum *vidisset* Jesus cogitationes eorum, dixit." But King

James's Translators in 1611 must have adopted the reading εἰδὼς (which is that of the Vatican and Sinaitic Manuscripts). And the Revisers of 1881 have kept them countenance, giving "*knowing* their thoughts" in their text, though their margin informs us that "Many ancient authorities read *seeing*." This brings us across the question what text was adopted by the Translators of 1611. And the answer given to this question in the Preface of the Revised Version is that "their chief guides appear to have been the later editions of Stephanus and of Beza and also, to a certain extent, the Complutensian Polyglott." A reference to Archdeacon Palmer's work ("The Greek Testament with the Revisers' Readings") will show that ἰδὼν, *not* εἰδὼς, was the reading of Stephanus's third edition (of 1550), the readings of which are "presumed, in the absence of evidence to the contrary, to have been accepted by the Translators of 1611." Why in the case before us they did NOT accept the reading of Stephanus, but were the first English translators to reject it, and what edition (or editions) of their day exhibit εἰδὼς, I must leave to persons versed in such subjects to say. Apart from any question of the reading, "seeing" seems to give a livelier idea of the Saviour's intuition into the heart than knowing. (3) *V.* 6. "But that ye may know that the Sonne of man hath power to forgive sinnes *in earth.*" Wycliffe, Tyndale, and the Genevan, as well as Cranmer, have all this order of the words, and "in" instead of "on" (see ἐπὶ τῆς γῆς rendered "*in* earth" by the Authorised Version in the Lord's Prayer, St. Matt. vi. 10, St. Luke xi. 2). As to the order of the words, it is by no means insignificant. The order in which the Authorised Version places them is doubtless the true one—"that the Son of man hath power *on earth* to forgive sins." One might readily suppose that the glorified and exalted Son of man possessed this power. But He claims while upon earth, in a body of humiliation, to have the right to exercise it.]

Sunday.—V. 2. "And, behold, they brought to him a man sick of the palsy, lying on a bed." The word translated "brought" is a sacrificial word, and might be rendered, "They offered to him." Many times in the Epistle to the Hebrews it is used of the sacrifices of the Mosaic law;[1] and in the Gospels also it is applied to the gold and frankincense, and myrrh, which the wise men pre-

---

[1] Thus v. 1 (ἵνα προσφέρῃ δῶρά τε καὶ θυσίας ὑπὲρ ἁμαρτιῶν), and v. 3, 7 ; viii. 3, 4 ; ix. 7, 9, 14, 25, 28 ; x. 1 ; xi. 4, 17, etc.

sented to the infant Saviour,[1] and to the offerings made
in the Jewish Temple,—"then come and offer thy gift."[2]
The Jews were forbidden to offer sacrificially any muti-
lated or defective victim; "If ye offer the blind for
sacrifice, is it not evil? and if ye offer the lame and sick,
is it not evil?"[3]   But the sick, the infirm, and, on one
occasion, young children[4] were offered or presented to our
Lord, as to One whose heart brimmed over with sympathy
and compassion for every malady and infirmity; and the
offering was most acceptable;[5] for he loved the opportunity of ministering relief to man and of furthering God's
glory thereby.[6]   Not one such offering did He reject;
not one of "the lame, blind, dumb, maimed" patients,
whom "the multitudes cast down at" His "feet,"[7] did He
send away without the healing, for which his friends sued
on his behalf,—sued sometimes without words, merely
leaving them in their misery exposed to the Saviour's
eye.—One great lesson of this narrative is, that we may
do much for friends in trouble or misfortune, and even
for such persons among our acquaintance, as, not recognising their need of spiritual healing, do not come to
Christ on their own account.   We may take them up in
the arms of prayer, and bear them into the Lord's presence, and commend their wants, infirmities, and sorrows,
to Him earnestly and perseveringly.   To do so were an
exercise, not of faith only, but of love.   And faith and

---

[1] St. Matt. ii. 11, ἀνοίξαντες τοὺς θησαυροὺς αὐτῶν προσήνεγκαν αὐτῷ δῶρα.

[2] St. Matt. v. 24, τότε ἐλθὼν πρόσφερε τὸ δῶρόν σου.

[3] Mal. i. 8 ; and see Lev. xxii. 21, 22, and Deut. xv. 21.

[4] See St. Mark x. 13, προσέφερον αὐτῷ παιδία.

[5] This thought is from Bengel's "Gnomon" *in. loc.*, but considerably
expanded.

[6] See the last verse of this Gospel, St. Matt. ix. 8; and also St. Matt.
xv. 30, 31.   [7] See St. Matt. xv. 30.

love have a peculiarly moving power with Him—cannot fail to elicit a response.

Monday.—V. 2. " And Jesus, seeing their faith, said unto the sick of the palsy ; Son, be of good cheer." Seeing the faith of those who brought the palsied man to Christ,—a faith the genuineness of which was attested, as two other Evangelists tell us,[1] by their breaking up the roof of the house in which our Lord was, in order to get access to Him. Here we have a glimpse of the great and deep truth, on which is founded the doctrine of the imputation of our sins to our Saviour, that God views and deals with men, not merely as individuals, but in their corporate capacity, as members of a family, a nation, a race, and that thus the consequences, both of sin and of righteousness, extend beyond the immediate agents to all who are in connexion with them. *As an undoubted fact,* we are bound up together in the reciprocal influence which we exert upon one another, and whereby we mould one another's opinions, and shape one another's practice. Why should it be so difficult to believe that Almighty God looks on us thus in our surroundings,—was ready to spare Sodom, if ten righteous men could have been found there,[2] and removed Judah " out of his sight, for the sins of Manasseh, according to all that he did ; and also for the innocent blood that he shed ?"[3] It is a very solemn thought that we all in a certain sense represent others, as well as ourselves, before God.— But I find in the words of the text, not only a profound principle of the Divine dealings with man, but also the justification of a particular application of that principle by the Church. We present little children to Christ in

---

[1] See St. Mark ii. 4 ; St. Luke v. 19.   [2] See Gen. xviii. 32.
[3] See 2 Kings xxiv. 3, 4.

Baptism, who are not of age to come to Him for them-selves.   We present them on the ground, not of their own faith, but of the faith of those who bring them.   And even where parents and sponsors may themselves lack true faith, still they are representatives of the Church of Christ, which has faith, and they appear at the font as the Church's representatives and agents.   And our firm belief, founded on such passages as that before us, is that the Lord, seeing this faith in His Church, grants to these infants, on the ground of it, remission of the guilt of original sin, and such an amount of grace as shall, if duly used and improved, correct their natural incapacity for holiness.

Tuesday.—V. 2. " He said unto the sick of the palsy; Son, be of good cheer ; thy sins be forgiven thee."   It is not only a word of absolution,—what might be called an official word,—but a word of absolution as from One who was God, prefaced by a bright word of cheer and en-couragement from One who was the Son of man also, and had a human heart brimming over with sympathy for the suffering members of the race.   And so, lower down, to the woman with an issue of blood the same word of encouragement is said ; " Daughter, be of good comfort."[1] How forcibly does our Lord thus teach us the lesson of doing good sympathetically, and especially of being bright, hopeful, and encouraging in our treatment of the sick and suffering !   And as to *the divinely spoken word of absolu-tion*—not, " The LORD hath put away thy sin,"[2] as the merely human prophet said to David, but " thy sins are forgiven thee," obliterated by me, the Son of God, from the book of God's remembrance,—what more consolatory

---

[1] See St. Matt. ix. 22, Θάρσει θύγατερ· ἡ πίστις σου σέσωκέ σε.

[2] See 2 Sam. xii. 13.

and encouraging lesson can I draw from it than that God is "always more ready to hear than we to pray, and is wont to give more than either we desire or deserve?"[1] Nothing had been asked of Christ in words; but a mute appeal had been made to His pity by the patient's being let down into the room before His eyes. The bodily healing of their friend was all that the bearers thought of or wished for. But their friend carried off a spiritual as well as a bodily healing. Our Lord, whose eyes were keener than theirs, saw that there was a burden on the man's conscience, the removal of which was a necessary condition of the enjoyment of health, possibly (for how powerfully do body and mind interact on one another!) of its restoration.—O how enriching is the trade with heaven! Solomon, asking wisdom only, receives also what he has not asked, "riches and honour."[2] The paralytic, a suitor for the health of the outer man only, receives an absolution also, which brightens the whole region of the inner man.

Wednesday.—V. 2. "Thy sins be forgiven thee." I find a most instructive lesson in the forgiveness of this man prior to his bodily cure, which I must by no means overlook. The sick of the palsy is the emblem of a sinner suffering from paralysis of the will, in regard of certain sins which he longs and strives to shake off, but finds evil habit again and again too strong for him. "To will is present with him; but how to perform that which is good he finds not. For the good that he would he does not; but the evil which he would not, that he does."[3] The will is stricken with a moral powerlessness, just as, when a paralytic patient would raise his hand, or

---

[1] Collect for the Twelfth Sunday after Trinity.
[2] See 1 Kings iii. 11, 12, 13.   [3] See Rom. vii. 18, 19.

would articulate clearly, he cannot. Is not this, more or less, the case with all of us ? Even if no particular sin has a persistent mastery over me, and mocks all my efforts to shake it off, even if my life in its main tenour is conducted on Christian principle, is not my will very torpid and sluggish, as regards the highest standard of holiness ? Am I "forgetting those things which are behind, and reaching forth unto those things which are before,"[1] with the energy I ought ? Now one lesson of the narrative before me is that moral paralysis cannot be cured except after and by the forgiveness of our sins, and the conscious reception into our hearts of God's forgiving mercy. All moral efforts and struggles will end in disappointment, which are not made in the strength of consciously received pardon.

Thursday.—Vv. 3, 4, 5, 6. "And, behold, certain of the scribes said within themselves, This man blasphemeth. And Jesus knowing their thoughts, said, Wherefore think ye evil in your hearts ? For whether is easier, to say, Thy sins be forgiven thee ; or to say, Arise, and walk ? But that ye may know that the Son of man hath power on earth to forgive sins, (then saith he to the sick of the palsy), Arise, take up thy bed, and go unto thine house." In one passage of his Epistles St. Paul beseeches his converts " by the meekness and gentleness of Christ."[2] What an illustration have we here of these features of character ! Let it be borne in mind that He was the Son of God, who had lain in His Father's bosom from all eternity,[3] and who, for God's glory and man's salvation, condescended to appear upon earth within the limits of a created nature. When He so appeared, He " counted it not a prize to be on an

[1] See Phil. iii. 13.   [2] 2 Cor. x. 1.   [3] See St. John i. 18.

equality with God "[1]; and here accordingly I do not hear Him say, " I forgive thee thy sins " (though that is implied), but " thy sins are forgiven thee." Unawed, however, by the marvellous displays of Divine power, which He had made in previous miracles, and in no measure softened by the gracious sweetness of His dealing with this poor patient, whose introduction to Him must have been a grievous interruption of His teaching, " certain of the scribes " throw out the wicked cavil, which jealousy and dislike had bred in their hearts; " This man blasphemeth." And yet, without the smallest trace of irritation with them, He proceeds to reason with them. " You are thinking," He says, " that the power of forgiving sins is a very easy claim to set up, as no one can bring it to the test. Behold, then, I claim another power, which *can* be brought to the test; and you shall judge from the effects following in that case whether my claim to forgive sins was unjustifiable." When it is considered who the Lord was, and what He was doing for man, His perfect command of temper in reasoning with His adversaries appears to be one of the most marvellous features of His human character.——Lord, how ready am I, either to fly off in a fit of invective, or to wrap myself in a mood of sullenness, if any one wounds my vanity, or does not give me credit for gifts which I am conscious of possessing! Instil into my heart one drop of that meekness and gentleness which filled Thine own, and which was an evidence that the Holy Dove of Thy Baptism brooded over Thee perpetually.[2]

Friday.——V. 6. " (Then saith he to the sick of the palsy), Arise, take up thy bed, and go unto thine house." Thus a short interval was made to intervene between the

---

[1] Revised Version of Phil. ii. 6.   [2] See St. Luke iii. 22.

spiritual and the bodily healing. The Divine Physician left the sweet peace of absolution to sink into the patient's soul, and to be cherished there awhile, before He caused him to experience bodily recovery. There is a profound connexion between sin as the cause, and disease as the effect and symptom, which is recognised everywhere in the Bible and Prayer Book. First, we have the juxta-position of the spiritual and bodily recoveries, the spiritual being placed first, in the hundred and third Psalm, " Forget not all his benefits; who forgiveth all thine iniquities; who healeth all thy diseases."[1] Then there is the patent fact that He who came to bring redemption, and to work out man's salvation, appeared upon earth as a healer of disease in every form which disease can assume, and that He bequeathed to His disciples, after His resurrection, not only the power to remit sins,[2] but also the power of miraculous healing,—" they shall lay hands on the sick, and they shall recover."[3] And then there is St. James's precept for the Visitation of the Sick, which also couples the spiritual with the bodily healing; " Is any sick among you ? let him call for the elders of the church; and let them pray over him, anointing him with oil in the name of the Lord : And the prayer of faith shall save the sick, and the Lord shall raise him up; and if he have com-mitted sins, they shall be forgiven him."[4] And though our English Church has discarded the anointing as the symbol of a miraculous healing, which cannot any more be looked for, yet traces are left in our Visitation Service of the original association of the bodily with the spiritual cure. Thus we pray in the Collect[5] that the patient " may

---

[1] Ps. ciii. 3.   [2] See St. John xx. 23.
[3] St Mark xvi. 18.   [4] James v. 14, 15.
[5] At '' the Communion of the Sick.''

recover his bodily health, if it be God's gracious will "; and in the noble benedictory prayer before the commendation of the patient to God, we pray that he may be made to " know and feel, that there is none other Name under heaven given to man, in whom, and through whom, he may receive *health* and salvation, but only the Name of our Lord Jesus Christ." What if it be God's will that, while the argument is proceeding between Christ and the powers which oppose Him, the patient should still linger on the bed of sickness all the days of his life ? If his sins have been forgiven him, and his conscience set at rest by absolving grace, this will—nay, must—draw after it in due time the resurrection of the body with new powers; for man, body and soul, is one whole, and any healing of the immortal spirit must issue, at a longer or shorter interval, in complete bodily restoration.

Saturday.—V. 8. " But when the multitudes saw it, they marvelled, and glorified God, which had given such power unto men." The power is not only, and I apprehend not chiefly, the power shown in restoring the paralytic, but the power of forgiving sins, Christ's claim to do which He had established by the miracle,—" but that ye may know that the Son of man hath *power on earth to forgive sins* (then saith He to the sick of the palsy), Arise." This power of forgiving sins, miraculously evidenced as it had been by the power of healing the body, the people believed to have been bestowed by God upon men ; and now, in virtue of His grant, to be in exercise among them. It had been exercised that day in their hearing and presence, the poor paralytic's sins having been lifted off from him, before he was enabled to spring from his couch and use his limbs. Nor was it only that the absolving power was given to Christ Himself; but a true instinct taught the people that *it was given to Him, as Son of man, for the behoof of the whole human family,* and therefore, in fact, given to them through Him,—a golden oil conveyed through the golden pipe of the Mediator's Person and work.[1]   The power of forgiving sins has been brought down from heaven to earth by the Son of God, and lodged in the Church; and in the ministry of the Word and Sacraments, as well as by formal absolutions, it is there dispensed.   Let but my faith claim the exercise of the power towards myself, and then my conscience shall experience it.

[1] See Zech. iv. 12.

CHAPTER LV

THE GOSPEL FOR THE TWENTIETH SUNDAY AFTER TRINITY.

St. Matt. xxii. 1 *to* 15
(leaving out the words " And . . . . answered and spake unto them again
by parables, and," in *v.* 1).

1, 2   Jesus said, The kingdom of heaven is like unto a certain king,
3 who made a marriage for his son ; and sent forth his servants to call them that were bidden to the wedding ; and they would not
4 come. Again, he sent forth other servants, saying, Tell them who are bidden, Behold, I have prepared my dinner ; my oxen and my fatlings are killed, and all things are ready, come unto the mar-
5 riage. But they made light of it, and went their ways, one to his
6 farm, another to his merchandise : And the remnant took his
7 servants, and entreated them spitefully, and slew them. But when the king heard thereof he was wroth ; and he sent forth his armies, and destroyed those murderers, and burnt up their city.
8 Then saith he to his servants, The wedding is ready, but they who
9 were bidden were not worthy. Go ye therefore into the high-ways,
10 and as many as ye shall find bid to the marriage. So those ser-vants went out into the high-ways, and gathered together all as many as they found, both bad and good ; and the wedding was
11 furnished with guests. And when the king came in to see the guests, he saw there a man who had not on a wedding garment.
12 And he saith unto him, Friend, how camest thou in hither, not
13 having a wedding garment ? And he was speechless. Then said the king to the servants, Bind him hand and foot, and take him away, and cast him into outer darkness : There shall be weeping
14 and gnashing of teeth. For many are called, but few are chosen.

[MISS. SAB.	1549.	1662 s.b.
In illo tempore, Loquebatur Jesus cum discipulis suis in parabolis dicens ; Simile factum est regnum cœlorum homini regi, qui fecit nuptias filio suo. (*Vulg.* Et respondens Jesus, dixit iterum in parabolis eis, dicens : Simile factum est regno cœlorum homini regi, qui fecit nuptias filio suo.)	Jesus said, The kingdom of heaven is like unto a man that was a king, Which made a marriage for his sonne, etc. (In the Black - Letter Prayer Book of 1636 [39 ?], the words "Jesus said" are in Roman type, *not in black letter*, probably to indicate that they are not found in the sacred text.)	Jesus said, The kingdom of heaven is like unto a certain king, who made a marriage for his son, etc. (*Gr.* Καὶ ἀποκριθεὶς ὁ Ἰησοῦς, πάλιν εἶπεν αὐτοῖς ἐν παραβολαῖς, λέγων· Ὡμοιώθη ἡ βασιλεία τῶν οὐρανῶν ἀνθρώπῳ βασιλεῖ, ὅστις ἐποίησε γάμους τῷ υἱῷ αὐτοῦ.)

The Parable of the Marriage of the King's Son, which furnishes the contents of this Gospel, is the last of a trilogy of Parables, all of which express by different similitudes the infidelity and rejection of the Jews, and the call and acceptance of the Gentiles. The first is the Parable of the Two Sons (Chap. xxi. 28 *to* 33), in which *the hypocrisy of Jewish professions of religion* is censured. ("He answered and said, I go, sir: and went not," *v.* 30). The second is the Parable of the Wicked Husbandmen (Chap. xxi. 33 *to* 45), in which the further charges are made against the Jews of *spiritual barrenness under the means of grace (vv.* 33, 34, 43) *and the persecution unto death of God's prophets and of His Son (vv.* 35 *to* 40). This Parable ended with the enigmatical warning of the danger of falling on the Stone and the still greater danger of being fallen on by it (*v.* 44) ; and when it was concluded, there was a brief pause, during which the chief Priests and Pharisees, aware of their being the object of our Lord's censures, "gave some indications of their designs against Him. As a last warning to them, He now proceeds to a third parable, similar in import to the last, but exhibiting God's relation to His chosen people under a more gracious image, no longer as a duty exacted by a householder from his labourers, but as an invitation to a feast issued by a king to his subjects." (Dean Mansel in the "Speaker's Commentary.") Here the charges against the Jews are *secularity of mind* (Chap. xxii. 5) and (as in the previous Parable) *persecution unto death of God's ministers and messengers* (*v.* 6). And the penalty, which in this Parable reaches its climax, is not only the destruction of the murderers themselves, but also the burning of their city (*v.* 7).—The "answered" in *v.* 1 ("Jesus *answered* and spake unto them again by parables ") is to be understood as an answer given not to the express words of the chief Priests and Pharisees, but to the evil designs, which by His divine intuition He saw working in their hearts. "He to whom ground for speaking is given," says Bengel, "no less than he who is asked, may be said to answer."—*Translation of* 1540. (1) *V.* 2. "The kingdom of heaven is like unto a man that was a king" (ἀνθρώπῳ βασιλεῖ). Cranmer varies here from Tyndale, who has, "a certayne kinge." The Genevan replaced "a certain king"; and the Authorised followed. "Personal nouns denoting office, character, etc., receive, with but slight extension of meaning, the general personal attributes in the substantives ἄνθρωπος, ἀνήρ, γυνή, etc." St. Matthew is rich in instances of this idiom ; see xiii. 45 ; xviii. 23 ; xx. i. ; xxi. 33. See Winer's Grammar of New Testament Greek (Ed. Moulton), Sec. LIX. 1. (2) *V.* 5. "One to his farm *place*, another to his merchandize." Tyndale and the Genevan both have "farm place." Wycliffe, as we have seen in a previous Introduction, has "oon into his *toun*." (3) *V.* 6. "and intreated them *shamefully*" (ὕβρισαν). The English versions here are very different ; Wycliffe having, "turmentiden hem"; Tyndale, "intreated them *ungodly*"; Genevan, "intreated them *sharpely*"; Rheims and the Authorised, "*spitefully*." The word ὑβρίζω (to outrage, insult) occurs four times elsewhere in the New Testament, once of the "despiteful treatment," which was one of the particulars of our Lord's Passion, and had a large element of *insolent contemptuousness* in it (St. Luke xviii. 32), once of the despiteful usage (accompanied with an attempt to stone) of St. Paul and St. Barnabas at Iconium (Acts xiv. 5), once of the *shameful* treatment of St. Paul and Silas at Philippi (1 Thess. ii. 2) ; and once in the modified sense of vehement objurgation, such as our Lord directed against the Scribes and Pharisees (St. Luke xi. 45). (4) *V.* 7. "he was wroth, and sent forth his *men of warre* (τὰ στρατεύματα αὐτοῦ). Here again we have diversity, Wycliffe and the Rhemish giving "hosts"; Tyndale and the Genevan, "warriors." "Hosts" or "armies" is certainly much preferable to the other renderings. (5) *V.* 12. "And he was *even* speechlesse" (ὁ δὲ ἐφιμώθη). What the "even" represents it is hard to see ; but it is found in Tyndale and the Genevan, as well as Cranmer. Wycliffe has, "and he was *doumbe*"; the Rhemish, "but he was dumme." (6) *V.* 13. "Then said the King to the *ministers*" (τοῖς διακόνοις. Note that the word is δοῦλος in verses 3, 4, 6, 8, 10,—a very interesting circumstance). Wycliffe has "servants" to represent δοῦλοι, "his ministers" to represent διάκονοι ; Tyndale, Cranmer, the Genevan, the same ; the Rhemish has "servants" for the first word, and "waiters" for the second ; the Authorised Version and Revised Version, "servants" in both places, the Revisers however distinguishing between the words by giving "bond-servants" as the marginal alternative of the earlier, and "ministers" of the later. But are we to learn anything from the employment of a different word to denote those servants who transact for the master in the conveyance of the invitation, and those whom he employs as executioners in the infliction of punishment? The one are called "bondservants," or "slaves," the other merely "attendants," "pursuivants." The one represent the human ambassadors of Christ (His bond-servants), who convey to their fellow-men the invitations of grace. But angelic, not human, ministers will, we are expressly told, be employed in inflicting the final punishment; "*The angels shall come forth*, and sever the wicked from among the just, and *shall cast them into the furnace of fire*: there shall be wailing and gnashing of teeth" (St. Matt. xiii. 49, 50). If there is any truth in this observation, it affords one of the many instances which show the extremely great care with which, under the guidance of Inspiration, the words of Holy Scripture have been chosen. Bengel's note on the difference of the words here employed is; "Δοῦλοι (Bond-servants) are sent forth. Διάκονοι (Domestics) minister at table. Cf. St. John ii. 5, 9; "His mother saith unto the servants (τοῖς διακόνοις), etc."; "the servants which drew the water (οἱ δὲ διάκονοι οἱ ἠντληκότες τὸ ὕδωρ) knew," etc.]

Sunday.—Vv. 2, 3, 4. "The kingdom of heaven is like unto a certain king, which made a marriage for his son, and sent forth his servants" (St. John the Baptist, the Apostles, and the seventy Disciples, in our Lord's lifetime), "to call them that were bidden to the wedding: and they would not come. Again, he sent forth other servants," (the Apostles after the day of Pentecost, St. Paul, and other Apostolic men) "saying, Tell them which are bidden, Behold, I have prepared my dinner; my oxen and my fatlings are killed, and all things are ready: come unto the marriage." "God's patience is not wearied by the denials and resistance of man's heart. He seems as earnestly desirous of uniting it to Himself, as if some great advantage would accrue to Him thereby; whereas in truth He finds in it nothing but poverty, misery, and corruption; and, on the contrary, the heart finds in Him wisdom, holiness, greatness, riches, and all things that make a perfect, infinite, and incomprehensible felicity."

(Quesnel.) The secret of God's earnest solicitations to sinners to be reconciled to Him is, that He finds His highest glory in the voluntary subjection of rational creatures. " The orbs of heaven revolve in obedience to a law which they know not. But God would be obeyed by the nobler attractions of the heart; He would have the willing service, in which love is the all-sufficing law, that preserves the spirits of the blessed revolving, in changeless harmony, around Himself as the centre of their regenerate life."[1]—O God, who condescendest to sue for the allegiance of my heart, enable me to give it Thee whole, undivided, and without reserve, and let Thy long-suffering in bearing with my refusals hitherto, touch me with " godly sorrow,"[2] and " lead me " at length to true and deep " repentance."[3]

Monday.—Vv. 5, 6, 7. " But they made light of it, and went their ways, one to his farm " (falling back on his earthly property to give him all the gratification which he cared to have), " another to his merchandise " (too immersed in money-making to have time or thought to spare for other engagements) ; " and the remnant " (manifested not an indifferent, but a decidedly hostile temper) " took his servants, and entreated them spitefully, and slew them. But when the king heard thereof " (it was a crying sin of defiance, which came up into his ears[4]), " he was wroth : and he sent forth his armies, and destroyed those murderers, and burned up their city." In the immediately preceding Parable of the householder who planted a vine-

---

[1] This, and other extracts in the present group of thoughts, are taken from Professor Archer Butler's very striking Sermon on "The Wedding Garment," the thirteenth sermon in the first series of "Sermons Doctrinal and Practical." [Cambridge : Macmillan, 1852.]
[2] See 2 Cor. vii. 10.   [3] See Rom. ii. 4.
[4] See James v. 4 ; Gen. iv. 10 ; Rev. vi. 10 ; Gen. xviii. 21, etc.

yard, and sent servants to the husbandmen to receive the fruits of it, I do not find that, though the servants were beaten, and killed, and stoned, the lord of the vineyard destroyed the husbandmen, but only sent another and larger body of servants, and, when they were similarly treated, sent his son.[1]   Whence, then, this severity of dealing with the invited persons in the following Parable? What makes the difference between them and the husbandmen?   The circumstance that the husbandmen were applied to for the payment of a debt, whereas the invited persons were not asked to do anything but come to the wedding,— that is, they were asked to receive, not to give. —The penalty of breaking God's law, of not meeting His requirements, will be severe ("He that despised Moses' law died without mercy under two or three witnesses"[2]); but how far more awful, hopeless, crushing, the penalty of making light of His invitations of grace!   It is God's highest prerogative to show mercy and grace to sinners; and accordingly it is the crime of high treason to "make light of" that proffered mercy and grace.   And let me remember that they do "make light of it," who do not cordially accept the mercy, and do not concur and co-operate with those movements of grace, which God makes in their hearts.—Lord, in proportion to the means of grace with which Thou hast surrounded me, and the attractions of grace, by which Thou hast sought to draw me to Thyself, is my present responsibility, and will be my future punishment, if Thy invitations and inspirations pass by me unheeded!

Tuesday.—V. 11. "And when the king came in to see the guests." This Parable was all, or nearly all, a prophecy when it was delivered. But since it was de-

---

[1] St. Matt. xxi. 33-45.   [2] Heb. x. 28.

livered, the world has seen the fulfilment of every scene in it, except the last. The Jews have rejected the Gospel, and they have been destroyed, and their city burned by the Roman armies, acting as God's executioners. The Gospel has been preached in the highways of the world to the Gentiles, and a large number, bad and good, have accepted its invitation of grace, and been gathered into the Church's fold. And now one point only remains to be accomplished,—the coming in of the king to see the guests,—the judgment which is to be made of the Church universal, corresponding to the judgment which has already been made of the Jewish Church. " Both were to come when our Lord spoke ; both were predicted in the self-same prophecy ; *one* has notoriously taken place ; who can doubt that the other is certain? He who was so fearfully right, when He predicted the one, was surely not mistaken in predicting the other." . . . " The felt reality which belongs to the one (for nothing is of such felt reality as what we know to be past) communicates itself with a most awful power to the other, and makes' the future as much a matter of downright historical certainty as the past event."[1]—Grant, Lord, that the large portions of Thy word which have already received their fulfilment, may confirm and strengthen my faith in those parts which are still unfulfilled !

Wednesday.—V. 11. " He saw there a man " (*one* put to represent in a close and individual manner, so as to bring the sad warning home to the conscience of each, the *many* which, having been called, are not chosen) " which had not on a wedding garment." " The marriage garment is well explained of Christian joy of heart, " the fruit of the Spirit is joy "[2]; and we may add, delight in

---

[1] Prof. Archer Butler. [2] See Gal. v. 22.

the presence of the Bridegroom ; for this it is which occasions this gladness of heart.   It is, in short, what St. Paul mentions as another requisite for receiving the crown.   " The Lord, the righteous judge," shall at that day give "a crown of righteousness," not to me only, but " unto all them also that love his appearing."[1]   To love His appearing, to look forward to it, and rejoice in His presence with spiritual joy, this must be the wedding garment of the soul.   The same temper, pervading our every day life, would be shown in what the Collect expresses by cheerfulness,—" that we, being ready both in body and soul, may *cheerfully* accomplish those things which God would have done."—(Isaac Williams.)

Thursday.—V. 12. " And he saith unto him, Friend, how camest thou in hither not having a wedding garment?" " The guest is reproved for having entered the banquet hall without the wedding garment.   He should, it seems, have sought it before he came.   He should have brought it with him from that earthly scene, which is but the ante-chamber of heaven ; it is not, ' How, *after* thou hadst reached my presence, soughtest thou not the fitting vestment for my feast ? ' but, ' How *camest thou in* hither not having a wedding garment ?'   The wedding garment, then, must be woven and fashioned on earth.   It must be brought from thence with each happy spirit to heaven."[2] It is then, I see, a very critical question for me how far there is at present an element of joy in my religion. Paul and Silas at Philippi were so filled with this spirit, that they were lifted up by it far above all the discomforts and sufferings of outward circumstance, and burst forth into hymns of praise, so that the prisoners heard them.[3]   Is there in me even the germ of such spiritual

---

[1] 2 Tim. iv. 8.   [2] Prof. Archer Butler.   [3] See Acts xvi. 23, 24, 25.

joy? "My life is decorous,—yes, but is it spiritually joyful? My religious observances are regular,—yes, but are they the delighted utterance of gratitude and praise? I violate no plain precept among the Commandments,—but do I *rejoice* in keeping them? I exhibit the deportment of a Christian, I wear the outward costume and apparel of moral propriety,—yes, but where shall we look for the brighter apparel of the soul, the brilliancy and beauty of the festive robes of rejoicing saintliness, the glory of ' the wedding garment ?'[1]"

Friday.—V. 12. "Friend, how camest thou in hither not having a wedding garment?" Let me meditate to-day on the Sacrament of the Lord's Supper,—that highest ordinance of our religion. It is evidently constructed to be a figure and a foretaste of that marriage supper of the Lamb,[2] the proceedings at which are here foretold by our Lord. It is truly a marriage supper; for, when duly received, it is the great means of cementing that union with Christ, which was brought about by the first Sacrament,—the closeness of the union being symbolized by the passage of the elements into the body, and their transmutation in due course into the substance of the body. And as the king made a scrutiny of the guests at the marriage supper in the Parable, and he who had not on the wedding garment was expostulated with for presuming to come in without it, so we are expressly warned that self-scrutiny must precede the reception of the earthly supper; ("But let a man examine himself, and so let him eat of that bread, and drink of that cup."[3]). Moreover, as in the parable both those who declined the invitation, and he who accepted it without the fitting attire, are punished, so in regard of this prefigurative

---

[1] Prof. Archer Butler,   [2] See Rev. xix. 9.   [3] 1 Cor. xi. 28.

ordinance there is but one right course, to attend it in a prepared frame of mind; and those who neglect it, and those who attend without preparation, are open to the same condemnation.—Lord, let my Communions be made in such a spirit of holy joy, through faith in Thy blood and righteousness, that each of them may be to me a preparation for that Supper at the end of time, which not we for Thee,[1] but Thou for us shalt make, and to which not we shall bid Thee by the invocation of Thy Spirit and mystical Presence, but Thou, manifested visibly, and no longer under the sacramental veil, shalt bid us with those words of blessing, " Come, ye blessed of my Father, inherit the kingdom prepared for you from the foundation of the world."[2]

Saturday.—V. 14. " For many are called, but few are chosen."   Those who make light of the invitation are not chosen ; those who despitefully use the persons conveying it are not chosen ; those who accept it, without having on a wedding garment,—a vast multitude, though symbolized here by a single man (in order to show the individuality of God's scrutiny),—are not chosen.—Lord, I have been called in every way in which Thy voice could reach me—by Baptism, by Confirmation, by sermons, by Communions, by Providential dispensations, by tender mercies, by solemn warnings, by chastisements, by bereavements, on all sides of me.   Let me give diligence, by adding to my faith all the virtues of the Christian character, to make my calling and election sure,[3]—that is, to make my calling sure, and by that my election ; for, the calling being made sure, the election follows of itself. " We are not to pry immediately into God's decree, but to read it in the performance.   Though the mariner sees not

<hr>

[1] See St. John xii. 2.   [2] St. Matt. xxv. 34.   [3] 2 Pet. i. 5-12.

the pole-star, yet the needle of the compass which points to it tells him which way he sails. Thus the heart that is touched with the lodestone of divine love, trembling with godly fear, and yet still looking towards God by fixed believing, points at the love of election, and tells the soul that its course is toward the haven of eternal rest. He that loves may be sure he was loved first, and he that chooses God for his delight and portion may conclude confidently that God hath chosen him to be one of those that shall enjoy Him and be happy in Him for ever, —for that our love and electing of God is but the return and repercussion of the beams of His love shining upon us."[1]

[1] Archbishop Leighton, as quoted in Vol. II. of Dr. Glentworth Butler's " Bible Reader's Commentary " [New York : 1879] on 2 Pet. i. 10.

CHAPTER LVI

THE GOSPEL FOR THE TWENTY-FIRST SUNDAY AFTER TRINITY.

St. John iv. 46 *to the end*

(leaving out the words, "So Jesus came again into Cana of Galilee, where he made the water wine. And," with which *v.* 46 commences).

46 There was a certain noble man, whose son was sick at Caper-
47 naum. When he heard that Jesus was come out of Judea into Galilee, he went unto him, and besought him, that he would come
48 down, and heal his son; for he was at the point of death. Then said Jesus unto him, Except ye see signs and wonders, ye will not
49 believe. The noble man saith unto him, Sir, come down ere my
50 child die. Jesus saith unto him, Go thy way, thy son liveth. And the man believed the word that Jesus had spoken unto him, and he
51 went his way. And as he was now going down, his servants met
52 him, and told him, saying, Thy son liveth. Then enquired he of them the hour when he began to amend: And they said unto him,
53 Yesterday at the seventh hour the fever left him. So the father knew that it was at the same hour, in the which Jesus said unto him, Thy son liveth; and himself believed, and his whole house.
54 This is again the second miracle that Jesus did when he was come out of Judea into Galilee.

[Miss. Sab.	1549.	1662 s.b.
In illo tempore, Erat quidam regulus cujus filius infirmabatur Capharnaum . . . . *down to end of v.* 53, credidit ipse, et domus ejus tota. (*Vulg.* Venit ergo iterum in Cana Galilææ, ubi fecit aquam virnum. Et erat quidam regulus, cujus filius infirmabatur Capharnaum.)	There was a certain ruler, whose sonne was sick at Capernaum . . . . *down to end of v.* 54, when he was come out of Jury into Galilee.	There was a certain noble man, whose son was sick at Capernaum . . . . *down to end of v.* 54, when he was come out of Judea into Galilee. (*Gr.* Ἦλθεν οὖν ὁ Ἰησοῦς πάλιν εἰς τὴν Κανᾶ τῆς Γαλιλαίας, ὅπου ἐποίησε τὸ ὕδωρ οἶνον. Καὶ ἦν τις βασιλικὸς, οὗ ὁ υἱὸς, ἠσθένει ἐν Καπερναούμ.)

By the addition to the Sarum Gospel of the last verse of the Chapter, the Reformers in 1549 certainly gave a finish and completeness to the extract. We are thus informed that the miracle, which forms the subject of the Gospel, was the second which our Lord wrought in Galilee, though several (which are mentioned only in the group) had been performed in Jerusalem during the first Passover of the Ministry (see Chap. ii. 13, 23). Bengel remarks that St. John, in recording the miracles of Christ, gives them in groups of three ;—three in Galilee, the turning of water into wine, the healing of the nobleman's son, and the feeding of the five thousand (Chap. vi.) ; three in Judæa, the restoration of the impotent man at the pool of Bethesda (Chap. v.), the cure of the blind man at the pool of Siloam (Chap. ix.), and the raising of Lazarus (Chap. xi.) ; and three manifestations of the Risen Saviour to His assembled disciples, to the disciples in the absence of St. Thomas (Chap. xx. 19 *to* 24), to the disciples in the presence of St. Thomas (Chap. xx. 26 *to* 30), and to the seven disciples on the shore of the sea of Tiberias (Chap. xxi. 1, 14). The addition of *v.* 54 reminds us that this was the second miracle of the first group. What immediately precedes and leads up to the narrative in this Gospel is the notice of the welcome which our Lord received from the Galilæans, when He returned into their country, after performing many miracles (of which they had been the witnesses) at the feast of the Passover in Jerusalem. Probably most of these miracles were cures ; and the nobleman of Capernaum having heard of the supernatural power being often exerted in this form, thought he would apply for its exercise on behalf of his son. Accordingly he journeyed to Cana, the scene of our Lord's earliest miracle, and where (as we are told in the first part of *v.* 46) our Lord then was.—*Translation of* 1540. (1) *V.* 46. "There was a certain *ruler*" (ἦν τις βασιλικὸς). Tyndale, Cranmer, and the Genevan, all have "ruler." Wycliffe ; "a litil kyng was." Rhemish ; "a certaine lord." Authorised ; "a certaine noble man" (two words in the Edition of 1611), with "*courtier* or *ruler*" as marginal alternatives. Revised ; "nobleman," with "king's officer" as a marginal alternative. Elsewhere in the New Testament the word βασιλικὸς is merely an adjective (= of, or belonging to, a king) ; thus, "the king's country" (βασιλικὴ χώρα), Acts xii. 20 ; "royal apparel" (ἐσθῆτα βασιλικὴν), *ib. v.* 21 ; "royal law" (νόμον βασιλικὸν), James ii. 8. (2) *V.* 47. "*Assoon* as *the same* heard." And so Tyndale and the Genevan. There is surplusage here, the original being merely οὗτος ἀκούσας. Wycliffe, always literal, gives, "whanne this hadde herde "; the Rhemish, "He hauing heard "; the Authorised and Revised, "when he heard." (3) *V.* 47. "that Jesus was come out of *Jury*" [see Introduction to Gospel for Sixteenth Sunday after Trinity. *Translation of*

1540.   (3) *V.* 17.]   (4) *V.* 47. "for he was *even at the point of death.*"
Tyndale had given, "even readie to die."   When Cranmer changed the
phrase to "at the point of death," the "even" became superfluous, and
ought to have been discarded.   The Genevan repeated Tyndale,—"he
was euen ready to dye."   King James's Translators, accepting Cranmer's
"at the point of death," and omitting the "even," which he allowed to
stand, have come as near to the force of the original ($\eta\mu\epsilon\lambda\lambda\epsilon$ $\gamma\grave{a}\rho$ $\grave{a}\pi o$-
$\theta\nu\acute{\eta}\sigma\kappa\epsilon\iota\nu$) as it is possible to do in English.   (5) *V.* 49. Sir, come down *or
ever that* my sonne die."   Tyndale and the Genevan also have, *or ever that.*
Wycliffe and the Rhemish "before that."   The form "or ever" may be
used not only with a verb denoting the action which came (or is to come)
subsequently, but with a noun specifying a certain point of time, as in
Milton's "Ode of the Nativity";

> "The shepherds on the lawn
> *Or e'er* the point of dawn
> Sat simply chatting in a rustic row."

Of the construction with the verb (but without *that*), there is a fine
instance in the description of the state of Scotland given by Rosse to
Malcolm and Macduff (*Macbeth*, Act IV. Scene iii.);

> . . . . the dead man's knell
> Is there scarce asked, for who ; and good men's lives
> Expire before the flowers in their caps,
> Dying *or ere* they sicken."

(But see *Introduction to the Gospel for the Fifth Sunday in Lent, on St. John
viii. 58.*)   (6) *V.* 50. "The man beleeved the word that Jesus had spoken,"
(omitting the "And," with which the clause begins in the Authorised
Version).   Wycliffe and the Rhemish agree with Cranmer in leaving out
the "And."   Tyndale however inserts it, and is followed by the Genevan
and the Authorised.   The Revisers of 1881 (omitting $\kappa a\iota$ from their text,
probably on the ground of its not being found in the Sinaitic and Vatican
Manuscripts) have gone back to Cranmer's translation—"the man believed
the word."   (7) *V.* 51. "As he was going down, *the* servants met him."
This is a variation from Tyndale, who has "*his* servantes," as also have
the Genevan, the Rhemish, the Authorised, and the Revised.   Wycliffe
however has, "*the* seruauntis camen agens him," as he, translating from
the Vulgate, (where the words are, "Jam autem eo descendente, servi
occurrerunt ei") would naturally have.   The Sinaitic Manuscript omits
the word $a\grave{v}\tau o\hat{v}$ after $o\grave{\iota}$ $\delta o\hat{v}\lambda o\iota.$]

Sunday.—V. 46. " There was a certain nobleman."   Our

Lord " is no respecter of persons."[1]   To the humble roof of the *centurion* of Capernaum, an inferior officer of the Roman army, He *proposed* to come, in order to heal his servant ; " Jesus saith unto him, I will come and heal him."[2]   To the villa of the nobleman of Capernaum, beautifully laid out perhaps with terraces and gardens by the side of the lake, He would *not* come, nor stir a step towards it, though strongly urged to do so.   Very probably there was some amount of the pride of station working in the nobleman's mind.   It may have been with him as it was with Naaman, who " came with his horses and with his chariot " (evidently seeking to make an impression by his retinue), " and stood at the door of the house of Elisha,"[3] and whose vanity was wounded, because the prophet did not appear in person, but merely sent him instructions by a messenger.[4]   And our Lord's dealing with him may have been meant to mortify his pride, as well as to enlarge and increase his faith.—Lord, when we come to Thee for the healing of our souls, we must lay aside our pride, whether it be pride of station, or of learning, or of self-righteousness, and must put ourselves on a level with the humblest, the most ignorant, the most sinful of our race.   And to impress upon us this lesson by an outward visible sign, Thou dost forbid us to give precedence in Thy house of prayer to the rich " man with a gold ring, in goodly apparel," over " the poor man in vile raiment."[5]

Monday.—V. 46. " There was a certain nobleman, whose son was sick at Capernaum."   I find several instances in which parents resorted to Christ for the cure of their children,—the case of the Syrophœnician woman,

---

[1] See Acts x. 34.   [2] St. Matt. viii. 7.   [3] 2 Kings v. 9.
[4] *Vv.* 10, 11, 12.   [5] James ii. 1, 2, 3, 4.

whose " daughter was grievously vexed with a devil"[1] ; of Jairus, whose " little daughter lay at the point of death"[2] ; of the father of the lunatic child, who had a dumb and deaf spirit, which threw him into convulsions.[3]   We may augur with certainty that such cases as these would specially touch the heart of our Saviour, and waken the chord of compassion there.   First, because God bears to His rational creatures the special relationship of Father, man, according to his mental and moral nature, having been made in the image of God[4]; and Christ is God, " the Everlasting Father,"[5] in virtue of His Deity. Secondly, because it is just the one feature of parental affection which our Lord singles out from the rest as a redeeming trait in fallen man ; " If ye then, being evil, know how to give good gifts unto your children : how much more shall your heavenly Father give the Holy Spirit to them that ask him ?"[6]—O Lord, let me lay to heart that the strong love of parents for children, such love as Jacob's for Benjamin, as David's for Absalom, is but an echo of that tenderness, which Thou hast for Thy rational offspring, and which led Thee to give Thine own Son out of Thy bosom to save them[7] from the ruin of sin.

Tuesday.—Vv. 47, 49. " When he heard that Jesus was come out of Judæa into Galilee, he went unto him, and besought him that he would come down, and heal his son." . . . Sir, come down ere my child die." " This ruler," says Bishop Hall, " was neither faithless nor faithful."   Had he been quite faithless, " he had not taken such pains to come to Christ : had he been faithful, he

---

[1] See St. Matt. xv. 22.

[2] St. Mark v. 23.

[3] St. Mark ix. 17, 18, 25.

[4] See Gen. i. 26, 27.

[5] See Isaiah ix. 6.

[6] St. Luke xi. 13.

[7] See St. John iii. 16.

had not made this suit to Christ when he was come; *Come down and heal my son, ere he die. Come down?* As if Christ could not have cured him absent. *Ere he die?* As if that power could not have raised him being dead." The ruler's faith being weak, then, I see what means our Lord uses to strengthen it. Had He gone with him to his house, this would have been to foster the erroneous impression which speaks out in the words, " Come down"; it would have left the ruler to conclude that our Lord was unable to work a miracle of healing at a distance from the patient. So Christ merely gives him the assurance that his son is restored, " Thy son liveth "; and the man believed that assurance, we are told, and " went his way," hereby putting forth a stronger faith than he had come with. And eventually, when he had made experiment of the truth of Christ's assurance, " he and his whole house believed,"—that is, believed in Jesus as the Messiah, and became His disciples. I see, to my great consolation, that God does not reject a sincere faith, however weak, however imperfect, however unformed, however much it may at present be as a dead seed, which has never sprouted in the heart or disentangled its germ. By His providential dealings, and by His word, He seeks to elicit such faith, to quicken it, to make it give evidence of vitality, " just as the fingers of the light go searching in the dark mould for the sleeping seeds, to touch and awake them "[1].—Lord, increase my faith, the first principle of spiritual life, even if, as the condition of this increase, Thou seest it to be necessary to submit me to a heart-searching discipline !

---

[1] This illustration is taken from the works of the Rev. George M'Donald, as quoted in Dr. Glentworth Butler's " Bible Reader's Commentary,' Vol. I., p. 107. [New York : D. Appleton & Co. 1878.]

Wednesday.—V. 48. " Then said Jesus unto him, Except ye see signs and wonders, ye will not believe." " The Jews require a sign."[1] Our Lord, unto whom the heart of every comer to Him was open, saw clearly that this nobleman was leaning too much to the evidence of miracles,—that although he had some weak faith, he would not be settled in the conviction of Christ's claims without the sight of a sign and wonder. Miracles are never creative of faith; they are merely helps, which a weak faith may confirm itself by, but a strong faith can dispense with. Though there is a sad tendency in the thinkers of these days to explain away the miraculous narratives of the Bible, and to pare down as much as possible the supernatural element in our religion, yet we have not rid ourselves of the craving after signs and wonders natural to the human heart, as is shown by the passion for what is called spiritualism, or communication with the spirits of the dead.——Lord, let my faith in Thee be rooted and grounded in the correspondence of Thy word with the felt needs of my heart and conscience ; and then, while I never decline (with presumptuous King Ahaz) such helps to faith as Thou graciously offerest,[2] I shall never be the victim of that morbid craving after the supernatural, which leads so many astray from the solid verities of religion.

Thursday.—V. 49. " The nobleman saith unto him, Sir, come down ere my child die." " They limited the Holy One of Israel."[3] What a limitation of the Saviour's power was it to conceive that He could not heal the child without going down to the coast for the purpose, and presenting Himself in the sick room ! And what a wonderful contrast was there between the thoughts en-

---

[1] 1 Cor. i. 22.   [2] See Isaiah vii. 10, 11, 12.   [3] Ps. lxxviii. 41.

tertained of our Lord's power by this nobleman, and those of the centurion, as if the two stories had been framed to throw one another into relief; " Lord, I am not worthy that thou shouldest come under my roof: but speak the word only, and my servant shall be healed."[1]   I see that the doctrine of Transubstantiation,—that is, the presence of the natural body of our Lord on the altar of the Church after the words of consecration have been pronounced,—really proceeds from weakness of faith, and is a limitation of the Saviour's power.   The strong craving for His bodily presence, as if He could not bless us from His heavenly throne, or receive our adoration there, is virtually saying to Him, " Sir, come down ere my soul die."—Nay, Lord, it is not necessary that Thou shouldest come down from Thy throne of glory to give us all the blessings which flow from Thy spiritual Presence, and to present Thyself to us for the acceptance of our homage.   For dost Thou not " fill heaven and earth ?"[2] and does not one single word, spoken by Thee in heaven, take effect with the rapidity of lightning in the remotest corners of the earth ?

Friday.—V. 50. " Jesus saith unto him, Go thy way; thy son liveth."   This word was not declarative only, like the similar word of Elijah, when he brought the widow's son down to his mother after restoring him to life, and said, " See, thy son liveth."[3]   It was effective also, and did that which it declared to be done, so that at the moment when Christ spoke the word, the patient recovered. This I gather from V. 53, which tells us that it was at the same hour, in the which Jesus said unto the nobleman, Thy son liveth, that " the fever left " his son,—did not go down and expire gradually, but left him all of a

---

[1] St. Matt. viii. 8.   [2] See Jer. xxiii. 24.   [3] See 1 Kings xvii. 23.

sudden, and left no trace of itself behind.   Verily, God's
" word runneth very swiftly."[1]   He " quickeneth the
dead " (and the dying), " and calleth those things which be
not as though they were."[2]   The form of Absolution used in
our daily Morning and Evening Service, as indeed that
in the Visitation Service also, when rightly understood, is
declarative ; " God pardoneth and absolveth all them that
truly repent, and unfeignedly believe his holy Gospel."
But if I come under the terms of it, when I hear it
recited, and have true repentance and lively faith, it is
doubtless effective also, and really conveys to me that
pardon which is the true life of the soul.—Oh, that I
might hear Christ saying to me by His ambassador,
" Thy soul liveth "!   It is only my want of faith which
prevents my hearing it ; for Christ really and truly dis-
penses blessings, where the two or three are gathered
together in His name.[3]

Saturday.—Vv. 52, 53. " Then enquired he of them
the hour when he began to amend.   And they said unto
him, Yesterday at the seventh hour the fever left him.
So the father knew that it was at the same hour, in the
which Jesus said unto him, Thy son liveth : and himself
believed, and his whole house."   God's words and His
works will both bear minute scrutiny ; and the examination of them, and the comparison of the words
with the works will open out new wonders, and tend
greatly under His blessing to strengthen and confirm
our faith.   The fulfilment of Prophecy is a department
of evidence in favour of revealed Religion, which is at
least as edifying and instructive to the believer, as it
is convincing to the unbeliever.   St. Peter seems to
assign to the study of Prophecy, notwithstanding all its

---

[1] Ps. cxlvii. 15.   [2] Rom. iv. 17.   [3] See St. Matt. xviii. 19, 20.

obscurities, a very high place in the spiritual illumination of the believer; "We have also a more sure word of prophecy; whereunto ye do well that ye take heed, as unto a light that shineth in a dark place, *until the day dawn, and the day star arise in your hearts.*"[1]   And what is the study of Prophecy but an inquiry into the Providence of God over the human race, as illustrating, and illustrated by, the predictions of Holy Scripture? And let me remember that Providence is not only admirable in those vast reaches of it, which History reveals, but admirable also when viewed through the microscope, as controlling and superintending the individual life.   Let me look narrowly, and in a devout spirit, into my own experiences of life, and assuredly I shall not fail to find many striking illustrations of God's word, fulfilments of its promises, and exemplifications of its maxims, and evidences, perhaps, that its warnings against certain evil courses are only too well founded.   "Like as the Lord of hosts thought to do unto" me, "according to" my "ways, and according to" my "doings, so hath he dealt with" me.[2]

[1] 2 Pet. i. 19.   [2] See Zech. i. 6.

CHAPTER LVII

THE GOSPEL FOR THE TWENTY-SECOND SUNDAY AFTER TRINITY.

ST. MATT. xviii. 21 *to the end*
(the words "Peter said unto Jesus" being substituted for "Then came
Peter unto him, and said," in *v.* 21).

21   Peter said unto Jesus, Lord, how oft shall my brother sin
22 against me, and I forgive him? till seven times? Jesus saith
unto him, I say not unto thee, until seven times; but until seventy
23 times seven. Therefore is the kingdom of heaven likened unto a
24 certain king, who would take account of his servants. And when
he had begun to reckon, one was brought unto him, who ought him
25 ten thousand talents. But forasmuch as he had not to pay, his
lord commanded him to be sold, and his wife and children, and all
26 that he had, and payment to be made. The servant therefore fell
down and worshipped him, saying, Lord, have patience with me,
27 and I will pay thee all. Then the lord of that servant was moved
28 with compassion, and loosed him, and forgave him the debt. But
the same servant went out and found one of his fellow-servants,
who ought him an hundred pence; and he laid hands on him, and
29 took him by the throat, saying, Pay me that thou owest. And his
fellow-servant fell down at his feet, and besought him, saying,
30 Have patience with me, and I will pay thee all. And he would
not; but went and cast him into prison, till he should pay the debt.
31 So when his fellow-servants saw what was done, they were very
32 sorry, and came and told unto their lord all that was done. Then
his lord after that he had called him, said unto him, O thou wicked
servant, I forgave thee all that debt, because thou desiredst me:
33 Shouldest not thou also have had compassion on thy fellow-servant,

34 even as I had pity on thee? And his lord was wroth, and delivered him to the tormenters, till he should pay all that was due unto him.

35 So likewise shall my heavenly Father do also unto you, if ye from your hearts forgive not every one his brother their trespasses.

[MISS. SAR.	1549.	1662 S.B.
In illo tempore, Dixit Jesus discipulis suis parabolam hanc; Simile est regnum cœlorum homini regi, etc. (*Vulg.* (v. 23) Ideo assimilatum est regnum cœlorum homini regi, qui voluit rationem ponere cum servis suis.)	Peter said unto Jesus, Lord, how oft shall I forgive my brother, if he sinne against me? till seven times? Jesus saith unto him, I say not unto thee, Untill seven times: but seventie times seven times. Therefore is the kingdom of heaven likened unto a certain man that was a king.	Peter said unto Jesus, Lord, how oft shall my brother sin against me, and I forgive him? till seven times? (*Gr.* Τότε προσελθὼν αὐτῷ ὁ Πέτρος, εἶπε· Κύριε ποσάκις ἁμαρτήσει εἰς ἐμὲ ὁ ἀδελφός μου, καὶ ἀφήσω αὐτῷ; ἕως ἐπτάκις;)

The prefixing to the Sarum Gospel *vv.* 21, 22 of St. Matt. xviii., as the compilers of King Edward's First Book did in this case, was a change proceeding on just the same principle, on which the author endeavours in these Introductions to point out the connexion of each Liturgical Gospel with its immediately foregoing context; only that here there is a much stronger case than usual for exhibiting the connexion. The Parable grew out of, and was in fact the answer to, a very remarkable question addressed to our Lord by St. Peter. This question, and the first part of the answer, are given in *vv.* 21, 22, without which therefore the Parable itself cannot be rightly understood. Yet, as the Parable stood in the Sarum Missal, it is severed altogether from the occasion which gave rise to it. Most judicious then was the alteration which exhibited that connexion, and for which we have to thank the Reformers of 1549.—But we may go back one step further, and ask what is the connexion indicated by "Then," when it is said, "*Then* came Peter to him, and" asked the question, in reply to which the Parable was given. The promise to *united* prayer, prayer in which the petitioners are *agreed* as to what they shall ask, had *immediately* preceded (*vv.* 19, 20); and this again had been preceded by instructions as to how to deal with a brother who should "trespass against thee" (*vv.* 15 *to* 19). Hence probably arose in St. Peter's mind a question about the limits of forgiveness,—a question which he may have heard agitated in the Jewish schools, and which he now refers to his Master for solution. It is thus that the late Mr. Isaac Williams understands the connexion [see his "Gospel Narrative of our Lord's Ministry harmonized,"

Vol. III., p. 149. (Rivingtons: 1849).] Bengel says that "this question took its rise from some sense of the superabundance of the Divine Grace, which had been so greatly extolled in the preceding discourses."—*Translation of* 1540. (1) *V.* 21. "Lord, how oft *shall I forgive my brother, if he sinne against me ?*" And so Tyndale and the Genevan. Wycliffe gives the more literal rendering, "hou ofte schal my brother synne agens me : and I schal forgeve hym ?" And Wycliffe is followed by the Rhemish and the Authorised. (2) *V.* 22. "I say not unto thee, Untill seven times : but seventie times seven times." The second "until" is improperly dropped by Tyndale and the Genevan, as well as by Cranmer. The Rhemish inserted it, as Wycliffe (ever literal) had done before ("I seye not to thee til senene sithis : but till seventi sithis senene sithis "). To omit it decidedly weakens the emphasis. (3) *V.* 23. "a certain man that was a king" (ἀνθρώπῳ βασιλεῖ). [See the Introduction to the Gospel for the Twentieth Sunday after Trinity. *Translation of* 1540. (1) *V.* 2.] (4) *V.* 23. "which would take *accompts of* his servants." Cranmer is following Tyndale, who has, "which wolde take a countis (*sic*) of his servauntis." The Genevan too has the plural, "acountes." The Rhemish is the first to give the singular,—"that would make *an account* with his seruants." May not Cranmer's plural have sprung from a misunderstanding of Tyndale ? "A countis" in Tyndale is written as two words. The word "account" is beyond doubt the Latin "computus" (*a reckoning, bill*) transferred into the English language. The shortened form of this would be "comptus" or "comptis," which soon passed into "countis." The "a" which Tyndale places before "countis" may be merely the definite article : but a copyist or printer, taking it to be the first member of the following word, may have attached it, and thus produce the word "acountis." Some five years after, the *s* of "acountis" may have been taken to be the sign of the plural, whereas really it was only a relic of the Latin word *computus.*—As for the orthography "accompt," it is to be regrétted that it should have passed out of use, because by dropping the *p,* the real etymology of the word (which undoubtedly is *computus*) is obscured. It was still "accompt" in the judicious Hooker's time ; (Ecc. Pol. v. 46)—"The soul may have time to call itself to a just *accompt* of all things past, by means whereof repentance is perfected."—It is to be regretted that King James's Translators did not follow the Rhemish in giving the preposition "*with*" instead of "of,"—"that would make an account *with* his servants." To "take account *of* his servants" *might* mean (though perhaps it did not necessarily do so in the English of 1611) to reckon up the number of his establishment, and see how many members it consisted of ; which of course is *not* the sense. The Revisers of 1881 have given us, "which would *make a reckoning with* his servants," going back most properly to the Saxon of Wycliffe ("that wolde rikene with hise scruauntes"), and discarding the Latin "computus" altogether. (5) *V.* 24. "which *ought* him ten thousand talents." This is the spelling adopted in all the English translations down to the Rhemish (1582), which first gave "owed." Indeed *the first Edition of the Authorised Translation* (1611) has "ought." And so in Shakspere (1 *Henry IV.*, Act III., Scene iii.) "*Prince Henry.* Thou sayest true, hostess ; and he slanders thee most grossly. *Hostess.* So he doth you, my lord ; and said this other day that you *ought* him a thousand pound." It is well to be incidentally reminded that what we *ought* to be and do, is in fact what we *owe* to God and to our neighbour.—(6) *V.* 25. "But for as much as he *was not able to* pay" (μὴ ἔχοντος δὲ αὐτοῦ ἀποδοῦναι). This "was not able to" is exclusively Cranmer's. Tyndale had given, "because he *had nought to paye*"; Wycliffe, "whan he hadde not wherof to yilde." Ἔχω with an infinitive of the aorist does of course frequently signify "to be able to"; (thus we have in Heb. vi. 13, "When God made promise to Abraham, because he *could* swear by no greater (ἐπεὶ κατ᾽ οὐδενὸς εἶχε μείζονος ὀμόσαι), he sware by himself"). But this sense of the word is derived from its radical sense of "having," inasmuch as one who *is able* to do a thing, *has* the means or power to do it. And whenever the radical sense can be exhibited, as here ("he *had not* wherewith to pay"), it is better to exhibit it. (7) *V.* 26. "The servant fell down." Cranmer, following Tyndale, has left out the "therefore" (οὖν), which appears in the original. The Genevan inserts the "therefore." Wycliffe and the Rhemish render it by "but," representing the "autem" of the Vulgate ("Procidens *autem* servus ille, orabat cum dicens, etc.") (8) *V.* 26. "The servant fell down, and *besought* him." And so Tyndale, the Genevan, and the Rhemish. Wycliffe has, "preied hym." King James's Translators, while retaining "besought" in the margin, give the more literal rendering of προσεκύνει ("worshipped him"), in their text. The Revisers have adopted "worshipped," but without any marginal alternative. (9) *V.* 27. "Then had the lord pity on that servant," instead of, "then the lord of that servant was moved with compassion" (Σπλαγχνισθεὶς δὲ ὁ κύριος τοῦ δούλου ἐκείνου). Wycliffe, Tyndale, Cranmer, and the Genevan, all seem to have regarded the genitive case, as governed by, and depending on, the verb σπλαγχνίζομαι not the noun κύριος. King James's Translators did not take that view, neither have the Revisers of 1881 done so. But Winer does so. He gives σπλαγχνίζομαι as one of the verbs of feeling, which take a genitive to denote the object towards which the feeling is directed,—the object which is conceived of as giving rise to the feeling.

["Grammar of New Testament Greek." Ed. Moulton. Edinburgh : 1877. P. 255.] Yet he admits (p. 277) that this construction is only found once in the New Testament (in the passage before us), σπλαγχνίζομαι usually taking ἐπί after it. It is used four times absolutely,—of the Lord's compassion for the two blind men at Jericho (St. Matt. xx. 34); and for the leper (St. Mark i. 41); of the good Samaritan's compassion for the wounded traveller (St. Luke x. 33); and of the father's compassion for the prodigal son (St. Luke xv. 20) : twice with ἐπί and a dative,—of the Lord's compassion for the multitudes who outwent Him when He sought privacy and rest (St. Mark vi. 34); and for the widow of Nain (St. Luke vii. 13): four times with ἐπί and an accusative,—of our Lord's compassion for the multitude before the feeding with the *five* loaves (St. Matt. xiv. 14), and again before the feeding with the *seven* loaves (St. Matt. xv. 32, St. Mark viii. 2); and in the father's prayer for the lunatic child, "have compassion on us" (St. Mark ix. 22): and once with περί and a genitive, —of our Lord's compassion on the multitudes, "because they fainted, and were scattered abroad, as sheep having no shepherd" (St. Matt. ix. 36).—It is worthy of observation that this beautiful word, in nine out of the twelve instances of its occurrence, denotes *the Divine compassion, as existing in God or Christ*, and that in the remaining three cases, the Parables of the Unforgiving Servant, the Prodigal Son, and the Samaritan, the king, and the father represent God, while the Samaritan represents Christ. We may almost say therefore that "yearning compassion" is an attribute which Holy Scripture ascribes, if not exclusively, yet at all events pre-eminently, to God. (10) *V.* 28. "and found one of his *fellows*." And so Tyndale and the Genevan. Wycliffe, always conscientious, must needs represent the *con* in the "conservis" of the Vulgate ; so he gives, "fond oon of his *euene* seruauntis." (11) *V.* 28. "Pay that thou owest." Tyndale had given "pay *me*"; and the Genevan also has the "me." Wycliffe and the Rhemish omit it, since it does not appear in the Vulgate, which has only "Redde quod debes." Our Revisers, having discarded from their text the μοι after Ἀπόδος (probably because of its omission by the Sinaitic and Vatican Manuscripts), have gone back to Cranmer's rendering, "Pay what thou owest." (12) *V.* 32. "O thou *ungracious* servant" (Δοῦλε πονηρέ). Tyndale and the Genevan give us "evil"; the Rhemish repeats the "*ungratious*" of Cranmer. The Authorised Version replaced the "wicked," which Wycliffe had given two hundred and thirty-one years before. "Ungracious" is as nearly as possible equivalent to "wicked" in *Lear*, Act IV. Scene vi. ;

> .   .   .   .   "and in the mature time,
> With this *ungracious* paper strike the sight
> Of the death-practised duke."

The "paper" in question was Goneril's letter to Edmund, urging him to destroy her husband. We are doubtless indebted to Christianity for this meaning of the word "ungracious." It is the Gospel that has taught us that all good in man is of God's grace, and that to be without that grace is to be bad or wicked. (13) *V.* 32. "I forgave thee all that debt *when* thou desiredst me" (ἐπεὶ παρεκάλεσάς με). "When" is peculiar to Cranmer. Wycliffe has, "for"; Tyndale, the Genevan, the Rhemish, Authorised, Revised, have all "because." There is one passage in the New Testament in which ἐπεὶ clearly denotes a relation of time. See St. Luke vii. 1, Ἐπεὶ δὲ ἐπλήρωσε πάντα τὰ ῥήματα αὐτοῦ ("Now *when* he had ended all his sayings"). But is there more than one? Usually it is causal in its meaning, and equivalent to "for," "for otherwise," "because." (14) *V.* 34. "And his Lord was wroth, and delivered him to the *jaylers*" (τοῖς βασανισταῖς). Tyndale, Cranmer, and the Genevan all have "jaylers." Wycliffe has, "tormentors" (the *tortoribus* of the Vulgate), which the Rhemish was the first to replace. (15) *V.* 35. "if ye from your hearts forgive not every one his brother their trespasses." In the 1st Edition of Cranmer's Bible (1539), as also in the Edition of 1541, the words "every one his brother" are in brackets,—a very important direction to be observed by those who read aloud.]

Sunday.—Vv. 21, 22. "Then came Peter to him, and said, Lord, how oft shall my brother sin against me, and I forgive him? till seven times? Jesus saith unto him, I say not unto thee, Until seven times; but, Until seventy times seven." Intelligent children learn much by questioning their parents and elders; and our Lord, one of whose titles is "the everlasting Father"[1] (compare, "Behold I and the children which God hath given me"[2]), used to call His disciples by the endearing name of "little children."[3] The Jewish doctors thought and taught that forgiveness was to be extended to an offending brother thrice.[4] St. Peter felt from the preceding conversation,

---

[1] Isaiah ix. 6.   [2] Heb. ii. 13.   [3] St. John xiii. 33; xxi. 5.

[4] "The Rabbinical rule was, to forgive *three times and no more;* this they justified by Amos i. 3, etc., Job xxxiii. 29, 30. LXX., and marg. E. V."—Alford, *in loc.*

and from the whole tone and tenour of our Lord's teaching, that His Master would demand a larger and more liberal measure.   So, founding his suggestion perhaps upon Prov. xxiv. 16, "A just man falleth seven times, and riseth up again," he suggests seven times as a suitable measure.   His Master's answer opens his eyes wide ; teaches him that he was fundamentally wrong in conceiving that there should be any limit at all; and in illustration of this a parable is elicited, which is one of the Church's greatest treasures, conveying, as it does, perhaps more of Christian doctrine and practice than almost any other.—Lord, though Thou art no longer upon earth, it is my mighty privilege to be able to consult Thy written word, which, being given by inspiration of God,[1] was written in the foresight of my circumstances, difficulties, trials, and which has somewhere made provision for them. If I am ever devoutly inquiring at these lively oracles, I shall grow in grace and knowledge,[2] and shall gain ever truer and deeper conceptions of Thy love for me, and of the extent of its requirements.

Monday.—Vv. 23, 24. " Therefore is the kingdom of heaven likened unto a certain king, which would take account of his servants.   And when he had begun to reckon, one was brought unto him, which owed him ten thousand talents."   This reckoning cannot be the final reckoning which is to take place at the end of time, when " every one of us shall give account of himself to God,"[3] because we find that after it the servant's probation continues, and an opportunity is afforded him of showing how little he appreciated the king's kindness to himself.   I must therefore interpret this reckoning as signifying some close dealing of God with the soul, as when He lays a

---

[1] 2 Tim. iii. 16.   [2] See 2 Pet. iii. 18.   [3] Rom. xiv. 12.

man upon what threatens to be a bed of death, and there seems to expostulate with him on his careless, godless life, or by some other providential means musters and arrays his past sins before his eyes. At first this close dealing seems to be attended with happy results. The man seems to find peace in his conscience through the blood of the cross, and is raised up from his sick bed, and death no longer stares him in the face. But the issue proves, alas! that the work upon his conscience had never gone deep enough; he was only frightened, not converted. —If at any time of my life, and by any means, I have been brought to see my need of God's mercy, and in a measure to taste its sweetness, how deep has this work penetrated into my soul? Has it been, indeed, the turning point of a new life, or has the prayer offered in those past moments been merely the prayer of the nine unthankful lepers,[1] wrung out from me by the pressure of alarm or trouble? How many spiritual processes and influences there are, which prove eventually abortive, never take hold of the will and the springs of the character!

Tuesday.—V. 25. " But forasmuch as he had not to pay, his lord commanded him to be sold." To be sold into slavery with all his family, that the sum so raised might go some way towards liquidating the debt,—this was the penalty of his fraud and embezzlement. Let me take occasion to meditate on those words of the Apostle, descriptive of man's state by nature; " I am carnal, *sold under sin.*"[2] The miserable effect of deliberate sin, unrepented of, and unforgiven, is that the sinner is thereby transferred, as if by a sale in a slave-market, to the service of Satan, a tyrannical and hardhearted master, exact-

---

[1] See St. Luke xvii. 13, 17, 18.   [2] Rom. vii. 14.

ing at all times, and whose wages decrease as people grow old in his service, till at length he withdraws from them altogether the stimulant of sensual and worldly pleasure. and they discover in their hearts a craving for solid and substantial happiness, but are fain to content themselves with the husks that the swine do eat.[1] Is it God's act, this sale of the sinner into the hands of the hard taskmaster? Not more than it is the sinner's own act; it is God's act of righteous retribution, pursuant upon man's deliberate choice of evil;—"Which of my creditors is it to whom I have sold you? Behold, for your iniquities have ye sold yourselves."[2] And in selling himself to Satan by deliberate sin, the sinner barters away the heavenly inheritance, to which his Baptism entitled him, for a transitory and fleeting indulgence,—it is profane Esau over again, selling his birthright to gratify a momentary craving of appetite.[3] The momentary gratification proves in the issue to be nothing, or nothing that can really satisfy the soul's craving; but this very nothingness of the wages of· sin (so exuberant are the riches of God's grace and mercy) is made the basis of a promise of free redemption; "Ye have sold yourselves for nought; and ye shall be redeemed without money."[4]—O God, against the murky background of our ruin and wretchedness how brilliant do the rainbow colours of Thy grace and mercy show!

Wednesday.—V. 27. "Then the lord of that servant was moved with compassion, and loosed him, and forgave him the debt." While this parable in its main scope is one of warning, and while it concludes with an awful menace, that our heavenly Father will deliver the unloving

---

[1] See St. Luke xv. 16.   [2] Isaiah l. 1.
[3] See Gen. xxv. 29 *to the end*; and Heb. xii. 16.   [4] Isaiah lii. 3.

and unforgiving into the hands of the tormentors, I yet find it full of grace and of the doctrine of grace. The servant carried away far more than he asked, more probably than he dared to hope for, when he prostrated himself at the king's feet. He had only asked for time, and promised payment, if time were given him; " Lord, have patience with me, and I will pay thee all." It was a rash vow enough ; for never could he have raised by his most strenuous exertions so large a sum; but the straits to which he was reduced, and the almost frantic earnestness of his appeal, touched the king's heart, and he granted him, not time to pay, but a complete release from all the obligations he had incurred. The debt was cancelled; the prison door flew open; and the debtor was a free man once more, and encumbered by no kind of embarrassments.—O God, how promptly and liberally does Thine heart of infinite compassion respond to any act of humiliation on the part of the sinner, if only it be sincere and earnest! Even wicked Ahab, rending his clothes, and fasting, and lying in sackcloth, elicits at once the response; " Seest thou how Ahab humbleth himself before me ? Because he humbleth himself before me, I will not bring the evil in his days."[1] For hast thou not promised to " look to him that is poor and of a contrite spirit, and trembleth at " Thy " word ? "[2] And art Thou not " always more ready to hear than we to pray, and wont to give more than either we desire, or deserve ?"[3]

Thursday.—V. 27. " Then the lord of that servant . . . loosed him, and forgave him the debt. But the same servant went out." I find in this Parable not only grace, but the doctrine of grace. For what can be more

---

[1] 1 Kings xxi. 27, 28, 29.   [2] See Isaiah lxvi. 2.
[3] Collect for the Twelfth Sunday after Trinity.

clearly taught than that we must first be forgiven freely, and discharged of our debt to God, before we can possibly walk in love, as Christ hath loved us,[1] and extend forgiveness to our brethren ? It is true, indeed, that our forgiving others is, and is represented in the Lord's Prayer to be, a condition of God's forgiveness; but this forgiving of others belongs to a subsequent stage of man's spiritual history: in the earlier stage of it, as this Parable most clearly shows, the man who is required to forgive, as the condition of retaining his pardon and having it ultimately assured to him, has first experienced forgiveness himself. This forgiveness sweetens his heart towards others, as the tree at Marah (the emblem of the cross) sweetened the bitter waters into which it was thrown[2]; and having tasted mercy, he is disposed to dispense it.   But alas ! too often the impression, which never penetrated deep enough, is obliterated, as marks on the sand are erased by the rising tide.   The man "goes out," and forgets what has passed in that hour of close reckoning between God and his soul.   He is like the nine unthankful lepers, whose gratitude for their restoration, if they had any, was so shallow, that it did not make them even turn back to acknowledge the favour, and give glory to God.[3]— O God, let my reception of Thy mercy sink to the depths of my soul, and sweeten the springs of my character !

Friday.—V. 29. "And his fellowservant fell down at his feet, and besought him, saying, Have patience with me, and I will pay thee all."   Here is another encouraging and consolatory thought arising from a parable, which vibrates with accents of solemn warning, not to say threatening.   It is but few persons who would under

---

[1] See Eph. v. 2.　　　　　[2] See Exod. xv. 23, 24. 25.
[3] See St. Luke xvii. 17, 18.

the circumstances act like the unmerciful servant. Very few would have the heart to do so. Generally speaking, anything like humiliation and a promise of amendment softens men at once, and induces them not to press (at all events not for the present) a claim, however just. Now man was made in God's image[1]; and the placability in man's heart is only a broken echo of the much tenderer, prompter, more compassionate placability in God's. Then, however grievous and multiplied my sins be, and however keen my sense of them, let me say with good Bishop Andrewes; "What hope remains to me? The hope that Thou wilt extend Thy mercy unto seventy times seven. For this measure Thou Thyself hast commended to us. Hast Thou done so, that we among ourselves should show it, but Thou Thyself shouldest not show so large a measure? Nay, but Thou wilt show it, —aye, and much more. Far be it from Thee that Thou shouldest require from us a higher perfection than is in Thyself,—that Thou shouldest require us to forgive until seventy times seven, but shouldest Thyself be unwilling to do so. For thy mercy as much exceedeth ours as Thou exceedest us!"[2]

Saturday.—V. 35. "So likewise shall my heavenly Father do also unto you, if ye from your hearts forgive not (every one his brother) their trespasses." "Every one his brother;"—I mark the individuality with which Christ presses home this requirement upon the consciences of His disciples, so that they might find no loophole to escape. In the former part of the Chapter I find Him speaking of Church censures ("If he neglect to hear the Church, let him be unto thee as a heathen man"[3]), and

---

[1] See Gen. i. 27.
[2] "Confessio Peccati," towards the end of the "Preces Privatæ."   [3] *V.* 17.

of Church absolutions ("Whatsoever ye shall loose on earth, shall be loosed in heaven "[1]).   But He would not have us merge in the general exercise of Church discipline a duty coming so close home to each one of us, so involving personal relations and personal feelings, as that of forgiveness.   This forgiveness must be ministered, not only by the priest, as the representative of the Church, but by " every one to his brother,"—by the party who has been made sore, irritated, wounded, to the brother who has wounded him.   And what an overwhelming weight is given to this precept—more than to any other—by the fact that our Lord has woven it into the texture of the Lord's Prayer,—has warranted our asking for the forgiveness of our own trespasses, only in the same measure as we extend forgiveness to others.[2]   And yet, since forgiving love is the burden of Gospel tidings, shall we be surprised to find that forgiving love is also the burden of Gospel requirements, — the supreme evangelical law ?— Lord, put this law of love into my mind, and write it in my heart ; and so fulfil towards me the terms of the New Covenant.[3]

[1] *V.* 18.   [2] See St. Matt. vi. 12 ; St. Luke xi. 4.
[3] See Heb. viii. 10.

Chapter LVIII.

THE GOSPEL FOR THE TWENTY-THIRD SUNDAY AFTER TRINITY.

St. Matt. xxii. 15 *to* 23.

15 Then went the Pharisees and took counsel how they might
16 intangle him in his talk. And they sent out unto him their disciples
with the Herodians, saying, Master, we know that thou art true,
and teachest the way of God in truth, neither carest thou for any
17 man: for thou regardest not the person of men. Tell us therefore,
What thinkest thou? Is it lawful to give tribute unto Cesar, or
18 not? But Jesus perceived their wickedness, and said, Why tempt
19 ye me, ye hypocrites? Shew me the tribute-mony. And they
20 brought unto him a peny. And he saith unto them, Whose is this
21 image and superscription? They say unto him, Cesars. Then
saith he unto them, Render therefore unto Cesar, the things which
22 are Cesars; and unto God, the things that are Gods. When they
had heard these words, they marvelled, and left him, and went their
way.

[Miss. Sar.	1549.	1662 s.b.
In illo tempore, Abeuntes Pharisæi consilium inierunt ut caperent *Jesum* in sermone, etc. . . . *down to end of v.* 21, et quæ sunt Dei, Deo. (*Vulg.* Tunc abeuntes Pharisæi, consilium inierunt ut caperent eum in sermone).	Then the Pharisees went out and took counsell how they might tangle him in his words, etc. . . . *down to end of v.* 22, they marvelled, and left him, and went their way.	Then went the Pharisees and took counsel how they might intangle him in his talk . . . *down to end of v.* 22, they marvelled, and left him, and went their way. (*Gr.* Τότε πορευθέντες οἱ Φαρισαῖοι, συμβούλιον ἔλαβον ὅπως αὐτὸν παγιδεύσωσιν ἐν λόγῳ).

The addition of *v.* 22, made by the Reformers in 1549, is obviously
right. For this verse records the impression made by our Lord's settle-

ment of the question propounded to Him on the subject of tribute to Cæsar.
and the amazed discomfiture of those who propounded it. What "they
marvelled" at doubtless was the wisdom with which He had extricated
Himself from the horns of the dilemma, in which they had hoped to entangle
Him. His decision had not made Him obnoxious to any party ; for
there was in it an obvious truth and rectitude, which must have approved
itself to both, and in which neither could find any ground for an accusa-
tion. This exhibition in the last verse of the Gospel of the defeat of His
enemies' contrivance is the suitable correlative to the first verse (15),
which records that contrivance.—As to the connexion of the passage with
what immediately precedes, which is pointed at by the opening word
"Then," the incident is introduced immediately after the Parable of the
Marriage of the King's Son. This is one of a trilogy of Parables (see the
Introduction to the Gospel for the Twentieth Sunday), in which the hypocrisy of the Jews and their bitter enmity to God's truth were censured,
and which we are expressly told (Chap. xxi. 45) that the chief priests and
Pharisees felt to be aimed at themselves. Frustrated in their desire of
employing *violence* against Him by the esteem in which the people held
Him (Chap. xxi. 46), they were soon afterwards infuriated to the last
degree by the way in which He seemed to detect and expose the murder-
ous intent, which was brewing in their hearts ("he destroyed those
murderers, and burned up their city," Chap. xxii. 7), and took counsel
with one another to supplant Him by *craft*. Our Gospel records the utter
frustration of their malignant scheme.—*Translation of* 1540. (1) *V.* 15.
"Then the Pharisees went *out*." So begins this Gospel in the Black-
Letter Prayer Book of 1636 [39 ?]. But in Cranmer's Bible (both in the
Edition of 1539 and in that of 1541) the words are "Then went the
pharises." Whence this discrepancy ? (2) *V.* 16. "And they sent out
unto him their disciples with *Herods servants*." And so Tyndale and
the Genevan. Wycliffe has, "erodianes ;" the Rhemish and Authorised,
"the Herodians." (3) *V.* 16. "for thou regardest not the *outward
appearance* of men." "Outward appearance" is peculiar to Cranmer.
Wycliffe has, "thou beholdist not the persone of men "; Tyndale, "thou
consydrest not mennes estate "; the Genevan, same as Tyndale ; the
Rhemish, "thou doest not respect the person of men "; the Authorised,
"thou regardest not the person of men." (4) *V.* 17. "Tell us therefore,
how thinkest thou " (τί σοι δοκεῖ ;). Tyndale and the Genevan both have
"how." The Rhemish, "what is thy opinion ?"—Wycliffe with his
usual punctual fidelity to the letter, "scie to us : *what it semith to thee* "
("quid tibi videtur," *Vulg.*) (5) *V.* 19. "And they *took* him a penny."
This is a variation from Tyndale. Tyndale and the Genevan both use the

verb "*bring*"; "thei *brougten* to hym," "they *brogt* him." Rhemish, keeping up the sacrificial meaning of the verb προσφέρω ; "they *offred* him a penie." ("At illi *obtulerunt* ei denarium," *Vulg.*) (6) *V.* 21. "*Give* therefore unto Cesar the things which are Cesars." ('Απόδοτε οὖν, etc.) Tyndale and the Genevan both have "give"; Wycliffe, "yield"; the Rhemish is the first to give "render." The Greek verb ἀποδίδωμι expresses something more than giving; it is giving *back* that which belonged originally to another person. Hence its frequent use in the sense of "paying" in the Parable of the Unmerciful Servant (St. Matt. xviii. 25, 26, 28, 29, 30, 34) ; and hence it is applied to Pilate's act in *giving back* the sacred Body of our Lord into the custody of the Jews, who had traitorously delivered it to the Gentiles ; "Then Pilate commanded the body—ἀποδοθῆναι—to be *given back*" (St. Matt. xxvii. 58). "The Jews," says Bengel, "had alienated the Body. Joseph, one of their senators, received it, as it were in the name of the nation, from the Gentiles ; and in association with Nicodemus, restored it to the Jews. It was buried 'as the manner of the Jews is to bury' (St. John xix. 40) ".]

Sunday.—V. 15. "Then went the Pharisees, and took counsel how they might entangle him in his talk." How easy do our spiritual enemies usually find it to "entangle us in our talk"! "Because the business of life cannot be carried on without speaking, there is always ample verge and scope enough for offences of the tongue. Speech is continually passing from us by a thousand avenues of occasion,"[1] and sin may insinuate itself at any one of these avenues. For which reason it is that the government of the tongue is a work of exceeding difficulty, and a test (according to St. James) of spiritual perfection ; "If any man offend not in word, the same is a perfect man, and able also to bridle the whole body."[2] "The good and pious," says Quesnel, "ought strictly to watch over their words, because the world" (like these Pharisees) "is always vigilant to make them serve its

---

[1] I venture to quote these words from my own book, "The Idle Word," first published many years ago.   [2] James iii. 2.

interests or passions. Set a watch, O Lord, before my mouth,[1] and secure it from being surprised either by the devil, or the world, or my own corrupt desires."

Monday.—V. 16. " And they sent out unto him their disciples, with the Herodians, saying, Master, we know that thou art true, and teachest the way of God in truth, neither carest thou for any man : for thou regardest not the person of men." These smooth words concealed a malignant hostility of design; they were a kind of prelude to the kiss of Judas, and his " Hail, master "[2]; " the words of his mouth were softer than butter, having war in his heart : his words were smoother than oil, and yet be they very swords."[3] And yet the words were absolutely true ; our blessed Lord's independence, integrity, incorruptibility, were doubtless leading features of His character. The devil can speak truth, just as he can quote Scripture, when it serves his purpose. He did so after our Lord's time, when the damsel possessed with the spirit of divination at Philippi followed Paul and Silas and the writer of the Acts of the Apostles, " and cried, saying, These men are the servants of the most high God, which shew unto us the way of salvation."[4] There could not be a truer description of the functions of these ministers of God. Why then was St. Paul so " grieved "[5] with the words which were put into the poor girl's mouth ? Because he saw at a glance that the object of the evil spirit was to bring discredit on the cause of the Gospel by seeming to ally himself with it, and applauding its ambassadors. The devil is as crafty as he is powerful. Let me not be ignorant of his devices, and so give him an advantage

----

[1] See Ps. cxli. 3.   [2] See St. Matt. xxvi. 48, 49.
[3] Ps. lv. 22, P.B.V.   [4] Acts xvi. 16, 17.   [5] *V.* 18.

over me.[1] From all " the crafts," as well as " the assaults of the devil, good Lord, deliver me."[2]

Tuesday.—V. 17. " Tell us therefore, What thinkest thou ? Is it lawful to give tribute unto Cæsar, or not ?" " In reading this account," says Mr. Isaac Williams, " what I think must most strike us, is not so much their malice and envy against Christ as the little, low, earthly thoughts which possessed them."[3] Our Lord has been speaking of the marriage supper at the end of time, from which all shall be excluded, who have not on the wedding garment.[4] " But their hearts are so full of things earthly, of their petty disputes about this world's politics, that they have no room there for "[3] such heavenly discourse. They were citizens of earth, not of heaven, and had their thoughts, desires, cares, affections, among things below.—Do I not too much resemble them on occasions, when some political crisis is imminent, and, thinking no affairs so important (as indeed no earthly and sublunary affairs are) as affairs of state, and the stability or insecurity of Governments, I allow my thoughts to be wholly swallowed up in it ? If my conversation were in heaven, and I were looking for the Saviour from thence,[5] could the politics and Governments of the earth ever bound my horizon, and shut out from me the sight of the heavenly Jerusalem ? Of every earthly throne God says that it will one day come down, or rather perhaps be occupied by the earth's rightful Sovereign ; " I will overturn, overturn, overturn, it : and it shall be no more, until he come whose right it is ; and I will give it him."[6]

---

[1] See 2 Cor. ii. 11.   [2] First Deprecation in the Litany.

[3] " Sermons on the Epistles and Gospels," Vol. II., p. 272. [Rivingtons: 1875.] I hope I shall be pardoned for having slightly altered the wording of the passage.   [4] See St. Matt. xxii. 2, 11, 12, 13.

[5] See Phil. iii. 20.   [6] Ezek. xxi. 27.

Wednesday.—Vv. 18, 19. " But Jesus perceived their wickedness, and said, Why tempt ye me, ye hypocrites ?   Shew me the tribute-money."   In sending forth His Apostles, our Lord had given them this instruction; " Behold, I send you forth as sheep in the midst of wolves : be ye therefore wise as serpents, and harmless as doves."[1]   How wonderfully does He here exemplify this precept in His own practice !   For, on the one hand, what wisdom is there in His answer, a wisdom whereby He entirely evades the snare laid for Him, and gives the enemy no handle whatever for laying hold of His words. And on the other hand, how much meekness and gentleness does He display in calmly arguing with these odious hypocrites, and seeking to convince them by argument how untenable would be the claim which some of them wished to establish, of exemption from tribute to Cæsar. " The very money you use shows that, as a fact, you are Cæsar's subjects.   If you had not submitted to him, never would you have admitted his currency.   Then, having submitted to him, you have no option but to pay those taxes, which every lawful Government has a right to impose."   Such is the argument; and it silenced them ; for they went their way.   But what absolute control of temper is shown in the willingness to argue, when His eye was resting upon their heart all the time, and He knew that their question was a mere pretext for destroying Him.—Lord, make me, too, " wise as the serpent and harmless as the dove," " in malice a child, in understanding a man."[2]   While I " walk circumspectly, not as fools, but as wise,"[3] may I be " gentle and patient toward all men !"[4]

---

[1] St. Matt. x. 16.   [2] See 1 Cor. xiv. 20.
[3] See Eph. v. 15.   [4] See 1 Thess. v. 14, and 2 Tim. ii. 24.

Thursday.—V. 20. "And he saith unto them, Whose is this image and superscription?" The soul of man was made originally in the image of God,[1] just as a coin, in the process of minting it, is impressed with the sovereign's image. The image, though not entirely obliterated, has been much blurred and worn away by the fall, and must be restored again in all its pristine sharpness and beauty by Divine grace. Now let me regard this question, "Whose is this image and superscription?" as one which will be put respecting myself at the last day, and by the answer to which my everlasting destiny will be determined. The superscription indeed I have upon me; for I have been baptized and confirmed, and thus admitted to all the privileges of the New Covenant, and made nominally and professedly a Christian. But what can I say in answer to, "Whose is this image?" Have I been, or rather am I being, "renewed in knowledge after the image of him that created"[2] me? Am I seeking to transcribe the features of my heavenly Father into my own character? Am I being "conformed to the image of his Son,"[3] which indeed is the Father's image, refracted in the crystal glass of a sinless humanity? Only those who can show God's image, as well as His superscription, legibly traced upon heart, character, conduct, will be rendered up at last into God's heavenly treasury.

Friday.—V. 21. "Then saith he unto them, Render therefore unto Cæsar the things which are Cæsar's." It was true that originally Israel had been under a theocracy, that is, governed by God Himself, until they had rejected that form of government, and asked to be put on a level with the nations around them by having an earthly

---

[1] See Gen. i. 26, 27.   [2] See Col. iii. 10.
[3] See Rom. viii. 29.

sovereign.[1]   It was true also that they had had in times past independent kings of their own race, "not a stranger, but one from among thy brethren "[2]; but it was equally true that for their grievous and multiplied sins God had sold them first into the hand of the Babylonians,[3] and afterwards into the hand of the Romans; and that being the case, they ought to have submitted themselves to the Roman, as the prophet Jeremiah had distinctly told them they must submit themselves to the Babylonian yoke,[4] as an act of religious duty and of humiliation for those sins, which had caused the yoke to be laid upon them. Meek payment of the tribute to Cæsar, and acknowledgment of his sovereignty, was the best proof they could give, and the proof which God required them to give, that their "uncircumcised hearts were humbled, and that they accepted of the punishment of their iniquity."[5]—O God, when we sin wilfully, Thou dost chastise and degrade us, and bringest us into captivity to those evil lusts which have led us astray. We are not thereafter free, but slaves; for "whosoever committeth sin is the servant of sin."[6] But a cordial acceptance, not indeed of sin's rule, but of all its galling providential consequences, and a heartfelt humiliation on account of it, is part of that grace of true repentance, whereby we may disentangle our necks from the yoke of Satan, and take upon us that "easy yoke and light burden" of the Redeemer, in bearing of which we may "find rest unto our souls."[7]

Saturday.—V. 21. "Render therefore unto Cæsar the

---

[1] See 1 Sam. viii. *passim.*   [2] See Deut. xvii. 15.
[3] See 2 Kings xxiv. 20, and xxv. 1-6.
[4] See Jer. xxi. 8, 9, 10 ; xxxviii. 2, 17, 18.   [5] See Lev. xxvi. 41, 43.
[6] St. John viii. 34.   [7] See St. Matt. xi. 29, 30.

things which are Cæsar's; and unto God the things that are God's." The creative work of God in the beginning consisted to a great extent in the separation one from another of the rudiments of the universe, as they lay before Him in their chaotic state, the division of the light from the darkness, of the waters under from the waters above the firmament, of the earth from the seas.[1] So here, by this great word of His, the Saviour marks out two separate and distinct spheres of duty—our duty to the State or earthly Government, and our higher duty to the Divine Government. And yet, like the Decalogue, which is divided into two Tables, and prescribes our duty both to God and our neighbour,—the duty to our neighbour however resting upon, and being part of, our duty to God (for " this commandment have we from him, That he who loveth God love his brother also "[2]),—so these two duties to the civil and the Divine Government rest upon, and are resolvable into, a single principle. We are called upon to obey Cæsar, not because he is in any way independent of God, but because he reigns by God's providence and ordinance, and because God hath said, " Render therefore to all their dues : tribute to whom tribute is due; custom to whom custom; fear to whom fear; honour to whom honour."[3] And thus the rendering to Cæsar the things that are Cæsar's is, in the higher aspect of it, a rendering unto God the things that are God's, Cæsar being himself God's ordinance and minister, and subjection to him being required on the ground that he is so.[4]—O God, let me never withhold from the civil power the acknowledgment, whether of tribute or reverence, which is its due, on the ground of Thy prior

---

[1] See Gen. i. 4, 7, 9.   [3] 1 John iv. 21.
[2] Rom. xiii. 7.   [4] See Rom. xiii. 1, 2, 4, 6.

claims, which would be like the hypocritical Jews saying "Corban" of any property whereby the wants of father and mother might be relieved[1]; and let me see in all government, civil as well as ecclesiastical, an image of Thy sovereignty, and yield to it accordingly a prompt and cheerful obedience.

[1] St. Mark vii. 10-14.

CHAPTER LIX.

THE GOSPEL FOR THE TWENTY-FOURTH SUNDAY AFTER TRINITY.

ST. MATT. ix. 18 to 27
("Jesus" being substituted for "he," and "John's disciples" for
"them," in v. 18).

18 While Jesus spake these things unto Johns disciples, behold, there came a certain ruler and worshipped him, saying, My daughter is even now dead; but come and lay thy hand upon her, and she
19 shall live. (And Jesus arose, and followed him, and so did his
20 disciples. And behold, a woman who was diseased with an issue of blood twelve years, came behind him, and touched the hem of his
21 garment: For she said within her self, If I may but touch his
22 garment, I shall be whole. But Jesus turned him about, and when he saw her, he said, Daughter, be of good comfort, thy faith hath made thee whole. And the woman was made whole from that hour)
23 And when Jesus came into the rulers house, and saw the minstrels
24 and the people making a noise, he said unto them, Give place; for the maid is not dead, but sleepeth. And they laughed him to scorn.
25 But when the people were put forth, he went in, and took her by
26 the hand, and the maid arose. And the fame hereof went abroad into all that land.

[MISS. SAR.	1549.	1662 S.B.
In illo tempore, Loquente *Jesu* ad *turbas*, ecce princeps unus accessit, et adoravit eum, dicens, etc., *down to end of v.* 22, — salva facta est mulier ex illa hora.	While Jesus spake° unto the people, behold, there came a certaine ruler and worshipped him, saying, etc. (In the Black-Letter Prayer Book of 1636 (39 ?), in	While Jesus spake these things unto Johns disciples, behold, there came a certain ruler and worshipped him, saying, etc., *down to end of v.* 26. And the fame hereof

(*Vulg.* Hæc illo loquente ad eos, ecce princeps unus accessit, et adorabat eum, dicens, etc.)

which the alterations were made in 1662, the words "unto the people" are crossed out, and in the margin is written, in Sancroft's hand, "° these things unto John's disciples") *down to end of v.* 26. And this noyse was abroad in all that land.

went abroad into all that land. (*Gr.* Ταῦτα αὐτοῦ λαλοῦντος αὐτοῖς, ἰδοὺ, ἄρχων ἐλθὼν προσεκύνει αὐτῷ, λέγων κ.τ.λ.)

The Reformers in 1549 did in every way wisely and well in adding to the Sarum Gospel the four verses (23, 24, 25, 26), which record the miraculous resuscitation of Jairus's daughter. In the first place, our Lord's earliest miracle of raising the dead is an incident of too much importance not to find a place among the Liturgical Gospels. Then again, there was a manifest incompleteness about an extract, which recorded an application made to Christ on behalf of one "at the point of death," without going on to record His gracious answer to the application. And again, the original Gospel, consisting only of five verses, was somewhat too short, and might well admit of a little extension. And, lastly, the two miracles,—that of the recovery of the woman with the issue of blood, and that of the resuscitation of Jairus's daughter, were so bound up together in their moral bearings, and probably also in their allegorical significance, that the accounts of them ought not to be severed. Not only was the delay entailed by the recovery of the woman, and the conversation with her which ensued, a severe trial of the faith and patience of Jairus (for we are certainly to understand that, when he left his house, his daughter was only "at the point of death" (see St. Mark v. 23), and therefore it might seem to him that a few minutes' delay on the part of the Saviour might place her beyond the reach of recovery), but, on the other hand, the miracle, which the woman with the issue of blood was made to avow that Christ had wrought upon her (St. Mark v. 32, 33), must have been an encouragement to him to hope and believe that even the greater miracle of raising a person in the last extremity was not beyond the power of this Wonderworker (see the Thought for *Sunday*). Add to this, that eminent theologians have seen in the woman afflicted with the issue of blood for twelve years (St. Mark v. 25) an allegory of the Gentiles, who, while Christ was passing on to resuscitate the defunct Jewish Church (represented by the dead girl of twelve years of age, St. Mark v. 42), stole from Him a spiritual healing, and afterwards confessed Him before men, and so came as it were into the place of "the lost sheep of the house of Israel to whom He was sent" (see St. Matt. xv. 24), which lost sheep, however, also shall be restored to spiritual vitality when "the fulness of the Gentiles is come in" (see Rom. xi. 25, 26). There is probably something more than fancy in this allegory, and if so, the two miracles cannot be severed without seriously injuring the mystical significance of the entire narrative.—As regards the connexion of this Gospel with what immediately precedes, I have taken the view (see the Thought for *Monday*), which any person having only St. Matthew's Gospel before him would naturally take, that our Lord was sitting at meat in St. Matthew's house (*v.* 10), and answering a question there put to Him by the disciples of St. John the Baptist (*v.* 14), when Jairus entered the house (many good Manuscripts read εἰσελθὼν, and this reading is adopted both by Tischendorf and Bishop Christopher Wordsworth) and prostrated himself at His feet with the request that He would come and lay His hand upon the expiring maiden. It is quite open to us to suppose, nevertheless, consistently with this view, that "the feast in Matthew's house did not immediately follow his call, but that the two events, from their connexion with the same person, were grouped together in an original narrative, oral or written, which in this case has been followed by all three Evangelists." [Dean Mansel, in the "Speaker's Commentary." *Note on the Chronological Order of Chap.* IX.]—*Translation of* 1540. (1) *Vv.* 20, 21. "touched the hemme of his *vesture.* For shee sayd within her selfe, If I may touch but even his *vesture* onely, I shall be *safe.*" *a.* Tyndale and the Genevan also have "vesture." Wycliffe, "the hemme of his *clothe.*" The Rhemish first gave, "garment," which the Authorised Version follows. "Vesture," *the more solemn and dignified word,* is reserved by King James's Translators for the clothing of the glorified Saviour, who "hath on his vesture (ἐπὶ τὸ ἱμάτιον αὐτοῦ) and on his thigh a name written, KING OF KINGS AND LORD OF LORDS," and yet whose heavenly vesture, as an ever-enduring memorial of His earthly passion, is "dipped in blood" (see Rev. xix. 13, 16). The Revisers have ruthlessly, it appears to me, given us "garment" here also (the Greek word being the same). The notion attaching to the word "vesture" as a garment of dignity and honour is brought out in an exquisite passage of Shakspere ;

> "She shall be dignified with this high honour,—
> To bear my lady's train ; lest the base earth
> Should from her *vesture* chance to steal a kiss,
> And, of so great a favour growing proud,
> Disdain to root the summer-swelling flower,
> And make rough winter everlastingly."
>
> (*Two Gentlemen,* Act III. Scene iv.)

b. "I shall be *safe*." All five English versions before the Authorised have, "I shall be *safe*." The Authorised changed "*safe*" to "*whole*." The Revisers have improved upon the Authorised by rendering σωθήσομαι, "I shall be *made* whole," and giving "saved" as a marginal alternative. (2) *V.* 24. "*Get you hence*" ('Αναχωρεῖτε). And so Tyndale and the Genevan. Wycliffe, "go ye awei." Rhemish, "Depart." Authorised and Revised, "Give place." (3) *V.* 25. "he went in, and tooke her by the hand, *and said, Damosell, arise.* And the Damosell arose." The words in Italics are not in the Greek text. Nor are they in any English version but Cranmer's. As his Bible is reprinted in Bagster's Hexapla, (from a fine copy of the first Edition, 1539), the words are within brackets and in italics. And in the Edition of 1541, they are within brackets, preceded by a sort of foliation, and *in a smaller and slenderer type.* Opposite Gen. i. in this Edition is the following advertisement to the reader; "Where as often tymes ye shall fynde a smal letter in the text, it sygnifyeth that so moche as" [is?] "in the small letter doth abounde and is more in the common translaciõ in Latyne, then is founde ether in the Hebrue or in yᵉ Greke." There is however no trace whatever in the "Latyne" of any such clause, the Vulgate Version being "intravit; et tenuit manum ejus. Et surrexit puella." Probably it appeared in some text which the Translators of 1539 used; but it is evidently a spurious insertion from St. Mark v. 41, "Damsel, I say unto thee, arise." (4) *V.* 26. "And this *noyse* was abroad in all that land." Tyndale, "and this was *noysed* through out all that lande." Genevan, the same as Tyndale. Rhemish, "and this *bruite* went forth into al that countrie." "Noise" in the sense of "rumour," "fame" was perhaps somewhat going out in 1611. We have the verb in Shakspere (*Henry VIII.*, Act I. Scene ii.); "*Wolsey.* Let it be *noised* That through our intercession this revokement And pardon comes."]

Sunday.—V. 18. "While he spake these things unto them, behold, there came a certain ruler, and worshipped him, saying, My daughter is even now dead: but come and lay thy hand upon her, and she shall live." By comparing the accounts of this incident given by St. Mark and St. Luke, I find that this ruler's daughter was not dead, but only at the point of death, when he came to Christ.[1] News came to him, before Christ could arrive

---

[1] "At the point of death," St. Mark v. 23; "she lay a dying," St. Luke viii. 42.

at his house, that she was dead, and that therefore he need not trouble our Lord further; whereupon our Lord said to him, " Be not afraid, only believe."[1] And there can be little doubt that one of the objects which our Lord had in view, in bringing the woman with an issue of blood to an open avowal of the miracle which had been wrought upon her person, was to strengthen the faith of Jairus under the tidings of his daughter's death; for it does not appear that Christ had ever raised the dead before, and therefore it might be a question in Jairus's mind whether His power was equal to so great a miracle as this. But St. Matthew passes over all these particulars, and gives a succinct and abbreviated account of the miracle, whereas the other two Evangelists enter into details. God's having given us four separate accounts of our Lord's life agreeing substantially, while they differ in particulars, is at once an evidence of the truth of the narrative, and an incitement to thoughtful and profitable study. For no matter of fact narrated by honest human witnesses is ever narrated in exactly the same words; if it were, we should be led to expect collusion. And the superficial discrepancies between Gospel and Gospel give occasion to the devout student to bring his mind into closer connexion with the details of the narrative than he would otherwise do, and thus to profit much by " comparing spiritual things with spiritual."[2]

Monday.—V. 19. " And Jesus arose, and followed him, and so did his disciples." Our Lord was at a great feast in St. Matthew's house, in which the society was very miscellaneous; " there was a great company of publicans and of others that sat down with them."[3] It was prob-

---

[1] See St. Mark v. 35, 36 ; St. Luke viii. 49, 50.
[2] See 1 Cor. ii. 13.　　　　　　　　　　[3] St. Luke v. 29.

ably the circumstance of our Blessed Lord's joining in this festivity that led to the question put to Him by John's disciples, " Why do we and the Pharisees fast oft, but thy disciples fast not ?"[1]　Jairus, whose business was urgent, and his anxiety about his daughter painted on his countenance, breaks through all usual forms, and gets access to the table, and prostrating himself before the couch on which our Lord was lying, prefers his request.　Immediately, without a moment's delay, our Lord " arose and followed him," to exchange the sounds of conviviality for those of mourning, the throng and hurry of the banquet for the stillness of the chamber of death.——O Lord, while I find in this alacrity of Thine to follow Jairus, a witness to the truth of the wise man's saying; " It is better to go to the house of mourning, than to go to the house of feasting : for that is the end of all men; and the living will lay it to his heart "[2]; and a warning that all merriment, however innocent, needs to be chastened and tempered with the thought of death, yet am I careful to note that Thou didst " adorn and beautify with Thy Presence "[3] the chamber of feasting no less than that of mourning, and to learn that all circumstances of human life, grave or gay, may be consecrated by the remembrance of Thy Presence in the midst of them.

Tuesday.——Vv. 20, 21. " And, behold, a woman, which was diseased with an issue of blood twelve years, came behind him, and touched the hem of his garment : for she said within herself, If I may but touch his garment, I shall be whole." " It was a poor conceit in this woman," says Bishop Hall, " that she thought she might receive so sovereign a remedy from Christ, with-

---

[1] St. Matt. ix. 14.　　　　　[2] Eccles. vii. 2.
[3] See Preliminary Address in "the Form of Solemnisation of Matrimony."

out His heed, without His knowledge." She seems to have fancied that the touch of the hem of His garment, on which He bore the fringes prescribed by the Law,[1] would act as a spell, independently of any exertion of will on His part, and even without His consciousness. But while He commends and responds to her faith, He corrects her error. He gives her to understand that, though His garment had been the channel through which the healing virtue resident in His sacred Person had reached her, it could have done nothing for her without her faith, much in the same way as we are assured that the consecrated elements in the Holy Communion can avail us nothing without a similar disposition. Nor does He suffer her to steal a blessing from Him, as she had thought to do; she shall not only believe in Him in her heart, but confess Him with her mouth before men.[2] "This is a most encouraging miracle for us to recollect," says Dean Alford, "when we are disposed to think despondingly of the ignorance and superstition of much of the Christian world,—that He who accepted this woman for her faith, even in error and weakness, may also accept them." And I am also hereby taught charity to devout Christians, whose minds are yet unenlightened on many points of Divine truth, as Henry Martyn the missionary, when he saw a poor old crone in a Spanish church devoutly kissing her crucifix and bathing it with tears, made the reflexion that, however much his understanding of the scheme of Redemption might excel hers, very probably in faith and love she was his superior. And it is through faith and love that we are accepted with Christ, and draw down blessings from Him.

Wednesday.—V. 22. "But Jesus turned him about,

---

[1] See Num, xv. 37-41; Deut. xxii. 12.   [2] See Rom. x. 9.

and when he saw her, he said, Daughter, be of good comfort; thy faith hath made thee whole." Our Lord was eager to arrive at Jairus's house; for the moment the dying state of the ruler's daughter had been announced to Him, He had risen from the table, and followed Jairus, who no doubt would urge Him on, and would naturally show himself very impatient of interruption. However, an interruption does arise, and our Lord stops a while, not so much to do a miracle of healing, as, when it was done, to say a word of sympathy, encouragement, and correction to her on whom it was wrought. With what natural sweetness and benignity does He do this, giving His full mind to the particulars of this fresh case, however eager to reach the ruler's house! One of the small, though at the same time, very real trials of a busy life is that of interruptions. We have some plan of usefulness for our day, which is all thrown out by a claim upon our attention or our compassion, quite unexpectedly made. How often have I shown myself irritable under such circumstances, and, if I have not met the applicant with a positive repulse, have given the most cursory consideration to his case, and that very peevishly !—Oh that by Thy Spirit, good Lord, one drop of the " meekness and gentleness "[1] which is in Thee might be instilled into my heart !

Thursday.—V. 22. The following beautiful thought is from Adolphe Monod's " Farewells," a series of addresses made by a pastor on his dying bed to such members of his flock as could be assembled in his bedroom. After telling them that one of his regrets was, that he had regulated his life too much on his own plans, and not with sufficient simplicity upon the plan which God unrolls before each of us in the order of His Providence, He

---

[1] See 2 Cor. x. 1.

refers to the Great Example, and says; " The good works of Jesus Christ were all given to Him one after another, were all put by God's hand before Him upon His road; and they follow one another so naturally, spring so easily one out of the other, that they never get entangled, even in the busiest days of His ministry. In a day, for example, like that described in the ninth Chapter of St. Matthew, in which He calls one of His Apostles, heals some sick folks, raises the dead, and in passing restores a woman who had laboured under a malady several years, there is not one instant of embarrassment or hesitation, either as to the manner of arranging the several things He does, or as to the time to be given to each of them, because Jesus Christ follows quite simply the plan of God, and God charges Himself with the business of conducting Him. When there is this perfect accord with the will of God, there is also on God's part a perfect clearness in conducting us; and thus is fulfilled in us an admirable and profound word of the Holy Ghost; ' we are his workmanship, created in Christ Jesus unto good works, which God hath before ordained that we should walk in them.'[1] The good works are presented to us, not as a road which we have to make for ourselves, but as a road which God has made, and in which nothing remains for us to do but to walk in it."

Friday.—Vv. 23, 24. " When he saw the minstrels and the people making a noise, 'he said unto them, Give place; for the maid is not dead, but sleepeth. And they laughed him to scorn." " The minstrels " were hired mourners, whom it was customary to send for upon a death in the family, that they might " take up a wailing "[2] for the dead, that is, sing dirges; and " the people " were

---

[1] Eph. ii. 10.　　　　[2] See Jer. ix. 17, 18.

a crowd which, hearing these lugubrious sounds, had collected in the court, some of them from idle curiosity, some from a desire to offer their condolence to the family of one who held a certain position. Mourners and crowd represent to us the world; and I will take occasion to reflect to-day on the utter hollowness of the world's sympathy. I find this hollowness in the words which follow, "And they laughed him to scorn." Misunderstanding our Lord, and supposing Him to have declared that the girl had never really died, they turned Him into ridicule; though the hardness of heart which could have turned into ridicule the doer of such works, and the sayer of such words as His, cannot fail to surprise us. But certainly the fact that the tears were changed all of a sudden into laughter and derisive jeers shows that they cannot have been very genuine. And this laughter, as it showed that there was no real sympathy, so it showed also that there was no real faith. Now, except to faith and love, the great manifestations of Divine power cannot be made. And therefore the Lord ejects these mourners, and closes the door of the death-chamber upon them. "Christ and the world," says Quesnel, " are incompatible visitors in the same heart." Begone, hollow courtesies, secret disbelief of all but what lies within man's experience; begone covetous and ambitious desires, and all else that takes up the room in the heart, which should be occupied by the Saviour! Then shall He come in to me, and I shall see and know the operations of His grace.

Saturday.—V. 25. " But when the people were put forth, he went in, and took her by the hand, and the maid arose." " Christ is now, as He was then, passing through the midst of men, if they would but see Him. Still they throng, and press, and draw nothing from Him, because

they bring no eye to discern, and do not feel that need
which opens the eyesight. We can take from Him only
what we perceive in Him, and must urge the prayer that
God would reveal His Son in us. . . . It is our hope and
joy to think, as we touch Him here with the hands of
dying men, that He is still passing on through the world
to perform His greatest work—to raise the dead. Many a
home, like that of Jairus, looks for His appearing. Himself the risen One, He is advancing to awake His friends
who have fallen asleep, and to comfort those who mourn
over them, and who wait for His coming. He spreads His
garment meanwhile, as He moves, to the touch of misery
and sin, and if He lingers in His progress to the homes of
the dead, it is but to gather in His train the fuller fruits
of His redeeming toil. His mercy and our need cause
the seeming delay. His work on the way must be finished
ere the close can come. Ere long He will enter that
highest house; and we shall possess the privilege of the
best-beloved, to enter the innermost chamber with Him,
where sorrow shall be turned into joy, and death into life;
where faith that touches the hem shall rise to vision that
beholds the face, and friends who part and weep at night-
fall shall meet at day-dawn, in a world where the voice of
crying shall not be heard any more, nor the shadow of
death fall upon the heart for ever." [Rev. John Ker,
D.D., as quoted in Dr. Glentworth Butler's " Bible
Reader's Commentary," Vol. I., p. 226.]

Chapter LX.

THE GOSPEL FOR THE TWENTY-FIFTH SUNDAY AFTER TRINITY.

St. John vi. 5 *to* 15.

5 When Jesus then lift up his eyes, and saw a great company
come unto him, he saith unto Philip, Whence shall we buy bread
6 that these may eat? (And this he said to prove him: for he him=
7 self knew what he would do) Philip answered him, Two hundred
peny=worth of bread is not sufficient for them, that every one of
8 them may take a little. One of his disciples, Andrew, Simon
9 Peters brother, saith unto him, There is a lad here, who hath five
barley loaves, and two small fishes; but what are they among so
10 many? And Jesus said, Make the men sit down. Now there
was much grass in the place. So the men sat down, in number
11 about five thousand. And Jesus took the loaves, and when he had
given thanks, he distributed to the disciples, and the disciples to
them that were set down, and likewise of the fishes, as much as
12 they would. When they were filled, he said unto his disciples,
Gather up the fragments that remain, that nothing be lost.
13 Therefore they gathered them together, and filled twelve baskets
with the fragments of the five barley=loaves, which remained over
14 and above unto them that had eaten. Then those men, when they
had seen the miracle that Jesus did, said, This is of a truth that
Prophet that should come into the world.

[Miss. Sar.	1549.	1662 s.b.
In illo tempore, Cum sublevasset oculos Jesus, et vidisset quia multitudo maxima venit ad	When Jesus lift up his eyes, and saw a great company come unto him, he saith unto Philip,	When Jesus then lift up his eyes, and saw a great company come unto him, he saith unto Philip,

eum, dicit ad Philippum; Unde ememus panes, ut manducent hi? (*Vulg.* Cum sublevasset ergo oculos Jesus, et vidisset quia multitudo maxima venit ad eum, dixit ad Philippum : Unde ememus panes, ut manducent hi?)

Whence shal we buy bread, that these may eate?

Whence shall we buy bread that these may eat ? (*Gr.* Ἐπάρας οὖν ὁ Ἰησοῦς τοὺς ὀφθαλμούς, καὶ θεασάμενος ὅτι πολὺς ὄχλος ἔρχεται πρὸς αὐτόν, λέγει πρὸς τὸν Φίλιππον· Πόθεν ἀγοράσομεν ἄρτους, ἵνα φάγωσιν οὗτοι ;)

There is a propriety, not difficult to discern, in the circumstance of the first four verses of St. John vi. being prefixed to the Liturgical Gospel on the Fourth Sunday in Lent, whereas they are omitted on the Twenty-fifth Sunday after Trinity. On the Fourth Sunday in Lent we are approaching Easter, and consequently the words of *v.* 4 ("And the passover, a feast of the Jews, was nigh") have then a point, which they would lack at another season of the Christian Year. At its latest season, and just before Advent, "Gather up the fragments that remain" (*v.* 12) and "This is of a truth that prophet that should come into the world" (*v.* 14) are the words which connect the Gospel with the occasion on which it is read [see the Thoughts for *Friday* and *Saturday*].—It may be observed as a minute point of discrepancy between the Liturgical Gospels, which profess to be taken from the Authorised Version of 1611, and our modern copies of that Version, that the first give us "lift" as the perfect tense of the verb "to lift" (both here, and also in the Gospel for the Fourth Sunday in Lent), whereas the New Testaments at present current have the modern form *lifted.*—The "then" (οὖν) in *v.* 5 glances back to what had been said in the immediately preceding verses. Our Lord in quest of rest and refreshment, had gone "by ship privately" "over the sea of Galilee" "into a desert place" (cf. St. Mark vi. 31, 32). The people, however, who habitually followed Him (the ἠκολούθει of *v.* 2 expresses "the habitual work, environment, and influence of Christ" [Prof. Westcott]) frustrated His design. On one occasion He went up into *the* mountain (*v.* 3, *Revised Version;* "the definite article implies an instinctive sense of the familiar landscape, the mountain-range closing round the lake"), and there He was sitting with His disciples, when His eye was caught by a great concourse of people, coming to Him, some on foot, some on boats across the lake,—pilgrims on their way towards the passover, the approach of which (as we are explicitly told in Chap. xi. 55) drew many "out of the country up to Jerusalem . . . to purify themselves."—*Translation of* 1540. *V.* 12. "When *they had eaten enough*" (Ὡς δὲ ἐνεπλήσθησαν). And so Tyndale. The Genevan gives, "And when they were *satisfied*"; the Rhemish, "And after they were *filled*"; Authorised Version, "When they were *filled*"; Revised Version (replacing the conjunction), "*And* when they were *filled*." And thus we come back at length to old Wycliffe ("And whanne thei weren fillid") after a lapse of five hundred and one years! Put not your faith in Revisers!

Other discrepancies between Cranmer's version of this Gospel, which was read in the Church for one hundred and thirteen years after the Reformation, and the Authorised Version which was made to supersede it in 1662, are given in the Introduction to the Gospel for the Fourth Sunday in Lent, to which the reader is referred.]

Sunday.—V. 5. "When Jesus then lifted up his eyes, and saw *a great company* come unto him." This refers back to the second verse, where we read that "*a great multitude* followed him because they saw his miracles which he did on them that were diseased." Their motive in following Him was not the highest motive conceivable. It was not because they had found His words come home to their hearts with peculiar power, and desired further instruction in "the things pertaining to the kingdom of God." Still it was a good motive, as far as it went. They had been arrested by the sight of His miracles; and their minds were open to conviction; they felt with Nicodemus that "no man" could "do" those "miracles that" Jesus did, "except God" were "with him."[1] Yet, though their motives were not as purely spiritual as they might have been, our Lord welcomed them gladly, "and spake unto them of the kingdom of God, and healed them that had need of healing."[2] And this He did, although, as we find from the accounts of the other Evangelists, He had retired with His Apostles to seek privacy and rest,[3] at a time when there "were many coming and going, and they had no leisure so much as to eat."[4] He so little discourages this

[1] See St. John iii. 2.   [2] St. Luke ix. 11.
[3] St. Matt. xiv. 13; St. Mark vi. 31; St. Luke ix. 10, 11.
[4] St. Mark vi. 31.

intrusion upon His privacy, that He may be said to en-
courage it very decidedly, by not only healing the sick
people they brought with them,[1] but by working a miracle
to supply their bodily wants. The lesson forcibly taught
us hereby is that nothing can please God more than our
importunity in seeking Him. The friend in the Parable,
dragged out of his bed at midnight to supply a sudden
need on the part of a neighbour, grants the request
reluctantly[2]; but God is "always more ready to hear
than we to pray, and " is "wont to give more than either
we desire or deserve,"[3] and there is no spectacle that
Jesus loves more than that of aroused and awakened
consciences, seeking further light.

Monday.—Vv. 5, 6. " He saith unto Philip, Whence
shall we buy bread, that these may eat? And this
he said to prove him." O Philip, thou hast already
some time back acknowledged thy convictions respecting
the Master, saying to Nathanael, " We have found him, of
whom Moses in the law, and the prophets, did write."[4]
If this be indeed the Messiah to whom Moses and the
prophets point, in their writings, He must be able to do
works at least as wonderful as the bringing down manna
from heaven to feed the people in the wilderness,[5] or as
the feeding a hundred men with twenty loaves of barley,
and full ears of corn in the husk thereof.[6] Now therefore, since thou hast avowed the convictions of faith, those
convictions shall be put to the proof. Is He whom thou
avowest to be Messiah, able to feed a multitude in the
wilderness with the slenderest stock of provisions ?—Let

---

[1] St. Matt. xiv. 14 ; St. Luke ix. 11.   [2] See St. Luke xi. 7, 8.
[3] Collect for the Twelfth Sunday after Trinity.
[4] St. John i. 45.   [5] See Exod. xvi. 4, etc
[6] See 2 Kings iv. 42, 43, 44.

me make the reflexion that, if I have faith, even in the lowest degree as a grain of mustard seed, God is sure to prove it. And His design in proving it is to strengthen it (just as bodily faculties are strengthened by exercise), and to open my mind to larger ideas of His power, wisdom, and love. Satan's design, on the other hand, in the temptations which *he* addresses to me, is to induce me to sin, and make me fall, though even Satan's temptations, malignant as their design is, are sometimes overruled by God's mercy and grace, to make men know themselves, and distrust altogether their own strength. I can form no better prayer than that God should show me myself, my feebleness, my vileness, the imperfection of my best graces, while at the same time He shows me Himself, His power, His all-sufficiency, His competency to all difficulties, and in all emergencies.

Tuesday.—V. 6. " For he himself knew what he would do." How careful is St. John to bring out the Divine nature of our Blessed Lord,—not to involve Him in any way in the ignorance and short-sightedness of His creatures.[1] Thus he tells us here that He asked Philip the question for the disciple's own good, not with the wish of gaining any suggestion as to how to act in the emergency. And (to take only one more instance), in giving us our Lord's fifth saying on the cross, " I thirst," the Evangelist is careful to point out that this cry was not wrung out of Him by the tortures of thirst, but uttered deliberately, with the view of eliciting a fulfilment of one small prediction, which alone was wanting to make the cycle of Old Testament prophecy shine out full-orbed in His

---

[1] Other instances in which this Evangelist draws attention to our Lord's insight and foresight, are to be found in *vv.* 61, 64 of this Chap., and also Chap. xiii. 3 ; xviii. 4 ; xix. 28.

career; "Jesus, knowing that all things were now accomplished, that the scripture might be fulfilled, saith, I thirst."[1]—Lord, when I approach Thee in prayer, let me bear in mind Thy foresight of all my future, and Thy pre-arrangement of all which concerns me. I do not pray, to inform Thee of my needs (for Thou knowest them before I lay them before Thee), but simply as a discipline of my own character, and as an acknowledgment of my dependence upon Thee. Thou foreseest the end of my career, knowest whether I shall persevere or fall away at the end. And often, when a great emergency in the future seems to press and threaten, it is only that Thou art proving me, to enlarge my conception of Thy power and love, and Thou hast pre-arranged all things for me, and hast in reserve Thine own method of extricating me from the difficulty in Thine own good time.

Wednesday.—V. 10. "And Jesus said, Make the men sit down. Now there was much grass in the place. So the men sat down, in number about five thousand." Hereupon Bishop Hall, with his usual devout quaintness, says; "They obey, and expect. O marvellous faith! So many thousands sit down, and address themselves to a meal, when they saw nothing but five poor barley loaves and two small fishes. None of them say, ' Sit down ? to what ? Here are the mouths, but where is the meat ? We can soon be set, but whence shall we be served ? Ere we draw our knives, let us see our cheer': but they meekly and obediently dispose themselves to their places, and look up to Christ for a miraculous purveyance." I call to mind that our Lord dealt in a similar manner with the ten lepers, bidding them go shew themselves to the priests, for examination and ceremonial cleansing, before they were

---

[1] St. John xix. 28.

actually recovered. " And it came to pass, that, as they went, they were cleansed."[1]　This was the Lord's response to an obedient faith, just as here He responded to the obedient faith of the multitude by feeding them miraculously.——In any emergency or trial which besets me, let me act upon the same principle, " Obey and expect." There is one command under such circumstances which may always be obeyed; " Be careful for nothing; but in every thing by prayer and supplication with thanksgiving let your requests be made known unto God."[2]　We obey this command, when we open our hearts to God, and make known to Him our wishes.　And having done this, we are bound to expect the fulfilment of the promise,——not indeed that God will grant whatever we ask for, to which He does not pledge Himself; but that His " peace, which passeth all understanding, shall keep" our " hearts and minds through Christ Jesus."[3]

Thursday.——V. 11. " He distributed to the disciples, and the disciples to them that were set down; and likewise of the fishes as much as they would."　Let me take a general survey of our Lord's miracles, as being all of them manifestations of His character and glory.　By far the greater number were cures, recoveries from malady, bodily or mental, or both, or recoveries from death.　It was sin which brought death into the world, and all those diseases, which are incipient death, and result in death. Accordingly the earliest character in which the great Deliverer must appear must be that of a Saviour of sinners (" Thou shalt call his name JESUS : for he shall save his people from their sins "[4]) and, in order to indicate this, His main miraculous work must be recovery

---

[1] St. Luke xvii. 14.　　　　[2] Phil. iv. 6.
[3] *Ibid. v.* 7.　　　　[4] St. Matt. i. 21.

from disease and death. But when a man has recovered bodily health, what does he still need? Sustenance of bodily life. The Saviour therefore must be shown to be not only the restorer of health, but the sustainer of life. And it is this character of Him which is indicated by the miracles of multiplication of food, the miraculous draughts,[1] and the miraculous feedings,[2] as also by the miraculous production of wine in Cana of Galilee.[3] The cycle of thought would not be complete without this latter miracle; for it must be shown somewhere in the miracles, not only that His flesh is meat indeed,[4] and that He is the Bread of life,[5] but also that His blood is drink indeed,[6] and that not only is He the soul's sustenance, but its joy. Even the two miracles of judgment—that upon the fig-tree,[7] and that upon the swine,[8]—are necessary to the completeness of the cycle; for judgment as well as mercy characterise the High and Holy One, just as the sunlight has sombre no less than brilliant rays in its constitution. " I will sing of mercy and judgment: unto thee, O LORD, will I sing."[9]

Friday.—V. 12. " Gather up the fragments that remain, that nothing be lost." This is evidently the God of Nature speaking. For Nature may be said to abhor waste, as she abhors a vacuum. There is no waste in Nature, but a constant husbanding of her resources. Matter having performed one function in the universe, passes off into some other form, and fulfils quite another function; not a jot of it is wasted. But, in connexion with the end of the Christian Year, at which we have now arrived, let

---

[1] St. Luke v. 6 ; St. John xxi. 6.
[2] St. Matt. xiv. 19, etc., and xv. 36, etc.   [3] St. John ii. 1-12.
[4] See St. John vi. 55.   [5] See St. John vi. 48.   [6] See St. John vi. 55.
[7] See St. Matt. xxi. 19.   [8] See St. Matt. viii. 32.   [9] Ps. ci. 1.

me make the reflexion that He, who shows Himself so careful that food should not be wasted, must be much more careful that our time, which is more precious than food, should be not only well spent, but thriftily husbanded, and every fragment of it made to go as far as it will go.   Only two days, the fragments and shreds of the old year, remain to us before a new Christian Year sets in with Advent Sunday.   With Thy help, O God, I will make the most of these two days, by doing something definite for God in them, for the advancement of His kingdom in my heart, or in that of my neighbour, and by throwing additional zeal and love into what I do ;

> "For Love too late can never glow ;
> The scattered fragments Love can glean,
> Refine the dregs, and yield us clean
> To regions where one thought serene
> Breathes sweeter than whole years of sacrifice below." [1]

Saturday.—V. 14.   " Then those men, when they had seen the miracle that Jesus did, said, This is of a truth that prophet that should come into the world." Literally, " This is of a truth the Prophet *that cometh* into the world."[2]   The Jews knew their Messiah under the name of " the Coming One " (" Art thou he that should come " ; the Coming One,—" or do we look for another ? "[3])   It is thus that this Gospel connects itself with Advent, sounding in these last words a note of the approach of the Coming One.   And let me remember that our Lord is still the Coming One.   The season of Advent is charged, as with memories of His first, so also

---

[1] " Christian Year."   Sunday next before Advent.

[2] This is the rendering of the Revised Version.

[3] St. Matt. xi. 3.   The rendering of the Revised Version is, " Art thou *he that cometh* ?"

with anticipations and hopes of His second Coming. Let me seriously ask myself whether hope and anticipation of the second Advent are an element in my religion ; for unless they be, is it not to be apprehended that my religion is not genuine, that it is a mere profession ? Faith cannot exist without giving rise to hope ; hope is the earliest blossom which faith puts forth. And without faith there is no real spiritual life. " Unto them *that look for Him* " (and to none but them) " shall he appear the second time without sin unto salvation."[1] " And not to me only " (shall He give the crown of righteousness), " but unto all them also *that love his appearing*."[2]

[1] Heb. ix. 28.   [2] 2 Tim. iv. 8.

INDEX.

ABSOLUTION, ministerial, II. 233, 234.

ἀγρὸς in St. Luke xv. translated by Wycliffe "*toun*," II. 113.

Alexander, Bishop, "Leading Ideas of the Gospels," quoted, I. 52, 57.

Alexandrine MS. I. 273; II. 183, 257.

Alford, Dean, on St. John v. 1, I. 263; on St. John viii. 59, I. 273; on St. John xvi. 31, II. 53; on the end of St. Mark's Gospel, II. 63; on St. Luke xvi. 4, II. 181; quoted, II. 325; II. 349.

Almsgiving, prayer, and fasting, linked together, I. 226.

Ambrose, St., quoted, I. 103.

Andrewes, Bishop, *Preces Privatæ*, quoted, I. 139, 258; II. 331.

Apollinaris, heresy of, I. 331.

Aposiopesis, meaning of, II. 191.

Aquinas, Catena Aurea, quoted, II. 128, 222, 223 n.

Articles, Thirty-nine, quoted, II. 100, 204, 225.

Asses, mentioned in the Old Testament; white asses for princes, I. 64, 65.

Augustine, St., quoted, I. 103, 232, 233, 258.

Avancini, quoted, I. 162 n.

Avaunt, whence derived, I. 235.

Avoid, used intransitively in 1 Sam. xviii. 11, and in Shakespeare, I. 235.

BACON, Lord, Advancement of Learning, quoted, II. 58.

Bagster's Hexapla, quoted, II. 52, 75, 173, 278, 346.

Baronius, his notice of St. Jerome's Baptism, I. 17 n.

Bĕnay-haṭṭōrah, Sons of the Law, I. 134.

Bengel, Gnomon Novi Testamenti, quoted, I. 142; on St. Matt. viii. 23, I. 161 and II. 288; quoted, I. 209; on St. Matt. iv. 10, I. 235, 238; on St. Matt. xv. 27, I. 243; on St. John vi. 1, I. 263; on St. John viii. 59, I. 273; on St. John viii. 51, I. 277; quoted, I. 326 n.; on St. Matt. xxvii. 51 n., I. 328, 329 n.; quoted, II. 87; on St. Luke xvi. 15-18, II. 103; quoted, II. 120; quoted, II. 154, 155; on St. Luke xvi. 1, II. 181; on St. Luke xix. 41, II. 191; quoted, II. 258; on St. Matt. ix. 1, II. 288; quoted, II. 290; quoted, II. 301, 302, 311; on St. Matt. xxi. 1, II. 322; on St. John xix. 40, II. 335.

Besant ; its value, II. 124.

Beza, quoted, I. 255 n.; II. 289. Codex Bezæ, I. 236, 273; II. 132.

Bible, Complutensian Polyglott, II. 289.

Bible, Coverdale's, I. 32.

Bible, Cranmer's, 1539; quoted, I. 32, 33 n., 37-40; II. 325, 334, 346.

Bible, Cranmer's, 1540; quoted, I. 31-34, 63, 74, 84, 94, 103, 115, 124, 133, 142, 150, 160, 177, 178, 187, 198, 209, 219, 235, 243, 252, 262, 272, 273, 285, 286; II. 2, 11, 21, 31, 40, 51, 52, 53, 63,

THE END.

Printed by R. & R. CLARK, *Edinburgh.*

New Edition. Square 16mo. 5s.

The Gospel of the Childhood : a Practical and Devotional

Commentary on the Single Incident of our Blessed Lord's Childhood (St. Luke ii. 41, to the end) ; designed as a help to Meditation on the Holy Scriptures, for Children and Young Persons.

New Edition, revised and enlarged. Small 8vo. 6s. 6d.

An Introduction to the Devotional Study of the Holy

Scriptures : with a Prefatory Essay on their Inspiration, and specimens of Meditations on various passages of them.

New Edition. Small 8vo. 6s.

The Acts of the Deacons; being a Course of Lectures,

Critical and Practical, on Acts vi., vii., viii., and xxi. 8-15. In two Books : Book I.—The Acts of St. Stephen the Protomartyr. Book II.—The Acts of St. Philip, Evangelist.

New Edition. Crown 8vo. 3s. 6d.

Family Prayers. Compiled from various sources (chiefly

from Bishop Hamilton's Manual), and arranged on the Liturgical Prin-ciple.

Also a Cheap Edition. 32mo. 1s.

New Edition. 32mo. 1s. 6d.

Short Devotional Forms : for Morning, Night, and Mid-

night, and for the Third, Sixth, Ninth hours and Eventide of each day of the week. Compiled and adapted from Bishop Andrews, and other sources. Arranged to meet the Exigencies of a Busy Life.

New Edition. Small 8vo. 4s.

Farewell Counsels of a Pastor to his Flock : Nine Ser-

mons preached at St. John's, Paddington, before quitting that Sphere of Ministerial Labour.

New Edition. Small 8vo. 1s. 6d.

A Manual of Confirmation ; comprising (1) A general

account of the Ordinance. (2) The Baptismal vow, and the English order of Confirmation, with short notes, Critical and Devotional. (3) Meditations and Prayers on Passages of Holy Scripture in connection with the Ordinance. With a Pastoral Letter instructing Catechumens how to prepare themselves for their First Communion.